THE GIANT BOOK OF FACTS

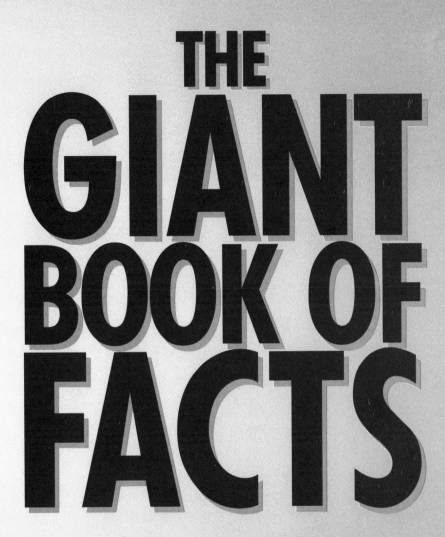

THE GIANT BOOK OF FACTS

OCTOPUS BOOKS

Contributors Bridget Ardley, Neil Ardley, Chris Burgess,
Jean Cooke, Derek Hall/Format Publishing Services, Keith Lye,
Ian Ridpath, Theodore Rowland-Entwistle
Illustrators Gill Tomblin, Janos Marffy
Designer Roger Kohn

First published in 1987 by
Octopus Books Limited
59 Grosvenor Street
London W1

Text and illustrations copyright © 1987 Octopus Books Limited

ISBN 0 7064 2657 6

Printed in Yugoslavia

CONTENTS

THE WORLD AND THE UNIVERSE

▲

The magma pillars of Devils Tower are over 182 m (600 ft) high.

GIANTS, DEVILS AND ALIENS

What is the Giant's Causeway? According to legend, an Irish giant, Finn MacCool, built a causeway between Northern Ireland and Scotland so that he could attack his enemy, the Scottish giant, Finn Gall. Fearing defeat, Finn Gall destroyed the causeway, though parts remained in both Scotland (the Isle of Staffa and Fingal's Cave) and on the Irish County Antrim coast. The remnants consist of mostly six-sided columns, which fit so neatly together that they could easily have been made by giants. However, they were actually formed naturally from basaltic lava, which shrinks and splits into columns of basalt when it cools.

Towering rocks Similar columns, like giant organ pipes, can be seen at Devils Tower, Wyoming, in the USA. This huge rocky stump, formed from magma, was the meeting place between humans and aliens in the film *Close Encounters of the Third Kind*.

HOT STUFF

What is a star? A glowing ball of hot gas, mostly hydrogen. Our Sun is a star. The stars we see at night appear as tiny points of light because they are much further away from us than the Sun. We could not land on the Sun, or on any other star. For one thing, a star has no solid surface, and it is so hot that it would melt our spacecraft.

Los Angeles, USA, veiled by smog.
▼

BIG BANG!

How did the Universe begin? Since the galaxies are currently moving apart, in the past they must presumably have been closer together. According to the most popular theory of the origin of the Universe, all matter and space was once concentrated into a superdense blob which, for some unknown reason, flew apart in an immense explosion known as the Big Bang.

The galaxies are the fragments from the Big Bang explosion, which have been moving apart ever since.

GALAXY OF STARS

How many stars are there? On a very clear night, away from the smoke and light of towns, you can see about 2,000 stars with your unaided eye. But these are only a fraction of the total number of stars. Binoculars and telescopes show many more faint stars.

Our Sun is one star in a gigantic collection of stars, called the Galaxy. Astronomers estimate that there are at least 100,000 million stars in the Galaxy. That's 20 stars for every person alive on Earth today.

BREATHING POISON

What is smog? Smog is a word made up from two other words: *smoky fog.* It occurs when smoke and poisonous gases from factories mix with fog. It can be dangerous, for example, a smog in Britain's biggest city, London, caused 4,000 deaths in 1952. London no longer has smogs, because its factories and homes now use smokeless fuels. Another kind of smog occurs in cities with many cars and is caused by exhaust fumes.

EXPLODING CONTINENTS

Where was Atlantis? The Greek philosopher Plato (427-347 BC) wrote about the mysterious continent of Atlantis, which people thought was destroyed in a single day by earthquakes and floods. Plato thought that Atlantis had been somewhere in the Atlantic Ocean.

Misinformed? Experts now think that Plato may have misunderstood information obtained by a traveller called Solon, who visited Egypt in about 590 BC. There Solon heard of a great civilization, west of Egypt, which had disappeared suddenly. This was probably the Minoan civilization based on Crete and other Mediterranean islands. It collapsed in about 1470 BC, when a massive volcanic eruption destroyed most of the Minoan island of Santorini (now called Thira). The eruption was the biggest in recorded history, five times more powerful than the 1883 Krakatoa eruption. Ash falls and destructive waves caused by the explosion of Santorini battered Crete and smashed its great palaces. The collapse of the Minoan civilization is the most likely origin of the Atlantis legend.

THE CONFETTI CROP

Which is the world's chief food crop? Nearly two-thirds of the world's farmland is used to grow cereals, including barley, maize, millet, oats, rye and wheat. However, the basic food of about half of the world's people is rice, which flourishes in warm, wet areas, especially in Asia. The popular custom of throwing rice at weddings probably originated in India.

AN ET'S-EYE VIEW

What would be a better name for our planet? Earth certainly isn't the best name, because water covers nearly 71 per cent of our planet's surface. An extraterrestrial being would probably call it 'Ocean'.

Earth's vast expanses of ocean can be clearly seen from space.
▼

FACT FILE: SPACESHIP EARTH

FACT The Earth is slightly flattened at the poles. It bulges near the equator, the greatest bulge being just south of the equator.

FACT The polar diameter (the distance between the poles through the centre of the Earth) is 12,713 km (7,900 miles).

FACT The polar circumference (the distance around the Earth via the poles) is 40,007 km (24,860 miles).

FACT The surface area of the Earth is 510,101,000 square km (196,951,000 square miles). Its weight (or mass) is about 6,600 million million million tonnes!

FACT The Earth's crust ranges in thickness from 60-70 km (37-43 miles) under high mountains to 6 km (4 miles) under the oceans.

FACT The mantle beneath the crust is 2,900 km (1,802 miles) thick.

FACT The Earth's dense core, composed mostly of iron and nickel, measures 6,920 km (4,300 miles) across. The outer core is liquid and the inner core solid. Temperatures in the centre probably reach 5,000°C (9,032°F)!

PUSHING BACK THE SEA

What is so unusual about Holland? There is a saying: 'God created the world but the Dutch created Holland.' Holland (more correctly called the Netherlands) is a low-lying country where more than two-fifths of the land is below sea-level at high tide. Since early this century Dutch engineers have reclaimed much of this flat land by building dykes (sea walls) to hold back the sea. The marshy areas behind the dykes, called polders, are drained and turned into fertile farmland. In this way, the Dutch have gradually increased the land area of their country.

A coastal dyke in the western Netherlands.
▼

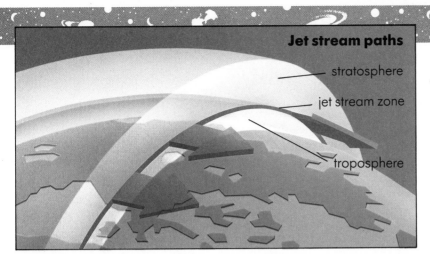

Jet stream paths

stratosphere

jet stream zone

troposphere

◀ The strong air currents known as jet streams occur in the upper troposphere and the lower stratosphere.

TAIL WINDS FOR HIGH FLIERS

What are jet streams? The lowest layer of the atmosphere is called the troposphere. Above it is the second layer, the stratosphere. Around the border between the two layers are strong winds, called jet streams, which blow mostly from west to east at over 160 km/h (100 mph). Pilots avoid flying into them, but they often use them as tail winds, so as to increase their speed and save fuel. Jet streams also influence the movements of weather systems in the troposphere.

ORGANIC ENERGY

What are fossil fuels? About 97 per cent of the energy we use in our homes and factories is generated from coal, oil and natural gas, which are called fossil fuels. These were all formed from organic (once-living) matter. Coal consists of the remains of land plants, while oil and gas were formed from the remains of tiny plants and animals which lived in lakes and seas. Oil and gas are more important fuels than coal. They are easier to extract and, by weight, they give out more heat.

WOBBLING LIKE JELLY

Why was Mexico City devastated by the 1985 earthquake? The centre of the severe earthquake that hit Mexico in September 1985 lay off the country's west (Pacific) coast, not far from the resort of Acapulco. The earthquake rocked the coastlands, but little damage was done. The greatest effects were felt in the capital, Mexico City, which was 400 km (249 miles) away from the earthquake's centre.

Background history To understand why Mexico City was badly hit, we must know something about its history. In the early 16th century, central Mexico was ruled by the Aztecs. Their capital, Tenochtitlán, stood on an island in Lake Texcoco. In 1520, Spanish soldiers led by Hernando Cortés attacked the capital and almost completely destroyed it.

The victorious Cortés then ordered that Mexico City should be built on the ruins of Tenochtitlán. The new city suffered from regular floods and so, in 1629, the Spaniards decided to drain Lake Texcoco. As the city grew, buildings were erected on the drained lake bed, although the soils were spongy and some large buildings sank into the ground.

Unstable Another problem faced by architects is that Mexico is in an unstable part of the world, where volcanic eruptions and earthquakes are common. In earthquake zones, the safest buildings are those based on solid rock. But the solid rock under Mexico City is buried by lake deposits up to 1.6 km (1 mile) deep. In 1985, the earthquake waves passed through the sand and silt under the city, making it shake like a bowl of jelly. Tall buildings swayed and collapsed, burying the people inside them.

The buildings on the old island site of Tenochtitlán fared much better. This is probably because the soils under this site have had a longer time to settle and become compacted and stable.

Even modern buildings collapsed in the 1985 Mexican earthquake. ▶

▲
Diamonds are often cut and polished to catch and reflect the light.

STRANGE RELATIONS

What is the hardest natural substance? The hardness of minerals is measured on a scale of 1-10, which was devised in 1822 by an Austrian, Friedrich Mohs. Number 1 on Mohs' scale is talc, an extremely soft mineral. Number 10 is diamond, the hardest natural substance.

When cut and polished, diamond is prized in jewellery, but the only thing that can be used to cut and polish diamond is diamond itself.

Chemical structure Diamond, which is about 40 times as hard as talc, is made of pure carbon. Chemically, it is exactly the same as graphite, the substance used to make pencil lead. Graphite has a hardness of between 1 and 2 on the Mohs' scale. The difference between hard carbon and soft graphite is caused by the arrangement of the carbon atoms. In graphite, the atoms are linked in flat planes which readily slide over each other. In diamond, which is formed in great heat and under intense pressure, the atoms are bound in a rigid structure.

Prized gems Diamond stones are popular in wedding rings because they wear well and won't dissolve in acid. However, strong heat can turn diamond into carbon dioxide, and heated without oxygen, the prized diamond will change into the humble graphite.

DOUBLE TROUBLE

What makes you see double? Calcite is a mineral which forms most of a common rock called limestone. A pure form of calcite, called Iceland spar, is transparent. If you placed a piece of it on this page, you would see two images of every word. This unusual feature is called double refraction.

INFLATION RATE

Did you know that the Universe is expanding? In 1929, the American astronomer Edwin Hubble discovered that the galaxies are moving apart from each other at high speed. The Universe is expanding like a balloon being inflated. The further apart the galaxies are, the faster they move. For instance, a galaxy 10 million light years away gets 300 km (187 miles) further from us every second. A galaxy ten times further off moves ten times faster, and so on.

THE DAWN OF TIME

How old is the Earth? Over the centuries, new ways to calculate the age of the Earth have often been proposed. In 1656, the Irish Archbishop Ussher announced that he had worked it out by adding up all the lifespans of the people in the Bible right back to Adam. He calculated that the Earth was created in 4004 BC. (Some people still agree with him.)

In the 19th century, scientists studying how rocks formed and changed thought that the Earth must be millions of years old. Then, in the early years of the 20th century, scientists began to date rocks by studying traces of radioactive elements found in some of them. Studies of meteorites and Moon rocks now indicate that the solar system and our planet were formed about 4,600 million years ago.

◀ A portrait of James Ussher, Bishop of Armagh, whose imaginative method of calculating the age of the Earth is still believed by some people today.

▲
The River Nile transforms the otherwise arid Egyptian countryside into fertile agricultural land.

FOOD FOR THOUGHT

Can farming produce enough of the world's food? Land covers just over 29 per cent of the Earth's surface. But about two-thirds of the land is too cold or too dry for farming. Of the remaining land, only one-third can be used for crops and the rest is grazing land. Will this be enough to feed the world's population as it soars towards 10,000 million?

Experts think that food yields can be increased in two main ways. First, scientists are producing new and more productive varieties of food crops. Second, farming can become more efficient if farmers use more modern machinery and follow better farming techniques. In many developing countries, wooden hoes are often more common than metal ploughs.

An animal shoulder blade embedded in permafrost in Alaska. ▶

DESERT WATER

Where is the largest oasis? Oases are places in deserts where there is fresh water. The largest oasis is the fertile valley of the River Nile in Egypt, which gets its water from the distant East African highlands.

REALLY COOL

Did you know that space is not totally cold? In 1965, two American radio astronomers discovered that a slight warmth pervades the Universe. The Universe today has a temperature of −270°C (−570°F), just three degrees above absolute zero, the coldest temperature possible. This feeble glow is energy left over from the Big Bang explosion.

OLD BUT TASTY

What is permafrost? In cold countries, the soil freezes hard in winter. In summer, the top few centimetres may thaw, while lower down the soil stays frozen. This permanently frozen soil is called permafrost. Several extinct woolly mammoths, which died about 45,000 years ago, have been dug out of the permafrost in Siberia. The meat of one of them, preserved in this natural refrigerator, was so fresh that dogs tucked into it!

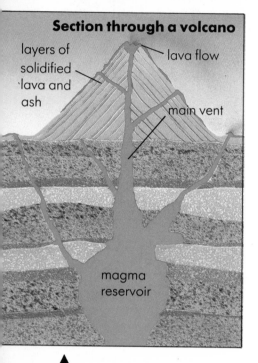

Section through a volcano

layers of solidified lava and ash

lava flow

main vent

magma reservoir

▲
A section through a volcano.

LOUDEST BANG

What explosion in Indonesia was heard in Australia? On August 27, 1883, the volcanic island of Krakatoa blew itself up The explosions, the most powerful in modern times, were heard 4,700 km (2,920 miles) away by puzzled Australian farmers from Perth to Alice Springs, and window frames rattled in Singapore, over 800 km (500 miles) away.

The cause Volcanoes explode when the magma (molten material) inside them is thick and pasty. Hot gases and steam trapped inside the magma gradually expand, until finally they explode. The explosions break the magma into fragments ranging from dust to brick-shaped lumps.

In big explosions, black clouds of dust and ash are hurled into the air. The 27-km (17-mile) high column of ash from Krakatoa spread around the world, causing vivid sunsets for three or four years afterwards.

JIGSAW MYSTERY

Can continents drift? If you look at a map of the Atlantic Ocean, you will see that the coastal shapes of the Americas resemble those of Europe and Africa. Might these continents have once been joined together like pieces in a giant jigsaw? A German meteorologist, Alfred Wegener (1880-1930), thought so. He wrote a book saying that, about 200 million years ago, all the continents were joined together. But this supercontinent later split apart and the pieces 'drifted' to their present positions.

Shifting plates The problem with Wegener's theory of 'continental drift' was that no one could explain how continents move. In the 1960s, scientists came up with an answer based on studies of the ocean floor. They suggested that the solid crust and part of the upper mantle are divided into large blocks, or plates. Beneath these plates is semi-fluid rock which moves around in slow currents. It is these currents which move the plates and the continents which rest upon them – very slowly.

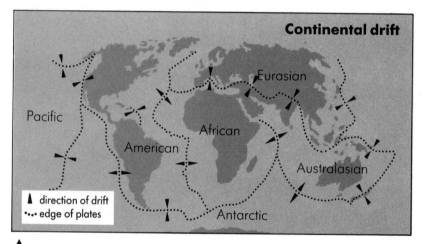

Continental drift

Pacific

Eurasian

African

American

Australasian

Antarctic

▲ direction of drift
•••• edge of plates

▲
Over many millions of years, movements in the Earth's crust resulted in continental drift. The main plates are still shifting today.

QUIZ: COUNTRIES

① Which country has been called 'the gift of the Nile'?
② Which country's name means equator?
③ Which British colony will be returned to China in 1997?
④ Which country is also the world's largest archipelago?
⑤ Which is the world's only officially atheist country?
⑥ Which African country had the same name as its neighbour until 1971?
⑦ Which country has more than 55,000 lakes?
⑧ Which country is named after a tree?
⑨ Which country is officially called the Hellenic Republic?

ANSWERS
① Egypt. ② Ecuador. ③ Hong Kong. ④ Indonesia.
⑤ Albania. ⑥ Zaïre (formerly Congo). ⑦ Finland. ⑧ Brazil (brazilwood). ⑨ Greece.

▲
A colourful display of the member countries' national flags outside the United Nations headquarters in New York.

CHANGING WORLD

What is the UN? Changes are taking place all the time in world geography and these changes are reflected in the United Nations (UN). The UN is an international organization set up on October 24, 1945 to work for peace and human dignity. Its first 50 members consisted of the Allies (the winning side in World War II), including the 'Big Three' – the UK, USA and USSR. Countries on the losing side joined later. Japan was admitted in 1956, while East and West Germany finally became members in 1973.

Steady growth The main changes since World War II, both in world geography and in the UN, resulted from the ending of the empires ruled by France, Portugal, Spain and the UK. These empires were based mainly in Africa and Asia, while small island colonies were scattered around the world. In 1945, only nine Asian and four African countries were members of the UN. But the desire for independence steadily increased throughout Asia and Africa. By 1959, the UN had 83 members, though there were still only 23 Asian and 10 African members.

Rapid expansion Major changes occurred in the 1960s when 43 countries joined the UN – 32 of them being former European colonies in Africa. On the UN's 40th birthday, it had 159 members, with 37 from Asia and 51 from Africa. By then, the world map looked very different from that of 1945.

BLAZING STREAMS

What are quiet eruptions? The volcanoes of Hawaii and Sicily's Mount Etna are called 'quiet volcanoes'. This is because they contain fluid, runny magma. Gases and steam can easily escape from runny magma and so 'quiet' volcanoes do not explode. Instead, they emit long streams of blazing hot lava. The lava often flows great distances before it cools and hardens.

BOOMS AND BANGS

Can sands boom? Yes. Loud booming sounds occur in deserts when sand dunes are disturbed and sand slips down the steep faces of the dunes.

Such roaring sounds have been compared with the noise of aircraft engines starting up.
At night, sounds like pistol shots may frighten travellers.

They occur when desert rocks crack and split. The cracking of rocks is caused by intense heating during the day, followed by rapid cooling after dark.

◀ Part of the expanse of sand forming Algeria's Grand Erg desert.

CELESTIAL SPARKLERS

Why do stars twinkle? The twinkle has nothing to do with the star itself. It happens as light from the star passes through the Earth's atmosphere. Moving currents of air bend the star's light, so that the star seems to flash rapidly. The effect is particularly noticeable near the horizon, where the star's light passes through the densest layers of atmosphere.

Bright stars close to the horizon often appear to flash many different colours from red to blue. The amount of twinkling varies from night to night, depending on how unsteady the atmosphere is.

FAR OUT

How far are the stars? The stars are so far away from us that astronomers do not use normal measurements such as kilometres or miles. Instead, they have invented a unit called the light year. This is the distance travelled in one year by a beam of light, which moves at the fastest speed in the Universe, 300,000 km (187,000 miles) per second. A light year equals 9.5 million million km (6 million million miles). The nearest star, Alpha Centauri, lies 4.3 light years away, or 40 million million km (26 million million miles).

That's 300,000 times further away from us than the Sun. The Space Shuttle, travelling at top speed, would take about 160,000 years to reach Alpha Centauri. Some of the stars you can see at night are so distant that their light has taken hundreds or even thousands of years to get here.

GIANTS AND DWARFS

How big are the stars? Stars, like people, come in different sizes. The largest stars are the supergiants. An example is Antares, the brightest star in the constellation of Scorpius, the Scorpion. Antares is about 420 million km (260 million miles) in diameter, 300 times the width of the Sun. That's large enough to swallow the orbit of the Earth.

If you could make a phone call from one side of Antares to the other, your voice would take more than half an hour to travel around the star.

The smallest stars are called dwarfs. Some of them, termed white dwarfs, are only about one per cent the diameter of the Sun — no bigger than the Earth.

▲
Star clouds in the Milky Way, towards the centre of our Galaxy.

THE WORLD'S HIGHEST MOUNTAINS

Mountain	Range	Height in m (ft) above sea-level
Everest	Himalayas (Asia)	8,848 (29,028)
K2	Karakoram (Asia)	8,611 (28,250)
Kanchenjunga	Himalayas	8,598 (28,208)
Lhotse	Himalayas	8,501 (27,890)
Makalu	Himalayas	8,481 (27,824)

A view of the south-west face of Mount Everest which ▶ lies on the border between Nepal and Tibet.

STANDING ROOM ONLY

Can populations explode? In AD 1, the world had a population of about 200 million. It took 1,400 years before the population doubled. But after AD 1400, the population increased rapidly. It reached 900 million in 1800, over 1,600 million in 1900, over 2,000 million in 1930, over 3,000 million in 1960, and over 4,000 million in 1975. This ever-increasing growth, called the 'population explosion', is still going on.

Predicted growth Some people fear that we will soon be threatened by overcrowding and food shortages, as is happening today in some poor African countries. There the populations are doubling every 20 years and famines are common. However, by the early 1980s, the populations of some rich countries, such as Britain, had stopped rising. And in others, including West Germany, the number of people was actually falling. Overall, it seems that the population explosion is slowing down. Experts now predict that the world's population will level out around AD 2100, when there will probably be about 10,200 million people on Earth.

HIDDEN MOUNTAINS

Which is the world's highest mountain? Some readers may think that this is the easiest question in the book. Surely everyone knows that the answer is Mount Everest, which rises 8,848 m (29,028 ft) above sea-level! But what about mountains that rise from the sea floor? If you take them into account, then Mauna Kea, Hawaii, is 1,355 m (4,446 ft) higher than Everest. Mauna Kea, a volcano, rises 10,203 m (33,476 ft) from its base, but only 4,205 m (13,796 ft) can be seen above sea-level.

▲
A crowd in New York, USA, a city with a population of over seven million people.

▲
Torrential monsoon rain flooding the streets of Calcutta, India.

FACT FILE: THE SOLAR SYSTEM

FACT Venus is enveloped in unbroken clouds composed of sulphuric acid, stronger than the acid in a car battery.

FACT Despite appearances, the Moon is not silvery. Its rocks reflect only 7 per cent of the light that hits them, so that they are actually dark grey.

FACT The largest volcano in the solar system is Olympus Mons on Mars. At 600 km (375 miles) in diameter and 26 km (16 miles) high, it is larger even than the volcanic islands of Hawaii on Earth.

FACT Saturn is of such low density that it would float on water.

FACT Asteroids are rubble left over from the formation of the solar system. Thousands of them orbit in a belt between the orbits of Mars and Jupiter.

FACT In 1910 the Earth passed through the tail of Halley's comet. But the gas of a comet's tail is far thinner than the Earth's atmosphere, so it had no noticeable effect on the Earth.

FACT Pluto is the only planet whose orbit crosses that of another. For part of its orbit Pluto is closer to the Sun than is Neptune, but Pluto's average distance from the Sun is greater than Neptune's.

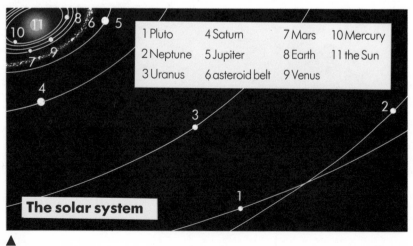

1 Pluto	4 Saturn	7 Mars	10 Mercury
2 Neptune	5 Jupiter	8 Earth	11 the Sun
3 Uranus	6 asteroid belt	9 Venus	

The solar system

▲
All the planets in the solar system orbit the Sun.

A MATTER OF LIFE AND DEATH

Where is the world's wettest place? Lots of people complain about the weather, especially when they get wet. But in tropical lands, rain is often a matter of life and death. For example, in India, farmers pray for the summer monsoon rains to help their young rice plants grow. North-eastern India is particularly wet, and the village of Cherrapunji holds the world record rainfall for one year. A total of 2,646 cm (1,042 in) of rain was recorded in 1860-61.

▲
A Basque shepherd and his flock.

SURVIVORS OF ATLANTIS?

Which European language is unique? Most Europeans speak one of the Indo-European languages. However, one language, Basque, which is spoken by people in north-eastern Spain and south-western France, isn't related to any other tongue. Its origins are shrouded in mystery and some people have even suggested that it was spoken in the 'lost continent of Atlantis'.

It now seems likely that the ancestors of the Basques, who belonged to an Upper Stone Age culture, settled in Spain long before the Indo-Europeans. Today, the Basques take pride in their strange language, and some would like to found a separate Basque nation.

WHICH INDIANS?

Who were the first Americans?
When Christopher Columbus
sailed across the Atlantic in
1492, he thought that the Earth
was much smaller than it actually
is. As a result, he believed that he
had reached India and that the
people in the Caribbean islands
were Indians. In fact, the
ancestors of these people came
from north-eastern Asia,
perhaps 40,000 years ago. They
spread southwards and reached
the southern tip of South America
over 8,000 years ago. Today many
scholars call the first Americans
Amerindians to distinguish
them from 'Indian' Indians.

SPEEDING UP NATURE

What is erosion? Natural forces
are constantly changing our
world. Some rocks are dissolved
by rainwater and others are split
by frost or rapid temperature
changes. Worn rock is then
carried away by running water,
glaciers and, in dry regions, by
the wind. Weathering, running
water, glaciers and winds are all
forces of erosion.

Natural erosion is slow. For
example, it takes 30,000 years
for 1 m (39 in) of ground to be
worn away from the eastern
USA. However, these natural
processes can be speeded up.
When people cut down forests
or plough up and overgraze
grasslands, they expose the soil.
The forces of erosion then
operate much faster, stripping
away the soil and making once-
fertile land useless.

The grooves and curves in this
sandstone cliff are the result
of weathering by rain and wind.
▼

SOLAR BLEMISHES

What is a sunspot? Dark patches mark the surface of the Sun. These sunspots are areas of cooler gas, caused by strong magnetic fields that temporarily block the outward flow of heat from inside the Sun. Individual sunspots can be up to 100,000 km (62,500 miles) in diameter, nearly ten times the width of the Earth.

A typical sunspot lasts for a week or two. The number of sunspots varies in a cycle lasting about 11 years. At the peak of the sunspot cycle, more than 100 spots may be visible at a time, whereas at sunspot minimum the Sun may be spotless for days.

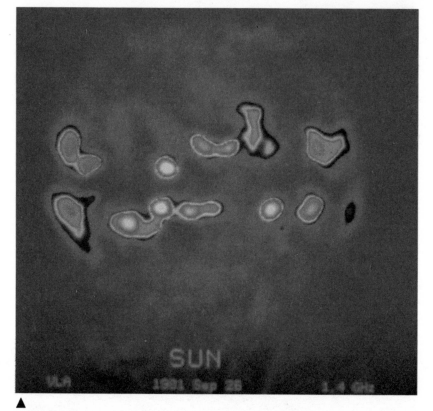

▲ A false-colour radio image of the Sun showing bands of sunspots along its equator.

OTHER FISH TO FRY

Why farm fish? Despite the use of modern instruments, such as radar and echo-sounders, fishing remains an unscientific industry compared with farming. Success still depends partly on luck. Fish farming, however, is an attempt to bring more science into the industry. It involves breeding fish and later transferring them to inland and coastal waters. Freshwater fish farming has proved profitable, although less success has been achieved with salt-water fish farming.

MARINE HAZARD

What causes whirlpools? Whirlpools are a threat to small boats. The whirlpools between Sicily and mainland Italy, named Scylla and Charybdis, were once thought to be the lairs of sea monsters that swallowed ships. Whirlpools are often caused when strong currents are confined between rocks or when two currents meet.

ENERGY SOURCE

What makes the stars shine? Stars are gigantic nuclear reactors. They produce energy at their centres by converting hydrogen, their main constituent, into helium. In the Sun, 600 million tonnes of hydrogen are turned into helium every second. But the Sun is so huge that it contains enough hydrogen to continue burning for thousands of millions of years yet.

SOLAR PUZZLE

Has the Sun stopped burning? Believe it or not, a tank of cleaning fluid buried underground is telling us about what goes on at the centre of the Sun. And the startling news is that the Sun may have stopped burning, albeit temporarily.

According to theory, the nuclear reactions inside the Sun should produce atomic particles known as neutrinos, which escape directly into space and reach the Earth. Neutrinos are difficult to detect, but some of them can be captured by chlorine atoms. A good source of chlorine is the liquid called perchloroethylene, which is used in dry cleaning.

Slow down An American scientist, Raymond Davis, has set up a tank of 400,000 litres (88,000 gallons) of this dry-cleaning fluid in a gold mine in South Dakota. It is placed 1.5 km (9/10 mile) underground to shield it from other forms of radiation. The experiment has detected far fewer neutrinos coming from the Sun than astronomers expected. One possible reason is that the Sun's nuclear furnace needs stoking.

SIXTH SENSE?

How can we foretell earthquakes? China has suffered some terrible earthquakes, and it isn't surprising that China's scientists want to find ways of forecasting them. In 1975, they were successful. They cleared the city of Haicheng two hours before a devastating 'quake and saved the city's population. Earthquake forecasting is, however, still inexact; the Chinese have failed to predict several earthquakes since 1975, but they have advanced the science of earthquake prediction.

Advance warnings We now know that small tremors (foreshocks) often occur before a larger movement. Changes also occur in the electric and magnetic properties of rocks, and growing tension often causes swellings and cracks in the ground. When rocks crack, a radioactive gas, radon, is often released. Radon dissolves in water and so, if the radon content in well water builds up, an earthquake may be on the way.

Chinese workers have also been asked to report strange behaviour by animals. Before 'quakes, dogs may howl, nervous animals run from buildings and fish thrash about in water. Perhaps they sense changes which we cannot detect.

THREE SCORE YEARS AND TEN?

How long do people live? The average lifespan of people varies from country to country. If you live in a developed country, then you can expect to live longer. For example, Australians live, on average, 76 years, West Germans and North Americans 75 years and Britons 74 years.

In poorly developed countries, where many people do not have enough to eat, suffer many diseases and lack good health services, lifespans are much shorter. Examples include Ethiopia, 43 years; Nepal, 46 years, and India, 55 years.

Women usually live longer than men. For instance, the average life expectancy at birth for women in the USA is 79 years — seven years more than men.

Contrasting faces of old age from rural Asia (left) and urban Europe (right).
▼

WELL DOWN

Where does all the rain go?
When it rains, some water flows into streams, some is absorbed by plants, some evaporates and some seeps into the ground. Some rocks are permeable— that is, they contain tiny pores or fissures (cracks) through which water can flow. Permeable rock layers containing water are called aquifers, and if you dig down to one of these, you create a well.

Rainwater will seep into permeable ▶ rock like this limestone outcrop.

◀ A forester preparing to fell a hardwood tree in Borneo.

TIMBER!

What are the main kinds of wood? The vast coniferous forests in the northern hemisphere contain evergreen trees, including cedars, firs, larches, pines and spruces. They are all called softwoods, though some are quite hard. But most are easy to work and have many uses, including the making of paper.

Deciduous, or broadleaved, trees grow in temperate lands. They include ash, beech, birch, chestnut, oak, sycamore and willow. These trees, which shed their leaves in winter, are often called hardwoods, though some are softer than pine. Valuable hardwoods, used to make expensive furniture, include ebony, mahogany and rosewood, which grow in tropical forests.

◀ A new road cut by lumberjacks as they move into isolated areas of the Brazilian jungle.

On maps and globes, lines of latitude and longitude are usually represented by a grid. Any point on the Earth's surface can be quickly located using degrees of latitude and longitude. ▶

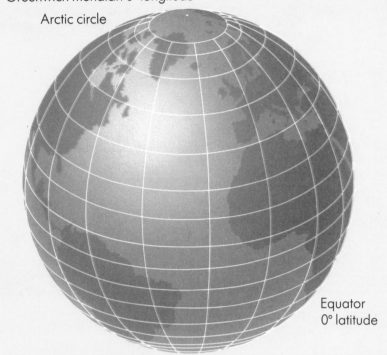

Greenwich meridian 0° longitude

Arctic circle

Equator
0° latitude

Lines of latitude and longitude

ICY ESCALATORS

How fast does ice move on land? Bodies of ice, ranging from vast ice sheets to valley glaciers move downhill because of gravity. In Antarctica the ice sheet moves by only a metre (39 in) or so a year, while most valley glaciers move the same distance in a day.

Special circumstances can speed up the movement of the ice. In 1936-37, Alaska's Black Rapids Glacier moved downhill at up to 60 m (197 ft) a day! This amazing rate was probably caused by an earthquake which shook huge amounts of snow on to the glacier's source. The snow rapidly compacted into ice, and its sheer weight propelled the glacier downwards at speed.

DEEP DOWN DIAMONDS

Where is the Big Hole?
Kimberley, South Africa, is called 'the diamond capital of the world'. One mine, opened in 1871, yielded about three tonnes of diamonds before it was abandoned in 1914. Called the Big Hole, it is the world's largest man-made hole. Largely dug by hand, it has a perimeter of 1.6 km (1 mile). It was 800 m (2,625 ft) deep, with shafts leading down to 1,100 m (3,609 ft). Water is now steadily filling in the Big Hole.

GLOBAL LINES

What are lines of latitude and longitude? These are the lines you will find drawn on a globe, running from east to west or north to south.

Latitude The line drawn halfway between the poles is called the equator. Other lines parallel to the equator are called parallels, or lines of latitude. They are measured north and south of the equator (0° latitude) to the poles (90° North and 90° South). Every place has its own latitude. For example, Montreal, Canada, is 45½° North; Buenos Aires, Argentina, is 34½° South.

Longitude On globes, there are also lines running at right angles to the equator. These lines, all of which pass through the poles, are lines of longitude, or meridians. By international agreement, the prime meridian (0° longitude) passes through Greenwich, a borough of London, England. The other lines of longitude are measured 180° east and 180° west of the prime meridian.

QUIZ: GEOLOGY

① What do geologists call molten rock *inside* the Earth?
② What do geologists call streams of molten rock that spill *out* of volcanoes?
③ What is the name for fractures (breaks) in rocks along which the rocks have moved?
④ What icicle-like rock structures hang down from the roofs of limestone caves?
⑤ What are cracks in the surface of glaciers called?
⑥ What porous volcanic rock floats on water?

ANSWERS
① Magma. ② Lava. ③ Faults. ④ Stalactites. ⑤ Crevasses.
⑥ Pumice.

GETTING THE WIND UP

Which are the worst storms? On average, 45,000 thunderstorms occur somewhere around the world every day. They may cause damage, as when lightning starts forest fires, but two other kinds of storms are even more dangerous.

Hurricanes The hurricane, which is also called a typhoon, a tropical cyclone or, in Australia, a willy-willy, is one deadly storm. Hurricanes are rotating low air pressure systems which form over tropical seas. As they approach land, fierce winds, which may reach 300 km/h (186 mph) drive waves inland, causing floods and devastation. In 1970, one such storm killed about a million people on the flat islands bordering the Ganges delta of Bangladesh. Hurricanes are between 160 and 500 km (99-311 miles) across. On satellite photographs, which are used to track their movements, they resemble whirlpools of clouds.

Tornadoes Another storm, the tornado, is a narrow column of swirling air, which seldom measures more than 0.4 km (¼ mile) across. Yet winds in tornadoes may reach 650 km/h (over 400 mph), ripping trees out of the ground and lifting people into the air. The south-eastern USA has over 500 tornadoes a year, and one in 1925 killed 689 people.

A convoy of cattle transporters on an American highway.
▼

WET UP AND DRY DOWN

What is a rain shadow? When winds blow from the sea up high coastal mountain ranges, they shed much of their moisture as rain or snow. However, when they blow down the leeward (sheltered) slopes of the range, they get warmer and pick up moisture, so the leeward side of the range is dry. It is said to be in a rain shadow area.

◀ The 'eye' of the storm: swirling Cyclone Rita seen from space.

TAKING TO THE ROAD

Why is road transport so important? The use of trucks has caused a revolution in land transport. Trucks can carry goods quickly from door to door, while trains must be loaded and unloaded at often inconvenient locations. Trains and barges are still used for carrying bulky goods of fairly low value, such as metal ores, but smaller items of higher value now go by road.

The growth of highway networks in many countries reflects the importance of the truck. The USA's highway network is, for example, the world's most highly developed, and North Americans are probably more dependent on cars and other road vehicles than any other society.

▲ Africa's rift valley — seen here in Kenya — occurs where two of the Earth's plates meet.

The Baluchi nomads of Pakistan follow a fairly traditional lifestyle, relying on camels for transport.
▼

DEEP DEPRESSIONS

What are rift valleys?
Movements of plates in the top layers of the Earth's crust create enormous tension, which sometimes makes long cracks, or faults, in rocks. Continuing tugging movements make blocks of land sink down between roughly parallel sets of faults, forming troughs called rift valleys.

The world's biggest rift valley runs from south-eastern Africa, through East Africa and the Red Sea to Syria. This long gash in the Earth contains the Dead Sea, a lake whose shoreline is 400 m (1,312 ft) below sea-level. This is the world's deepest depression.

CHANGING LIFESTYLES

What are nomads?
People who move around making use of land which is unfit for farming are called nomads. The term is applied especially to people whose livelihood depends on animals. Some, like the Lapps of northern Europe, follow the yearly migrations of animals, such as reindeer. Others, like the Bakhtiari in Iran, drive herds of domesticated animals from place to place in search of pasture.

Many nomads are now abandoning the wandering life. For example, many Bedouins who once travelled on camels – the 'ships of the desert' – have now settled down to enjoy the riches that come from Arabia's oil.

MISLEADING PICTURES

What do hot deserts look like?
From watching cinema films, you could be forgiven for thinking that all deserts are covered by sand. However, sand deserts make up only a fifth of the world's deserts. The rest are covered by small stones or just bare rock. Desert landscapes are called by Arabic names. Sand desert is called *erg*, stony desert *reg*, and areas of bare rock *hammada*.

◀ Scott Base in Antarctica. The pressure ridges where the ice shelf meets land can be seen clearly in the background.

NO ESCAPE

What is a black hole? It is the grave of a massive star. If the shrunken core left behind by a supernova has a mass of more than three Suns, its gravitational pull is so strong that nothing can escape, not even the star's own light. The object is invisible – a black hole. A black hole can swallow up gas and even passing stars, like a plug hole in space. Gas falling into a black hole heats up to millions of degrees, at which temperature it emits X-rays, which can be detected by satellites orbiting the Earth.

In this way at least one black hole, called Cygnus X-1, has been detected. The largest black holes, containing the mass of millions of Suns, are thought to lie at the heart of galaxies.

HOW COLD?

Which is the coldest continent? 'Great God! this is an awful place,' wrote the British explorer Captain Scott at the South Pole on January 17, 1912. The average temperature at the South Pole is −50°C (−58°F) and the low temperatures in Antarctica are made worse by blizzards – high winds that whip up powdery snow and reduce visibility to zero.

The coldest weather ever recorded was at the Russian Vostok Station, east of the South Pole, in 1983. The thermometer, protected from the wind behind a screen, showed a temperature of −89.2°C (−128.6°F)!

A fossilized insect.
▼

FACT FILE: FOSSILS

FACT Fossils are evidence of ancient life. The oldest are the remains of reefs built by bacteria. They are called stromatolites and are around 3,500 million years old.

FACT Fossils are rare in Pre-Cambrian rocks (rocks formed before the start of the Cambrian period, 570 million years ago).

FACT Some extinct animals have been preserved in tar pits. And mammoths which lived 45,000 years ago have been found in the frozen soil of Siberia. Such fossils are rare.

FACT Fossil moulds are common. They form when the hard parts of animals are buried and later dissolved away. This cavity forms the mould of a fossil cast if it is filled by minerals.

FACT Permineralized fossils are those in which minerals have filled the pores in buried bones and shells, making them stone-like.

FACT Petrified fossils are formed when minerals replace all the original cells. For example, petrified logs show every detail of the original wood.

FACT Plant leaves may be preserved as carbon smears.

FACT Trace fossils include petrified eggs, burrows and footprints.

CHANGING TABLES

Why do wells dry up?
Rainwater that seeps into the ground filters down to the zone of saturation, where every crack in the rock is filled with water. (Below this point compact rocks stop the water going any deeper.) The top level of the zone of saturation is called the water table. This level rises and falls according to the weather, and wells sunk down to it in wet weather may dry up during times of drought.

ROLLING STONES

What is an erratic? In many parts of the world, you can find large boulders, called erratics, which rest on rocks of a different kind. How did they get there? One idea popular in the early 19th century was that they had been rolled there by strong currents during Noah's Flood!

In the 1830s, a Swiss professor, Louis Agassiz, studied the glaciers which move slowly down mountain valleys in the Alps. He saw that glaciers carried loose rock (moraine) ranging in size from fine particles of clay to boulders. Could ice, not water, have moved the erratics? Agassiz finally decided that, at some time in the past, there had been an Ice Age and ice had spread over a much larger area than it does today. The erratics, he argued, were moved at that time. His ideas, published in 1840, finally won the day.

GRUB UP

How many people can a farmer feed? The average farmer in the USA produced about enough food for four people in 1850. Because of the use of farm machinery, fertilizers, improved varieties of plants and scientific care of animals, the average American farmer can now feed 80 people. Although far fewer people work on farms than in the past, they are so productive that the USA is now the world's top food exporter.

Wheat harvesting in America is a highly mechanized process.
▼

WORKING TOGETHER

What is the EEC? Since World War II, many countries have joined common markets. These organizations try to develop the economies of the member countries, especially by removing all trade restrictions between them. The European Economic Community (EEC) was founded in 1957 by Italy, France, Belgium, Luxembourg, the Netherlands and West Germany. Six nations joined later: Denmark, Ireland and the UK in 1973; Greece in 1981; and Portugal and Spain in 1986.

The EEC: 1 Britain; 2 Ireland; 3 Denmark; 4 The Netherlands; 5 Belgium; 6 Luxembourg; 7 West Germany; 8 France; 9 Portugal; 10 Spain; 11 Italy; 12 Greece.

▼

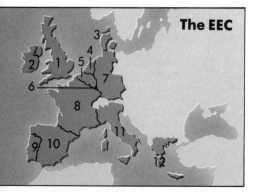

The EEC

MARTIAN MIRAGE

Who thought there were people on Mars? Percival Lowell, an American astronomer, thought he saw canals criss-crossing the deserts of Mars, when he observed the planet through his telescope early this century. He believed that these canals were built by a Martian civilization to bring water for irrigation from the planet's polar caps.

However, space probes have shown that the canals were simply optical illusions, and that Mars is too hostile for any form of life.

SMOKE THAT THUNDERS

▲ The Victoria Falls, Zimbabwe.

How are waterfalls formed? Many waterfalls occur where rivers flow over hard rocks which overlie softer ones. The hard rocks resist erosion, while the softer rocks are worn away. The hard lip of the waterfall often overhangs the softer rock and slabs of hard rock sometimes break off and crash downwards. In this way, waterfalls, like southern Africa's Victoria Falls (whose African name means 'the smoke that thunders'), gradually move upstream. Other waterfalls occur along cliffs, like those bordering steep-sided valleys, or ice-worn troughs.

The biggest fall The highest waterfall, Angel Falls in Venezuela, was named after an American pilot, Jimmy Angel, who was the first non-Amerindian to see it. Its total height is 979 m (3,212 ft), with one unbroken drop of 807 m (2,648 ft).

FIERY FATE

How will the Sun die? A few thousand million years from now, the Sun will run out of hydrogen at its centre. Then the nuclear reactions will spread outwards into the region surrounding the Sun's core. With more hydrogen to burn, the Sun will produce more energy, and it will swell up into a red giant star.

As the Sun gets bigger and brighter, the Earth will be roasted to a cinder. When the Sun has swollen to its largest, perhaps 100 times the size it is now, its outer layers will drift off into space, like a celestial smoke ring. The core of the former red giant will be left behind as a small condensed star called a white dwarf.

▲ The 'Frost Fair' held on London's River Thames in 1684.

CLUES TO ANCIENT CLIMATES

When was the Little Ice Age? We expect the day-to-day weather to change, but we expect the climate (the average or usual weather) to stay more or less the same from year to year. About 12,000 years ago, northern North America and northern and central Europe were in the grip of a bitterly cold Ice Age. By contrast, about 10,000 years ago, the climate was probably warmer than it is today. Between the 15th century and the mid-19th century, however, there was a Little Ice Age.

Contemporary records There are no climatic records for this time, but European artists have provided useful clues. Many of their paintings in the 16th and 17th centuries show rivers, which never freeze today, covered by thick ice.

Other evidence of climatic differences comes from the writings of travellers. It suggests that not only was Europe colder, but that all the climatic zones moved south. Why should this happen? No one knows for sure. Perhaps it was caused by wobbles in the Earth's axis or variations in the Earth's path around the Sun.

CHIPS WITH EVERYTHING

Where is Silicon Valley? A new industrial revolution began in the 1960s. One of its main centres is just south of San Francisco, California, USA. Here in Santa Clara County, a fertile fruit-growing region, is Silicon Valley. You won't find this name on any map. Silicon Valley is the region between Palo Alto and San Jose where silicon chip computer technology was pioneered. Its main rival is Japan.

THE LONG AND THE SHORT OF IT

Who are the tallest and shortest people? The Tutsi of Burundi and Rwanda, who are noted for their dancing and high jumping, are, on average, the world's tallest people. Men average over 183 cm (6 ft) in height. The world's shortest people also live in Central Africa. These are the pygmy hunters and gatherers in the forests. Pygmy women average only 135 cm (4 ft 5 in) and men 137 cm (4 ft 6 in)!

The spectacular Tutsi dancers in ▶ their full regalia.

▲
Some rocks are formed today
when molten lava solidifies.

HOT ROCKS?

Where are the world's oldest rocks? Rocks that were formed in the last 2,800 million years can be found in every continent, but rocks more than 3,500 million years old are extremely rare. Some rocks in the American Minnesota River valley and others in western Greenland have been dated at about 3,800 million years. The world's oldest rocks, however, are probably in Australia, where, in 1983, scientists claimed they had found crystals of the mineral zircon that were 4,200 million years old.

Molten surface The reason why extremely old rocks are so rare is probably because the surface of the Earth was molten for many millions of years after its formation. Whenever the surface cooled and hardened, it was broken up and remelted. It now seems certain that the Earth had a solid crust by about 3,800 million years ago and that, by 2,500 million years ago, about half of the present continents had been formed.

Oceanic rocks The oceans are, by contrast, recent features. About 275 million years ago, all the land areas were fused in one super-continent, surrounded by one vast ocean. This continent broke up about 180 million years ago and the pieces drifted slowly to their present positions. So most oceanic rocks were formed in the last 200 million years.

LUNAR SCARS

What caused the craters on the Moon? The surface of the Moon is scarred by craters up to 250 km (160 miles) in diameter, the result of meteorites smashing into the surface long ago.

There has also been some volcanic activity, for dark lava flows cover the lowland areas of the Moon, forming the familiar pattern known as 'the Man in the Moon'. The Moon's surface is incredibly ancient. The youngest rocks brought back by the Apollo astronauts are more than 3,000 million years old!

The surface of the Moon is pitted ▶
with craters of all sizes.

DRIED UP

Where is the world's driest place? Many deserts – places which have less than 25 cm (10 in) rainfall a year – are, in fact, dry for years and then a freak storm causes floods. Or heavy rains can transform some deserts, as in Namaqualand, South Africa, into a sea of flowers, bringing new life to seeds which may have been dormant for years. Elsewhere, drought-resistant plants like cacti soak up rainwater in their swollen stems. Such events are, however, unknown in Chile's Atacama Desert. This is the world's driest place where no rain has fallen in 400 years!

Desert extremes The world's largest desert, the Sahara, covers about 8,400,000 square km (3,250,000 square miles). It is a hot desert, though it may be freezing cold at night because there are no clouds to stop heat escaping into space.

In Antarctica, Greenland and the northern USSR there are cold deserts, where the average annual rainfall (or the equivalent in snow) is as low as in a hot desert. Here, the snow blown into your face during blizzards isn't usually falling from above – it is simply loose snow swept up from the surface of the ground.

▲ Spring flowers in Namaqualand.

North Sea fishermen preparing ▶ to land their catch.

UNDERWATER BANKS

What are the Grand and Dogger Banks? Around the continents are shallow seas covering the continental shelves. These seas contain most of the world's chief fishing grounds, some of which are called banks. The Grand Banks, off the south-east coast of Newfoundland, Canada, extend across about 360,000 square km (139,000 square miles). With an average depth of 110 m (361 ft), they yield more than 800,000 tonnes of fish, especially cod, a year. Fishing in the Grand Banks can be dangerous and sailors must beware of fogs, icebergs and fierce storms.

The Dogger Bank in the North Sea, about 160 km (110 miles) east of the coast of North Yorkshire in northern England, is another rich fishing ground. Between 15–37 m (49–122 ft) deep, it is best known for its cod and herring.

QUIZ: PLANETS

1 Which is the smallest planet in the solar system?
2 Which planet is called the Red Planet?
3 Which planets have no moons?
4 Which planet is named after the god of the sea?
5 Which planet appears as the brilliant morning or evening 'star'?
6 Which is the only planet not mentioned in Holst's *Planets* suite?

ANSWERS
1 Pluto. 2 Mars. 3 Mercury and Venus. 4 Neptune. 5 Venus. 6 Pluto (it was not discovered until 1930, after the music was written).

cirrus

cirrostratus

cirrocumulus

altostratus

altocumulus

stratocumulus

cumulus

cumulonimbus

Common cloud formations

nimbostratus

SHAPES IN THE SKY

What makes clouds? When warm air rises, it cools. Eventually, the invisible water vapour in the air condenses (liquefies) to form water droplets, so tiny that they do not fall to the ground. At higher levels, the water vapour condenses and freezes into ice crystals. Clouds are formed from masses of these water droplets or ice crystals.

Some clouds, called *cumulus*, look like fluffy heaps. Others, called *stratus*, are thin sheets. *Cirrus* (a Latin word meaning curl) is a fibrous cloud, the highest in the sky. The tallest clouds, measured from their base to their often anvil-shaped top, are *cumulonimbus* or thunderclouds.

◄ Cloud formations vary considerably.

BASIC HUMAN NEEDS

Which farm products are used to clothe us? Several plants and animals are raised to produce fibres, which are then made into fabrics, yarn and other textiles. Major plant fibres include cotton, flax, hemp, jute and sisal. Wool is the chief animal fibre, while silk is made from the cocoons of silkworms.

Modern textiles Many fibres today are, however, artificial. For example, rayon is made from wood pulp and nylon, polyester and acrylic from petrochemicals.

Textile industries are as widespread as food industries, because both supply basic human needs. Even the poorest developing countries have factories that produce fabrics and clothes in order to save the high cost of importing textiles.

▲ A total solar eclipse.

LIGHTS OUT

What causes an eclipse? Both the Sun and the Moon can be eclipsed. An eclipse of the Sun (a solar eclipse) occurs when the Moon passes between us and the Sun, blocking off its light. A partial solar eclipse can last several hours, but a total eclipse, in which the Sun is completely blotted out, lasts no more than a few minutes.

An eclipse of the Moon (a lunar eclipse) occurs when the Moon enters the Earth's shadow. Lunar eclipses can last several hours. At least two solar eclipses and two lunar eclipses occur each year, although they are not all visible from any one place on Earth.

FLAT OUT

Where might you go to break the world land speed record? Obviously somewhere flat! Playas are large, flat depressions which are sometimes filled with water, but more often are dry. When the water evaporates in a playa, it often leaves behind a glistening crust of salt, so that many playas are called salinas, or salt flats. Such places, including the Bonneville Salt Flats, in Utah in the USA, and Lake Eyre, a playa in Australia, have proved good spots for the record breakers.

▲
A close-up view of salt flats in California, USA.

JUST SLEEPING

What is a dormant volcano? There are about 500 active volcanoes around the world, not including those hidden by the sea. A few, such as Stromboli, a volcanic island off the north-eastern coast of Sicily, are active nearly all the time. But most undergo long periods when they are dormant, or sleeping. Some volcanoes stay dormant for so long that they are thought to be extinct and it comes as a terrible shock when they unexpectedly erupt again.

LAND OF SAND

What is the Empty Quarter? Southern Arabia contains one of the world's bleakest deserts, which is visited only by the hardiest Bedouin nomads. Like all deserts, this is a place of extremes, and they must be prepared to risk hunger and thirst, and exposure to heat by day and bitter cold by night. The region is the Rub al Khali, or the Empty Quarter. Much of this 647,500 square km (250,000 square miles) is covered by drifting sand dunes up to 200 m (656 ft) high.

Ploughing on flat land is unlikely to cause problems with soil erosion.
▼

SOIL SAVING

What is contour ploughing? This is an important technique in modern farming, which was developed as farmers learnt from the mistakes made in the 19th and early 20th centuries. Then many people thought that the Earth's resources were boundless, and in colonies and other territories around the world, they cleared forests and grasslands to make way for new farms. At first, yields were high, but many farms became infertile. Soil erosion – the rapid removal of fertile topsoil by wind or rain – was the main culprit.

Soil erosion is especially severe on sloping land, when farmers plough furrows straight down the slope. This creates gullies which rainwater quicky deepens. Contour ploughing, a way to stop this form of erosion, involves ploughing along contours, so that the furrows follow lines linking points of the same height. Such furrows halt the downward flow of water and so reduce erosion.

THE ABYSS

How deep is the ocean? The oceans contain three main zones: a gently sloping continental shelf, covered by a shallow sea; a steep continental slope, which is the true edge of the continents; and the abyss, or ocean deeps. The abyss contains mountain ranges, called ocean ridges, volcanic mountains and deep trenches.

The average depth of the oceans is about 3,550 m (11,647 ft). The deepest point is 10,915 m (35,810 ft) in Challenger Deep – part of the Marianas Trench in the North Pacific Ocean.

A section through the ocean (artist's impression)

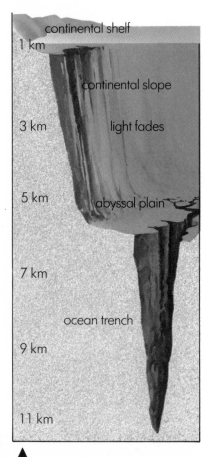

continental shelf
1 km
continental slope
3 km   light fades
5 km   abyssal plain
7 km
ocean trench
9 km
11 km

▲
The oceans contain more than 96 per cent of the world's water.

FACT FILE: RIVERS AND LAKES

FACT The longest river is the Nile in north-eastern Africa. The second longest river, the Amazon in South America, has the greatest flow.
FACT The power of rivers depends on their volume and speed. At 0.5 km/h (0.3 mph), rivers move sand. At more than 30 km/h (19 mph), they can shift large boulders.
FACT The Mississippi River in the USA carries over 700 million tonnes of eroded rock into the Gulf of Mexico every year.
FACT The world's largest lake is the salty Caspian Sea in the southern USSR and Iran. It covers about 170,000 square km (65,600 square miles).
FACT The largest freshwater lake is Lake Superior in North America. It covers 31,820 square km (12,286 square miles).
FACT The deepest lake, Lake Baikal in Siberia, is 1,940 m (6,365 ft) deep.

MAJOR RIVERS

River	Location	Length in km (miles)
Nile	NE Africa	6,679 (4,150)
Amazon	Brazil	6,276 (3,900)
Mississippi-Missouri-Red Rock	USA	6,115 (3,800)
Yangtze (Ch'ang Chiang)	China	5,472 (3,400)
Ob-Irtysh	USSR	5,150 (3,200)
Hwang Ho (Huang Ho)	China	4,667 (2,900)
Zaire (Congo)	Central Africa	4,667 (2,900)
Amur	China/USSR	4,506 (2,800)
Lena	USSR	4,506 (2,800)
Mekong	SE Asia	4,506 (2,800)

REVERSING FALLS

Can tides make rivers flow backwards? Tides are rises and falls of the oceans. They are caused approximately every 12 hours by the gravitational pull of the Moon and Sun on seawater. The highest (spring) tides occur twice a month, when the Sun, Moon and Earth are in a straight line and the gravitational pull of the Sun and Moon are combined. The lowest (neap) tides also occur twice a month, when the Sun, Earth and Moon form a right angle, so that their gravitational pull is opposed.

Tidal bores In some coastal areas, the height of tides is raised when the water is funnelled in narrow inlets. Rising spring tides sometimes build up a wall of water, called a bore, as much as 3 m (10 ft) high, which will rush inland up river valleys. When tidal bores surge from the Bay of Fundy, Canada, up the St John River, the water actually flows up some 5-m (17-ft) high rapids. This backward flow is called the Reversing Falls.

BLAZING WATER

Can rivers catch fire? Cleveland, Ohio, is one of the USA's leading industrial cities. Through it flows the Cuyahoga River, into which factories have poured their wastes for many years. The river did actually catch fire in 1969 and it is now so polluted that it is classed as a fire hazard!

ADVANCING DESERTS

Can people create deserts? Bordering the southern edge of the Sahara is a region called the Sahel. It extends from Mauritania and northern Senegal through Mali, Burkina Faso, Niger and Chad into Sudan. The Sahel has an average annual rainfall of between 100 and 400 mm (4-16 in) and, in the past, it was grazing land.

From the 1960s, this zone has suffered droughts, so that over large areas all the plants have died and the Sahara has been advancing southwards by 10 km (6 miles) or more a year. Droughts are only partly responsible for this disaster, in which millions of cattle and thousands of people have died of starvation. The people themselves have played a part by overgrazing the land, and removing shrubs and trees for use as firewood.

ONE CROP FARMS

What is plantation agriculture? Most farmers in the tropics used to grow a variety of produce, sufficient to feed their families. During the colonial era, Europeans combined these small family farms into large plantations to produce one crop, such as coffee. Plantations became important, because, in many developing countries, they produced the leading exports. After independence, the governments of many new nations took over the foreign-owned plantations.

VIOLENT VOLTS

What is the connection between thunder and lightning?
Lightning is a discharge of static electricity in clouds. The sudden heating of the air along the channel of the flash makes the air expand and heated molecules collide with cold ones, causing thunder.

We see lightning before we hear thunder, because light travels faster through air than sound. If you count the seconds between lightning and thunder, you can work out how far away you are from a storm. Thunder travels 1 km in 3 seconds (1 mile in 5 seconds). If you count 12 seconds, the storm is 4 km (2⅖ miles) away.

A tea plantation in Darjeeling, India, and Kenyan tea-pickers (inset). ▼

SECRET ARMY

What is maquis? In World War II, French underground fighters called their secret army the *Maquis*. This is the name of heathland vegetation in dry areas in Mediterranean countries, which used to be a hideout for bandits, because it was difficult to clear and so of little use. The same type of vegetation is called *chaparral* in California, *fynbos* in South Africa, and *macchia* in Italy.

Maquis on the Corsican hillsides.
▼

FAIR SHARES

What is OPEC? American and European oil companies once controlled most of the developing world's oil industry. In an attempt to gain control over the pricing and production of oil, five developing countries – Iran, Iraq, Kuwait, Saudi Arabia and Venezuela – set up OPEC (Organization of Petroleum Exporting Countries) in 1960.

In the 1970s, when world demand for oil increased, OPEC members raised the price of oil. Their income from the oil greatly increased, and they were able to set up development projects and welfare services for their people. By the mid-1980s, OPEC had 13 members – the original five and Algeria, Ecuador, Gabon, Indonesia, Libya, Nigeria, Qatar and the United Arab Emirates. Together these 13 nations formed a powerful economic force, which controlled about 45 per cent of the world's trade in oil in the mid-1980s.

◀ Yellowstone National Park, USA, is a place of great natural beauty containing huge waterfalls, river canyons and the world's largest geyser basins.

GOUGING GLACIERS

How can ice shape the land? The surfaces of valley glaciers are littered with rocks which have tumbled down the mountainsides. Other rocks are frozen into the sides and bottoms of glaciers. These rocks turn the glaciers into gigantic files, because, as the glaciers move, the rocks scrape away at the land and gouge out more and more rocks. When the ice melts, steep-sided, U-shaped valleys are striking evidence of the cutting power of glaciers.

SAVING NATURE

Which was the world's first national park? As the world becomes more crowded, nature is threatened. Some scientists think that the destruction of forests and other areas could cause the extinction of a tenth of all plant and animal species on land within the lifetime of most people alive today. Many people believe that we must take urgent action to protect our planet home.

The idea of conservation isn't new. The 13th-century Mongol emperor, Kublai Khan, protected several beauty spots, and Switzerland founded a game reserve in 1542. National parks, however, originated in the USA, where the Yellowstone National Park was set up in 1872. Since then, national parks and reserves have been established throughout the world.

LIGHT AND REFLECTIONS

What's the difference between a star and a planet? Stars are hot bodies that give out light of their own, whereas planets shine only by reflecting light. Stars are composed of gas, but planets can be either gaseous or solid.

The Earth is a solid planet. Jupiter is a gaseous one. Nine planets orbit the Sun. In order of distance from the Sun, they are Mercury, Venus, Earth, Mars, Jupiter, Saturn, Uranus, Neptune and Pluto.

FAMILY OF THE SUN

How did the planets form? When the Sun was born from an immense cloud of gas and dust 4,600 million years ago, it is thought to have been surrounded by a disk of surplus material. Gradually, this disk formed into a number of smaller, cold bodies orbiting the Sun. The planets were born. Hence the planets are the left-overs from the birth of the Sun. Together, the Sun and planets make up the solar system.

MOVING POLES

What are the magnetic poles? The Earth is a giant magnet. The magnetism, which is probably caused by movements in the Earth's molten outer core, is concentrated at the two magnetic poles. The north magnetic pole is about 1,600 km (1,000 miles) from the true North Pole, while the south magnetic pole is about 2,570 km (1,600 miles) from the South Pole.

Although their positions vary from time to time, the magnetic poles are useful in modern navigation, because magnetic compass needles point north. However, the needles would have pointed south on some occasions in the past, because the Earth's magnetic field is periodically reversed. The last reversal occurred 30,000 years ago. The cause of these reversals is still a mystery.

FUTURE FOOD

What are the main vegetable oils? When prehistoric people learnt how to make fire and realized that cooked food was more digestible than raw food, they needed fats for cooking.

Today, cooking fats come from animal products and plant seeds, including coconut, cottonseed, groundnuts, olives, palm kernels, rapeseed, soya beans and sunflower seeds.

COMMUNISTS COMBINE

What is COMECON? The 12 western European nations of the EEC are not the only ones to have formed an economic alliance. The USSR and its allies have set up a similar organization. Founded in 1949, the members of the Council for Mutual Economic Assistance (COMECON) are Bulgaria, Cuba, Czechoslovakia, East Germany, Hungary, Mongolia, Poland, Romania, the USSR and Vietnam.

▲
Frost crystals on a window pane.

INVISIBLE SHIELD

Why is ozone so important? The atmosphere consists mainly of three gases: about 78 per cent nitrogen, 21 per cent oxygen and 1 per cent argon. The remaining ingredients include the carbon dioxide we breathe out and which green plants absorb, plus traces of helium, hydrogen, krypton, methane, neon, ozone and xenon.

Ozone, which some people wrongly think is the refreshing air at the seaside, is a poisonous type of oxygen. At ground level, ozone makes up less than one part per million of the air. But a thin layer of ozone, about 24 km (15 miles) above ground level in the stratosphere, blocks out most of the Sun's burning ultraviolet rays. If these rays reached the ground, they would kill all land animals and plants, so this ozone layer is essential to our well-being.

FREEZING WEDGES

How does frost split rocks? Frost is frozen moisture. It forms when invisible water vapour in the air changes directly from a gas-like state into ice crystals. In mountains, moisture in cracks in rocks freezes at night. Because ice occupies more space than water, the ice exerts a wedge-like pressure inside the cracks, widening them until the rocks split. This is called frost action.

JOURNEY THROUGH TIME

Which is the world's biggest gorge? About six million years ago, the Colorado plateau in the south-western USA was a flat coastal plain. Winding slowly across it was the Colorado River. Gradually, earth movements pushed the plain upwards, making the river run faster and faster. The force of the flow began wearing out the Grand Canyon.

This, the world's largest gorge, is 446 km (277 miles) long and 1.6 km (1 mile) deep in places. Exposed on the canyon walls are layers of rock, the oldest at the bottom being about 2,000 million years in age. Resting on them are younger and younger rocks. In some ways, climbing up or down the canyon and past the rocks from different periods is like a journey through time.

▲
The Grand Canyon in Colorado is one of the USA's most spectacular areas of natural beauty.

URBAN EXPLOSION

Which is the world's largest city? For many years, Tokyo and Shanghai headed the world league table of the largest cities, but in the early 1980s Mexico City pulled ahead. Present forecasts suggest that it will have 30 million people by AD 2000. The expansion of Mexico City is part of a trend throughout developing countries for poor people to leave the hard life in the countryside and seek better opportunities in the cities.

In Mexico, 55 out of every 100 people lived in urban areas in 1965. By 1983, the figure had risen to 69. This trend is even more marked in some other nations. For example, the percentage of city dwellers in Brazil increased from 51 per cent in 1965 to 71 per cent in 1983. Many cities in developing countries do not have enough houses, jobs or social services for the new immigrants, so slums develop on the outskirts, and disease and crime become serious problems.

MAJOR CITIES

City	Country	Population (1986)
Mexico City	Mexico	16,000,000
Shanghai	China	11,859,000
Tokyo	Japan	11,807,000
Cairo	Egypt	11,000,000
Paris	France	10,073,000
Buenos Aires	Argentina	9,677,000
Peking (Beijing)	China	9,231,000
Calcutta	India	9,200,000
Moscow	USSR	8,546,000
São Paulo	Brazil	8,491,000
Seoul	South Korea	8,367,000
Bombay	India	8,300,000
Tianjin (T'ienching)	China	7,390,000
New York City	USA	7,071,000
Surabaya	Indonesia	7,028,000
London	UK	6,776,000
Jakarta	Indonesia	6,503,000
Chiongqing (Ch'ungch'ing)	China	6,200,000

QUIZ: CITIES

① Which city is called the Big Apple?
② What is the diamond capital of the world?
③ Where is the Venice of the North?
④ What is the world's highest national capital city?
⑤ What is the Eternal City?
⑥ Which city is called 'Australia's front door'?
⑦ Which city is called the 'Windy City'?
⑧ Which former capital was called the 'Forbidden City'?
⑨ Where is the Granite City?

ANSWERS
① New York City, USA. ② Kimberley, South Africa. ⑤ Rome, Italy.
③ Stockholm, Sweden. ④ La Paz, Bolivia. ⑧ Lhasa, Tibet.
⑥ Darwin, Australia. ⑦ Chicago, USA.
⑨ Aberdeen, Scotland.

THE ISOLATED GUANCHES

Who were the Guanches? The Canary Islands, now part of Spain, lie about 100 km (62 miles) off the north-west coast of Africa. When the Spaniards arrived there in the 15th century, the islands were inhabited by people called the Guanches, who lived at a 'Stone Age' level. Their origins are unknown, and their primitive lifestyle probably continued because they were not a seafaring people. No pure-bred Guanches survived, but because many intermarried with Spaniards, there are now tall, fair-haired Canary Islanders whose appearance recalls the mysterious Guanches.

Crowds in a Shanghai street.
▼

◄ Old Faithful geyser, Yellowstone, USA regularly shoots thousands of gallons of steaming water high into the air.

YOURS FAITHFULLY

What are hot springs? Springs are flows of water from the ground. Sometimes they contain hot water which has been heated by molten rock left over by some extinct volcano. Geysers are special kinds of hot springs, in which water is heated into explosive steam. Every now and then, geysers erupt and hurl columns of steam and hot water into the air.

Geysers are found in Iceland, New Zealand and the Yellowstone National Park in the USA. Yellowstone's Old Faithful is the world's most famous geyser. It erupts every 65 minutes, shooting up columns of water between 37 and 46 m (120-150 ft) into the air.

DUST OF DEATH

What creates a dust bowl? In 1934, people in the city of Boston in the north-eastern USA watched in amazement as clouds of choking yellow dust passed over them on their way to the Atlantic Ocean. The dust had come from the Great Plains in the American Midwest. These plains are generally treeless, because the average yearly rainfall is less than 500 mm (20 in) and droughts are common.

The plains were formerly grasslands that supported herds of buffalo, but from the late 19th century they were turned into farmland. Some areas were ploughed and others became cattle ranches. Overgrazing and ploughing removed the grasses, whose roots had bound the soil together. Strong winds blew the dry, loose soil about, breaking it down into fine dust which was blown away by westerly winds. Formerly fertile soil ended up on the seabed, and the Great Plains were turned into an infertile dust bowl.

In recent years, similar dust bowls have been created in the drier parts of Africa.

A dust storm in the Sudan, Africa.
▼

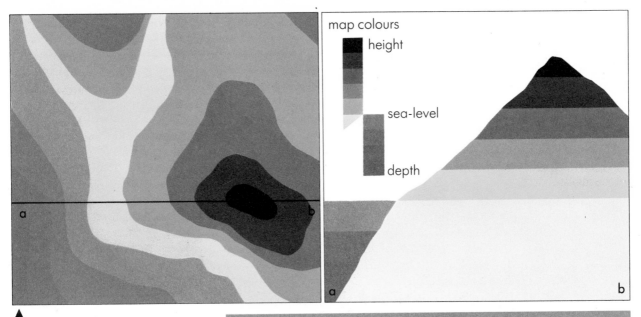

map colours
height
sea-level
depth

▲
An area of land represented from above (left) and as a cross-section (right) using colours to indicate heights between selected contours.

GIANT ICE-CUBES

Where do icebergs come from?
In polar regions, such as northern Greenland, ice extends right to the coast. In Antarctica, ice shelves extend out to sea for great distances. Periodically, icebergs (huge masses of glacial ice) break away and drift out to sea, slowly melting as they reach warmer waters.

Icebergs are a danger to ships, particularly because about eight-ninths of the ice is hidden below the water. It was an iceberg that sank the liner *Titanic* in 1912, and today patrols keep watch on the tall, jagged icebergs that drift into North Atlantic shipping lanes.

North Atlantic icebergs rise up to 120 m (394 ft) out of the water, while icebergs from Antarctica are usually low and flat-topped. The world's largest iceberg came from Antarctica. It covered 31,000 square km (about 12,000 square miles) – an area larger than Belgium.

HIGH AND LOW

What are contours? Maps portray the world, or part of it, on flat surfaces. They employ lines, words, colours and symbols to show land features. The height of the land is depicted in several ways. Many maps show the actual heights of peaks in metres or feet. These are called spot heights. Too many figures would make a map confusing, so many atlases show the height of the land by shading, which gives the impression of a 3-dimensional model, or by colouring.

General reference, or topographic, maps cover much smaller areas than atlas maps. They often use contours to show heights. Contours are lines, usually drawn in brown, that link places of the same height.

LONG DISTANCE

How can we talk to the stars?
If other beings existed in space, we could talk to them via radio waves, which travel at the same speed as light. Astronomers have begun to listen for possible incoming radio messages from the stars, although nothing has been heard so far.

In 1974, the first deliberate radio message from Earth was beamed towards a star cluster called M 13 in the constellation of Hercules. Even if there is anyone at home to receive the message, and even if they reply immediately, M 13 is so far away that we will not hear from them until about the year AD 50,000.

NOT ALONE?

Is there other life in space?
Astronomers estimate that one star in ten is accompanied by planets. Not all those planets will be like the Earth, but the chances are that some of them will have the right conditions for life. Even if life arises on only a small fraction of those suitable planets, that still means there could be a lot of inhabited planets throughout the Galaxy. According to an estimate by the American astronomer Carl Sagan, as many as one million other civilizations, similar to or more advanced than our own, may exist at present in the Galaxy.

FACT FILE: RICH AND POOR NATIONS

FACT In terms of their per capita (per head of population) GNPs, the poorest countries are Ethiopia, with a per capita GNP of $120. Bangladesh ($130), Mali ($160) and Nepal ($160). Amounts are in United States dollars.

FACT Rich, developed countries include Switzerland, with a per capita GNP of $16,290, the USA ($14,110), Norway ($14,020), Sweden ($12,470) and Canada ($12,310).

FACT Middle income countries include oil exporters, such as Iran and Venezuela, and countries which export manufactured goods, including Argentina, Brazil and South Africa.

FACT In the poor countries of Africa south of the Sahara, people eat only 91 per cent of the calories they need. In developed countries, people consume, on average, 133 per cent of the calories they need.

FACT In poor countries, children are lucky to get a proper education. In Bangladesh, only 68 per cent of boys of primary school age and 51 per cent of girls were attending school in 1982. And only 15 per cent of children of secondary school age were at school.

NATIONAL WEALTH

What is the GNP? One measure of a country's wealth is its gross national product (GNP). This is the total value of all the goods and services produced in a country in a year (or the gross *domestic* product), plus foreign output claimed by residents of the country. It is often called the national income.

To find the *average* income of a country's citizens (though it will not show how the wealth is distributed) you simply divide the GNP by the population. The GNPs of some countries are based on inadequate information, for many developing countries have never had a complete census (count of their population). When we study GNP figures, we must remember that they are a useful but rough guide to a country's wealth.

Powerful waves have created this unusual rock stack.

▼

VANISHING GAUCHOS

Where would you find a gaucho? The gauchos of South America were cowboys who rounded up wild cattle and horses, bringing down running animals with weighted slings, or bolas. They once roamed the pampas – the vast temperate grasslands of central Argentina. Today, only a few gauchos remain, working on cattle ranches.

WEARING WAVES

How does the sea form a 'blow hole'? In stormy weather, powerful waves hurl loose rocks at the shore, undercutting cliffs. While soft rocks are worn back to form bays, hard rocks often survive as headlands in which waves then hollow out caves. If the roof of a cave collapses, a 'blow hole' is formed in the ground above. When waves break in the cave, clouds of spray burst through these holes.

Caves on opposite sides of headlands often meet to form arches. When arches collapse, a rocky island, or stack, is left behind, but this, too, will eventually be removed by the relentless waves.

PICTURES IN THE SKY

Can you spot the dragon, the unicorn and the giraffe in the sky? These animals are all represented by star patterns known as constellations. A total of 88 constellations fills the entire sky, and some of them have very odd names. The most famous constellations date back to the ancient Greeks and Romans, but imaginative astronomers have introduced additional ones since then.

Among the constellations is a dragon, called Draco, coiled around the north pole of the sky; a unicorn, Monoceros; and a giraffe, Camelopardalis. Other constellations include a chameleon, a lizard, a toucan, a fly, and even an air pump.

▲
A false-colour photograph of the Milky Way, taken looking towards the centre of the Galaxy. The constellation of Scorpius, the Scorpion, can be seen on the right of the image.

SLIPPERY SLOPES

What is a glacier and how does it move? Glaciers form when snow piles up in mountain hollows, called cirques. The snow is gradually compacted into a white substance, halfway between snow and ice. As the pressure increases, the ice crystals become closely interlocked, while water, seeping down from above, refreezes and binds the crystals together. Finally, the compacted snow is pressed into clear blue ice.

Exactly *how* ice flows downhill isn't completely clear, but it does seem that stress and pressure release molecules of water between the ice crystals, so that they slide over each other. Melting and refreezing of the ice underneath the glacier also helps it to slide slowly downhill.

WAY TO THE NORTH

How can you find the north pole star? If you live in the northern hemisphere, you can always find north at night, because there is a star very near to the north pole of the sky. This star is called Polaris, and during the night all other stars appear to circle around it as the Earth turns.

To find Polaris, first locate the familiar saucepan shape of seven stars that make up the Plough or Big Dipper (actually, a part of the constellation Ursa Major, the Great Bear). Two stars in the bowl of the saucepan point towards Polaris.

A glaciated valley in Alaska.
▼

GETTING TOGETHER

Did you know that many stars come in families? Most stars are not single, as they appear at a casual glance, but are actually twins, triplets or members of larger families. A large group of stars is termed a cluster, such as the Pleiades, or Seven Sisters, so named because seven main stars are visible to the naked eye. Binoculars and telescopes, however, show dozens of fainter stars in the cluster.

GLOW AND FADE

Did you know that some stars change in brightness? Not all stars are constant in brightness. Some of them, known as variable stars, get brighter and fainter every so often. In many cases, the brightness variations are caused by actual changes in the size of the stars, which get brighter and fainter as they swell and shrink. In other cases, one star is periodically eclipsed by a close companion star, which means that light from the star is blocked off until the eclipsing companion moves aside.

TAKING A STAR'S TEMPERATURE

Did you know that stars have different colours? Stars appear in different colours, depending on the temperature of their surface. The coolest stars, with temperatures of about 3,000°C (6,030°F), glow red. The hottest stars, with temperatures of 10,000°C (20,000°F) and above, glow blue. The Sun, whose surface temperature is 5,500°C (11,030°F), appears yellow-white.

By measuring the colour of a star, astronomers can tell how hot it is. The colours of stars are not very noticeable to the naked eye, but they become more prominent through binoculars and telescopes.

STELLAR NURSERY

How are stars born? Enormous clouds of gas and dust in space, called nebulae, are the birthplaces of stars. The word 'nebula' comes from the Latin meaning mist. One of the most famous star-forming regions is the great nebula in the constellation of Orion, where stars are being born today. The Orion nebula contains enough gas and dust to make a cluster of thousands of stars.

Our own Sun is thought to have been born from such a cloud, about 4,600 million years ago. By studying the Orion nebula, we are in effect turning back the clock to watch how the Sun came into being.

The Great Nebula of Orion consists of gases lit up by young stars in its centre.
▼

TIME WILL TELL!

Where and what is the San Andreas fault? Running through south-western California is a 960-km (600-mile) long crack in the ground, called the San Andreas fault. This fault is the boundary between two plates in the earth's crust, which are moving alongside each other. Plates do not move smoothly. Instead, their jagged edges become jammed together until so much pressure builds up that the jams break and the plates lurch forward.

'Quake town It was a sudden movement along the San Andreas fault, averaging 4 m (13 ft), which rocked the city of San Francisco with an earthquake in 1906. Electrical short-circuits and broken gas pipes caused fires which raged for three days. About 700 people died and 300,000 were made homeless.

Many small tremors have occurred in the city since then. But some scientists think that another major 'quake is likely before long. Modern buildings in San Francisco have been specially designed to withstand earthquake shocks. Only time will tell if the builders have got it right.

The San Andreas Fault

R. Sacramento

Sierra Nevada

San Francisco

R. San Joaquin

fault line

Pacific Ocean

Los Angeles

▲
San Francisco after the 1906 earthquake (top).

BURSTING BANKS

What causes floods? Major floods can occur in several different ways. For example, in 1840, an earthquake caused a landslide in the Himalayas, damming the upper course of the River Indus, so that a lake soon formed. The lake was 64 km (40 miles) long and over 300 m (984 ft) deep, and when this natural dam broke, flood water swept down the valley, destroying all in its path.

Other floods occur when artificial dams are breached and when storm winds or *tsunamis* drive seawater inland. Farmers who cause soil erosion help to make floods occur, because the loose soil gets into rivers and raises the level of their beds until they overflow. This factor was involved in the world's worst flood. This occurred in 1887 when China's Hwang Ho burst its banks and drowned 900,000 people.

Each year the fields of north-east ▶
India are flooded by the
torrential monsoon rains.

WORKING WATER

What is irrigation? About 5,000 years ago, civilizations were springing up in river valleys in China, India, south-western Asia and north-eastern Africa. The farms which provided the food for these civilizations were mostly irrigated (watered) by canals that carried river water to the fields. Irrigation not only played a major part in the development of civilization, but it is still important today. About 13 per cent of the world's cultivated land is irrigated.

Canals are used to irrigate these terraced rice fields in Bali.

▼

FLASH POINTS

Where do volcanoes occur? We know that the Earth's crust and the top part of the mantle are split into rigid sections, called plates, which are up to 70-100 km (43-62 miles) thick. Beneath the plates, temperatures are high and the rocks are semi-molten. Currents in the molten material are moving the plates about. Plates are moving apart along the ocean ridges. When they move, molten material wells up to fill the gaps. Sometimes, lava piles up into volcanoes which may, like Surtsey (off Iceland) reach the surface as islands. So, the ocean ridges are one place where volcanoes occur.

Another place is beside ocean trenches. Here one plate is being pushed beneath another. Descending plates are melted, creating magma at temperatures about 1,090°C–1,200°C (1,994°F–2,192°F). Some of this magma rises and emerges through volcanoes as lava. Many volcanoes are of this type. For instance, Indonesia – which lies above a descending plate – has 167 volcanoes, 77 of which have erupted in historic times.

A few volcanoes, like those in Hawaii, are far from any plate edge. Scientists think they are fuelled by 'hot spots' in the Earth's mantle.

◀ Deep crevasses are often hidden by a layer of snow.

REFRIGERATED RAM

What are crevasses? These are deep cracks found in glacial ice. They are especially dangerous when they are hidden by snow. In 1933, the body of a mountain ram appeared at the end of the Lyell Glacier in California. The animal belonged to a species which had become extinct 50 years earlier. Scientists decided that it had fallen into a crevasse near the head of the glacier about 250 years earlier. It had taken all that time for the glacier to carry the body to its final resting place.

APPLE A DAY?

Why is fruit good for you? Many fruits contain large amounts of Vitamin C (useful in helping wounds heal and in preventing some virus infections), as well as sugar which provides energy. However, they do not make a balanced diet, because most contain little protein. Prehistoric people collected fruit which grew wild. Today, fruits are grown scientifically. Fruits vary from region to region, according to the climate. The main types are temperate fruits, such as apples; subtropical fruits, such as oranges; and tropical fruits, such as bananas.

WET BLANKETS

What is a depression? Cold air flows outwards from the poles, while warm subtropical air moves polewards. The cold and warm air meet along a line called the polar front. Because of the great difference in temperature, the cold and warm air do not mix. Instead, warm air flows into bends in the polar front and cold air flows in behind it. This sets up a rotating low pressure air system, called a depression or cyclone, which has warm, light air at its centre.

    The front edge of the warm air is called the warm front. Ahead of the warm front, the warm air flows upwards over the dense, cold air. As it rises, a blanket of cloud forms and rain starts to fall from it. The advancing edge of the cold air, behind the warm air, is called the cold front. Here, cold air pushes under the warm air and thunderclouds often form as the warm air rises. Depressions, therefore, bring stormy, unsettled weather as they move across the land.

QUIZ: THE WEATHER

1. What instruments are used to measure air pressure?
2. What is the name for a high air pressure system?
3. What do we call a low air pressure system?
4. What instruments are used to measure wind speeds?
5. What scale is used to classify wind speeds?
6. What do meteorologists (people who study the weather) call a thundercloud?
7. What is the name for charts that show weather conditions at a particular time?
8. What do we call invisible moisture in the air?

ANSWERS
1 Barometers. 2 Anticyclone. 3 Depression or cyclone.
4 Anemometers. 5 Beaufort scale. 6 Cumulonimbus.
7 Synoptic chart. 8 Water vapour.

Pears and apples (temperate fruit).
▼

▲
Ploughing with oxen is still common in rural Africa.

UFOs OR WHAT?

What is the Bermuda triangle? Near the end of the film *Close Encounters of the Third Kind*, some American pilots from 'Flight 19' are released from an alien spacecraft. This scene refers to the sudden disappearance of Flight 19, a group of five US torpedo bombers that vanished without trace on December 5, 1945, in the 'Bermuda triangle'.

The Bermuda, or Devil's, triangle is part of the North Atlantic Ocean, roughly between Florida, Bermuda and the Sargasso Sea. A number of aircraft and ships have vanished there, and it has been suggested that the triangle may be a landing area for UFOs. Other theories are that the accidents are caused by unusual magnetic forces, rays from lost Atlantis, or by space-time warps. But scientists who have studied the evidence don't agree. They say that no more accidents have occurred in the Bermuda triangle than anywhere else. They put down the disappearances to bad weather, human error and mechanical failure. It has been said that some people will begin to believe anything if it is repeated often enough.

DESTRUCTION

Which were the world's worst earthquakes? Japan has, on average, 1,000 noticeable earthquakes a year. In 1923, about 575,000 houses were destroyed in Tokyo and Yokohama by the most destructive 'quake in recorded history. The damage was estimated at £1,000 million – it would be more than four times as much today. Nearly 143,000 people died in this disaster. But in 1556, an earthquake in Shensi province, China, caused about 800,000 deaths – the greatest recorded loss of life in any earthquake.

CHANGING JOBS

How many of the world's people are farmers? In most poor countries, farming is the chief occupation. For example, in 1980, 65 per cent of Africa's and 58 per cent of Asia's workforce was engaged in farming. By contrast, only 16 per cent of European workers lived by farming. In many middle income countries, such as Brazil, the percentage of farmworkers is falling and the percentage in industry is rising. However, in rich countries, the percentages of people in farming *and* industry, both of which are being increasingly automated, are falling at the expense of service industries.

WHITE TERROR

What is pack ice? Large blocks of floating ice, called pack ice, cover much of the Arctic Ocean and the seas around Antarctica. Pack ice was a problem for explorers. In 1915, the *Endurance*, the ship used by Sir Ernest Shackleton to reach Antarctica, was crushed by pack ice and sank. The first ship to reach the North Pole was the Russian atomic icebreaker *Arktika* in August, 1977.

Local wildlife showing an interest in an ice-bound ship.
▼

TOURIST TEMPERATURES

What makes Mediterranean lands tourist attractions? Most places around the Mediterranean Sea have hot, dry summers and mild, moist winters. These regions are tourist magnets, mainly because of the climate. The same climate occurs in California, central Chile, parts of southern Australia, and the south-western tip of South Africa.

BACK IN TIME

How far can a telescope see? Telescopes are like time machines. The farther off in space they look, the farther back in history they go, because of the time that light takes to reach us from distant objects.

The farthest galaxies and quasars visible in the Universe are so far away that their light has taken over 10,000 million years to reach us. Therefore we see them as they appeared early in the history of the Universe, not long after the Big Bang.

MEASURING HUNGER

What is malnutrition? Many people throughout the world suffer from malnutrition – that is, they are undernourished. Undernourishment causes ill-health, starvation and death. The FAO (Food and Agricultural Organization) has worked out how the calorie intake of people compares with what they need for good health.

The worst malnutrition occurs in developing countries. For example, the average calorie intake per person in Ghana in 1983 was only 68 per cent of a person's needs, whereas in the USA, it was 137 per cent. Yet Ghana, in 1980, had only one doctor to every 7,100 people, as compared with 1 doctor to every 520 people in the USA.

DRIPS AT WORK

How are limestone caves formed? Coastal caves are worn out by waves, lava caves form in lava flows, and ice caves occur in glaciers. But the largest caves are in limestone, a rock consisting mainly of the mineral calcite, and a related rock, dolomite.

Limestone caves are formed when rainwater, which contains carbon dioxide dissolved from the air or soil, reacts chemically with calcite and enlarges cracks in the rock, widening them into deep shafts, passageways and chambers. Many caves contain icicle-like, hanging stalactites and column-like stalagmites. Both are made of calcite deposited from the dripping water. The largest cave system lies below the Mammoth Cave National Park in the USA.

◄ These immense stalagtites and stalagmites have formed slowly over the centuries.

Shifts in the Earth's plates create mountains and rift valleys.
▼

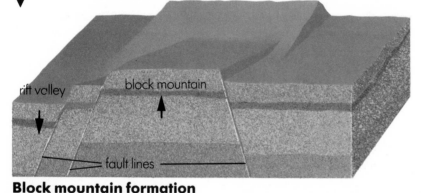

Block mountain formation

BETWEEN FAULTS

What are block mountains?
When the huge plates that cover the Earth move, they create enormous tension that cracks rocks, forming long faults. Blocks of land pushed up between roughly parallel sets of faults form block mountains. Examples include the Ruwenzori Mountain range in Central Africa and the Sierra Nevada in the south-western USA.

SUN SPOT

Where is the world's sunniest place? We listen to weather forecasts to find out how warm and sunny, wet or windy the weather is likely to be. People in the eastern Sahara, in North Africa, don't have this problem. This is the world's sunniest place, with an average of over 4,300 hours of sunshine a year – nearly 12 hours a day!

THE NAME GAME

Where is Burkina Faso? Maps must be revised all the time to take account of place name changes. Since 1950, many colonies have gained independence and changed place names that they associate with the past. For example, the French colony of Upper Volta, which took its name from the River Volta, became independent in 1960, but it took 24 years before it was renamed Burkina Faso, which means 'land of the upright men'.

Not all new place names win approval. For instance, the English county of Shropshire adopted an older name, Salop, in 1974. But this proved unpopular and the name Shropshire was restored in 1980.

Block mountains such as the Sierra Nevada range (below) are often found in the centres of continents. ▼

FACT FILE: SUN AND STARS

FACT The brightest star in the night sky is Sirius, in the constellation of Canis, Major, the Great Dog.

FACT It would take over a million Earths to fill a sphere the size of the Sun.

FACT Gases boiled off from the Sun flow past the Earth, forming the so-called solar wind. In a sense, we live inside the thin outer atmosphere of the Sun.

FACT The Sun takes 220 million years to orbit the centre of the Galaxy. So far, it has been around the Galaxy 20 times.

FACT The temperature at the centre of the Sun is 15 million °C (30 million °F). A pinhead at this temperature would incinerate everything for several kilometres around.

FACT Red supergiant stars are huge, but their outer layers are very rarefied – far thinner, in fact, than the Earth's atmosphere. The outer layers of a red supergiant are, in effect, a red-hot vacuum.

FACT About ten stars are 'born' each year in our Galaxy. That's almost one a month. But a similar number of stars die each year.

FACT The farthest object visible to the naked eye is the Andromeda galaxy, 2.2 million light years away.

LAND BUILDING

How does the sea create new land? Most people are familiar with the idea of the sea eroding or destroying land. For example, storm waves can remove rock from many coasts. Some loose rock is swept out to sea, but some is moved along the shore. Groynes, or sea walls, which jut out from the coast in many resorts, are built because of this movement. Without them, the waves would periodically remove the beaches.

In places where the coast changes direction, however, as at headlands, the waves often drop their loads and form new land. The long fingers of sand, gravel and pebbles dumped by the waves are called spits. Some spits join two headlands, creating lagoons. Others link the mainland to islands, forming natural bridges.

'WILD MEN' OF ASIA?

What are the origins of modern man? Many unanswered questions still surround human evolution. People belong to the order of primates, which evolved about 60 million years ago. Apes belong to the same order, and their ancestors go back about 35 million years. The first recognizable human-like creatures (named *Homo*) were evolving about 2 million years ago. The species known as *Homo sapiens*, to which we belong, evolved perhaps half a million years ago.

Neanderthal man One type of *Homo sapiens*, the Neanderthals, appeared about 200,000 years ago. Most scientists think that the Neanderthals were extinct by 30,000 years ago, possibly because they couldn't compete with the ancestors of modern people (called *Homo sapiens sapiens*), who appeared more than 50,000 and perhaps as long as 100,000 years ago.

Survivors? In the 1970s, Russian and Mongolian scholars, who were studying evidence of mysterious creatures like the Abominable Snowman of the Himalayas, came across reports of sightings of 'wild men' from several parts of Asia. One report described a creature with a slanting forehead, protruding jaw and flat nose. These are features of Neanderthals. Is it possible that a few Neanderthals escaped extinction?

Modern man is directly descended from *Homo erectus*, but some people dispute whether *Homo habilis* is our ancestor.
▼

The probable evolutionary progress of man (the 'Homo' genus)

| Homo habilis | Homo erectus | Homo sapiens (archaic) | Homo sapiens (Neanderthal) | Homo sapiens (modern) |

▲
Prehistoric man hunted grassland animals in areas where there is now only arid desert.

YESTERDAY'S WEATHER

Can climates change? Scientists have found much evidence to show that climates have changed throughout Earth history. For example, coal is formed from plants that grow in warm, swampy conditions. They couldn't possibly grow in Antarctica today, yet coal is found there. And cave paintings in the heart of the dry Sahara show that it was grassland towards the end of the Ice Age.

Some mysteries can be explained by continental drift. Antarctica was probably much closer to the equator when the coal was formed. However, continental drift is slow and can't explain the radical changes in the Sahara. Some scientists think that changes were caused by variations in the Earth's path around the Sun or in the tilt of its axis. Others believe that long periods of volcanic activity threw up clouds of dust and blocked out the Sun's rays. Volcanoes also release carbon dioxide into the air. The higher the proportion of carbon dioxide, the hotter the atmosphere becomes. No group of theories is generally accepted, and this debate will continue for many years.

POISONOUS FISH

What is Minamata disease? In the early 1950s, a mysterious disease struck Japanese fishing families living around Minamata Bay, on Kyushu island. Some people died and many suffered unpleasant illnesses. By the late 1950s, some scientists suspected that the 'Minamata' disease was being caused by a chemical company that was pouring poisonous wastes into the bay. It was later shown that fish and shellfish absorbed the poisons, so that people who ate them were also poisoned. As many as 10,000 people were affected.

This is an example of water pollution, which has fouled many rivers, lakes and seas. Because of dangers to health and the environment, a number of governments have made strict laws to control water pollution.

COW COUNTRY

Where do you find most dairy farms? Dairy farms produce milk, butter, cheese and other items made from milk. Dairy farming is important in wet areas, with abundant pasture. Most dairy farms are near cities, which need daily supplies of fresh milk. Farther away from the cities, dairy farming is often combined with crop growing on mixed farms.

Cattle grazing in Russia.
▼

FLAT CURVES

Are maps completely accurate? Because the Earth's surface is curved, no world map can correctly show shapes, areas, distances and directions.

Mapmakers have devised map projections (ways of making maps) that preserve some of these features, but no one map gets them all right. The only true representation of the world is a globe. But globes can't show anything like as many details as maps. And what hiker wants to carry a globe around?

▲
Mount St Helens erupting.

UNCORKED VOLCANO

What was unusual about the eruption of Mount St Helens in 1980?
Mount St Helens, a volcano in Washington state in the USA, erupted on May 18, 1980, killing 60 people. Yet, unlike most eruptions, this had been forecast, for it was the most carefully studied volcanic event of all time.

Predicted eruption From 1969, scientists monitored the volcano, checking pressure and temperature changes inside it, analysing the gases that leaked out of it, measuring small swellings on its flanks, and recording tremors caused by movements of magma.

In March 1980, a small eruption occurred and in April one side of the mountain started to swell. The scientists issued warnings, asking people to clear the area.

Photographic record The eruption of May 18 was photographed by remote control, radio-operated cameras. The photographs showed that an earthquake had cracked the top of the mountain, starting a landslide. The landslide released the pressure inside the volcano. A surge of hot gases burst outwards, like the discharge from an uncorked bottle of fizzy liquid. Following the gases came a dense cloud of hot ash which raced downhill, burning all in its path. Finally a huge black cloud of ash was hurled into the air.

After the eruption was over, the height of Mount St Helens had been reduced by 400 m (1,313 ft). About 600 square km (230 square miles) of land was devastated.

ISLANDS UNITED

What is CARICOM? In 1973, four English-speaking Caribbean countries — Barbados, Guyana, Jamaica, and Trinidad and Tobago — founded the Caribbean Community (CARICOM). They were later joined by Antigua and Barbuda, the Bahamas, Belize, Dominica, Grenada, Montserrat, St Christopher-Nevis, St Lucia and St Vincent. All these developing countries, except the Bahamas, belong to the Caribbean Common Market, which aims at economic cooperation and industrial development. With their many similar traditions, CARICOM members are also trying to coordinate their foreign and social policies.

KILLER WAVES

How high can waves reach? The waves that break on the seashore are usually caused by winds blowing across the open sea. During storms, waves reach 12 m (39 ft) or more in height. The highest wave recorded in the open sea was 34 m (112 ft) high.

Other large and often destructive waves, called tsunamis, are triggered off by earthquakes or volcanic eruptions. They are low, fast waves, with immense energy. As tsunamis near land, they lose speed and their energy is converted into an increase in height. The highest recorded tsunami appeared off the Japanese Ryukyu Islands in 1971. It was 85 m (278 ft) high. In 1883, the volcanic explosion at Krakatoa set off tsunamis that drowned 36,000 people on nearby islands.

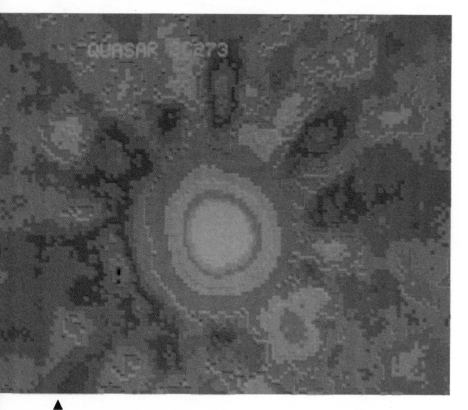

▲
An X-ray view of quasar 3C 273.

CLEAN COAL

How do plants become coal? When plants die, the remains usually rot and break down into water, carbon dioxide and simple salts. But in swamps and bogs, layers of rotting plants are often buried and the decay is halted. Slowly, these plant remains are pressed into a compact substance called peat.

When peat is dug up, 90 per cent of its weight is often water. However, when it is dried, up to 60 per cent of its weight is carbon, and so it is a useful fuel. As the plant remains are buried deeper and deeper, the pressure increases and the peat changes into lignite, which still contains a lot of water, then bituminous coal, and finally anthracite. Carbon forms up to 95 per cent of anthracite. This hard, shiny coal doesn't dirty your hands when you pick it up, and burns slowly giving out intense heat.

USE AND MAKE

What are consumer and capital goods? In industry, people talk of two kinds of manufactured goods. First, consumer goods, such as clothes and washing machines, which are bought by people. Second, capital goods, including machinery and tractors, which are bought by firms and used to produce other goods.

POWERHOUSE

What is a quasar? In the 1960s astronomers discovered a number of objects that looked like faint stars, but which actually turned out to lie far off in the Universe, among the galaxies. They were called quasars, short for quasi-stellar objects.

Quasars are stupendous powerhouses. They give out as much energy as hundreds of galaxies from a volume of space only a light year across. Astronomers think that the energy output of quasars is caused by immense black holes, which swallow up stars and gas from their surroundings.

Quasars are probably young galaxies in the early stages of formation. Perhaps the centre of our own Galaxy was once like a quasar.

LAVA FLOW

What are fissure eruptions? In volcanoes, lava emerges through a pipe in the top of the mountain. Sometimes, lava also reaches the surface through long cracks in the ground, called fissures. In 1783, lava spilled out of a 32-km (20-mile) long fissure in Iceland and buried 565 square km (218 square miles) of land.

ROCKS IN VARIETY

What are the main types of rocks? The three main types of rock are known as igneous, sedimentary and metamorphic rocks. Igneous rocks form from molten material. Basalt is an igneous rock which forms from lava on or near the Earth's surface. Granite is another, but it forms at great depths.

Many sedimentary rocks are formed from worn fragments of other rocks, which pile up in water. For example, clay is compacted into a rock called shale. Limestone, another sedimentary rock, often consists largely of the remains of sea creatures, such as shells.

Metamorphic rocks are the third type. They are rocks which have been changed by great heat and pressure. The hard slate used on many roofs is a metamorphic rock formed from the much softer shale.

QUIZ: MINERALS

1 What mineral feels soapy to the touch?
2 What is bauxite?
3 What mineral is used to make Plaster of Paris?
4 What types of the hard mineral corundum are prized as gemstones?
5 What is the name for bits of magma, ranging from volcanic dust to loaf-sized volcanic bombs, that are hurled from volcanoes?
6 What sedimentary rock consists mainly of worn fragments of quartz?
7 What rock is formed when limestone or dolomite are subjected to great heat and pressure?
8 What instrument is used to locate radioactive minerals?
9 What mineral tastes salty?

ANSWERS
1 Talc (or soapstone). 2 Aluminium ore. 3 Gypsum.
4 Ruby and sapphire. 5 Pyroclasts. 6 Sandstone.
7 Marble. 8 Geiger counter. 9 Halite (or rock salt).

Igneous, sedimentary and metamorphic rocks: (from left to right) basalt, china clay and marble.
▼

MOVING ON

What is shifting agriculture? In poor developing countries, some farmers grow only enough food to feed their families, with a little left over to barter or sell for such things as clothes. This is called subsistence farming. In tropical countries, subsistence farmers clear plots in the forests or savanna and farm them for a few years. When the soil begins to become infertile and crop yields fall, they move on and clear new plots. This simple form of farming is called shifting agriculture.

The world's ten largest islands. The two main kinds of island are 'continental' (rising from the continental shelf) and 'oceanic' (mostly volcanic in origin). ▶

HAVES AND HAVE-NOTS

What is the North-South divide? In the 1970s, an international committee produced a report that divided the world into two parts: the rich (developed) North and the poor (developing) South. This division, which often appears in books and newspapers, is a little confusing. This is because the 'North' includes Australia and New Zealand from the southern hemisphere, along with North America, Europe, the USSR and Japan.

However, the North-South divide is, as the report argued, of great importance to us all, because the poverty and hunger experienced increasingly in the 'South' is likely to become a major threat to world peace.

ALL AT SEA

What are the main kinds of islands? Some islands are really parts of the continents, separated from the mainland by shallow seas. About 11,000 years ago, during the Ice Age, the sea-level was much lower than it is today, because so much water was frozen in ice sheets. At that time, Great Britain was joined to mainland Europe. As the climate got warmer, the ice melted and the sea-level rose. In about 5500 BC, the rising waters encircled Great Britain, which has been an island ever since.

Other islands rise from the ocean deeps. Some, such as Surtsey, are volcanoes and some are made of coral. Atolls are circular or horseshoe-shaped groups of low coral islands that have formed on the tops of submerged volcanoes.

The world's ten largest islands (drawn to scale)

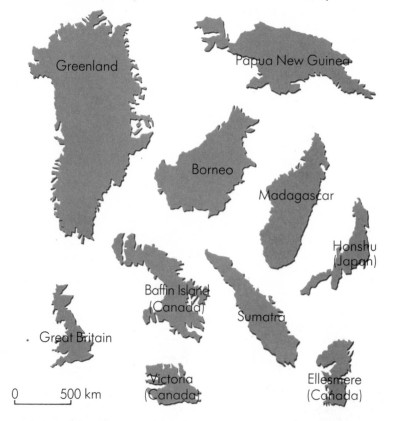

MAJOR ISLANDS

Island	Ocean	Area in sq. km	Area in sq. miles
Geenland	Arctic	2,175,590	840,000
New Guinea	Pacific	789,946	305,000
Borneo	Pacific	751,097	290,000
Madagascar	Indian	587,039	226,657
Baffin Island	Arctic	507,451	195,928
Sumatra	Indian	422,168	163,000
Honshu	Pacific	230,092	88,839
Great Britain	Atlantic	229,848	88,745
Victoria	Arctic	217,290	83,896
Ellesmere	Arctic	196,236	75,767

POLAR FIREWORKS

What is an aurora? Colourful glows in the Earth's atmosphere, called aurorae, are seen from time to time near the Earth's poles. They are caused by atomic particles, thrown out from storms on the Sun, which hit the atmosphere and make it glow like a neon tube at heights of several hundred kilometres.

Aurorae are usually green, yellow and red in colour, and they often look like curtains hanging down from the sky, moving and shimmering mysteriously. The Earth's magnetic field focuses the atomic particles from the Sun into the regions near the Earth's poles.

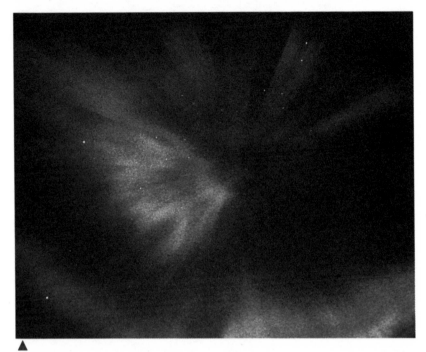

▲ A brilliant aurora photographed above Antarctica.

EARTHQUAKE FOCUS

What is an epicentre? The point of origin of an earthquake inside the Earth is called the focus, and the point on the surface directly above it is the epicentre. Severe earthquakes are usually shallow focus – that is, they occur within 60 km (37 miles) of the surface.

GENTLE BREEZES

How does the sea affect climates? On hot days at the seaside, cool breezes blow inland from the sea. This is because land warms up faster than water. Hot air over the land rises, and cool air from the sea is sucked in. At night, the reverse happens, because the land cools faster than water. In this way, the sea moderates the climate of coastlands.

Ocean currents also play a part. Onshore winds are warmed or chilled by ocean currents, and the effects of these winds are felt some way inland.

The effect of the oceans is slight in the hearts of continents. Central Asia and North America have extreme continental climates. Winters are far colder and summers hotter than coastlands in the same latitude.

ADAPTED TO SURVIVE

What is taiga? South of the treeless tundra in northern North America and Eurasia are huge tracts of coniferous forests, called the taiga. Most trees are evergreens, including fir, pine and spruce. These trees begin growth as soon as it becomes warm enough in spring, and they take full advantage of the short growing season. They are adapted to survive bitterly cold winters. Most of the trees have thick barks, and their conical shapes prevent overloading by snow.

▲ Sparse coniferous forest at the northern edge of the Alaskan taiga.

FLOOD DANGER

Where is the world's largest delta? Deltas are plains near the mouths of some rivers, made of sediment dumped there by the rivers. The world's largest delta is the Ganges-Brahmaputra delta, which lies partly in Bangladesh and partly in India. This low-lying fertile plain is one of the world's most densely populated areas. It has also been the scene of many disasters when storms in the Bay of Bengal have driven seawater inland, causing great loss of life.

◄ A false-colour satellite photograph of the Ganges delta.

▲ Islanders leaving Tristan da Cunha.

THE QUIET LIFE

What is the world's remotest inhabited territory? In the South Atlantic Ocean, about halfway between Africa and South America, are the British islands of Tristan da Cunha. Their nearest neighbour is St Helena, another British island 2,120 km (1,317 miles) away. In 1961, a volcanic eruption forced the Tristan islanders to leave for Britain. But life in crowded Britain lacked appeal and most of them went home in 1963. The 300 or so islanders on Tristan da Cunha, a dependency of St Helena, are happy to live on the world's most remote inhabited territory.

RACE EXTINCTION

Who were the first Australians? Truganini, the 73-year-old daughter of a Tasmanian chief, died in 1876. She was the last Tasmanian Aborigine. It is likely that her ancestors were Australia's first inhabitants, who had probably been driven south into Tasmania over 11,000 years ago by the ancestors of the Australian Aborigines.

In 1803, when the first European settlement was established in Tasmania, there were about 2,000 Tasmanian Aborigines. By 1830, only 200 remained. As is happening to the inhabitants of the rain forests today, brutal treatment and contact with European diseases were major factors in their decline. Truganini witnessed many atrocities, including the stabbing of her mother and the shooting of her father by European settlers.

FACT FILE: HIGHLIGHTS IN EARTH HISTORY

FACT The first living things, bacteria, probably evolved about 4,000 million years ago.

FACT Many-celled algae evolved about 2,000 million years ago. They produced oxygen, which gradually made the atmosphere breathable.

FACT The first known vertebrates (animals with backbones) were fishes. They appeared about 500 million years ago.

FACT Plants were growing on land by 430 million years ago.

FACT The first land vertebrates, amphibians, evolved about 370 million years ago.

FACT The first large land animals, reptiles, had evolved by about 310 million years ago.

FACT The dinosaurs became extinct about 65 million years ago. This enabled mammals to develop.

FACT Early apes appeared about 21 million years ago.

FACT Modern human beings appeared about 50,000 years ago.

SHORT CUT

What is a Great Circle? A straight line drawn between two places on a world map looks like the shortest distance between them. But this usually isn't so, because most maps are distorted. Take a look at a globe. If you stretch a piece of string over the globe, joining Japan and Denmark, you will see that the shortest route runs over the North Pole, not from east to west. The curved line joining Japan and Denmark is part of a Great Circle. This is any circle that divides the globe into two equal halves. Aircraft and ships often follow Great Circle routes.

Amazonian Indians, plants and wild animals are all threatened by the steady destruction of rain forests.
▼

AT OUR PERIL

What is happening in the world's rain forests? In the hot and wet parts of the tropics, there are vast areas of dense rain forest. The largest forests are in South America, especially in the Amazon River basin, with other areas in central Africa, south-eastern Asia and on some Pacific islands. The rain forests cover only about 2 per cent of the Earth's surface, but they contain 40 to 50 per cent of all living plant and animal species. Scientists think that the Amazon basin alone may contain up to 50,000 plant species which have never been named or studied.

Today, these forests are being destroyed at a rate of about 75,000 square km (about 29,000 square miles) a year to make way for cattle ranches, mines, reservoirs and cities. This is almost the same area as the country of Scotland.

Destructive progress Many forest people are dying in clashes with outsiders, or of common European diseases to which they lack resistance. At the start of the 20th century, about 230 separate Amerindian communities lived in the Amazon basin. Today, only 144 remain – the rest are extinct.

Another problem is that plant breeders, who produce improved food plant varieties, need genes from wild species – many of which are now becoming extinct. And more than 40 per cent of the drugs we use are made from wild plants, many of which come from the rain forests. Plants which could be used to save lives are now becoming extinct.

A final problem is that rain forests absorb carbon dioxide from the air and put oxygen back into it. If the forests vanish, the amount of carbon dioxide in the air will probably increase. This could change world climates, possibly with disastrous results.

The planet Uranus and space probe *Voyager 2*.

ON ITS SIDE

Which planet has been knocked over? Uranus seems to have fallen on its side, for the planet's axis of rotation lies almost in the plane of its orbit around the Sun. At times the Sun can appear overhead at one pole of Uranus while the other pole is in complete darkness, so seasons would be extreme on Uranus.

Uranus orbits the Sun so slowly that summer in one hemisphere lasts 42 years, to be followed by 42 years of winter. Why Uranus leans on its side is a mystery. Perhaps it was once hit by another celestial body that knocked it over.

IN REVERSE

Which planet spins backwards? Unlike the Earth and the other planets, which spin from west to east, Venus spins from east to west. It also does so very slowly, taking 243 days to turn around once. This is longer than the 225 days it takes to orbit the Sun.

Venus is the only planet that takes longer to spin on its axis than it does to orbit the Sun. No one knows why Venus spins so slowly, or why it does so in the reverse direction to all the other planets.

LIQUID BALL

Which is the biggest planet? Of the nine planets in the solar system, by far the largest is Jupiter. A line of 11 Earths would be needed to equal its width of 142,000 km (88,000 miles). Jupiter weighs two and a half times as much as all the other planets put together. Yet Jupiter is not solid. Its surface is a swirling mass of clouds. Beneath the clouds, Jupiter consists of hydrogen in liquid form.

HOME ON THE RANGE

What are prairies? Known to TV addicts as the home of cowboys and Indians, the prairies are the vast grassy plains that stretch from south-central Canada through the central USA. Trees are rare because the rainfall is light, but the sunny summers make the prairie grasslands one of the world's leading wheat-producing regions.

HOLY COWS

Which country has the most cattle? Cattle are important farm animals, because they supply meat, dairy products, leather and other materials. They are reared in many parts of the world, with India being top of the cattle league.

Although they are used as beasts of burden, most Indian cows are thin and produce little milk. In fact, Hinduism, the religion of 83 per cent of India's people, forbids the killing of cows or any other animal for food. To Hindus, cows are sacred symbols of Mother Earth. In India, you will often see cows in city streets. They may even pause for a snack, lifting vegetables from a street stall, but no one stops or harms them.

▲
In India, sacred cows are a common sight, even on busy city streets.

▲
High-speed trains like this may revive interest in rail travel.

RAIN OF DEATH

What is acid rain? Car exhaust fumes and smoke from factories and power stations release chemicals, including sulphur dioxide and nitrogen oxides, into the air. The chemicals react with water vapour to form specks of sulphuric and nitric acid. These acids return to the ground in raindrops, snowflakes and other types of precipitation.

The acid kills fish and other animals in lakes and rivers. It damages the soil by destroying the bacteria in it and it harms plants. Acid rain is a serious problem in North America and in central and north-western Europe. For example in the mid-1980s, West German experts estimated that one-third of their trees were dying because of acid rain. The governments of many industrial nations are now trying to find ways of reducing this form of pollution.

RAIL HITS BACK

Will railways survive? Railways became a major form of transport in the Industrial Revolution, because they could transport the heavy materials needed by factories. They were later important in opening up remote areas in the hearts of continents. Although railways carry passengers, most of their income still comes from transporting bulky raw materials and manufactured goods.

Road transport has now taken much trade from the railways and, in some developed countries, people travel more by car or airlines. Many unprofitable railway lines have been closed. However, new fast passenger trains and improved freight cars are being introduced to meet the competition.

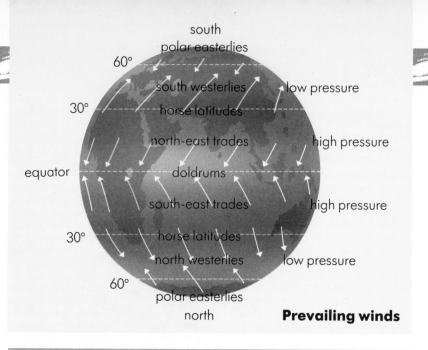

Winds are always named after the ▶ direction from which they blow. Their boundaries are not clearly defined, so that variable weather conditions may be experienced at the fringes of the different wind zones.

south
polar easterlies
60°
south westerlies
low pressure
30°
horse latitudes
north-east trades
high pressure
equator
doldrums
south-east trades
high pressure
30°
horse latitudes
north westerlies
low pressure
60°
polar easterlies
north

Prevailing winds

PLAYING WITH FIRE?

What causes savanna?
Savanna is tropical grassland, ranging from dry regions with short grass and thorn bushes, to areas of open woodland with grasses reaching about 3 m (10 ft) high. It usually occurs in warm places with marked wet and dry seasons.

Why doesn't woodland spread into the wetter parts of the savanna? Some experts think that it is not so much the climate as human interference, which includes deliberate burning, overgrazing and cultivation. Grazing wild animals may also have played a part, especially in Africa, the continent with the greatest area of savanna.

Zebras grazing on African savanna.
▼

AIR IN ACTION

What are prevailing winds? These are the usual, or dominant, winds in their respective latitudes. The air is always moving in different directions around the Earth. Warm air flows from the tropics towards the poles, and cold air flows from the poles towards the tropics. This heat-exchange system is powered by the Sun.

Changing currents At the equator, the heat of the Sun on the Earth's surface is intense. Warm air rises and this creates a low pressure zone called the doldrums. The rising warm air finally cools and spreads out north and south.

Around latitudes 30° North and South, the air sinks downwards, creating two zones of high air pressure, called the horse latitudes. (This odd name probably comes from the days of sailing ships, because, when ships were delayed by calm conditions, horses were thrown overboard to save drinking water.) From the horse latitudes, air is drawn back towards the doldrums, replacing the rising air. These air currents are the trade winds.

Polar flow Air also flows from the horse latitudes towards the poles. These currents form the westerly winds. The warm westerlies eventually meet up with cold, easterly winds, flowing from the polar regions. The trade winds, the westerlies and the polar easterlies are all prevailing winds in their particular latitudes.

CHILDREN OF THE STARS?

Did you know that some of the atoms in your body may have been made inside stars? Some scientists believe that we are all incredibly ancient. They think that the atoms in our bodies were formed inside stars that lived and died over 5,000 million years ago, before our Sun was born.

Stars over ten times as massive as the Sun end their lives in a violent explosion called a supernova. In the eruption, all the chemical elements of nature are produced by nuclear reactions and are scattered into space. There, they mix with the existing clouds of gas from which new stars and planets will later form. Without supernova explosions in the past, the Earth and the life on it might not be here.

Airborne industrial waste may gradually be changing our climate. ▶

LIGHTHOUSES IN THE SKY

What is a pulsar? A supernova leaves behind a tiny object termed a neutron star, far smaller than the Earth. It is the core of the star that exploded. The protons and electrons of its atoms have been squashed together by the force of the supernova, to form the atomic particles known as neutrons.

A neutron star is unimaginably dense. It contains the mass of the Sun, squeezed into a ball 20 km (12½ miles) across. Neutron stars are so small that they can spin very rapidly, once a second or faster. Some of them flash each time they spin, like a lighthouse. Such flashing neutron stars are termed pulsars.

PREDICTING DISASTER

How might the changing atmosphere affect our climate? The composition of the air around us is constantly changing. Industrial processes such as the burning of oil, gas and coal help to increase the amount of carbon dioxide in the atmosphere. People and animals breathe in oxygen and breathe out carbon dioxide, while green plants absorb carbon dioxide and give off oxygen when light falls on them.

The amount of carbon dioxide in the air affects temperatures. This is because carbon dioxide absorbs some of the heat that is radiated from the Earth's surface, stopping it escaping into space. The higher the content of carbon dioxide in the air, the more heat it retains.

Possible consequences Some American scientists have estimated that the amount of carbon dioxide in the atmosphere may double between 1980 and 2030, particularly if the tropical rain forests disappear. Were this to happen, the temperature of the air might rise by 2°C (3.6°F). This would alter world climates, making dry regions drier, and melting the ice in polar regions. The rising seas would then flood some of the world's biggest cities.

QUIZ: ASTRONOMY

① What is an astronomical unit?
② Can you see farther during the day or at night?
③ Which star is called the Dog Star?
④ Which constellation is known as the bull?
⑤ What type of telescope collects light with a mirror?
⑥ What creature is represented by the constellation Cygnus?
⑦ What caused the Crab nebula?
⑧ Which constellation contains the stars Castor and Pollux?

ANSWERS
① The distance from the Earth to the Sun, 150 million km (93 million miles). ② At night! ③ Sirius. ④ Taurus. ⑤ A reflector. ⑥ A swan. ⑦ A supernova. ⑧ Gemini, the twins.

▲ An open-cast Australian coal mine.

◀ In undeveloped countries some prospectors continue to rely on age-old methods of gold-panning.

DEEP NOT CHEAP

Where is the world's deepest mine? The world's deepest mine is at Carletonville, South Africa. The lowest point in this gold mine is 3.777 km (2³⁄₁₀ miles) below the surface. Such underground mining was once hazardous. But though accidents still occur, modern mines have complex safety precautions.

Other methods The cheapest, not the deepest, form of mining is surface mining. Open-cast mining involves the removal of rocks from the surface, as in Western Australia where whole mountains rich in iron ore are being dug away. Dredging involves the mining of gravels containing fragments of minerals, such as diamonds, while quarries are surface excavations to obtain building stone, such as granite and limestone.

SCIENTIFIC SEARCHING

How has mineral prospecting changed? As the world's population grows, so also does the demand for fossil fuels, metals and other minerals. Until the 20th century, the search for minerals was largely hit-or-miss. Prospectors wandered around looking for signs of minerals, such as grains of gold in riverbeds. If they were lucky, they hunted in the right places. Today, there is usually a much more scientific approach to prospecting.

Instruments and information Modern prospectors are armed with detailed geological maps and air or space photographs, which often supply clues. They also use scientific instruments, including seismographs. Seismographs record small earthquake waves caused by explosions. The passage of these waves through the ground yields information about the rock structures below the surface. Other instruments include geiger counters to detect radioactive rocks, and magnetometers for metals with magnetic properties, such as iron.

Chemistry also helps. Chemical analysis of the soil or plants often provides information about the nature of the rocks below.

STORMY WEATHER

What are the main types of rain? Rainclouds are formed when moist air rises. This happens in three main ways. First, intense heating of the ground by the Sun makes warm air rise in strong currents. This rising air frequently causes thunderclouds, and rain formed in this way is called *convectional* rain. *Orographic* rain occurs when winds are forced to rise over mountain ranges. The third main type of rain, *cyclonic* rain, occurs when warm air rises over cold, dense air in depressions.

LORD OF THE RINGS

How did Saturn get its rings? Saturn's equator is girdled by a beautiful set of rings, made of countless ice-coated moonlets orbiting the planet. Saturn's rings measure 275,000 km (172,000 miles) from rim to rim, yet they are only 100 m (328 ft) thick. On the same scale of width to thickness, a long-playing record would be nearly 3 km (2 miles) in diameter.

Saturn's rings are probably the building blocks of a moon that never formed. Alternatively, they could be the remains of a former moon that broke up.

EXTREMES

Where are the hottest and coldest places in the solar system? Venus is the hottest of the Sun's planets. Space probes have measured the temperature on its surface as a scorching 460°C (950°F). The reason is that Venus is surrounded by a dense atmosphere of carbon dioxide, which traps the Sun's heat like a greenhouse. The coldest planet is distant Pluto, whose surface has a temperature of −230°C (−490°F).

CHANGING SEASONS

What are solstices and equinoxes? The Earth's axis is tilted so that the northern hemisphere leans towards the Sun for half the year and the southern hemisphere for the other half. This explains why we have seasons. On about June 21, the northern hemisphere leans towards the Sun to the greatest extent, and the Sun is overhead at the Tropic of Cancer (latitude 23°27′ North). This day is the summer solstice in the northern hemisphere and the winter solstice in the southern.

On about December 21 – the winter solstice in the northern hemisphere and the summer solstice in the southern – the Sun is overhead at the Tropic of Capricorn (latitude 23°27′ South).

The equinoxes are on about March 21 and September 23. On these days, the Sun is overhead at the equator and the length of day and night is everywhere the same – 12 hours. This explains the word equinox, which means 'equal night'.

The alignment of the rising Sun's ▶ rays and certain stones at the ancient site of Stonehenge, England, at the summer solstice is thought once to have had some astronomical or religious significance.

GOOD NEWS AND BAD

Why is the Nile delta retreating? This is a result of natural erosion combining with the effects of modern technology. The building in the 1960s of the Aswan High Dam on the River Nile in Egypt was a great achievement. The power station at the dam now supplies much of Egypt's electricity.

Irrigation works using water from Lake Nasser (the lake behind the dam) have doubled Egypt's farm production.

Much of the fertile silt, which was once spread over the Nile valley during the yearly floods, now piles up on the lake bed. As a result, Egyptian farmers must now use more artificial fertilizers.

Before the dam was built, the silt also reached the coast. Some was dumped in the Nile delta, balancing the land lost by wave erosion. However, the coast along the delta is now being worn back and there is a danger that salt water will begin to penetrate inland and ruin good farmland.

▲
The Aswan dam provides water for hydroelectric power, industry and irrigation.

ENERGY FAMINE

What is the energy crisis? Most of the world's electricity is generated by oil, gas and coal in power stations. These fossil fuels are being used up quickly, and some experts have predicted that an energy crisis will occur before long. At the present rates at which we are using oil and natural gas, the known reserves will run out in the early 21st century. Coal reserves are expected to last 300 to 400 years, but even they will be used up one day.

Alternative sources In some countries, water power is used to produce hydroelectricity, but this is only possible in places with mountains and plenty of rainfall. Other countries are developing nuclear power stations, but nuclear energy is costly and problems remain, such as how to get rid of dangerous radioactive wastes safely.

Scientists are now studying other forms of energy production, including the harnessing of the Sun's radiation and tapping the heat inside the Earth. Improved windmills, tidal and wave power, and even the cultivation of seaweed to use as a fuel are some of the other ideas being explored to meet the energy crisis.

BEYOND PLUTO?

Is there a 10th planet? Since the discovery of the outermost planet, Pluto, in 1930, astronomers have wondered whether another planet might exist unseen in the outer darkness. They have looked, but nothing has been found.

Clyde Tombaugh, the man who discovered Pluto, photographed the entire sky in search of extra planets. He concluded that if any other planets existed they must either be very small, or very far away. Most astronomers think that the solar system ends with Pluto.

FIERY SPACE DUST

What is a shooting star? It has nothing to do with real stars at all. Shooting stars are actually bits of dust from space, burning up by friction as they plunge at high speed into the Earth's atmosphere, 100 km (62 miles) or so above our heads. Their fiery death produces a streak of light in the sky, usually lasting no more than a second or so. Half a dozen shooting stars can be seen per hour on a clear night.

Astronomers term them meteors. Several times a year the Earth passes through swarms of dust left by comets, and the resulting dust storm produces a meteor shower, during which dozens of shooting stars may be seen in an hour.

Each year Rotterdam Europoort handles many thousands of barges and ocean-going vessels.
▼

FACT FILE: TOWN AND COUNTRY

FACT The first cities grew up in south-western Asia. By about 3500 BC, Babylon, on the River Euphrates, had a population of about 80,000.

FACT Today, in developed countries, a large proportion of the people live in urban areas. For example, 91 per cent of the people in Britain live in cities and towns.

FACT In poor countries, more people live in country areas. For example, 85 per cent of Ethiopians live in the countryside.

FACT In developed countries, farming is so efficient that few farmworkers are needed. In the USA, only 2 per cent of the workforce is employed in farming. By contrast, 93 out of every 100 people in Nepal work on the land.

FACT Many cities in poor and middle income countries are now expanding quickly, because they offer the chance of higher standards of living than the countryside. But there are often too few houses and jobs for the newcomers, and so slums are increasing.

ARTIFICIAL HARBOUR

Which is the world's busiest port? There are many thousands of different ports throughout the world. Some lie inland on rivers and lakes, and can be reached by boats big enough to carry raw materials and manufactured goods. On coasts, there are fishing ports and seaports which handle trade. Seaports are situated on natural or specially built harbours, which offer safe anchorage for ocean-going vessels. The world's busiest port is the artificial harbour of Rotterdam-Europoort, in the Netherlands.

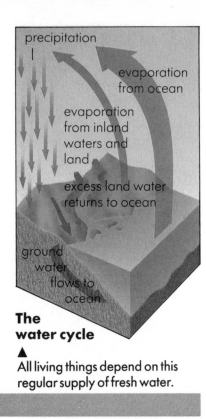

precipitation

evaporation from ocean

evaporation from inland waters and land

excess land water returns to ocean

ground water flows to ocean

The water cycle
▲
All living things depend on this regular supply of fresh water.

THE VITAL CYCLE

What is the water cycle? Water can be a liquid, a solid (ice) or a gas (water vapour). The oceans contain about 97 per cent of the world's water supply, and about another 2 per cent is ice. Only 0.001 per cent of the world's water is in the form of vapour, yet without it there would be no life on land. Animals and plants need a regular supply of fresh water and, surprisingly, this comes from the salty oceans through the water cycle.

Rising and falling Water vapour is formed when the Sun heats wet surfaces, especially the oceans, and water is evaporated. Air currents carry the vapour upwards, where it condenses (liquefies) to form clouds. Winds blow the clouds over the land, where much of the moisture falls as rain, snow or some other kind of precipitation. Some of this fresh water runs into rivers and lakes, and some sinks into the soil, where it may be absorbed by plants. Yet more water seeps farther down and percolates through pores and cracks in rocks. This 'ground' water may return to the surface through springs (the sources of rivers).

Ceaseless process The influence of gravity ensures all the water eventually gets back to the oceans, completing the continuous process of the water cycle. The constant recycling of water means that some of the water coming from your taps today may have been in the River Nile a month ago!

BOMBARDMENT

Did you know that rocks from space hit the Earth? Several times a year, lumps of rock and metal plunge to Earth. They are called meteorites, and they are debris left over from the formation of the planets.

Meteorites have been known to crash through the roofs of houses, and one in 1954 badly bruised a woman in Alabama. If a meteorite is moving quickly enough when it hits the Earth it can gouge out a crater, like the one in the Arizona desert which is over 1 km (⅝ mile) wide. The largest known meteorite lies where it fell in prehistoric times, at Grootfontein in Namibia, Africa. It is made of iron and nickel and is estimated to weigh 60 tonnes.

HEAVENLY MISSILE

What hit the Earth in 1908? On the morning of June 30, 1908, a brilliant fireball blazed through the skies over Siberia, exploding above the Stony Tunguska river with the force of a 12-megaton bomb. The blast knocked down trees for up to 30 km (19 miles) around, set the forest ablaze and caused shock waves like an earthquake.

Astronomers think that the Tunguska object was a fragment from the head of a comet. It was about 100 m (330 ft) across and weighed a million tonnes. Another such object could hit the Earth at any time. If it descended over a city, it would cause massive devastation.

◀ Buildings at the centre of this meteor crater in Arizona, USA, give some idea of its massive size.

▲
An Alaskan lake and swampy tundra in spring.

SUMMER RESIDENTS

Where is tundra found? In the Arctic lands of North America and Eurasia that have long, cold winters. Snow blankets the ground from September to April or May, but during the cool summers, the snow and the icy top of the soil melts. Flat areas become swamps, filled by swarms of insects which provide food for many feathered visitors. Also, mosses, lichens, grasses and some flowering plants flourish in summer, attracting grazing animals, such as caribou, musk oxen and reindeer, from the south.

The southern hemisphere doesn't have a tundra region, because there are no landmasses in the appropriate latitude. There are, however, zones of treeless tundra near the tops of high mountains throughout the world.

SUGAR FOR ENERGY

Where does sugar come from? Sugar is a food that people use for energy. Each person in the USA uses, on average, about 41 kg (90 lb) of sugar a year. All plants produce sugar, but the main sources of commercial sugar are sugarcane, a type of grass plant grown in tropical and subtropical regions, and sugar beet, a root crop grown in temperate areas.

Sugar cane being sold at a ▶
market in Bahia, Brazil.

OVERVIEW

What are the uses of air photographs? Photographs of the ground taken by high-flying aircraft were used in wartime to obtain information about enemy territory. After World War II, air photography became the chief method of mapping the detail of the land. Because overlapping photographs viewed through a stereoscope produce a three-dimensional image, air photographs can also be used to measure the height of points on the land.

LEAVE US BE

How have the Mbuti pygmies preserved their lifestyle? The Mbuti pygmies live in the Ituri rain forest in north-eastern Zaire, Africa. They live by hunting, and gathering fruit and roots. They have kept up their old way of life by supplying their neighbours, Bantu-speaking farmers, with all the forest products they need. To outsiders, the pygmies may seem to behave like servants. However, by doing this, they ensure that their neighbours have no reason to enter the forest and upset the pygmy way of life.

Pygmy villagers preparing a meal.
▼

QUIZ: FOSSILS AND PREHISTORY

1. In what type of rock are fossils most common?
2. What was the largest flesh-eating dinosaur?
3. What fake 'human fossil', made up of a human skull and an orang-utan's jawbone, fooled scientists between 1912 and 1929?
4. What is the name of the earliest known bird?
5. What is the name of the dog-like ancestor of the horse which lived in the early Eocene epoch?
6. What was the heaviest known dinosaur?
7. In what transparent substance were insects often fossilized?
8. What do we call the study of fossils?
9. What are the oldest rocks in Earth history in which fossils are common?

ANSWERS
1 Sedimentary rocks. 2 Tyrannosaurus rex. 3 'Piltdown Man'. 4 Archaeopteryx. 5 Eohippus. 6 Brachiosaurus. 7 Amber (hardened resin). 8 Palaeontology. 9 Cambrian rocks.

MEMBERS OF THE COMMONWEALTH

Antigua and Barbuda
Australia
Bahamas
Bangladesh
Barbados
Belize
Botswana
Brunei
Canada
Cyprus
Dominica
Fiji
Gambia
Ghana
Grenada
Guyana
India
Jamaica
Kenya
Kiribati
Lesotho
Malawi
Malaysia
Malta
Maldives
Mauritius
Nauru
New Zealand
Nigeria
Papua New Guinea
St Christopher-Nevis
St Lucia
St Vincent and the
    Grenadines
Seychelles
Sierra Leone
Singapore
Solomon Islands
Sri Lanka
Swaziland
Tanzania
Tonga
Trinidad and Tobago
Tuvalu
Uganda
United Kingdom
Vanuatu
Western Samoa
Zambia
Zimbabwe

A FREE ASSOCIATION

What is the Commonwealth of Nations? By the late 19th century, the British Empire covered about a fifth of the world's land area. But as countries began to win their independence, the Empire began to evolve into a free association, called the Commonwealth. In 1931, the Commonwealth's founder members were Australia, Britain, Canada, Ireland, New Zealand, Newfoundland and South Africa. Ireland and South Africa later withdrew and Newfoundland became part of Canada.

Expansion From 1947, the membership of the Commonwealth steadily expanded, because most former British colonies joined it when they gained independence. Many of the new countries became republics. But the British monarch remains Head of State in 18 Commonwealth countries, and all member countries recognize Queen Elizabeth II as Head of the Commonwealth.

A useful alliance British traditions and the English language help to bind the Commonwealth countries together. The Commonwealth now contains nearly a fourth of the world's inhabitants. It is not a military alliance, but it makes important political and economic decisions. For instance, a Commonwealth conference in 1979 produced the plan to bring about the independence of Zimbabwe.

▲
Water filled an extinct volcano dome to create Crater Lake, Oregon.

COLLAPSING MOUNTAINS

What causes craters? Craters are depressions in the Earth's surface. Some, like the pit filled by Lake Bosumtwi in Ghana, were formed when large meteorites crashed to the ground. But far more craters form in volcanoes, when the magma in the pipe sinks and the top of the volcano collapses inwards. Crater Lake, Oregon, USA was formed in this way 6,600 years ago. Water later filled the hole, forming a 52 square km (20 square mile) lake.

Large craters are called calderas. The world's largest caldera is Toba, in Sumatra, Indonesia. It has an area of 1,775 square km (685 square miles).

STARDUST TRAIL

What is the Milky Way? Across the sky on a clear, dark night stretches a misty band of light. The ancient Greeks called it the Milky Way, and in their legends they explained it as a splash of milk from the breast of the sky goddess, Hera.

In 1609 the Italian astronomer Galileo turned a telescope on the Milky Way, and found it consisted of innumerable faint stars. All the stars of the Milky Way are members of our Galaxy – written with a capital G to distinguish it from any other galaxy.

ANIMAL, VEGETABLE AND MINERAL

What are elements, minerals and rocks? Elements are the basic chemical substances that make up all matter. Some 92 elements occur naturally in the Earth's crust. The commonest are oxygen, which makes up 46.60 per cent of the weight of the crust, silicon (27.72 per cent), aluminium (8.13 per cent), iron (5 per cent), calcium (3.63 per cent), sodium (2.83 per cent), potassium (2.59 per cent) and magnesium (2.09 per cent). The other 84 elements account for only 1.41 per cent of the crust's weight.

Minerals are mostly chemical combinations of two or more elements. They are inorganic (lifeless) substances with a definite chemical composition. Coal, oil and natural gas are not minerals, because they are formed from vegetable and animal material.

Rocks are made of minerals, but they do not have a definite chemical composition. This is because the proportions of minerals in rocks vary from one kind of rock to another.

COLD CAPS

Where are the biggest ice blocks? About 2.15 per cent of the world's water supply is frozen. Most of the ice is locked in two great ice sheets, the largest blanketing most of Antarctica and the other in Greenland. Smaller ice caps occur on northern islands, including Iceland, Spitzbergen and various islands in northern Canada. Valley glaciers are smaller still. They are found on mountain slopes throughout the world.

The icy wastes of Antarctica.
▼

▲ A spiral galaxy.

ISLANDS IN THE UNIVERSE

What is a galaxy? Galaxies are immense aggregations of millions or billions of stars. Our Sun is a member of a galaxy, the rim of which we see as the Milky Way. In fact, the word 'galaxy' comes from the Greek meaning milk, in reference to the Milky Way.

Spirals and ellipticals There are two main types of galaxy, spirals and ellipticals. The elliptical galaxies are shaped like gigantic rugby balls and they include the largest known galaxies in the Universe, containing a million million stars.

Spiral galaxies are shaped like Catherine wheels. Our home Galaxy is a spiral. It contains at least 100,000 million stars, and is 100,000 light years across. We lie in one of the spiral arms, 30,000 light years from the centre.

▲ The different time zones are shown on clocks at the London Stock Exchange.

TIME PIECES

What are time zones? Times differ around the world and because the Earth spins once on its axis every 24 hours, we experience day and night. The world is divided into time zones, which are about 15° longitude wide. This is because 15° is the equivalent of one hour of time (360° divided by 24 hours). The actual boundaries between time zones often follow the frontiers of countries, which prevents one small country having two separate times.

INSTANT DATE CHANGE

Where can one lose or gain a day? Time is measured east and west of the prime meridian (0° longitude), an imaginary line that passes through Greenwich, England. East of Greenwich, the time advances by one hour for every 15° of longitude. To the west, one hour is lost for every 15 degrees. At 180° East, the time is 12 hours *ahead* of Greenwich, while at 180° West, the time is 12 hours *behind* Greenwich.

But 180° East and West are the same line. So, there is a difference of 24 hours between the two sides of this line, which is called the International Date Line. Crossing it from west to east, you gain one whole day, but going from east to west, you lose a day. The International Date Line does not follow the 180° line of longitude exactly. It is adjusted so that it does not pass through land areas.

DATING BY DECAY

How are the ages of rocks measured? In the 19th century, geologists could tell whether one rock layer was older or younger than another by the fossils they contained. But they could not measure the absolute ages of rocks until after the discovery of radioactivity in the 1890s.

Radioactive substances, which are occasionally found in rocks, give off high-energy rays and decay (break down) at a fixed rate. For instance, as the radioactive element uranium decays, it changes into lead. If you measure the amount of lead in a uranium sample, you can then work out its age. The uranium-lead method is used for extremely old rocks.

For substances up to 50,000 years old, scientists use carbon-14 dating. Carbon-14 is a radioactive element that is present in all living things. When organisms die, the carbon-14 in the tissues decays. Half of the carbon-14 decays every 5,700 years. Knowing this, scientists can work out the ages of old bones or logs.

DRINKS THAT CHEER

Where do the leading beverages come from? Today many different countries produce the natural ingredients for the world's most popular drinks. Cocoa originated in tropical South America and coffee in Ethiopia. The first use of tea as a drink is supposed to have been in 2737 BC in China, although much tea is now produced in India. Grapes used for wine require hot summers and so vineyards are common in Mediterranean lands. Hops used to make beer grow in cooler, wetter climates.

FACT FILE: MINERALS AND ROCKS

FACT Geologists have classified nearly 3,000 minerals.
FACT Of the 92 elements (basic chemical substances) that occur naturally in the Earth's crust, 22, including gold and silver, are sometimes found in a pure state. The others occur in combinations with one or more other elements.
FACT Sedimentary rocks (formed from compressed rock fragments) cover about 75 per cent of the world's land areas.
FACT Igneous rocks (formed from solidified lava) and metamorphic rocks (those charged by great heat or pressure) make up 95 per cent of the top 16 km (10 miles) of the Earth's crust.
FACT The Moon rocks collected by astronauts are igneous in type. There are no sedimentary rocks on the Moon. This is because the Moon has no atmosphere, and so weathering and erosion do not occur.

Crystals of the minerals malachite (green) and azurite (blue).
▼

DIVIDED RULE

When is a country not a country? Occasionally, civil wars occur which lead to a country being divided in two. For example, a war in Pakistan in 1971 led to the creation of the new nation of Bangladesh. Not all new countries, however, win international recognition. For instance, Cyprus has been divided, though the breakaway Turkish Republic of Northern Cyprus, established in 1983, is recognized only by Turkey.

Other places with a doubtful status are the 'Homelands' set up in South Africa for black people. South Africa's government has granted independence to four of them: Bophuthatswana (1977), Ciskei (1981), Transkei (1976) and Venda (1979). However, no country other than South Africa considers the Homelands to be independent. The UN sees them as part of South Africa's apartheid, or separate development, policy which it opposes.

▲
A crowded Chinese street market.

BURIED ALIVE

What causes landslides? These sometimes deadly landslips are often the result of rainstorms. For example, in September 1963, heavy rain soaked the slopes of Monte Toc in northern Italy. Water seeped down through the top layers of limestone to a deeper layer of clay. The top of the clay became increasingly slippery and on October 9, the top layers of rock slid downwards over the clay into a reservoir. The concrete dam holding the reservoir held. But a huge wave of water, containing millions of tonnes of rock, swept over the dam, burying the town of Longarone lower down. More than 2,000 people died. Heavy rains also cause earthflows, which are torrents of water mixed with soil, clay or volcanic ash.

Mudflows caused by the eruption of the Nevado del Ruiz volcano in Colombia in 1985 killed more than 20,000 people. Earthquakes have caused many great landslides. One in Kansu province, China, in 1920 killed about 180,000 people.

This house is being destroyed by landsliding cliffs. ▶

REDUCING REPRODUCTION

How has China reduced its birth rate? China contains about a fifth of the world's people and for some years its government has been trying to cut the birth rate. In the 1970s, the government encouraged people not to marry until they were in their late twenties and, by law, no woman may marry until she is 20 and no man until he is 22. Married couples in cities and towns are asked to have only one child, though people in the countryside are allowed two. People who have more children than allowed suffer penalties and loss of benefits.

The policy was successful. The birth rate fell from 2.8 per cent in 1964 to just over one per cent by the mid-1980s. But success brings new problems. The percentage of elderly people will increase rapidly after the year 2000. This will place a great burden on their children and the government, which will have to provide increasing benefits.

MOUNTAIN MEN

Who are the Sherpas? On May 29, 1953, Sir Edmund Hillary, a New Zealander, and Tenzing Norgay, a Sherpa, became the first people to scale Mount Everest. The Sherpas live in Nepal in the shadow of the Himalayas. They have won fame as sturdy porters, guides and skilled mountaineers.

UNITY IN DIVERSITY

What country has three official names? It is Switzerland, a country whose three official languages are German, French and Italian. The country's three names are Schweiz (in German), Suisse (French) and Svizzera (Italian).

The Swiss are a united people, proud of their long history of freedom and neutrality. Elsewhere, language differences within countries have sometimes caused strife. For example, in Belgium, the Dutch-speaking Flemings have often clashed with the French-speaking Walloons.

▲
Sherpas are skilful and efficient mountain porters.

INITIAL ORGANIZATIONS

What are the OAU and OAS? Newspapers often refer to large organizations by their initials. This can be confusing, especially when groups with different aims have similar initials. One important national body is the OAU, or the Organization of African Unity. It was set up by 32 African countries in 1963 to promote political, economic and social development throughout Africa. Its members do not always agree. For instance, in 1984, Morocco left the OAU when it was criticized for annexing Western (formerly Spanish) Sahara.

The similarly named OAS, the Organization of American States, is a regional branch of the United Nations, and it includes 31 Latin American countries and the USA. It, too, has problems. For instance, Cuba is a member, but it is barred from taking an active part because it has a Communist government.

SAME BUT DIFFERENT

What is a race? The word race is often wrongly used. For example, the Jews are not a race, but a religious and cultural group, who, in racial terms, are exactly the same as the Nazis who persecuted them. Many scholars say that there is only one race – the human race. However, the human family can be divided into several groups according to such features as skin, eye colour and hair type. The four main groups are: Caucasoids, Mongoloids, Negroids and Australoids, who include Australian Aborigines.

The four main ethnic groups

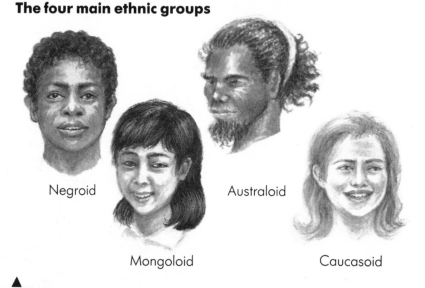

Negroid

Australoid

Mongoloid

Caucasoid

▲
People belong to one species but many different races.

MOBILE CONTINENTS

What was Pangaea? Because of continental drift, the world's surface is always changing. About 300 million years ago, there were two continents. One, called Gondwanaland, contained parts of South America, Africa, India, Australia and Antarctica, which were then joined together. The other, called Laurasia, was made up of North America and Eurasia.

About 275 million years ago, Gondwanaland and Laurasia collided and joined up to form a single supercontinent, Pangaea, a Greek name meaning 'all the Earth'. In the last 170 million years, Pangaea has broken up and the continents have drifted slowly apart.

LAND YIELDS

What kind of farming is the most productive? When land is scarce, farms must be as productive as possible. For example, less than 15 per cent of Japan is suitable for farming. But through intensive farming, using fertilizers, irrigation, machinery and improved plant varieties, yields are high, and Japan produces 70 per cent of the food it needs.

Another example of intensive agriculture is market gardening – the production of flowers, fruit and vegetables on small plots near cities. Market gardens often cover only 0.4 ha (1 acre) but they are highly profitable. By way of contrast, a sheep ranch in a dry grassland region requires four times as much land to graze one animal. Sheep ranching is an example of extensive agriculture.

▲
The open spaces of a sheep farm in Australia (above) contrasted with a patchwork of intensively farmed Japanese fields. ▶

AID IN ASIA

What is the Colombo Plan? The Colombo Plan, an organization founded in 1950, is named after the city in Sri Lanka which contains its headquarters. The 26 member countries work together to promote economic and social development in southern Asia and the Pacific area.

Aid comes mainly from the six developed members: Australia, Canada, Japan, New Zealand, the UK and the USA. The other members are Afghanistan, Bangladesh, Bhutan, Burma, Fiji, India, Indonesia, Iran, Kampuchea, South Korea, Laos, Malaysia, the Maldives, Nepal, Pakistan, Papua New Guinea, the Philippines, Singapore, Sri Lanka and Thailand.

FLYING FOREIGN FLAGS

Which country has the largest merchant fleet? Japan is the world's leading shipbuilding country, though its merchant fleet ranks third in size after Liberia and Greece. The size of a merchant fleet is measured by its gross tonnage – that is, the total space within the hull and the enclosed deck space – rather than the number of ships. Liberia itself owns few ships, but it operates a flag of convenience. This means that most of its fleet is owned by foreign companies. These companies register ships in Liberia because of the country's lower taxes and less strict laws on wages and safety precautions.

QUIZ: OCEANS AND SEAS

① What is the name for the shallow areas around continents?
② What do we call (a) the highest and (b) the lowest tidal ranges?
③ What two elements give seawater a salty taste?
④ What are the deepest parts of the oceans?
⑤ What craft was used by Jacques Piccard and Donald Walsh in the record descent of 10,917 m (35,817 ft) into the Marianas Trench?
⑥ What instruments are used to map the ocean floor?
⑦ What is the cause of surface ocean currents?
⑧ What ocean current moderates the weather in north-western Europe?
⑨ What volcanic island emerged off Iceland in 1963?

ANSWERS
① Continental shelves. ② (a) spring tides; (b) neap tides. ③ Sodium and chlorine. ④ Ocean trenches. ⑤ US bathyscaphe *Trieste*. ⑥ Echo sounders. ⑦ Winds. ⑧ The Gulf Stream (and its extension, the North Atlantic Drift). ⑨ Surtsey.

SHORT CUTS

Which are the world's leading ship canals? The world's busiest big ship canal is the Panama Canal, linking the Atlantic and Pacific oceans. Completed in 1914, it saves ships going from New York City to San Francisco, a journey of 12,600 km (about 7,830 miles) around South America.

With a length of 163 km (101 miles), the longest big ship canal is the Suez Canal. Opened in 1869, it links the Mediterranean and Red seas.

Up to 12,000 ships pass through ▶ the Panama Canal each year. Their average journey time is eight hours.

THE OCEANS

Ocean	Area in sq. km (sq. miles)	Greatest depth in metres (ft)
Pacific	166,240,000 (64,186,300)	10,915 (35,810)
Atlantic	82,217,000 (31,744,000)	9,200 (30,184)
Indian	73,481,000 (28,371,000)	8,047 (26,400)
Arctic	14,056,000 (5,427,000)	5,450 (17,880)

MINING THE ABYSS

What are manganese nodules? As metals are used up at an increasing rate, scientists have been studying new sources of supply. For example, bromine, magnesium and salt are extracted from seawater, which also contains more dissolved gold than all the gold in human possession (though it is far too expensive to extract).

On parts of the ocean bed, there are large numbers of potato-shaped lumps of metal, called manganese nodules. These nodules are also often rich in cobalt, copper, iron and nickel. At present, they can't be brought to the surface economically. But it is hoped that one day huge pumps will suck them up into the holds of ships, thus utilizing another of the world's natural resources.

NATURAL FOUNTAINS

What is an artesian well? The mountainous Great Dividing Range gets plenty of rain, but the interior plains of east-central Australia are dry. Some rainwater in the mountains seeps into porous rock strata which extend beneath the dry plains. These porous rocks are aquifers (water-bearing layers) enclosed above and below by compact rocks which stop the water escaping.

In places like the Australian interior (and similar locations throughout the world), farmers sink artesian wells down to the aquifer. Because the source of the water is higher than the well, the water gushes upwards under pressure. Sometimes, it even shoots forth as a fountain. However, as water is removed, the pressure falls and finally the water must be pumped up.

The word artesian comes from the French province of Artois, where some early artesian wells were dug.

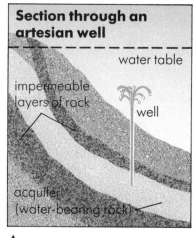

Section through an artesian well

- water table
- impermeable layers of rock
- well
- aquifer (water-bearing rock)

▲ A typical artesian well.

BEFORE THE PLOUGH

African bushmen and Australian aborigines continue to use bows, arrows and spears when hunting for food.
▼

Why was the invention of farming so important? Farming began in south-western Asia between 8,000 and 9,000 years ago. We know this because a farming settlement dated at about 6700 BC has been found in southern Turkey. The invention of agriculture was a major landmark, because for the first time people had more food than they needed. Because it was no longer essential for everyone to be engaged in the daily search for food, the development of civilization became possible.

Hunters and gatherers Before this great event, small bands of people roamed around hunting animals and gathering seeds, berries and roots. The way of life of our distant ancestors can be observed today among such peoples as nomadic Australian Aborigines, Bushmen in southern Africa's Kalahari desert, pygmies in Central Africa, and some Amerindian groups in the Amazon basin. The hunting and gathering way of life may seem primitive, but it is based on an extremely deep knowledge and understanding of the workings of nature.

VALUE PLUS

What is meant by 'value added'? When iron and manganese are mined, they have a certain value or worth. If they are used to make high-grade steel, value is added to them. More value is added when the steel is used to make a machine. The end product, the machine, may be more than 100 times as costly as the materials used to make it. This added value reflects such things as the cost of labour, management and transport.

Rich and poor nations Value added is important in understanding the relationship between rich and poor countries. For example, some developing countries have rich deposits of metal ores. But they cannot afford to build the factories to process the ores and make things with them. Instead, they sell them to developed countries, where they are often turned into products, such as farm machinery, that may be sold in the same developing country that produced the original materials.

POWER SOURCES

How does the world generate its electrical energy? Most of the world's electrical energy is generated by power stations burning fossil fuels such as coal. But some mountainous and well-watered countries have hydroelectric power stations. These produce, for example, 92 per cent of Norway's electricity supply and 92 per cent of Brazil's.

In industrial countries, another source of electrical energy is nuclear power. Although this is costly, it accounts for 40 per cent of the electricity produced in France, 15 per cent in Japan, 14 per cent in West Germany and the United Kingdom, and 12 per cent in the USA. Generating nuclear power does, however, pose some problems. One is that radioactive nuclear wastes do not become safe for hundreds of years.

WET AND WINDY

What are monsoons? In winter, dry north-east winds blow across India from the cold interior of southern Asia. In summer, the land is intensely heated by the Sun. The hot air rises and a low pressure air system develops. Warm, moist south-east trade winds that blow across the equator are drawn into the low pressure system, replacing the rising hot air. In doing so, they become south-west winds, a complete reversal of the winter winds. Such seasonal reversals of wind direction are called monsoons, although the heavy rains brought by the summer winds are more commonly associated with this name.

GHOSTLY WANDERERS

What is a comet? Comets are the ghostly wanderers of the solar system. They loop around the Sun on hairpin-shaped paths, often taking centuries or more to complete one trip. When far from the Sun, a comet is thought to resemble a dirty snowball of frozen gas and dust, a few kilometres across.

The coma As it approaches the Sun, the snowball warms up, releasing gas and dust to form a glowing head known as the coma, up to ten times the width of the Earth. Gas and dust flow away from the comet's head to form its transparent tail, which can stretch as far as the distance from the Earth to the Sun. Comets are among the debris left from the formation of the solar system.

◀ An artist's impression of a comet passing across the sky above Egypt in 1882.

▲
The world's tallest mountains, the Himalayas in Nepal, are fold mountains.

GIANT WRINKLES

What are fold mountains? On exposed cliff faces, you will often see that the rocks are arranged in layers, rather like a sliced loaf placed on end. The layers, or strata, may be level, tilted or bent into rounded wrinkles, or folds. Folds are caused by sideways pressure from colliding plates in the Earth's crust.

Fold mountains – created by rocks thrown up and distorted by colliding plates in the Earth's crust – form the world's most extensive and highest ranges.
▼

Imposing ranges The tremendous pressure created by sideways moving plates can squeeze otherwise level rock strata into gigantic folds which form lofty mountain ranges. The world's highest ranges, including the Himalayas – where the rock layers have been compressed by as much as 650 km (about 400 miles) – are fold mountains. Upfolds are called anticlines and downfolds are synclines.

MOUNTAIN WORLD

What causes mountain climates? A trip up a high mountain near the equator takes you through a series of climatic and plant zones that resemble those you would meet on an overland journey from the equator to the poles. This is because temperatures fall by about 6°C for every 1,000 m (roughly 1°F for every 300 ft), so that climates change as you climb upwards. You leave a hot equatorial climate at the bottom and reach a polar climate at the top of the mountain.

Fold mountain formation

eroded jagged peaks

gentle slopes

pressure from plate movement

BABYLESS STATE

What is the world's smallest independent country? Vatican City (also called the Holy See), an independent country situated in north-western Rome, in Italy, which covers only 44 hectares (108.7 acres). This tiny state is extremely important as the centre of the government of the Roman Catholic Church, headed by the Pope. Its population, including Church officials and members of the Swiss Guard, stood at 1,008 in 1984. There were no recorded births.

LIMITED WEALTH

What is the world's smallest republic? Nauru is a coral island which lies close to the equator in the western Pacific Ocean. In 1968, it became independent as the world's smallest republic. Among independent countries, only Vatican City and Monaco are smaller.

Nauru has only one natural resource – phosphates, which are used to make fertilizers. Nauru's government is using money from phosphate sales to create new industries, including canoe building and fishing, but time is running short for the 8,400 citizens, because the phosphate supplies are expected to be exhausted by the mid-1990s.

◄ St Peter's Square, the Vatican City.

FACT FILE: RELIGIONS AND LANGUAGES

FACT The world's major religions, in order of their founding, are Judaism, Hinduism, Buddhism, Confucianism, Taoism, Shinto, Christianity and Islam.

FACT In the early 1980s, an estimated 1,056,693,000 people (22 per cent of the world's population) were Christians.

FACT After Christianity, Islam (11.8 per cent) and Hinduism (9.8 per cent) had the most followers in the early 1980s.

FACT The number of languages around the world is thought to be about 3,000. But many dialects are regarded as languages and some estimates of the number of languages are as high as 10,000.

FACT About half of the world's people speak languages belonging to the Indo-European family. One of them, English, which is spoken by about 409 million people, is the world's leading business language.

FACT Mandarin Chinese, a language of the Sino-Tibetan family, is spoken by 755 million people!

FACT Other languages with over 100 million speakers are Russian (280), Spanish (275), Hindustani (275), Arabic (166), Bengali (160), Portuguese (157), Malay-Indonesian (122), Japanese (121), German (118) and French (110).

CONES AND DOMES

Do all volcanoes look alike? Volcanoes vary in shape, because they are formed in different ways. Some steep-sided ash and cinder cones are made of small fragments of magma exploded out of the vent (opening).

On the other hand, quiet volcanoes emit streams of molten lava. If the lava is thick and pasty, it flows only a short distance before cooling. This lava creates steep-sided mountains. Runny lava spreads out over large areas before cooling. Layer upon layer of this lava piles up in broad domes, or shield volcanoes, such as Mauna Loa in Hawaii. Most volcanoes are composite cones, consisting of alternating layers of ash and hardened lava.

CRACKING THE CODE

What is a Csa climate? Unless you are a meteorologist (a person who studies the weather), it is unlikely that you will know that this is, in fact, a coded description of the climate of the Mediterranean regions. Devised by a Russian meteorologist, Vladimir Köppen, in the early 20th century, the code (see below) is based mainly on temperature and rainfall and is now used by climatologists throughout the world.

The climatologist's code
Main groups

A tropical rainy climates
B dry climates
C mid-latitude climates
D cold snowy climates
E polar climates
H mountain climates

Rainfall features of area

s dry steppeland
w desert
f rainfall throughout the year
m marked rainy and dry seasons
s dry summers
w dry winters

Other symbols

a hot summers
b warm summers
c cool summers
d cold winters
h hot and dry climates
k cold and dry climates

DANGEROUS VIBRATIONS

What causes avalanches? Avalanches are masses of snow, ice and rock that thunder down mountain slopes, sometimes blocking roads and burying villages. Most avalanches occur in spring, when melting creates moist surfaces over which snow and ice can slide. Earthquakes, explosions, rifle shots, the sounds of vehicles and even a shout can set up vibrations that start avalanches.

MADE BY ICE

What are fiords? Some of the world's most beautiful coastlines include long, narrow, steep-sided inlets, called fiords. These inlets are deep troughs worn out by glaciers during the Ice Age. When the Ice Age ended, the rising sea flooded the lower parts of these valleys.

Mountains and the sea meet at ▶ fiords like this in Greenland, New Zealand and Norway.

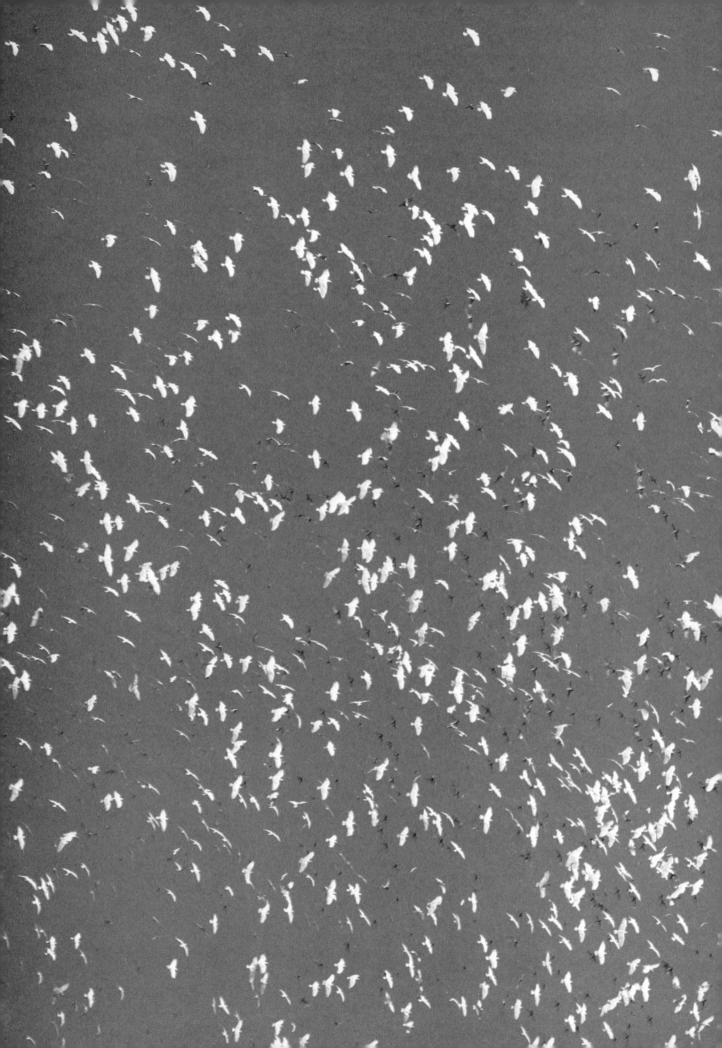

NATURAL HISTORY

GNAWING JAWS

How common are shark attacks? Although attacks on humans by sharks often make headline news, they are not, in fact, very common occurrences. The chances of being attacked by a shark are surprisingly low – about 30 million to one against! Most attacks happen in quite shallow water, and are usually the result of a hungry shark coming close to the shore and snapping at the arms and legs of a swimmer.

The man-eaters Several types of shark are known to attack man, including the hammerhead, the carpet shark and the tiger shark. But the most fearsome of the so-called man-eaters is the great white shark. This massive fish can grow to a length of 7.6 m (25 ft). Although its exploits have been exaggerated many times in films and books, it is, in fact, an extremely dangerous creature whose sheer size means that it can normally despatch any prey – human or otherwise.

Divers suspended inside steel cages in order to study the great white shark often tell hair-raising stories of huge specimens trying to lunge through the bars of the cage, or grabbing the cage in their mighty jaws and shaking it violently as if frustrated at not being able to eat the occupants.

▲
The great white shark is a fierce predator of fishes and other sea creatures such as whales, porpoises and turtles.

SOME NECK!

How many bones has a giraffe in its neck? Surprisingly, the giraffe has just seven bones in its neck, the same as we do.

blue whale

LIFESPANS

Which animal lives the longest? Here is a 'league table' of animal lifespans:

Galapagos tortoise 150 years

blue whale 90 years

Indian elephant 70 years

rhinoceros 50 years

African elephant 50 years

swan 40 years

camel 40 years

killer whale 35 years

tiger 30 years

penguin 25 years

deer 25 years

baboon 20 years

giraffe 20 years

seal 20 years

lion 18 years

cheetah 15 years

wolf 15 years

flamingo 10 years

mouse 6 years

octopus 3 years

monarch butterfly 1 year

housefly 17 days

MASSIVE MAMMALS

Which is the largest living animal? The prize for this achievement doesn't go to the elephant, as you might imagine, but to the blue whale. These huge animals roam the oceans of the world feeding on nothing larger than krill, a tiny shrimp-like creature.

Look, no teeth! When a blue whale feeds it swims through huge shoals of krill with its mouth open, and gulps in thousands and thousands at a time. It also gulps in great amounts of sea water, but this is pushed out at the sides of the whale's mouth.

Instead of teeth, the blue whale has large brush-like plates hanging down inside its mouth. These strain the water out, but prevent the krill, which the whale then swallows, from escaping.

Amazing dimensions Blue whales are not only big on the outside – their insides are also impressive! Some of their blood vessels are wide enough for a child to crawl through, and their massive stomachs can contain as much as 2.5 tonnes of food at any one time.

Land giants On land, the biggest – or at least heaviest – animal is the elephant. Of the two kinds of elephant the African elephant is the larger, with males sometimes reaching a weight of 12 tonnes.

Most zoos have elephants, but they are usually the smaller Indian variety. So, next time you see one of these and marvel at how big even that is, remember that a blue whale is about 20 times heavier!

pygmy shrew

Indian elephant

▲
Some of the world's greatest and smallest living creatures.

0   1 m
scale

The poor-will has the unusual habit of nesting on the ground. The bird is well camouflaged, so that it can remain hidden by day and hunts insects only in the twilight or at night.

SLEEPING BEAUTY

Do birds hibernate? Yes, they do. Or at least, *one* does. This bird is called the poor-will, and it is a North American species related to the nightjar. The poor-will hibernates during the winter when its normal diet of insects is in short supply; its temperature drops very low and it appears virtually lifeless. There are a number of remarkable stories about apparently 'dead' birds – taken inside to be examined – suddenly waking up in the warmth.

CATNAP?

How much time do cats spend sleeping? Humans spend about eight hours in every twenty-four hours asleep. Cats sleep a great deal longer than that. They spend sixteen out of every twenty-four hours asleep – they are awake for only *one-third* of their lives.

TRUE OR FALSE?

Why did the dinosaurs die out? No one really knows the answer to this mystery. How could a huge group of highly successful reptiles, including the fearsome meat-eating *Tyrannosaurus* and the armour-plated *Stegosaurus*, vanish suddenly, after ruling the earth for millions and millions of years?

Various theories Many theories have been suggested, some possible and few less likely. Some scientists believe that the meat-eating dinosaurs ate all the plant-eating ones and so they in turn died out.

Another theory suggests that the small, furry mammals which lived at the same time raided all the dinosaurs' eggs and ate the young! Then there are those who think the vegetation changed, and the plant-eating dinosaurs starved because their teeth were not suited to the new woody stemmed plants. None of these theories really fits the facts, however. For instance, if furry mammals ate the eggs and caused the extinction of the dinosaurs, why did the sea-dwelling reptiles (whose eggs were less accessible) also die out?

Perhaps the most widely accepted theory is that a giant meteorite hit the earth, sending up vast clouds of dust. This may have blotted out the sun's rays, causing the plant life to die. Or the cloud of dust may have insulated the earth so effectively, that it grew steadily hotter, and the dinosaurs just died because they overheated.

The face of a vampire, the most notorious of all bats. The sharp incisor teeth are used to pierce its victim's skin.

FACT FILE: BATS

FACT Although most bats cannot see well, they *do not* catch in your hair! Bats always avoid any obstacles in their way.

FACT There are two main kinds of bat: the Megachiroptera (fruit-eating bats or flying foxes) and the Microchiroptera (smaller, insect-eating bats that find their way about by echolocation).

FACT Bats which fly by echolocation literally 'shout' as they fly. If they receive an echo, they know something is in their path.

FACT Vampire bats live in Mexico and South America. They drink the blood of animals by first puncturing the skin, and then lapping up the blood which flows from the wound.

FACT Vampire bats are extremely small and light, measuring only 7 cm (2¾ in) or less.

FACT One old country name for a bat is 'flittermouse', because people mistakenly used to think that they were flying mice.

FACT Bats hang upside down when resting, and use a specially enlarged claw to obtain a good grip wherever they are roosting.

FACT The fish-eating bat catches fish near the water's surface by flying low over the water and snatching the fish with its feet.

FACT Bats which live in the cooler parts of the world hibernate in the winter.

FACT The largest bat is the fruit-eating kalong bat. It is 40 cm (16 in) long, and has a wingspan of over 150 cm (59 in).

FACT The bones which support the bat's wings are really specially elongated finger bones.

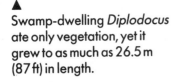

▲ Swamp-dwelling *Diplodocus* ate only vegetation, yet it grew to as much as 26.5 m (87 ft) in length.

FROM TREE TO TYRE

Where does rubber come from? Real rubber is made from the sap, or latex, of certain types of trees which grow in tropical countries like South America and Malaya. When the tree is still growing, workers make long v-shaped cuts in the trunk. The latex then flows out of these cuts where it is collected in special containers placed at the bottom of the tree. The latex is processed into rubber in factories.

WAY OF THE WOLF

Which is the largest member of the wild dog family? The biggest members of the wild dog family are timber wolves, which grow to a length of 1.4 m (4½ ft) and weigh about 68 kg (150 lb).

Lifestyle Timber wolves generally live in packs, or groups, and patrol a territory. Within the pack there is a very definite social structure, with dominant and submissive members. Wolves communicate with each other by a complicated system of facial expressions and body patterns; they are also extremely vocal on occasions, and their plaintive howls can be heard over long distances.

The main food of wolves is caribou, deer and horses, but they will also eat smaller prey such as squirrels, insects, worms and even berries.

▲
Latex being collected at a rubber plantation in West Java.

NUMBERS GAME

Can you give the correct number to each of the following?
1. The number of legs on an adult insect.
2. The number of humps on a dromedary.
3. The number of legs on a mite.
4. The number of eggs in a black swan clutch.
5. The life expectancy of a blue whale.
6. The number of arms on a squid.
7. The distance, in metres or feet, which an adult red kangaroo can jump.
8. The number of wings on a housefly.
9. The number of different species of sloth.
10. The number of petals on a buttercup.

ANSWERS
1. 6. 2. 1. 3. 8. 4. 5 to 7. 5. 90 years. 6. 10. 7. 6 m (20 ft).
8. 4 (2 pairs). 9. 2. 10. 5.

ALL WIRED UP

What is the western magpie's nest composed of? Most birds build their nests of twigs, grass, feathers and bracken. Some prefer ready-made nest sites like tree holes, which they then line with a soft bedding material for the young chicks. The western magpie, however, a bird of Australia and New Zealand, prefers to use rather more robust materials. It is particularly fond of pieces of metal, such as wire and tin. The nest of one western magpie was found to contain 6.3 kg (13¾ lb) of assorted pieces of wire. Placed end to end these bits and pieces extended to a length of 45 m (138 ft)!

BRANCHING OUT

What tree needs supports for its branches? The Indian banyan tree is a large evergreen which can reach a height of 26 m (86 ft). Its huge horizontal branches grow aerial roots which hang down and eventually act as supporting struts.

Considered a sacred tree in India, the banyan tree often resembles something from a science-fiction film. ▼

MUTUAL AID

How do ants protect plants? Most plants have developed some way of avoiding being eaten. You only have to think of stinging nettles, roses or brambles to be painfully reminded that any creatures interfering with them can be stung or scratched quite severely.

Many species of plants produce natural insecticides which keep unwanted insects at bay, but some tropical palms and acacias have enlisted the help of certain species of insect to act as *protectors*. These plants have colonies of insects living among their leaves and, should any other animal attempt to eat the leaves, the ants drive them off. In reality the ants are just protecting their home as they would any other sort of nest, but it gives the plant a very useful form of protection, too.

CLAWS FOR SPEED

Which is the only cat that cannot retract its claws? You've only to look at your own pet cat as it lies comfortably on the carpet to see how its claws can be extended or retracted at will. Cats often push their claws in and out as they stretch after a good sleep. The ability to retract the claws means that they are always sharp when needed for fighting or killing prey. The cheetah, however, is the only cat which *cannot* retract its claws — they are used to help it grip the ground when hunting at speed.

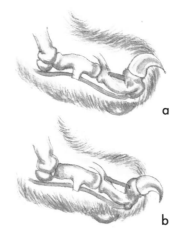

a

b

▲
The cat's versatile claws shown retracted (a) and extended (b).

SNAP ANSWER

Which is the world's largest reptile? The largest *living* reptile is the estuarine or saltwater crocodile, which is found in many parts of Asia and Australasia, including India, China, Northern Australia and Papua New Guinea. Adult males of this species can reach lengths of 5m (16ft) and weights of over 500kg (1,100lb). But even larger examples of this species have been recorded. There is evidence that a monster of 8.5m (28ft) was shot by an Australian woman in 1957. Unfortunately, it was too big to be carried back for preservation, but a photograph was taken to prove the size of the creature.

THE CRUSHER

Which is the world's heaviest snake? The South American anaconda, a snake that kills its prey by crushing it, rather than by biting it and injecting it with poison. Anacondas live near large rivers and swamps, where they prey largely on pigs and other mammals. Some of the largest anacondas can reach a weight of nearly 270kg (600lb).

▲
The estuarine crocodile's size enables it to make long sea journeys.

NIGHT VISION

How do cats see in the dark? In fact, cats do not see in the dark. If a cat were to be placed in a *totally* dark room, it would see no better than you would.

However, out in the open, even at night, it is seldom totally dark. The moon, street-lamps or light from houses all help to provide some illumination at night. What the cat does extremely well is use whatever light is present. In poor light conditions, the cat's eye is able to multiply the effect of the light by means of a special layer of cells at the back of the retina. It is this layer, shining with a green glow, that we sometimes see if we shine a light on a cat's eyes in the dark.

▲
A cat's eyes. The dilated pupils (below) will let in more light.

BIRD BRAIN

Which is the most intelligent bird? It is very difficult to evaluate intelligence in terms of animals such as birds. In the wild, there are birds that use small sticks in their beaks to poke insects from the bark of trees and, in urban areas of some countries, others which peck the tops from milk bottles, in order to reach the cream.

Tests Both these examples must be a form of intelligence, since the birds have worked out for themselves how to reach the food. Scientists have actually devised a series of tests to try and gauge the relative intelligence of various species of birds. These involve the birds performing such feats as manipulating levers and rods in order to release a peanut or similar food item.

In a series of tests carried out in Great Britain, it was discovered that the bird which solved most of these puzzles the quickest was the blue tit. This bird was then awarded the title 'Bird Brain of Britain'!

▲ A blue tit supplementing its diet with a drink of milk.

BIG EATERS

Which is the biggest eater in the animal kingdom? In terms of sheer bulk, the blue whale must take the prize. Every time it takes a mouthful of shrimp-like krill, it swallows literally thousands upon thousands of individuals. When full, the blue whale's stomach can hold as much as 2.5 tonnes of krill.

Frequent meals At the other end of the scale, the pygmy shrew – just about the world's smallest mammal – must consume twice its own weight of food every day. The pygmy shrew is a nervous, constantly active little creature that must feed every few hours to give itself the necessary energy to stay alive.

DEEP SEA DIVER

How deep can whales dive? Many whales can remain submerged for long periods of time, hunting for food or simply cruising along. However, when it comes to deep diving, one species of whale stands – or should it be sinks? – head and shoulders above all the others. The sperm whale can dive to depths of 3,193 m (10,476 ft).

▲ Many whales have 'baleen' teeth which they use to sieve their food.

QUIZ: INSECTS

1. How many species of insect are there in the world today?
2. Which is the world's heaviest insect?
3. How fast can a honey-bee fly: is it 8 km/h (5 mph); 11 km/h (7 mph); or 16 km/h (10 mph)?
4. What types of insects are the painted lady, the Camberwell beauty and the common skipper?
5. What sort of insect does a leatherjacket turn into?
6. Which insect swims upside down on its back?

ANSWERS
1. Over one million have been identified and named. Many scientists believe there could be as many as two or three million other species not yet discovered. 2. The African goliath beetle. It weighs 100 g (3½ oz) and measures up to 11 cm (4¼ in). 3. 11 km/h (7 mph). 4. They are all butterflies. 5. A type of beetle. 6. The water boatman.

HAVE POUCH, WILL TRAVEL

What are marsupials? Marsupial mammals are found mainly in Australasia, although one or two species live in South America, and one species has managed to colonize North America. They are different in several ways from the more advanced placental mammals (animals like lions, dogs, rabbits and mice). To begin with, marsupials only have one full set of teeth throughout life, whereas placental mammals – including humans – have two.

In the pouch The most unusual feature about marsupials, and the reason why they are so called, is because the embryo animals complete their development within the mother's pouch or marsupium. Within the marsupium the embryo obtains milk from its mother and steadily grows until it is large enough to leave the pouch and fend for itself. In placental mammals the young embryo remains within its mother's placenta until ready to be born.

Among the most famous marsupials are kangaroos, wallabies and koala bears. There are also marsupial bats and marsupial moles. There was even, until recently, a marsupial wolf called the thylacine, although it is thought that this animal is now extinct.

Survival So why are marsupials only found in Australasia and parts of America? Many millions of years ago, a number of continents were joined together in a large land mass. At that time the more advanced placental mammals had not yet evolved, and so the many marsupials in this area flourished and exploited all the available habitats and food sources.

Then the continents began to move apart. Australia became separated from the rest of the world by vast oceans. When the placental mammals evolved, they were better able to compete for food than the marsupials, and gradually the marsupials died out.

But the placental mammals could not reach Australia, nor for many years could they reach South America, for this was separated from North America by an ocean, too. So in these areas the marsupials continued to flourish. The few marsupials in South America today are the last species which have managed to survive in the face of competition from the placental mammals.

▲
A female wallaby and her offspring, nicknamed a 'joey'.

BIG DIFFERENCES

How do you tell the difference between Indian and African elephants? The Indian elephant has smaller ears than its African cousin, and it also has a higher forehead. Also, the end of an Indian elephant's trunk has only one 'finger'; that of an African elephant has two.

◄ The African elephant (right) is generally more heavily built than the Indian elephant (left).

STRICTLY NON-VEGETARIAN

Can plants eat animals? Yes, some can! There is a group of plants known as carnivorous plants, which digest tiny animals to obtain from their bodies the nitrogen they need for healthy growth. Carnivorous plants live in places which are boggy or otherwise lacking in the vital nitrogen they need. Once an unsuspecting animal has been trapped by a carnivorous plant, special digestive juices are released which dissolve the animal. The juices are then taken into the plant's own tissues, together with the vital nitrogen.

Cunning traps Many different kinds of carnivorous plants exist, and they have all devised cunning ways of luring and trapping their prey.

The sundew is a small plant which grows on boggy heaths. All its leaves are covered with long sticky hairs. When an insect lands on a leaf, these hairs 'glue' it to the leaf while it is digested.

The Venus fly trap has leaves which are hinged in the centre, and around the edge of each leaf is a series of long spiky hairs. If an insect, attracted by the bright red leaves, lands on a leaf, the leaf quickly snaps shut, trapping the insect in a sort of cage.

In some tropical countries there lives a carnivorous plant called the pitcher plant. The leaves of the pitcher plant are shaped like deep vases or pitchers. If any insect or small animal clambering about the pitcher falls in, it is unable to get out. The inside of the pitcher is coated with tiny slippery scales. These stick to the victim's feet, preventing it from obtaining a grip on the sides of the pitcher.

Beware, bubbles! Perhaps the most unusual carnivorous plant is the bladderwort. This plant floats in fresh water. Beneath the water surface is a series of bubble-like bladders, which are individual traps. If a small aquatic creature like a water flea should come too close and brush against the bladder, it suddenly opens, sucking in its victim.

▲
The lure of the Venus fly trap proves fatal for unlucky insects.

FLY WEIGHTS

Which is the heaviest flying bird? You probably think that it is one of the big birds, such as a golden eagle, albatross or condor. All of these animals do have huge wing spans and are among the biggest of flying birds. However, the heaviest flying bird is, in fact, the mute swan. An adult may weigh as much as 18 kg (40 lb).

MUSCLE BOUND

Which has most muscles – a man or a caterpillar? Surprisingly, the answer is the caterpillar! A caterpillar has almost four times as many muscles as we do.

FACT FILE: DINOSAURS

FACT One of the largest dinosaurs was *Brachiosaurus*. It weighed an estimated 80 tonnes – about the same weight as 20 elephants.

FACT Some scientists believe that many dinosaurs were warm-blooded, like us.

FACT All dinosaurs lived on land. Marine reptiles such as *Plesiosaurus*, and airborne reptiles such as *Pteranodon*, lived at the same time, but were not dinosaurs.

FACT The smallest dinosaur ever discovered was no bigger than a thrush.

FACT Prehistoric man never did hunt or fight dinosaurs. They all died out some 60 million years before man walked on the Earth.

FACT Not all dinosaurs were giant, flesh-eating monsters. Some, like the three-horned *Triceratops*, ate vegetation and roamed in herds, just like modern-day cattle.

FACT The first fossil dinosaur bones were found in 1822 in Sussex quarries (in southern England) by Mary Mantell. These bones were from the plant-eating dinosaur *Iguanodon*.

FACT Most dinosaur eggs were only about the size of an ostrich egg. This is because the egg shell of a very large egg would be so thick that the young dinosaur would be unable to break its way out.

FACT Believe it or not, birds are probably the dinosaurs' closest living relatives.

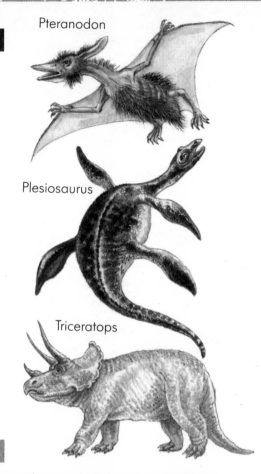

Pteranodon

Plesiosaurus

Triceratops

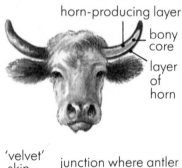

horn-producing layer

bony core

layer of horn

'velvet' skin

junction where antler separates

bony knob on skull

▲ The main differences between horns (above) and antlers (below) can be seen in these cross-sections.

BUMPS ON THE HEAD

Do you know the difference between antlers and horns? Antelopes, cows, goats and sheep have horns. Horns are composed of a bony central core attached to the skull and covered in a horny sheath. The horny sheath is 'grown' by a layer of tissue covering the bony core. Horns continue to grow throughout the life of the animal. (When people used horns for drinking from, it was the horny sheath that was used; the bony core would have been discarded.)

Antlers are found on deer, moose and caribou. Only the males of these animals have antlers, whereas horns may grow on both males and females. Antlers grow from a bony core on the skull, covered with skin. This is richly supplied with nerves and blood vessels. Eventually the bony core produces the branching antlers; and these remain covered with skin.

When the antlers are fully grown, the blood and nerve supplies are cut off and the skin peels away. After the mating season the antlers are shed, leaving just a bony stump, and the whole process begins again the following year.

False horns The 'horns' of rhinocerous are not really true horn at all. They are composed of densely packed keratin – the same material from which our own nails and hair is produced. Despite the fact that rhinocerous horn is not composed of bone, it is an extremely hard structure, and is used as a formidable weapon.

▲
The zebra's disruptive colouration is most effective in a group.

DEFENSIVE SHELL

How strong are eggs? Eggs seem to break all too easily, but they are really quite strong. They can withstand firm pressure exerted on them without shattering. Try breaking a chicken's egg by squeezing its ends – you'll find it almost impossible to break it this way.

SCOOP

Why has the flamingo got such a curious beak? The strangely shaped beak is designed to help it catch its food. The flamingo feeds by sweeping its bill from side to side, disturbing small animals and plant debris by using a paddling motion with its feet at the same time. Water and food particles are drawn into the mouth, where bristles on the edge of the bill trap the food. Water is strained out through slits near the top of the bill. The flamingo's tongue then collects the trapped food particles, which are swallowed.

PROBLEM OF STRIPES

Do all zebras have the same coat pattern? No, the various species of zebra – Burchell's, mountain and Grévy's – all have different coat patterns. (So also, do the various subspecies such as Chapman's.) Thus, although all zebras look superficially the same, scientists can tell them apart by comparing the width of the stripes and the overall patterning.

Awkward target But why *do* zebras have stripes to begin with? You might think that a black-and-white striped body would be very easy for a predator to spot in the African bush.

The reason for the striping is that zebras display a form of camouflage called disruptive coloration. Zebras roam the bush in herds, and when they are close together their patterning makes it very difficult to spot individual animals clearly. Because individual zebras cannot be identified, a predator finds it difficult to pick a 'target' for his meal. All he sees is a mass of black-and-white patterns.

◄ The flamingo's unusually shaped bill only comes into its own when the bird feeds with its head upside-down in the water.

ONE LUMP OR TWO?

How do you tell the two species of camel apart? There are two types of camel, the bactrian camel of Asia, and the dromedary or Arabian camel. The bactrian camel has two humps on its back. It is found mainly in the Gobi Desert. The dromedary has one hump on its back. This species is now completely domesticated and is used by man as a beast of burden and for riding.

MISTAKEN IDENTITY

How did the goose barnacle get its name? The goose barnacle, a tiny marine animal related to shrimps and crabs, originally received its name from the fact that it looks rather like a goose's head and neck. Long ago, it was thought that these barnacles grew into geese.

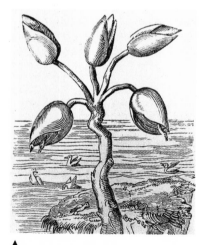

▲
The mythical goose barnacle.

SEA CHANGE

What is the difference between a seal and a sea lion? Sea lions have external ear-flaps, but seals do not. Also, sea lions can pull their hind limbs forwards to use as 'back legs' when on land. Seals cannot do this.

If necessary, the bactrian camel (right) and the dromedary (below) can use the fat in their humps as a food reserve.
▼

A LITTLE MONKEY BUSINESS

Which is the world's smallest monkey? The pygmy marmoset. This tiny animal is only 12 cm (5½ in) long and weighs a mere 70 g (2½ oz).

BIG BABY

Which animal produces the biggest baby? The animal which is bigger than all others when fully grown – the blue whale. When baby blue whales are first born, they weigh over 3,000 kg (3 tonnes), about the same weight as a fully grown hippopotamus.

Once born, a baby blue whale takes two years to reach a weight of 26,000 kg (26 tonnes). No other living creature grows so quickly.

▲
A South American pygmy marmoset, the world's smallest monkey.

TIGER RANGE

Where do tigers live? You probably know that tigers live in jungles, and you may know that some come from India, but do you know that there are *eight* distinct races of tiger scattered throughout Asia? The tiger ranges from Iran to Turkestan, Mongolia, Siberia and Korea. It is also found throughout India, Tibet, China, Thailand and Indo-China. Some even reach as far as the Malay Peninsula, Sumatra and Java.

However, throughout this huge geographical range the tiger is very rare. Hunting and persecution by farmers, as well as destruction of its habitat as forests are cleared for farming, has meant that the tiger is now an endangered species in the wild. Strict conservation measures are in force to help preserve its remaining numbers and habitat, and to try and ensure that it is no longer hunted for sport.

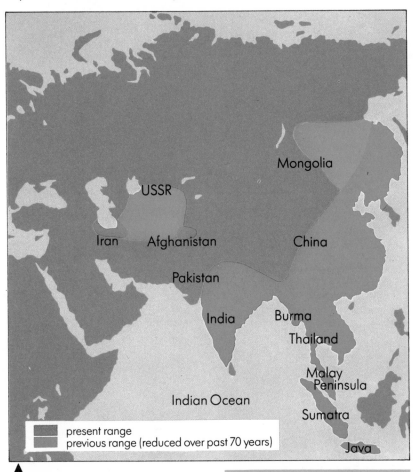

present range
previous range (reduced over past 70 years)

▲
Tigers are now found in very few areas of the world.

OLD TIMER

How old is the world's oldest tree? In California's Wheeler Park, there is a bristlecone pine tree with an estimated age of 5,000 years. And what's more, it is still alive.

BIG HUNGRY CATS

How much can a tiger eat?
Tigers have very big appetites indeed. A full-grown tiger may eat as much as one fifth of its own body weight at one sitting. If a man of 76 kg (12 stone) were to try to eat an equivalent amount, he would need to consume a mighty 15 kg (2½ stone) meal at one sitting.

GROUP NAMES

Here are some of the names by which collections of animals are known:

Animal name	Group name
asses	pace
bees	swarm
boars	sounder
cats	clutter
cattle	drove, herd
cockles	bed
colts	rake
coots	covert
crows	murder
dogs	kennel
doves	flight
ducks	team, flush
elks	gang
ferrets	business
finches	charm
fishes	school, shoal
foxes	skulk
frogs	colony
gnats	cloud, horde
hares	drove, kindle
hens	brood
herons	sedge
horses	harass, team
hounds	pack
jellyfishes	stuck
kittens	litter
larks	bevy
magpies	tiding
moles	labour, company
mules	pack, span
mussels	bed
otters	bevy
peacocks	muster
porpoises	school, pod
rabbits	colony
ravens	unkindness
rooks	building
seals	herd, pod
sheep	flock, drove
snakes	den
snipe	wisp, walk
sparrows	host
spiders	clutter
stoats	pack
swans	herd, drift
teal	spring
toads	knot
vipers	nest
wolves	pack
wrens	herd

BOLT HOLE

What is a mouthbrooder? A mouthbrooder is a kind of fish which has a most unusual way of looking after its young. When the young are still quite small, they swim in a tight shoal around their parents' heads. If danger should threaten – perhaps a predator appears – all the tiny young of the mouthbrooder dash quickly into the mouth of one of their parents. They are not eaten by the adult, just carried to safety and then released back into the water.

The moment of danger has passed and this mother mouthbrooder gently releases her tiny young back into the water.
▼

QUIZ: TERMITES

1. What are termites?
2. How many species of termite are there? Is it 5,000, 9,800 or 1,700?
3. How high is the biggest termite mound?
4. Do any animals eat termites?
5. Where do termites live?
6. What are 'magnetic termites'?

ANSWERS
1. Termites are pale, soft-bodied, ant-like social insects which comprise the order Isoptera. Termite colonies consist of workers, soldiers, reproductives, a king and a queen. 2. 1,700. 3. The mounds, or nests, of the Australian termite *Nausutitermes* may be over 8 m (26 ft) high. 4. The giant anteater of South America is a particularly important predator of termites. It rips termite mounds open with its strong, hooked claws and licks up the termites, using its long, sticky tongue. Some birds also feed on termites occasionally. 5. Termites are found mainly in the tropics, and the continents of North America, Australia, Africa and South America. 6. 'Magnetic termites' get their name from the fact that their nests always face in a north-south direction, so that the broadest part of the nest is exposed to the maximum heat of the sun's rays.

▲
The two 'spires' of this termite mound in the Transvaal, South Africa, have reached an incredible height of 4.6 m (15 ft).

LIVING AEROFOILS

How are birds able to fly? To start with they need wings, but how do wings actually work? If we look at a cross-section of a bird's wing we see that it is shaped rather like a very flattened oval, rounded at the front edge, but more tapering and pointed at the rear. Also, the whole wing is slightly curved. This shape is known as an aerofoil, and many years ago scientists copied the shape when they first produced aircraft wings.

Lift When air flows over an aerofoil, the shape causes the air to travel faster over the top than over the bottom. This causes a difference in pressure between the top and bottom of the aerofoil, which in turn makes the air beneath the aerofoil rise, pushing it upwards.

The part of the bird's wing responsible for creating this lift lies between the body and elbow. As the bird flaps its wings and rises, the rest of the wing is used mainly to push the bird forwards through the air.

Close fit All the feathers on a bird's body fit together very precisely, creating a smooth surface. This is important, since a smooth surface is necessary to ensure that the bird moves through the air without causing turbulence, which would seriously impair its flight.

Built for flight As well as feathers and wings, birds have other features which help them to fly and land safely. They have very light bones, extremely powerful chest muscles for effortless wing beating, and large eyes so that they can judge distances well.

▲
An airborne great
egret makes an
impressive sight.

angle at leading
edge of wing

lift

air stream

drag

a

leading
edge
of wing

b

c

direction of lift
direction of drag
direction of air stream

▲
During flight, birds adjust the angle of their wings to control lift. The 'aerofoil' wing causes a difference in pressure above and below the wing, creating lift (a). If a wing's angle is too low (b), lift is decreased and drag is increased. But if the angle is too great (c) the airflow is broken up, reducing lift and increasing drag.

WINGS TO THE SUN

How many birds fly south for the winter? Every year 5,000 million birds – songbirds, cuckoos and others – leave Europe and Asia to spend the winter in the warmer climate of Africa.

The human body

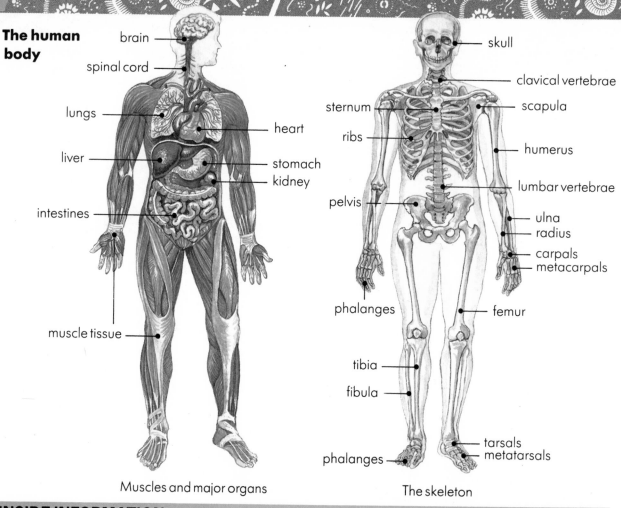

brain
spinal cord
lungs
liver
heart
stomach
kidney
intestines
muscle tissue

skull
clavical vertebrae
sternum
scapula
ribs
humerus
lumbar vertebrae
pelvis
ulna
radius
carpals
metacarpals
phalanges
femur
tibia
fibula
tarsals
metatarsals
phalanges

Muscles and major organs

The skeleton

INSIDE INFORMATION

What do you know about yourself? Probably quite a bit. You know what you look like on the outside – the colour of your eyes, how many fingers and toes you have, for instance – but do you know much about what you are like inside?

Did you know, for example, that the brain of a human is about ten times the size of a gorilla's brain and weighs about 1.4 kg (3 lb)? Or that we have about 96,560 km (60,000 miles) of arteries, veins and blood capillaries in our bodies?

Vital statistics Here are some more facts. The human skeleton is made up of 206 bones. The cardiac cycle, or heartbeat, occurs between 50 to 80 times a minute in normal adults. The average weight of an adult human liver is 2 kg (4½ lb). The

small intestine is approximately 6 m (20 ft) long.

Usually our lungs take in about half a litre of air when we breathe gently, but very deep breaths can result in an intake of up to 5 litres!

Ten per cent of our body weight is fat, and most of this is absorbed into the blood as tiny globules. Fat provides the major energy source for the body.

Taste Our tongues are able to distinguish only four basic sensations – sweet, sour, salt and bitter – but we can still taste a huge range of flavours.

Muscle We have several different kinds of muscle: voluntary muscle forms the major muscle system for our bodies, and enables us to move our arms and legs, for instance; involuntary muscle – under direct

control of the central nervous system – surrounds many of the organs of the body, and assists in such functions as the passage of food down the alimentary canal; cardiac muscle is found solely in the heart. It has the ability to contract rhythmically without fatigue, so enabling the blood to be pumped continuously around the body.

Cell statistics The average diameter of the cells within our bodies is between 1/50 and 1/100 mm, but certain brain cells may be as small as 1/200 mm. The human body has about 13,000 million nerve cells, and in every cubic millimetre of blood there are about six million red cells, and between 5,000 and 10,000 white cells. Altogether, the human body is composed of 100 million million cells!

SPOT THE ODD ONE OUT

Which is the odd one out among:
1. Capercaillie, Dugong, Pangolin, Hyrax.
2. Oak, Ash, Lime, Larch, Birch.
3. Cheetah, Serval, Lion, Jaguar.
4. Emu, Kiwi, Rhea, Pigeon.
5. Banana, Potato, Yam, Celeriac.
6. Sea urchin, Dogfish, Cockle, Whelk, Roach.
7. Beetle, Spider, Dragonfly, Mayfly, Weevil.
8. Dog, Elephant, Emu, Cockroach, Trout.
9. *Brontosaurus, Stegosaurus,* Pterodactyl, *Iguanodon.*
10. Lynx, Wolf, Llama, Bear, Seal.

ANSWERS
1. Capercaillie. It is the only bird. All the other animals are mammals. 2. Larch. It is the only cone-bearing tree. All the other trees are angiosperms, or flowering plants. 3. Serval. All the other animals are 'big cats'. 4. Pigeon. It is the only bird of the group which can fly. 5. Banana. All the others are vegetables. 6. Roach. All the other animals live in the sea; the roach is a freshwater fish. 7. Spider. All the other animals are insects. 8. Cockroach. All the other animals are vertebrates (animals with backbones). 9. Pterodactyl. It is the only one of these extinct animals which is not a dinosaur. Also, the pterodactyl was the only one which could fly. 10. Llama. All the other animals are meat-eaters; the llama eats only vegetation.

STRIPPED PINE

What does a red squirrel eat?
Red squirrels, like their cousins the grey squirrels, eat a variety of food ranging from eggs raided from birds' nests to nuts and pine cones. Pine cone seeds form the major part of their diet. These are methodically stripped from the pine cone. The squirrel nibbles out the seeds along one edge, and then, rotating the cone with its front paws, it strips out another line of seeds.

What may surprise you, however, is the amount of pine cones that a squirrel eats. It has been calculated that a single squirrel can eat its way through 40,000 pine cones in a year.

A native of North America, the grey squirrel (right) has taken over much of the territory of the red squirrel (left) since being introduced to Europe.
▼

FACT FILE: SCORPIONS

FACT Scorpions are members of the Arachnida, the group of invertebrate animals which includes spiders.

FACT Some of the largest species of scorpion measure as much as 25 cm (10 in) from the end of the sting to the tips of the pincers. The largest specimens come from India.

FACT Not all scorpions are deadly dangerous. Some have stings which merely produce a temporary and painful irritation in man.

FACT The most feared scorpion is the fat-tailed scorpion of the Atlas Mountains in the Sahara. The sting, carried in the tail, can produce a venom capable of killing a man in about four hours.

FACT Stories about scorpions stinging themselves to death if surrounded by a ring of fire, are untrue. Scorpions are immune to their own venom. However, a cornered scorpion would be quite likely to stab wildly with its sting, perhaps giving the impression that it was stinging itself.

FACT Throughout the warmer parts of the world, there are more than 750 species of scorpion.

BUSY BEE

How far must a bee travel to make 500 g (1 lb) of honey? Honey is made from nectar, which some species of bee collect from flowers. Only a small amount is collected each time, and so a honey bee must travel from flower to flower, and from flower to hive and back again, many times in order to produce a large quantity of honey. A single bee would have to cover a distance of over 75,000 km (46,500 miles) in order to make 500 g (1 lb) of honey.

LIGHT CONTROL

Why are our pupils small in bright light and large in dim light? Try this simple experiment. Stand in front of a mirror and cover one of your eyes with the palm of your hand. After a few seconds, quickly remove your hand and watch what happens to the pupil – the dark-coloured central portion – of the eye you were covering.

The pupil will suddenly get smaller; you can actually see it happening. It is the pupil which controls the amount of light that enters the eye and strikes the retina. When the eye was covered, the pupil became quite large to allow the maximum amount of light to enter. When the hand was removed, it compensated for the extra available light by becoming smaller and allowing less light to enter.

After gathering nectar, the honeybees empty their honey in the cells of the comb (inset).
▼

HARDLY WEEDY

Why are 'weeds' so successful? If someone is called a 'weed', it usually means that they are rather weak, but, in fact, weeds are among the most successful and hardy of plants. The word 'weed' really just refers to any plant growing where humans don't want it to grow. So, attractive thistles, or patches of clover growing in a garden, are considered weeds when they are simply wild flowers in a place other than their usual habitat.

Ensuring success Many so-called weeds do seem to have special ways of ensuring their own success. Firstly, weeds are among the first plants to colonize bare ground and they are also very quick to produce seed – and plenty of it. A single poppy may produce 20,000 seeds in one season.

Weeds are also able to tolerate a wide range of conditions. Many species can live in places that are too shady, too cold or too dry for the survival of other plants. Even the method of growing is often designed for success. Plants such as daisies have very flat leaves which shade out the competition, and also prevent themselves from being easily eaten by animals. Weeds like dandelions and thistles have spiky stems or leaves which prevent many animals from choosing them for a meal.

GREEN THIRST

How do trees manage to get water all the way up the trunk? All trees must take water from the soil and transport it up to the leaves and branches – even to those at the very top. Running throughout the roots, stem, branches and leaves is a series of tiny tubes. Some of these are called xylem, and some are called phloem. Xylem tubes are responsible for carrying water up the plant, and phloem is responsible for transporting dissolved food to various parts of the plant.

Water enters the root by root pressure. It does this because the cells of the plant within the root have a higher osmotic pressure and act with a sort of sucking action, drawing in the soil water. This is then drawn steadily up the trunk by the process called transpiration pull. Water evaporating from the leaves draws more water into the leaves, and this water is in turn replaced by water which is being drawn up the stem.

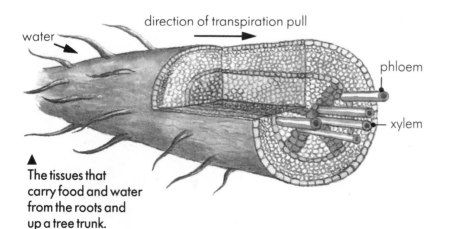

direction of transpiration pull

water

phloem

xylem

▲ The tissues that carry food and water from the roots and up a tree trunk.

FOREST GIANT

How high is the tallest tree?
An American coast redwood reaches a height of 110 m (362 ft).

▲ Towering giant sequoias (redwoods) like this grow only in the mountains of California.

TRUE OR FALSE?

1. Some fish can fly.
2. A female whale is called a cow.
3. The spores of some fungi have been found floating as high as 11,000 m (36,000 ft).
4. Crocodiles cry when they eat a meal.
5. The largest primate (monkeys and apes) is the orang-utan.
6. Dogs are members of the mammalian group the Carnivora.
7. Some mammals can lay eggs.
8. The noise made by a rattlesnake is produced by scales on its tail.
9. The record height of a sunflower is nearly 4 m (13 ft).
10. A camel can drink over 90 l (90 gals) of water in ten minutes.
11. All birds can fly.
12. Penguins live in the Arctic.
13. Some fish deliberately live out of water for periods of time.
14. The only mammal known to have lived for over a hundred years is man.
15. The world's most common coniferous tree is the larch.
16. A cross between a lion and a tiger is called a ligon.
17. The only cat which cannot retract its claws is the cheetah.
18. There are four types of rhinoceros alive in the world today.
19. Some lizards are poisonous.
20. All snakes are poisonous.

ANSWERS

1. True. No fish can truly fly like birds, but some species of fish can glide on outstretched fins. 2. True. 3. True. 4. False. This is an 'old wives' tale'! 5. False. The biggest primate is the gorilla. A fully grown male gorilla may stand as high as 2 m (6½ ft) and can weigh 225 kg (496 lb). 6. True. 7. True. The spiny anteater and platypus are both egg-laying mammals. 8. True. 9. False. Sunflowers have been grown to a height of 6.5 m (21 ft). 10. True. 11. False. There are many species of flightless birds, including penguins, ostriches, emus, and rheas. 12. False. Penguins live in the Antarctic and along the coasts of some countries in the southern hemisphere, such as New Zealand. 13. True. Species such as the mudskippers deliberately haul themselves out of the water for a time to feed on small animals in the mud. 14. True. 15. False. The world's most common coniferous tree is the Scots pine. This tree ranges from the Pacific to the Atlantic coasts and from the Arctic down to southern Spain. 16. True. 17. True. 18. False. There are five species of rhinoceros. There are three in Asia and two in Africa. 19. True. 20. False.

RARE BIRD

Which is the world's rarest bird? There are several species of bird which are extremely rare, but the rarest may well be the Hawaiian Oaaa bird, which, in 1977, had a world population of just two! It is not known whether this pair has managed to breed since then. If they have not, it is very likely that the species is now extinct.

SINK OR SWIM

Does all wood float? Wood, the hardened material of which trees are composed, is made up of millions of tiny tubes or fibres packed together. The air between the tubes allows wood to float. However, some trees — the box tree, for example — have such densely packed tubes that there is insufficient air to allow the wood to float, and so it sinks in water.

GAME SNAKE

Why is the ball python so called? The royal python, a snake of equatorial West Africa, has an unusual way of protecting itself when disturbed. It can roll up into an almost perfect ball, and so has earned itself the name of ball python. Tame specimens can even be rolled along in this undignified manner!

This royal python has assumed ▶ a far from regal position in order to protect itself.

RIGHT OR LEFT?

Do snail shells coil to the left or to the right? Most snails have a right-handed spiral. This is called a dextral spiral. But a few snail shells are 'left-handed'. Spirals that are left-handed are called sinistral.

A REAL TURKEY

Which is the most stupid bird in the world? It must be the domestic turkey. Some have been known to drown in a heavy rain shower because they didn't realize that it would be dry and safe inside their hutches! Others are so brainless that they can't even remember how to eat, and must be fed by the farmer.

▲
The banksia's striking and colourful flowers secrete honey, hence the plant's alternative name of the Australian honeysuckle tree.

FIERY BIRTH

Which tree needs fire in order to reproduce? Strange as it may seem, some plants need fire before they can complete their life cycles. Banksia trees, which grow in the semi-desert regions of Australia, need a fire, such as a bush fire, to take place in order that their seeds will split open and germinate.

TEEMING MILLIONS

How common are insects and spiders? The answer to this is – very common. In fact, more common than you might imagine. Think of how many tiny spiders' webs you can see on a bramble bush on a dewy morning, for instance. If you had a long, long time to spare and could discover a way to count them all, you would find that just 0.4 hectare (1 acre) of meadowland contains over one million spiders, ten million insects and over 600 million mites.

QUIZ: MAMMALS

1. What is the heaviest land mammal?
2. How many species of mammal are there in the world: 2,000, 4,500, 8,000, or 15,000?
3. How do you tell the difference between a black rhinoceros and a white rhinoceros? (Clue: it's nothing to do with the colour.)
4. Which mammals lay eggs?
5. Which is the fastest land mammal?
6. Which mammal is man's closest relative: chimpanzee, gorilla or orang-utan?

ANSWERS
1. The African elephant, which may weigh up to 12 tonnes. 2. There are about 4,500 species of living mammals. 3. Look at their top lips. The white rhinoceros has a square-shaped lip, and the black rhinoceros has a triangular-shaped lip. In fact, the 'white' rhinoceros is so-called because the word 'white' is a misuse of the Afrikaans word *wijd*, or 'wide', which describes the shape of the top lip. 4. The platypus, and the spiny anteater or echidna. 5. The cheetah. It can attain speeds of 96 km/h (60 mph) for short distances. 6. The chimpanzee.

◀ The amazing variety of the insect world is shown here. A giant centipede (top left), a delicate lacewing (below left), a mantis (left) and a spider (below).

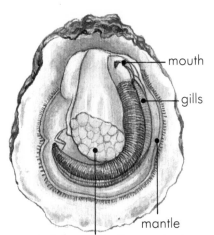

mouth

gills

mantle

muscle (clamps shells together)

IRRITATED OYSTERS

How is a pearl formed? Pearls are produced when a tiny piece of grit or sand becomes trapped inside the shell of an oyster. This irritates the oyster, which then produces a layer of mother of pearl around the particle to prevent it harming the oyster's internal organs. (Mother of pearl is a hard, iridescent substance produced by the oyster normally to coat the inside of its shell.) Layer upon layer of mother of pearl is coated around the particle until a pearl is formed.

In time, an irritant introduced into an oyster will produce a pearl (see stages 1-3, below).
▼

mantle epithelium

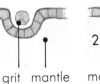

fully formed pearl

grit   mantle

1

mother of pearl
forming

2

fully formed pearl
embedded in mantle

3

FILLING THE BILL

Why are bird beaks all different? If you compare the beaks of, say, a duck, an eagle and a blackbird, they are all quite different. This is because, unlike humans, birds are fairly specialized feeders. Most species eat only a few kinds of food items, and so they have beaks (or bills) specially designed to cope best with these.

Purpose built One of the most specialized types is that of birds of prey. An eagle or a falcon has a large hooked beak. This is used for tearing pieces of meat from the prey.

Ducks and many other waterbirds have broad, flattened bills to help them sieve small food particles from the water.

Specialized seed eaters like finches have short, conical bills which are ideal for tearing open seeds and pine cones.

Birds such as the blackbird and thrush are more generalized feeders. Their 'all-purpose' bills enable them to feed on a variety of food items, including seeds, worms, insects and berries.

Shore birds Birds which probe the mud of the seashore or estuary often have long, pointed bills which they push deep into the mud to grab worms and shellfish. Birds with this sort of beak include redshank and dunlin. Avocets also feed near the seashore, but they wade into the water and sift tiny floating food particles, using their slender, upturned bill which they sweep from side to side as they walk along.

Variety There are many other sorts of bill to be seen in the bird world; parrots have bills suited to eating fruit, pelicans have deep-pouched bills for collecting fish, and hummingbirds have thin, needle-like bills for taking nectar from flowers. When you next see birds, try to work out what sort of food they eat by looking at their bills.

duck

eagle

avocet

blackbird

▲
Designed for different diets:
the varied bills of a duck (a),
an eagle (b), an avocet (c) and
a blackbird (d).

EASY DOES IT

Which animal lives upside down? The sloth. It lives in the forests of South America, and spends almost its entire life hanging upside down from the branches of trees as it wanders slowly about, looking for leaves and fruit to eat.

So completely at home is the sloth in its upside-down world, that it has several remarkable adaptions to this way of life. To hang on to the branches the sloth has huge curved claws which act like hooks, ensuring that it always maintains a firm grip on the branches. When it rains, the water just runs off the fur because the hairs on its body grow from the belly towards the back. Another curious feature of the animal is the fact that, because of the tiny algae coating its fur, the sloth always looks green.

◄ This lethargic two-toed sloth seems unperturbed by its topsy-turvy view of life.

PARTNERS

What is a lichen? A lichen is a curious plant that is really a mixture of two other plants, an alga and a fungus. Several different types of algae and fungi may combine to form lichens. This association becomes so close that both plants are unable to exist without each other.

Layers Under a microscope, a section cut through a lichen shows a complicated layered structure. The outer layers are produced by the fungus, whose hyphae (the thin threads of which the fungus is composed) also make up a proportion of the central layer. The alga, consisting usually of numerous spherical green cells, is found within the central portion.

Advantages So what advantages are there to the fungus and the alga in this relationship? Most lichens grow in locations which other plants cannot tolerate – extremely hot or cold places, on mountainsides, on roofs, walls, and the bark of trees. Fungi or algae alone would be unable to live in many of these places, but by sharing their biological properties, they can colonize apparently inhospitable places.

The fungus provides the alga with a protective layer in which to grow, and also takes up water and mineral salts and passes these to the alga. The alga manufactures food by photosynthesis, and releases some of this manufactured food to the fungus, which is unable to make its own food. This sort of mutual partnership is called symbiosis.

There are three main sorts of lichens. Foliose lichens look like spreading fingers. Fruticose lichens may often be branched, and resemble tiny bushes. Crustose lichens are flatter, and often appear on rocks as a kind of shapeless yellow, orange or black crust.

Section through a typical lichen

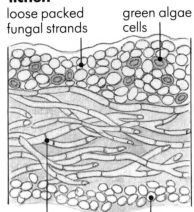

loose packed fungal strands

green algae cells

enmeshed fungal hyphae

thin layer of fungal strands

▲ Lichens like this usually grow on rocks, trees and boards exposed to the sun and wind.

▲
The venom from any of these arrow-poison frogs could prove fatal to another creature.

DEADLY FROGS

Can frogs kill humans? Yes, some kinds of frog can. Some of the brilliantly coloured frogs of Central and South America produce a highly poisonous venom. In the wild, this venom is used to deter the frogs' natural predators like snakes, which recognize the venomous frogs because of the vivid warning coloration which they display.

Poison Natives living in the rain forests catch these frogs and extract the poison to coat the tips of their darts. Frogs whose venom provides this coating are actually called arrow-poison frogs. The most poisonous frog is the kokoi, which lives in Columbia. Although only 2.5 cm (1 in) long, its skin can provide sufficient poison to kill 50 men.

THESE EYES HAVE IT

Which animal has the largest known eye in the animal kingdom? The eyes of the giant squid measure an incredible 40 cm (16 in) across! These massive eyes belong to an equally massive creature, for the giant squid can grow to a length of over 9 m (29½ft) – indeed, it is quite possible that even larger specimens lurk in the deep oceans in which the giant squid lives. Possibly the very large eyes are a necessity for an animal living in such a dark and gloomy habitat, to enable it to see in the poor light conditions.

Sailors used to tell tales of giant squids attacking their ships.
▼

DO NOT TOUCH

Can fish produce electricity? Some can, and one – the South American electric eel – can produce sufficient electricity to light up ten electric light bulbs. The electricity is produced in special electric organs within the body. The current can measure up to 500 volts, and is sufficient to kill any unwary swimmer who touches the fish.

Usually the electric eel, which grows to a length of about 2.5 m (8¼ ft), uses the electricity which its body produces to stun other fishes, which it then eats. It is also thought that the fish is able to use the electric field with which it surrounds its body for navigation in the dark, turbid waters of its river habitat.

▲
A sea creature to avoid – the deadly electric eel.

WRITE OR WRONG?

Can you write with a sea pen? No. Sea pens are feathery corals which live on the seabed. They get their name from the fact that the sea pen colony does indeed look rather like an old-fashioned quill pen. Despite this similarity you would have a job to write with a sea pen.

▲
A delicate sea pen coral on the seabed.

PLANT PUZZLER

Are fungi plants? Some scientists do not believe fungi – the group which contains mushrooms and toadstools – really are plants. They do not produce green leaves and so cannot make their own food. Instead, fungi must obtain their food ready made, just as animals do.

Parasites Fungi are what is known as saprophytes or parasites. Saprophytes feed on dead and decaying organic matter (such as rotting tree stumps), and parasites feed on living tissue. They feed by absorbing dissolved food substances which they have first made soluble by covering the food in digestive juices.

Because fungi do not make their own food, they do not need to obtain the energy from sunlight in the way that green plants do. So fungi can live in dark, damp places – in fact many species prefer these.

Reproduction For most of the year fungi exist below ground as a mass of tiny white thread-like structures, called hyphae. But, at certain times of the year – usually autumn – the hyphae produce a fruiting body. This withers away, having shed masses of tiny reproductive spores which, in turn, produce new hyphae and the process starts again.

Majority viewpoint So, are fungi plants? Overall, most scientists believe they have more in common with the plant kingdom than with the animal kingdom, and still tend to regard them as plants, although there is no doubt that they are very strange ones.

◀ The colourful fly agaric fungus is poisonous to many animals.

FACT FILE: FLOWERS

FACT A flower is the reproductive organ of a flowering plant. Most flowers contain both male (stamens) and female (ovary) parts. Pollination occurs when pollen from a stamen is deposited on to the stigma, the top of the female part of the plant.
FACT The largest flower in the world belongs to a parasitic plant called *Rafflesia*. The flower grows up to 1 m (3¼ ft) in diameter.
FACT Familiar flowers such as the primrose, buttercup and daisy all belong to a group known as dicotyledons. They have a pair of seed leaves (or cotyledons) which nourish the young seedling.
FACT The oldest known petal (one of the parts of a flower) comes from Cretaceous rocks found at Dakota, USA. It belonged to a plant called *Magnolia palaeopetala*, which lived some 100 million years ago.
FACT There are over 230,000 species of flowering plants in the world.
FACT Some of the drugs used in medicine come from flowers. Opium, for example, comes from a species of poppy.
FACT The flower of a plant such as a daisy is in fact made up of many tiny individual flowers called florets. Plants which have flower heads of this type also include dandelions, marigolds and sunflowers; together they form a family called the Compositae.
FACT The flowers of some orchids mimic the insects which pollinate them. In the bee orchid, the lower lip of the flower is shaped and coloured like a bee's abdomen. Other bees are attracted to the flower and in so doing help to pollinate it.

▲
The world's largest flower – the colourful rafflesia.

FINDING A BIGGER PLACE

Which crab has a 'mobile home'? The hermit crab. Instead of scuttling about protected by its own tough shell like other crabs, it has a soft body which it protects inside the empty shells of whelks and other molluscs. The hermit crab finds a suitable shell and eases its body inside. Then, with just its head and legs sticking out, it trundles about the seabed looking for food.

Animal lodger Even more remarkable is the fact that it frequently shares the shell with another animal – a sea anemone. It is thought that the sea anemone's stinging tentacles give some extra protection to the crab. The sea anemone benefits by obtaining tiny particles of shedded food which result from the crab's untidy feeding habits.

Removals So important is this relationship that, when the hermit crab outgrows its shell and looks for a larger one in which to live, it encourages the anemone to swap homes, too. The anemone is coaxed from the old shell and on to the new one by the hermit crab. Once both animals are safely installed, they carry on their lifestyle as before.

▲
Different types of feathers: primary covert (a), secondary (b), contour (c) and down (d and e).

INSULATION

How many feathers does a bird have? The swan has over 25,000 feathers on its body, providing it with good, year-round insulation in cold northern climates. The larger the bird, the greater the number of feathers it has.

Small songbirds like sparrows and thrushes have between 1,500 and 3,500 feathers on their bodies. In fact, smaller birds have more feathers per square centimetre than larger birds because they lose heat from their bodies more quickly and therefore need much greater insulation.

◀ Hermit crabs and sea anemones often enjoy a mutually beneficial relationship.

SOLAR POWER?

Where do insects go in the winter? In temperate countries, one of the better things about winter is the absence of flies – in fact, the lack of most flying insects is quite noticeable. But why is this? Well, the main reason is the fact that it is colder.

Insects need warmth to enable them to fly, and once the temperature begins to drop most species find somewhere to hibernate for the winter; others simply die out, leaving eggs which will hatch the following spring. Sometimes, on cool spring and summer mornings in temperate climates, you can see butterflies gently flapping their wings as they wait for the sun's rays to warm their bodies up so that they can begin flying.

TURNED-ON WORM

When is a worm not a worm? When it is a glow worm. The glow worm is, in fact, a type of beetle.

Only the female produces the greenish-yellow glow which you can sometimes see in hedgerows on warm summer nights. She produces this glow to attract a mate. The glow is caused by a substance in the glow worm's body, called luciferin.

This almost magical effect (far ▶ right) is produced by dozens of individual glow worms (right).

NO FUSSY FEEDER

Which animal is a glutton? The glutton is an alternative name for an animal called the wolverine, a lumbering bear-like predatory animal which lives in the Arctic wastes. It is one of the least fussy feeders in the animal kingdom, devouring a wide range of prey including berries, frogs, fishes, lemmings – even animals as large as a moose. Any food it encounters is greedily gobbled down – hence the name is also applied to people who eat their food in a similar manner.

▲
A wolverine in search of food. This creature is mainly a scavenger and, when hunting, depends more on stealth than speed.

THE PLANT WORLD

How are plants grouped together, or classified? There are several distinct groups of living plants, each of which is quite different from all the others.

Simple plants The most primitive types of plant are called thallophytes. They have a simple structure, with no true root, stem or leaves. The two most common groups of thallophytes are the algae and the fungi. Bacteria, too, are sometimes also included in this group.

The algae are found mainly in the sea and on the seashore, most commonly as seaweeds, although a few are found in fresh water. Some species are even found coating the bark of trees.

The fungi are a curious group of plants which are composed of a mass of compact tubes called hyphae. These usually exist underground or among the rotting tissues of trees or other organisms, and at certain times of the year, they produce fruiting bodies such as mushrooms.

Algae make their own food because they contain the green pigment, chlorophyll, although other pigments may make some seaweeds appear red, or brown. Fungi cannot make their own food since they do not process chlorophyll, and so they feed on the tissues of living or dead organisms.

Green plants The next group of plants is the bryophytes. These green plants usually have a stem and may have leaves. Bryophytes generally like damp places. They are divided into two main groups: the mosses and the liverworts.

Another group of green plants is the pteridophytes, which includes ferns, club-mosses and horsetails. These more advanced plants generally have true stems, leaves and a proper root system. Pteridophytes live in a variety of habitats; some, like the horsetails, grow by water; others, like the ferns, in woodland clearings or in tropical forests. Ferns reproduce by scattering spores.

Seed-bearers The final group of plants, the spermatophytes, is divided into two main sections; the gymnosperms and the angiosperms. These are seed-bearing plants with a well-developed stem, leaves and roots. There is a huge variation in size and shape, and members of the group range from minute plants that float on water to the mighty redwood trees.

Most gymnosperms are conifers and bear their seeds in cones. Plants like the cycads and yews are included in this group.

The angiosperms are the other major section within the spermatophytes. Familiar trees like the oak, ash, elm and beech, flowering plants like daisies and tulips, and cereals (like maize), grasses and rushes, are just a few of the many thousands of plants in this group.

Angiosperms bear their seeds enclosed within a protective structure called the ovary. They are the most advanced, and the most successful, of all the plants living today.

QUIZ: REPTILES

1. All lizards are non-venomous (non-poisonous). True or false?
2. What is a slow-worm?
3. Which snake can raise a 'hood' behind its head?
4. How do boas and anacondas kill their prey?
5. What are terrapins?
6. To which group of reptiles do caimans belong?

ANSWERS
1. False. There are two species of venomous (poisonous) lizard: the gila monster of southern USA and the bearded lizard of Mexico. 2. The slow-worm is not really a worm at all, nor is it particularly slow. It is a variety of lizard, but it has no legs. 3. The cobra. 4. They kill their prey by squeezing, or constricting, it. 5. Terrapins are aquatic reptiles related to tortoises. 6. Caimans belong to the group called the crocodilians, which also includes the crocodile, alligator and gharial.

The 'classification' of plants is ▶ the grouping and naming of them in such a way that those most nearly related are placed together. Modern classification was founded by a Swedish botanist called Carolus Linnaeus. The chart on the opposite page depicts some typical plants from each of the major groups of the plant kingdom.

Plant classification

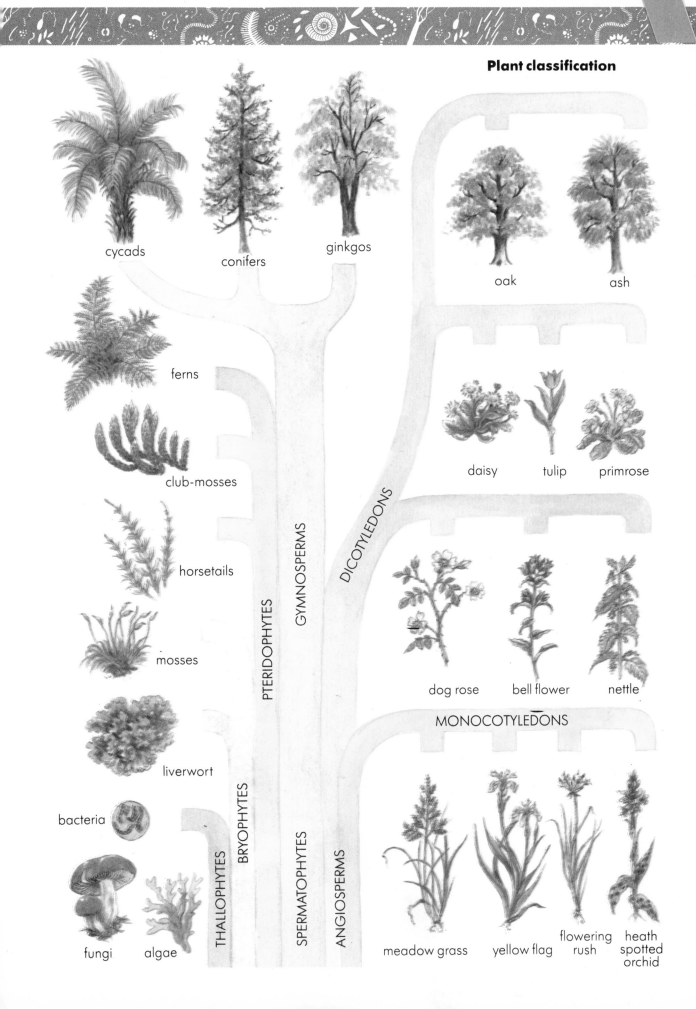

cycads

conifers

ginkgos

oak

ash

ferns

club-mosses

horsetails

daisy   tulip   primrose

DICOTYLEDONS

mosses

dog rose   bell flower   nettle

liverwort

MONOCOTYLEDONS

bacteria

PTERIDOPHYTES

GYMNOSPERMS

BRYOPHYTES

SPERMATOPHYTES

ANGIOSPERMS

THALLOPHYTES

fungi   algae

meadow grass   yellow flag   flowering rush   heath spotted orchid

FAMILY PRIDE

How many species of cat live in groups? Surprisingly, only one species of cat lives in a well-ordered and organized group, and that species is the lion. Groups of lions are called prides, and they usually consist of one or two males together with several lionesses and their cubs.

The hunt The organization of lions is seen to good effect during a hunt. They co-operate closely to drive herds of antelope or zebra towards other members of the pride, which then single out old or weak individuals to attack. Although the lionesses often do most of the work, the lions also take part in the hunt.

Lion hunts often end in failure, but when a kill is made, all the pride gorge themselves on the meal and then spend several days sleeping it off! A lion may eat over 30 kg (66 lb) of meat at one sitting.

Breeding Lionesses leave the pride to give birth to their cubs. At first, the cubs have spotted coats. This helps to camouflage them. Even so, when the lionesses and their cubs rejoin the pride, more than half the original number of cubs may have died through starvation, disease or predation by animals such as hyaenas. It takes about 18 months for cubs to become useful hunters for the pride.

BRAVE BABY

Who is afraid of snakes? Many people show a great aversion to snakes. Is this a natural fear, or do we become frightened of snakes because we are taught to fear them? It seems as though we are taught to be afraid of them, for a tiny child shows no fear of snakes at all.

A baby chimpanzee, on the other hand, even if it is reared from birth in a cage, will show marked signs of fear and alarm if it is placed near to a snake. This shows that the baby chimpanzee has an innate or in-bred fear of snakes, probably because baby chimpanzees would be likely to encounter snakes in the wild which would be potentially dangerous to them.

SPEEDY SWIFT

Which is the fastest animal? You might think that the fastest animal is the cheetah, for it can sprint for short distances at speeds up to 96 km/h (60 mph). But if we include the birds in our quest for the fastest animal, the record goes to the spine-tailed swift. This creature is the fastest of all living animals. It has been recorded flying at speeds of up to 170 km/h (102 mph).

▲
A spine-tailed swift perching on a rock.

	cheetah		gazelle	horse
	96 km/h (60 mph)		88 km/h (55 mph)	56 km/h (35 mph)

UNDERWATER HORRORS

What dangers lurk in the water? When we think of danger in the water, our minds usually turn to sharks. Some, such as the great white shark, are highly dangerous. But if we eradicated all sharks, would the underwater world be safe for humans?

Definitely not. Although the chances of being attacked or eaten by creatures living in water are rare, there is nevertheless a huge collection of venomous and otherwise downright unpleasant animals to be considered. Indeed, the world's most poisonous creature is a kind of jellyfish called the sea wasp, which is often found floating in coastal waters around Australia. Other highly venomous invertebrates include the blue-ringed octopus and a species of cone shell related to snails.

Who's for a swim? Also lurking in the sea are several other species of dangerous fish – apart from sharks. The large moray eel is armed with sharp teeth, and has been known to come out of the water and chase an intruder back up the beach! Other dangerous sea creatures include electric eels, poisonous stonefishes, seasnakes, estuarine crocodiles, bluefish and barracuda.

Jaws of the rivers In fresh waters the situation is a little less dangerous, but there are reports of people being pulled into dark, muddy South American rivers by huge anacondas (a type of constricting snake that spends much of its time lurking in the water for prey). Crocodiles and hippopotamuses are to be avoided, too.

Perhaps the most feared river animal is the piranha. In the South American Amazon basin shoals of these voracious feeders swarm on to any animal unfortunate enough to fall into the water. Within minutes the razor-sharp teeth of these fish can reduce a victim the size of a cow to nothing more than a skeleton.

▲
A fish has fallen victim to this venomous sea wasp.

◄ Most creatures can only maintain their top speeds (shown below) over limited distances.

dog	man	tortoise
48 km/h (30 mph)	32 km/h (20 mph)	1·5 km/h (1 mph)

WHICH IS WHICH?

How can you distinguish a butterfly from a moth? Well, to start with, colour is not a good guide. There are dull-coloured butterflies and brightly coloured moths, and vice versa. Many butterflies rest with their wings folded over their bodies, but not all. Similarly, many moths rest with their wings folded flat, but not all. And of course most butterflies fly by day, while most moths are active at night, but again there are the exceptions.

Perhaps the best way to tell butterflies and moths apart is to examine their antennae. The antennae of butterflies are club-shaped, whereas those of moths are usually elaborate, plume-shaped structures.

small tortoise-shell butterfly

emperor moth

▲
Similar, but different. A moth (below) and a butterfly (above).

GENTLE GIANTS

Are gorillas man-eaters?
Stories of great gorillas attacking and eating explorers are very much in the realms of fiction, for gorillas are strictly vegetarian. Despite their huge size they eat mainly twigs and leaves. The fearsome-looking canine teeth which they possess are used for threat displays, and for settling disputes among their own kind. On the whole, gorillas are shy, retiring creatures which have shown an amiable curiosity towards the few humans who have been able to get close to them in the wild.

Mountain gorillas like this are now in danger of extinction.
▼

redshank

sand dune

razor shell

seaweed

▲
Some common sights at seashore locations (above). The wildlife along the strandline (below) has to be able to tolerate extreme conditions.
▼

1 mussels
2 mermaid's purse
3 whelk eggs
4 cockles
5 crab
6 razor shell

HIGH LIVING

Which species of fish lives at the highest altitude? The Tibetan loach. This fish is found in water at an altitude of 5,200 m (17,060 ft) in the Himalayan mountains.

FACT FILE: THE SEASHORE

FACT Shorebirds like the redshank feed on tiny crustaceans called *Corophium*, which live in the mud of estuaries and seashores. As many as 40,000 of these crustaceans can be eaten by one bird in a single day.

FACT Some cockle beds can contain as many as 3.6 million individual cockles per hectare.

FACT Sand dunes on the coast actually move! A strong wind coming off the sea and blowing against a dune can cause it to move inland at speeds of up to 7 m (23 ft) per year.

FACT The razor shell, which lives upright in wet sand, digs itself into the sand whenever danger threatens. By using a large muscular foot at the bottom end of the shell, it can bury itself faster than someone trying to dig it out.

FACT Of all seashore plants, seaweeds are best able to tolerate long periods out of water, followed by long periods covered by water. Their different positions on the beach are determined by their varying tolerance to exposure.

FACT The sea anemone, despite its name, is really an animal and not a plant. It belongs to a group of animals called cnidarians, which includes jellyfishes and corals.

FACT The curiously named mermaid's purse is actually the egg case of the common dogfish. You find these rectangular brown objects washed up on the shore, especially after stormy weather.

FACT Some marine animals are nocturnal (active at night). Crabs and some molluscs such as whelks, which hide by day under rocks and seaweed, clamber about at night looking for food.

FACT The rise and fall of the tides is caused by the moon's gravitational pull.

BIG LAYERS

Which bird lays the biggest egg? The ostrich. An average egg measures 15×14 cm (6×5¼ in) and weighs 1.6 kg (3 lb 10 oz). The shell is so thick that it can support the weight of a man.

The largest egg produced by any bird relative to its own size is that of the New Zealand brown kiwi. A hen weighing about 1.7 kg (3 lb 12 oz) can produce eggs of 510 g (18 oz)! In other words, a bird the same size as a domestic chicken can lay an egg ten times bigger than a chicken's egg.

FEEDING FEET FIRST

How does a barnacle feed? Barnacles are a common sight on rocks, piers and jetties. Usually, all you see is the conical white shell of the animal. The delicate creature inside remains 'locked up' when the tide is out, to avoid drying out.

As soon as the sea covers the barnacles, however, they open their shells and out pop their legs. It is with their legs that they actually feed. They do not use their legs for walking, for they are fixed permanently to one spot. So the legs are modified to 'kick' food particles into the mouth from the surrounding sea.

▲ Barnacles feeding.

▲ A fried ostrich egg (above) easily fills the pan.

A typical ostrich nest in Zimbabwe (right). It is little more than a scrape in the ground. ▶

LIFE ON EARTH

What is the geological time-scale? It is the time span used by geologists, palaeontologists and other scientists to measure the age of the earth, especially in relation to the plants and animals that have existed.

The earth is thought to be at least 4,000 million years old, and the earliest forms of life are recorded in rock about 2,000 million years old. Here is a diagram showing the major divisions of the geological time-scale, together with the plants and animals that evolved at certain times.

Millions of years ago	Period	Plants	Animals
2	Quaternary	arctic flora appears	mammals dominant
65	Tertiary	flowering plants dominant	mammals radiate to fill dinosaur niches
136	Cretaceous	flowering plants appear	dinosaurs die out, mammals and birds flourish
190	Jurassic	conifers abundant	'Age of reptiles', birds appear
225	Triassic	cycads appear	dinosaurs appear, first mammals
280	Permian	conifers, ginkgos	reptiles abundant
345	Carboniferous	seed ferns, giant lycopods	first reptiles, winged insects
395	Devonian	ferns, horsetails, lycopods	'Age of fishes', first amphibians
430	Silurian	seaweeds, first land plants	fishes first appear
500	Ordovician		first vertebrates
570	Cambrian	bacteria, algae, fungi	corals, echinoderms, graptolites, trilobites
	Precambrian	very primitive life-forms	

DELICATE DRINKER

How does an aye-aye drink?
First of all, what is an aye-aye? It's a kind of rare Madagascan monkey, and it drinks by dipping one of its fingers into water, and then drawing the finger across its mouth.

TAIL'S AWAY

How does a lizard escape?
Lizards have evolved an ingenious way of escaping from predators. Their first line of defence is, naturally enough, to run for cover, but should they be caught by the tail, they have one trick left. The tail has a specially weakened bone in it which immediately breaks at this point, allowing the lizard to scuttle for safety, and leaving the predator holding just a stump of tail. In time, the lizard grows a new tail.

▲
A blue-tailed skink escaping after shedding its tail in self-defence.

CLOSE RELATIONS

Which is the elephant's closest relative? You might think that the elephant's nearest relative would be another big lumbering animal of the African or Indian bush, but in fact its 'nearest and dearest' is a tiny creature called a rock hyrax. Rock hyraxes live in rocky or wooded regions in parts of Asia and Africa. They couldn't look less like an elephant, either, for they are very similar to hamsters in appearance. The reason why rock hyraxes and elephants are related is that both have hoof-like nails on the toes of their front feet.

The burrow-dwelling rock hyraxes ▶ are also able climbers.

OPEN WIDE

How can a snake swallow something bigger than itself? Some snakes can eat prey which seems far bigger than themselves. A snake is a long, thin animal with a fairly narrow head, and yet some species eat birds' eggs and other animals which are far broader than their own bodies. They can do this because their jaws are not rigidly fixed together, but are merely connected by ligaments which can stretch, allowing the snake to force its mouth right over the bulkiest of prey.

A snake's stomach can also stretch enormously, allowing the prey to be swallowed whole. A snake which has just eaten a big meal looks very strange indeed. Its head and neck are the normal size, then there is a huge bulge where the prey is located, before the body tapers to its usual size towards the tail.

Snakes that swallow eggs whole have a unique way of breaking them open once they are inside their bodies. They have special bones in their throats which they squeeze against the egg until it breaks.

EATEN OUT OF HOUSE AND HOME

What is a caterpillar's first meal? For many species of caterpillar, the first meal is their own egg shell. It is thought that the shell contains vital food substances.

This adder's specially hinged jaw enables the snake to tackle food the size of an egg.
▼

hinge

INSECTS GALORE

Which is the most abundant group of animals? In terms of numbers of species, the answer is insects. Although no one is really sure just how abundant they are, for new species are discovered almost every year.

Estimates of the number of different species of insect range from well over a million to nearly three million. Whatever the true number, there are at least three times as many different kinds of insects in the world as there are every other species of animal put together!

If you could place every single insect in the world on one side of a huge pair of scales, and every single animal in the world on to the other side, the insects would weigh more.

▲
Some striking members of the insect world – a well-camouflaged stick insect (top right) and two large scarab beetles (above).

NOSE FOR FOOD

How keen is a shark's sense of smell? The reason why a shark is able to come so quickly on to the scene when an injured animal starts to bleed, is because of the shark's phenomenal sense of smell. Sharks can detect a single drop of blood in water from a distance of 200 m (656 ft).

QUIZ: FISH

1. What is the biggest fish in the world?
2. Of which species of fish is the goldfish an ornamental variety?
3. Why does a shark sink when it stops swimming?
4. Which fish uses a fishing rod to catch its prey?
5. How many eggs does a sturgeon lay, and what do we call the eggs when we eat them?
6. Name the 'living fossil' first discovered in 1938.

ANSWERS
1. The 43 tonne, 18.5 m (60 ft) long whale shark. 2. The common carp. 3. Because it has no swim bladder, the buoyancy organ found in other types of fish. 4. The angler fish. 5. Up to 2.5 million. They are eaten as caviar. 6. The coelacanth.

ALIVE AND WELL

What is a living fossil? Despite the contrary-sounding name there are such things as living fossils – living animals which were thought to have become extinct many millions of years ago.

Ancient fish Perhaps the most famous living fossil is the coelacanth, a kind of fish. The first recorded instance of a coelacanth being discovered occurred in 1938 when some fishermen working off the coast of South Africa found one in their nets. They showed this strange creature to some scientists, who proclaimed it to be a member of a species thought to have become extinct over 70 million years ago.

The coelacanth certainly bears little resemblance to other modern-day fishes. It has large, fleshy, lobe-like fins, a curious tail shape and large, heavy scales on its body. It represents one of the earliest stages in the evolution of the bony fishes, and yet, somehow, it has managed to survive to the present day. Since that first specimen was caught, several other coelacanths have been discovered.

Sole survivor Another animal which could be described as a living fossil is the tuatara. This is a lizard-like reptile found in parts of New Zealand. It is the sole survivor of an ancient group of reptiles that lived 170 million years ago. It shows several very unusual features: it has a pineal eye – a sort of third eye; it has the lowest body temperature – 11°C (52°F) – of any living reptile; it can go for 60 minutes without breathing; it has the longest incubation period of any living reptile (15 months); it shows almost no reaction to pain; it grows very slowly and only reaches sexual maturity after 20 years.

Perhaps its most endearing quality, however, is the fact that it often shares a burrow with a shearwater – a species of bird!

A rare photo of a coelacanth.
▼

MUSCULAR GENERATOR

Why do we shiver when we are cold? When we become too cold, the normal body processes begin to slow down. Before this temperature drops to a dangerous, critical level the body tries to raise its own temperature by shivering. Shivering is the rapid contraction of muscles, and this contraction generates heat within the body.

LIGHT AND STRONG

Which weighs more: a bird's skeleton or its feathers? Surprisingly, the feathers of a bird weigh more than its skeleton. Bird skeletons must be incredibly light in order that the bird may fly without expending huge amounts of energy. But the skeleton must also be strong, and bird skeletons have special supporting struts within the bones to give them strength.

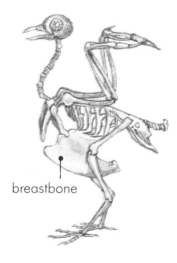

breastbone

▲
Powerful flight muscles attach to a bird's breastbone, the most specialized part of its skeleton.

HUNGRY BABY

Which young animal eats the most food? Relative to its size there can be only one contender for the title, greediest young animal. The larva of the polyphemus moth of North America is capable of consuming the equivalent of 86,000 times its own weight of food within the first 48 hours of its life. In human terms, that is equivalent to a 3.5 kg (8 lb) baby eating 301,000 kg (688,000 lb) of food in the same period of time!

UNSEEN MULTITUDE

What is the world's most common single animal? Although insects are the most abundant form of life in terms of overall numbers of species, the single most common species of animal in the world is a kind of nematode worm. Although most people in the world have never even seen one, it is estimated that there are 40 million million million million million million million million million individuals of this animal alive.

VARIETY OF LIFE

How many different kinds of plants and animals are there? Throughout the whole world, there are well over 20 million species of animals and plants alive today.

A nematode worm swimming in a pond. These worms are found in every conceivable habitat and may often be parasitic.
▼

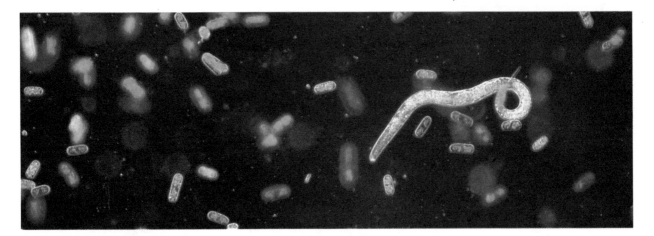

MASSES OF MOSS

How many mosses? How many different types of moss are there in the world? You can probably name several types and can perhaps recognize a few others, but did you know there are over 14,500 types known?

FEATHERWEIGHT

Is there a bird that weighs less than an insect? Believe it or not, the answer is yes. The bee hummingbird weighs less than the sphinx moth.

A rare example of an insect that ▶ is larger than a bird.

bee hummingbird

Privet hawk moth (Sphinx moth)

ALL ROUND VIEW

How does a fly see the world?
Through a pair of very complex
eyes known as compound eyes.
The eyes are composed of many
tiny cells, each with its own
honeycomb-shaped lens.
When light falls on to the eye a
message is sent to the brain
relaying the image seen by each
cell. The brain then builds up a
complete picture of what all the
eyes see.

▲
The fly's compound eyes give
a wide field of vision.

FACT FILE: BIRDS

FACT There are nearly 9,000 species of birds throughout the world.
FACT The bird with the largest wingspan is the wandering albatross,
with a wingspan of 3 m (10 ft).
FACT The smallest living bird is the bee hummingbird. It measures just
5.7 cm (2¼ in) in total length – half of which is taken up by the bill and
tail. The ostrich, the world's largest living bird, is 97,000 times bigger
than a bee hummingbird.
FACT The fastest running bird is the ostrich, which can reach speeds of
up to 48 km/h (30 mph).
FACT Birds have a body temperature of about 41°C (106°F). They
need this high temperature to ensure their muscles work at maximum
efficiency when flying.
FACT Birds have a poor sense of smell, but very good hearing and
eyesight. A blackbird can hear an earthworm tunnelling underground,
and birds of prey like the kestrel can spot a beetle or tiny mammal in the
grass while hovering 12 m (40 ft) or more above the ground.
FACT The largest marine bird is the emperor penguin, which is found in
Antarctica. Adults reach a height of 1.2 m (4 ft) and may weigh 32 kg
(70.5 lb).
FACT The world's most abundant species of bird is the African red-
billed quelea. It is estimated that the total population of this species
exceeds 10,000 million.
FACT The rarest bird of prey in the world is the Mauritius kestrel; only a
few pairs are believed to still exist.
FACT The oldest captive bird was an Andean condor which died in
Russia's Moscow Zoo in 1964. This bird was over 72 years old.
FACT The longest incubation period for a bird's egg is that of the
wandering albatross, which takes about 82 days to hatch.

NO BEAUTY

***Which is the ugliest of all
mammals?*** Throughout the
animal kingdom there are
several strange-looking
animals, and a few which are
distinctly unpleasant to look at.
Among mammals the ugliest
must surely be the appropriately
named warthog.

It is difficult to think of anything
about this poor creature which is
not ugly. Its body is covered with
sparse, coarse bristly fur
sprouting out of an otherwise
rather naked skin. The warthog
actually gets its name from its
face. This is huge, with large
warts and growths arising from
it, as well as large crescent-
shaped canine tusks.

▲
The warthog's name emphasises its unattractive and fearsome appearance.

GETTING A GRIP

Which bird has claws on its wings? The little-known hoatzin which lives in the mangrove swamps of Venezuela. Young hoatzins have two small claws on their wings, and they use these to help grip the branches as they clamber about the trees.

They are poor fliers even when adult. When the chicks grow up the claws drop from their wings. Watching a hoatzin chick clambering through the branches is like going back in time, millions of years, to when the first known bird appeared. This bird was called *Archaeopteryx* and it, too, had claws on its wings, and quite possibly also clambered about the branches in the same way as the young hoatzins.

▲
A young hoatzin using its wing-tip claws to help it climb.

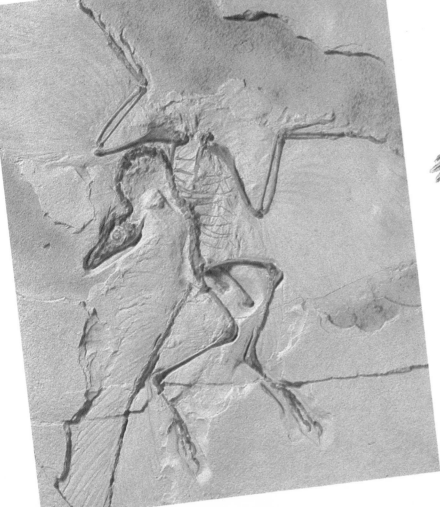

▲
The hoatzin shares a number of features with the long extinct
◄ *Archaeopteryx* (above and left), including claws on its wings and an inability to fly well.

GECKO FACTS

How can a gecko climb walls?

Geckos are tropical lizards which often enter houses in search of insects to eat. The remarkable thing about them is that they can climb up vertical walls – and can even walk across a ceiling. The gecko has muscular suckers on its feet which enable it to grip. It also has minute scales that can hook into any irregularity in the surface, giving it an even firmer grip.

Welcome visitors Geckos are often quite welcome in houses, for they are interesting to watch, and help to keep down the population of troublesome insects such as mosquitoes. The only problem is their habit of occasionally letting out a loud 'gecko' call, from which they get their name. Although some other lizards can make hissing sounds, geckos are the only lizards which possess a true voice.

Designed for climbing – here the ▶ gecko clings to a window-pane.

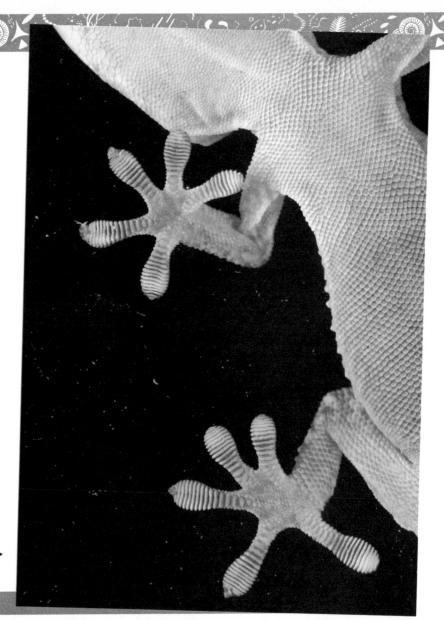

SWIMMING SHELLFISH

How do scallops get about?

Scallops belong to the group of animals known as molluscs. These particular molluscs are known as bivalves; in other words, they have a shell composed of two halves or valves. Most bivalves spend their time attached to rocks, or hidden in the sand. If they are threatened, most bivalves just dig deeper into the sand to escape. The scallop can also do this, but it has a more ingenious method of getting away. It vigorously claps its valves together, causing it to rise from the seabed and swim off to safety.

▲ A queen scallop swimming swiftly away from a predatory starfish.

DOUBLE DEFENCE

How does the ringhals protect itself? The ringhals is a kind of cobra, and it has two methods of self-defence. When danger first threatens, the ringhals pretends to be dead. It turns its body over, and lies there with its mouth open. Sometimes this has the desired effect and the would-be predator goes away.

But if the predator persists the ringhals has another way of defending itself – it spits venom into the eyes of its attacker. There are holes situated at the base of its fangs, and the venom is sprayed through these for a distance of up to 2.4 m (8 ft). No wonder that the ringhals' other name is the spitting cobra.

ONE ONLY

Can you name the only bird that can eat cuckoo-pint berries? The cuckoo-pint is an unusual plant of hedgerows and woodsides, which produces bright red berries in the autumn. The berries are extremely poisonous to all birds, except the thrush.

RIP VAN DORMOUSE

How long does the dormouse sleep for? The dormouse gets its name from its habit of sleeping for much of its life. (In French, 'dormir' means 'to sleep'.) The hazel dormouse hibernates for six months of the year!

▲ A common dormouse sleeping peacefully in its nest.

JUST THINKING

What is meant by 'chewing the cud'? Deer, giraffes and domestic animals like cows belong to the group of mammals known as ruminants. When ruminants feed, they bite off and swallow as much grass, twigs and leaves as they can, as quickly as they can, and then go off to find somewhere safe.

Once in a safe place, they sit down, return the food to their mouths and chew it again, properly and thoroughly this time. The food returned to the mouth for this second chewing is termed cud. So the food is really chewed twice. After it is swallowed for the second time, the food passes through a very complicated four-part stomach which is designed to extract all the goodness from the food.

When we talk about people 'ruminating' we mean that they are thoughtfully 'chewing over' something in the manner of ruminants, which seem thoughtfully to watch the world go by as they chew the cud.

MATCHING PAIRS

Match the males and females of these animals together:

Males	Females
1 Drake	A Cow
2 Boar	B Jill
3 Cock	C Pen
4 Bull	D Hind
5 Stag	E Hen
6 Buck	F Sow
7 Jack	G Vixen
8 Dog	H Nanny
9 Billy	I Doe
10 Cob	J Duck

ANSWERS
1 J; 2 F; 3 E; 4 A; 5 D;
6 I; 7 B; 8 G; 9 H; 10 C.

Section through the four chambers of a cow's stomach

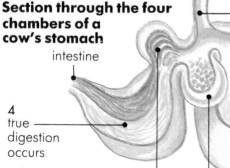

intestine

4 true digestion occurs

3 food is rubbed into a paste

2 liquid moistens cud

gullet

1 chewed food is turned into balls of cud

◄ The four chambers of a cow's stomach enable it to extract all the goodness from its food.

TWO-WAY BREATHER

Which fish breathes air? Most fish breathe by extracting oxygen from water, by means of their gills. Gills are delicate filaments of tissue through which blood passes. As water flows over the gills, oxygen diffuses into the blood.

However, some fish have an additional method of obtaining oxygen; they use a lung, just as we do. Fish which breathe in this way are, not surprisingly, called lungfish. The lung is formed from a modified swim bladder, the organ usually used to help a fish maintain buoyancy in the water.

Versatility Found in Australia, South America and Africa, lungfish live in places which may become very dry during drought. They use their gills to breathe when water is plentiful, but as drier conditions prevail they take in air from the surface into their lungs, or they sometimes bury themselves in the mud and breathe through a small tube until water returns. Some lungfish live in stagnant water, and use their lungs as well as their gills all the time.

The increasingly rare Australian lungfish is now a protected species.
▼

QUIZ: FLIGHT

① How fast does a stooping (or swooping) peregrine travel?
② A hoverfly can fly backwards as well as forwards: true or false?
③ A flying squirrel can perform flapping flight: true or false?
④ How far does a willow warbler travel in a year?
⑤ Name the large, flightless bird of Australia.
⑥ How many primary feathers are there on a duck's wing: 5, 10, 15 or 20?

ANSWERS
① 362km/h (225mph) ② True. Sideways too! ③ False. It can only perform gliding flight. ④ At least 16,000km (9,600 miles) – from northern Europe to southern Africa and back. ⑤ The emu. ⑥ 10.

VICTIMS OF VENOM

How common are deaths from snake bites? Throughout the whole world, about 35,000 people die each year from snake bites. Most of these deaths occur in Africa, Asia, Australia and parts of America.

Generally, snakes try to keep out of the way of humans, and most deaths occur when a snake is deliberately provoked, or when accidentally trodden on.

The country with the highest rate of deaths from snake bites is Burma. The place you are most likely to be bitten by a snake is on the Amami Islands in the western Pacific. One in every 500 of the population stands a chance of being bitten by a snake there.

BEWARE OF THESE SNAKES!

Most venomous snake
Sea Snake (*Hydrophis belcheri*)
Location Timor Sea, off the coast of North West Australia

Most venomous land snake
Small Scaled or Fierce snake
Location Australia (Queensland and South Australia)

Longest venomous snake
King Cobra or Hamadryad. It can reach a length of over 5.5m (18ft)
Location Philippines and south-east Asia

Fastest venomous snake
Slender Black Mamba. It has been known to achieve a speed of 11km/h (7mph)
Location Africa

The world's most venomous snakes are not necessarily the most dangerous. Other factors, such as which snakes are found in highly populated areas, always have to be taken into consideration, too.

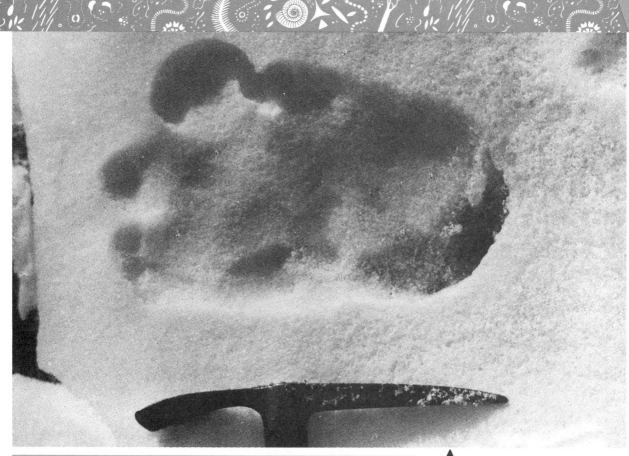

▲
The footprint of a yeti, or was this just a hoax?

FACT OR FICTION

Does the abominable snowman exist? Legend has it that a huge, hairy man-like creature lives in the high frozen wastes of the Himalayan mountains. The native Tibetans called it the Yeti, and many of them claim to have seen it. It is even thought by some people to be a sort of 'missing link' between man and the apes.

Evidence? In one of the temples in Nepal there is an object reputed to be a Yeti scalp, although it is more likely to be just the skin of some smaller mammal.

Some years ago, a group of European mountaineers on an expedition to Mount Everest found a huge footprint outside their camp one morning. They even took a photograph of it, with an ice-pick alongside for comparison. It was very large, and unlike any footprint seen before.

There was immediate speculation that this was a Yeti footprint, but, unless it was a hoax, it is most likely to have been made by a large bear. Although no known bear is capable of making a print of the size discovered, it is possible that the snow thawed around the edge of the print, making it appear larger than it was initially.

No proof So far, no one has been able to prove the existence of a Yeti by either capturing one or taking a conclusive photograph. In the inhospitable landscape of the Himalayas, it might be possible for such a creature to live practically undetected, since few people would consider seriously mounting an expedition to explore such dangerous terrain for something that may not even exist.

Several years ago great excitement was generated when a 'missing-link' creature, which had been pestering local girls, was captured near a remote village in China. Scientists who travelled to the village to try to identify this creature found it to be a monkey!

MONSTER MOTH

Which insect has the largest wingspan? It is the atlas moth. This huge insect, which lives in the tropical rain forests of Asia, has a wingspan of 30 cm (12 in).

▲
The striking and beautiful atlas silk moth.

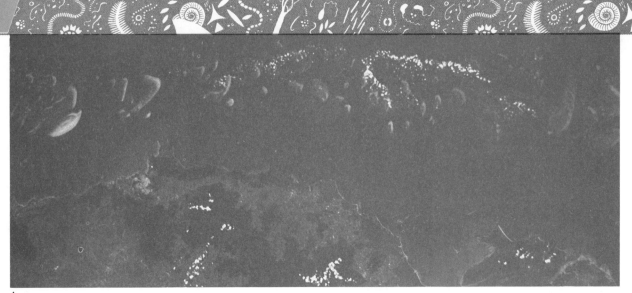

▲
Recognizable even from space – the remarkable expanse of the Great Barrier Reef.

A WORLD WONDER

What structure made by animals can be seen from outer space?
Astronauts on space flights were amazed that from their space rockets they could clearly see one particular feature of the earth's surface. The object was the 600-million-year-old Great Barrier Reef.

The Great Barrier Reef extends for 2,028 km (1,260 miles) along the coast of Queensland, in north-eastern Australia. It covers an area of 208,000 square km (80,000 square miles) and supports a greater density of life per given area than anywhere else on earth.

This amazing structure is a vast coral reef, consisting of millions and millions of tiny stony cups, within which live coral polyps – small animals related to anemones and jellyfishes. As polyps die, new polyps build their own little stony cups, gradually building the reef up into an enormous structure.

The reef is one of the most fascinating places in the world as it is a vital haven for hundreds of species of fish and other marine creatures.

ON THE HOOK

How did the butcher bird get its name? The butcher bird has developed a cunning way of keeping its prey safe until it is ready to eat it. The shrike (the proper name for the butcher bird) lives in habitats where gorse bushes and thorny shrubs are common. When a butcher bird catches a meal such as a lizard or beetle, it sometimes stores its prey by impaling it on a thorn. You may possibly come across one of these rather gruesome 'larders', with its collection of dead prey waiting to be eaten.

BELL AND TENTACLES

How big can a jellyfish grow? Jellyfishes are not very substantial creatures; they are thin, delicate animals with two body layers separated by a jelly-like layer from which they get their name. However, the trailing tentacles which contain stinging cells for catching food may be extremely long, and the top of the animal, which is known as the bell, may also be quite broad.

The largest jellyfish is the arctic giant jellyfish. This animal is found in the shallow waters of the Atlantic Ocean from Greenland to parts of North America. A massive specimen of the arctic giant jellyfish found in Massachusetts Bay in the last century had tentacles 36.6 m (120 ft) long, and a bell measuring 2.3 m (7½ ft) across. Most jellyfishes are, of course, considerably smaller than this, although even in European waters specimens such as the lion's mane jellyfish can reach a length of 13.7 m (45 ft).

▲
Impaled on a thorn, this insect is part of a shrike's larder.

KILLING WAYS

Do all spiders spin webs? No. Although we usually think of a spider spinning a silken web and then lying in wait until some unsuspecting insect becomes trapped on the sticky strands; many species of spider build no web at all, but rely on other methods of catching their prey. For instance, the crab spider disguises itself as the central portion of a flower and waits for unsuspecting insects to come within range of its legs, which shoot out to grab the prey.

Hunting methods An important group of spiders that do not spin webs are the wolf spiders. They rely on their keen eyesight and their ability to run quickly. When they spot a likely meal, they chase it and overpower it with a venomous bite.

The trapdoor spiders use the element of surprise. They lie in wait in burrows in the ground which are covered by flaps. As soon as a small creature passes within range, the flap flips open and the spider rushes out to grab its victim, which is then dragged back into the burrow to be devoured.

A much more ingenious method of catching prey is shown by the spitting spider. It actually spits sticky threads at flies, pinning them to the spot. Then there are spiders which lasso their prey using a sticky thread, and other species which spin a sort of net and throw it over their victim before rushing up to finish it off.

LONELY LEMUR

Name the world's rarest monkey. The rarest monkey in the world is the hairy-eared mouse lemur, which lives in the rain forests of eastern Madagascar. Only one live specimen has ever been found.

LONG IN THE TOOTH

How long were mammoth tusks? Mammoths were huge elephant-like mammals that once roamed the ice and snow-covered wastes of parts of Europe and America. The longest mammoth tusks ever discovered are from Germany, and were from a species called *Palaeoloxodon*. Some of these tusks were 5m (16½ft) long. The heaviest tusks on record weighed 150kg (330lb).

SPARE SPORES

How many spores does a mushroom produce? During the few days in which a mushroom or toadstool sprouts above the ground, it can produce a huge number of spores. A typical fruiting body (the dome-shaped structure at the top of the mushroom or toadstool's stalk) can produce over 1,500 million spores. Of course, very few spores land in an environment suitable for germination.

◀ The wolf spider is unusual in that it actively hunts down its prey, aided by the large eyes which give it exceptionally keen sight.

FACT FILE: WHALES, DOLPHINS AND PORPOISES

FACT Whales are divided into two groups: the toothed whales or odontocetes, and the whalebone (baleen) whales or mysticetes. Odontocete whales include the killer whale, sperm whale, narwhal, dolphins and porpoises. Mysticete whales include the blue whale, rorqual and right whale.

FACT All whales are intelligent creatures, and many kinds – such as dolphins, porpoises and killer whales – can be taught to perform complicated tricks.

FACT Although they cannot live anywhere but in water, whales are mammals. They breathe air just as we do, they suckle their young and they give birth to live young.

FACT Whales can communicate over huge distances. Some species can call to others of their kind making sounds that travel for hundreds of kilometres through the water.

FACT Dolphins can navigate by echo-location, emitting a series of high-pitched clicks (really sound waves), which bounce off obstacles in their path.

FACT Sperm whales can remain under water for nearly an hour and can submerge to depths of 3,193 m (10,476 ft) when feeding.

FACT Whales 'spout' by expelling spent air from their blow-holes at the surface. The hot breath condenses on contact with the cooler air and forms the characteristic plume or spout.

FACT The world's largest whale is the blue whale; it measures 30 m (100 ft) in length.

FACT The world's smallest whale is Commerson's dolphin, which only grows to a length of 1.3 m (4 ft).

Whales, dolphins and porpoises spend most of their time near the surface of the sea. They propel themselves through the water by beating their tails up and down.
▼

common porpoise

white-sided dolphin

bottle-nosed dolphin

La Plata dolphin

blue whale

right whale

killer whale

sperm whale

pilot whale

DEADLY NOOSE

How does a fungus catch a worm to eat? Some kinds of fungi are able to grow nooses which they use to trap tiny soil-dwelling worms. If a worm wriggles through the fungus noose, it grips the worm tightly. The helpless worm is then digested by the fungus.

FLOWERING PEBBLE

What is a living stone? This is a plant that looks exactly like a small pebble or stone. Living stones, or lithops, are found in the hot dry deserts of southern Africa. They are succulents, with a thick cuticle which lets in sunlight for photosynthesis. Lithops grow quite slowly, dividing in half every so often. They need very little water, as their thick cuticle prevents them from drying out in the heat. Their appearance so closely matches the desert floor that they are very hard to see, unless they are in flower, when for a brief time they bring a splash of colour to the dry landscape.

SQUATTER

Which bird does not build a nest of its own? The familiar cuckoo, whose song heralds the arrival of spring in northern Europe. Cuckoos belong to a group of birds known as egg parasites; they lay their eggs in the nests of other birds, normally warblers and other songbirds. The eggs which cuckoos lay very cleverly mimic the colour and size of those in the nest. The cuckoo steals one of the eggs, so that the owner does not realize that there are now too many in the nest.

Big chick Cuckoo eggs hatch before their companions, and the new-born chick instinctively heaves any other eggs out of the nest.

The cuckoo chick is quite a handful for its parents to feed, as it grows rapidly and has a truly voracious appetite. When 18 days old, it is about five times the weight of its foster parents, and becomes too big for the nest; it sits on it, rather than in it. Finally, it leaves the nest after about three weeks, and makes the long trip to southern Africa in the autumn, having never seen its real parents.

▲
A young cuckoo dwarfing its meadow pipit foster parent.

SUPREME TUSKER

What is the length of the longest elephant tusks? The longest elephant tusks ever found belonged to an African elephant, and measured an amazing 3.4 m (11 ft) and 3.5 m (11½ ft) long.

GIANT VERSION

Which is the largest rodent in the world? Most rodents we can think of are quite small; mice and rats for instance are small enough to sit on our hands. But can you imagine a rodent almost big enough for you to sit on? Well, there is one: the South American capybara can reach a size of 1.4 m (4½ ft) and a weight of 55 kg (121 lb). Even larger specimens have been recorded in captivity: a breeding female in Evansville Zoo, in Indiana, USA, weighed 79 kg (174 lb).

The capybara usually spends much ▶ of its time submerged in water.

▲
The distinctive face of a male proboscis monkey.

DO NOT TOUCH

How does a stinging nettle sting you? Stinging nettles are covered with special glands which contain an acidic substance. The glands are shaped like hollow hairs with a very brittle tip which breaks off when touched. When these glands on the leaves and stems are brushed against, they inject their acid, causing a painful stinging sensation.

NO SOLUTION

Which tree would 'puzzle a monkey'? The monkey puzzle tree of South America is a conifer with thick triangular leaves, packed densely along the branches, almost like a green coat of armour. The branches grow in a regular pattern, but are so intertwined that the tree can take on some bizarre shapes. Some people think that the tree is so called because to climb it would puzzle even a monkey. Or it may be named after its jumbled mass of branches, which look rather like green monkey tails.

BIG HOOTERS

Which monkey has the biggest nose? This distinction belongs to the proboscis monkey, an inhabitant of the coastal mangrove swamps of Borneo. The males have a bulbous flexible nose which may measure 8 cm (3 in) long. Proboscis monkeys live in small family groups and feed on the leaves, flowers and fruits of the mangrove trees.

DANCING BEES

What is the language of honey bees? Honey bees are colonial insects which live in a hive. The hive contains a single queen whose eggs are fertilized by a few males called drones. The worker bees guard the hive, feed the larvae and the queen and, most importantly, forage for pollen and nectar.

In 1919 a scientist, Karl von Frisch, noted that when the bees returned to their hive from a foraging expedition, they performed a kind of dance. He discovered that this dance was the language of the bees, for it communicated information about the location of plants on which the worker had found food to other bees in the hive. They, in turn, performed a similar dance on their return to the hive. In this way, the bees managed to locate and feed off flowers perhaps up to 3.2 km (2 miles) from the hive.

Dance patterns There are basically two types of dance. In the round dance, the worker scuttles in a circle, changing direction after every revolution. This tells the other bees that food is available within about 50 m (164 ft) of the hive, but does not pinpoint its location.

For food further afield, a more precise dance called the waggle dance is used. The bee performs the 'waggle' by vigorously shaking its abdomen whilst performing the crossover part of a figure-of-eight movement. The direction of this waggle run corresponds to the direction the bees must fly in order to find the food, and the longer the crossing over 'waggle run', the further away the food is. As a general rule, the closer the food is to the hive, the more frequently the bees dance.

In its complexity and precision, the language of bees is one of the most fascinating means of communication in all the animal kingdom.

▲
This bee's tail-wagging dance indicates that food is to be found some distance away in the direction of the sun.

SMITHY BIRD

Which bird uses an anvil? The European song thrush uses a flat stone as an anvil on which to smash snail shells. Thrushes often have a favourite site for this purpose and may bring snails there from a distance. They leave behind a mass of broken and splintered snail shells as evidence of their favourite food.

A hungry song thrush using a stone as an anvil to smash the shell of a snail.
▼

▲

For members of the Loch Ness Investigation Team (top), patience can be as useful as scientific equipment. A convincing but inconclusive photograph of the 'monster' taken in 1934 (above).

MONSTER MYSTERIES

Does the Loch Ness Monster exist? Over the years many people have reported seeing the Loch Ness Monster. Some of these sightings may have been dreamed up to help the tourist trade, or just as tricks, but some very respected people have reported sightings, and a few people have even taken photographs of what they claim is the monster. Unfortunately none of these photographs has ever proved conclusive, and many have been identified as semi-floating logs and other structures.

Monster seekers Many scientific studies have been conducted to try and establish whether or not there is some truth in the legend. There has been ultrasonic scanning, underwater photography and mini submarine investigations, as well as the time-honoured loch-side vigils at well known 'monster' sighting places, such as at the ruins of Urquhart Castle. So far all that has been proved is that there are a lot of people willing to spend a lot of time looking!

Speculation So what do those scientists who believe in the existence of a monster think it is, and how could one be there anyway? First, let us look at the nature of the Loch itself. Loch Ness is a large lake some 37 km (23 miles) long and reaching a depth of 228 m (750 ft). Within these dark and cold waters a large animal could probably go undetected, feeding on the fishes that also inhabit the Loch.

If the Loch Ness Monster really does exist, most theories tend to suggest it is a plesiosaur – a type of massive reptile which is believed to have become extinct (died out) at the end of the Cretaceous Period, some 65 million years ago. Of course, one plesiosaur could not live for 65 million years! It would require the presence of a whole breeding colony to produce generation after generation of plesiosaurs to enable individuals to still be alive today.

Sadly, although evidence has suggested that something big is in Loch Ness, it is more likely to be the remains of a crashed aeroplane, a large shoal of fish, or a huge submerged tree than a real live monster.

FLYING FEATS

How many kinds of animals can fly? Well, birds of course, and bats and insects, but did you know that many other kinds of creature can also fly? They may not be able to perform 'flapping flight' or remain in the air for as long as they wish, but they can glide superbly for long distances.

Fishes There are several species of flying fish living in the Atlantic and Indian Oceans, that can glide for long distances. They do this by swimming very fast and then breaking the surface of the sea and gliding on outstretched fins. It is thought that they do this to escape from predators.

Amphibians and reptiles The flying frogs of tropical regions jump from tree to tree, and glide by using the large webs of skin between their outstretched fingers and toes. The golden tree snake of Indo-Malaya takes off from the tops of trees and glides down to lower branches, by making its body as flat as possible, thereby slowing its descent.

Mammals Apart from bats, there are other mammals that can fly. The flying squirrel of Australia, and the flying lemur of the Philippines can both glide through the air, using flaps of skin between their front and back legs like a kind of parachute. The flying lemur can leap distances of up to 50 m (192 ft).

FLOWER POWER

Which group of plants is the most common? By far the most abundant and widespread group of plants is the Angiosperms, or flowering plants. They include familiar examples such as dandelions, roses, and buttercups, as well as trees like the ash and oak.

Flowering plants flourish in hot places, in cold places, up mountains and even on the seashore. There are over 250,000 different types of flowering plants in the world today.

Four-winged flying fish skimming across the ocean waves.
▼

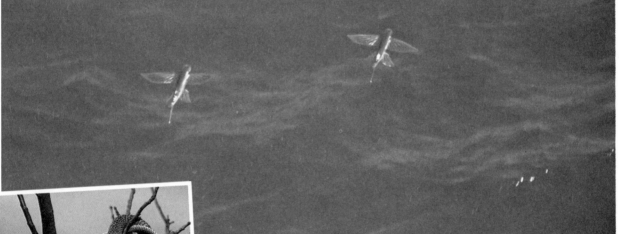

▲
A golden tree snake prepares for lift-off.

QUIZ: BIRDS

1 Which is the heaviest flying bird?
2 Which bird lays the smallest egg?
3 Which is the heaviest flightless bird?
4 Where do penguins come from – North Pole or South Pole?
5 What is the earliest known bird called?
6 What sort of bird is a saddlebill?

ANSWERS
1 The mute swan. It weighs over 18 kg (40 lb).
2 The bee hummingbird. It lays eggs into a nest no bigger than a thimble. 3 The ostrich. The ostrich of the grasslands of Africa and Arabia may weigh over 150 kg (254 lb). 4 South Pole.
5 Archaeopteryx. 6 A type of stork.

PLACE OF HIS OWN

Is it only birds that make nests? The stickleback is a common fish found in streams and rivers. In spring, this remarkable fish does something that we normally associate with birds – it makes a nest. During the breeding season each male stickleback guards a small territory on the stream bed. There, with a mixture of sand and mud, held together by mucus, he builds a small, tubular nest.

When he has finished this task, he lures a female stickleback into the nest, where she lays the eggs, and he then fertilizes them. Rather surprisingly, after this he drives her away and guards the nest until the young fish are ready to swim away.

LEFT, RIGHT . . .

What is the difference between a centipede and a millipede? Centipedes and millipedes belong to an invertebrate group called the myriapods, which literally means 'many legs' – but counting the legs is not a reliable way of telling them apart. The best way to identify them is to look at the number of legs attached to each segment of the body. Centipedes have one pair of legs to each body segment, and millipedes have two pairs.

In the tropics, millipedes can reach an enormous size and specimens have been caught which measure over 28 cm (11 in) in length.

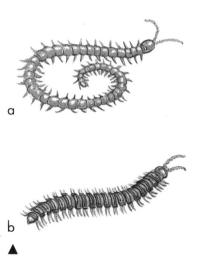

▲
Unless you look at their legs, a centipede (a) and a millipede (b) are difficult to tell apart.

THE GREAT FERTILIZERS

How many earthworms are there in your back garden? The figure will depend upon the nature of the soil and drainage, but it has been estimated that there are between ½ and 2½ million worms in an acre of pasture land. Burrowing through the soil, earthworms are mainly active at night. They drag organic debris such as rotting leaves and grasses into their burrows and this is of great benefit to man in keeping the soil fertile. By bringing up soil from the subsoil layer, earthworms add about 2.4 cm (1 in) to the topsoil in a year. In Europe, the familiar earthworm is only about 15 cm (6 in) long, but in the tropics they can grow to a length of 1.7 m (5½ ft)!

◀ The male stickleback drives the female away after spawning.

A LOT OF IT ABOUT

What is a virus? Sometimes when we feel ill we are told by our doctors that we have a virus infection, but what does that mean? Viruses are the simplest known forms of life, so simple that some scientists argue that they should not be called 'living' at all.

They only become active when they invade a host tissue and cause a disease or viral infection. These microscopic organisms have no nucleus or cell membrane normally associated with plants and animals. Instead, they have a protein shell, inside which is a nucleic acid. Once inside the host, the virus interferes with the normal metabolism of the cells, causing the symptoms of disease.

HONEY UP!

What is a honeyguide? This is a small bird which feeds upon the honey from the bees and wasps nests in the tropics. The bird is unable to break open these nests itself, and has evolved an ingenious method of obtaining its food. When the honeyguide spots a likely looking nest, it makes an alarm call which is recognized by a honey badger, a lumbering animal which also feeds on honey. The badger breaks open the nest with its strong claws, and both badger and bird get themselves a meal.

SAFETY CATCH

What is a trigger fish? This strange fish lives in tropical seas around coral reefs. Its name probably arose because of a curious shaped dorsal fin which looks like a spike or trigger. This can be erected at will and locked into position. When danger threatens, the trigger fish dives into a crevice in the coral and erects its trigger fin. It is now securely wedged into position and no predator is able to dislodge it.

The brilliantly coloured clown trigger fish.
▼

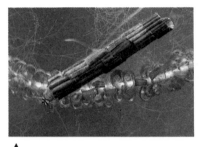

▲
A well-concealed caddis fly nymph.

AT HOME

Which insect builds itself a house? We normally associate house-building with people, but it also goes on among other animals, and even in some insects. Caddis flies are rather dull moth-like insects which are found near fresh water, and are easily overlooked. They do, however, have remarkable larvae which live in the water, and make a protective home for themselves.

Depending upon the species and the type of stream or pond that they are in, the caddis larvae glue together pieces of sand or plant, to form a long protective tube in which they live. Only their head and front legs protrude to allow them to move and feed.

IN THE AIR

Why do insects have antennae? Insects use their antennae as we use our noses – to 'smell' the world around them. Many male moths use them to detect females so that they can mate. The male emperor moth, one of Britain's most colourful species, can smell a female from a distance of 1.6 km (1 mile), if she is downwind of him. The antennae on this moth are very large and feathery, and this improves its ability to smell by enabling even the slightest odour to be detected.

Other insects, such as crickets, have very long, thin antennae, which they use to 'touch and taste' the environment in their search for food. To make sure that this essential sense is in perfect working order, the insect often spends long periods cleaning the antennae with its mouthparts.

Second sense Everyone knows how keen the sense of smell is in a housefly. Within minutes of opening a pot of jam, dozens may have descended upon it. However, flies have a second means of tasting their food, and the organs are found not in their head, but in their feet. Quite sensible really – when you walk all over your food!

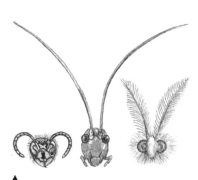

▲
The contrasting antennae of a wasp (left), a cricket (centre) and an emperor moth (right).

BODY SNATCHERS

What is a sexton beetle? If you come across the corpse of a dead small mammal or bird, try carefully turning it over with a stick. You may be lucky enough to see boldly marked black and red beetles underneath. These are sexton beetles, so called because they are attracted to dead bodies, which they bury.

These beetles have a remarkable sense of smell, and can detect the odour of a rotting mouse up to 3.25 km (2 miles) away. They are active fliers and will 'home-in' on the corpse. If a male and female meet, they employ team-work to bury the body and lay their eggs on it. If the soil is too hard, they drag it away – quite a feat when you consider that the body may be five or six times heavier than the beetle! When the larvae of the sexton beetle hatch, they eat the corpse and finally emerge the next year as adults.

▲
Sexton beetles scavenging for food.

TURNCOATS

Which animal is brown in summer and white in winter? Several. Animals that live in areas which are covered in snow in winter change the colour of their coat according to the seasons. The arctic hare does this, and so does the stoat. In summer both these animals have brown fur, but this changes to white at the onset of winter. This helps the hare to remain concealed and avoid predators, and helps the stoat to sneak up on its prey unseen! In its winter coat, the stoat is called an ermine.

In its winter coat the stoat blends in with the snowy landscape.
▼

FACT FILE: LIFE IN CAVES

FACT No green plants can grow deep inside caves, because there is insufficient light for photosynthesis (the process in which the plant uses sunlight to make its own food).

FACT Plants such as fungi have no problem growing in caves because they do not need sunlight, and shade-tolerant species like ferns often grow well in partly lit caves.

FACT Oil birds live in South American caves. To find their way about in the dark, they emit rapid clicks, which send back echoes, telling them of anything in their path.

FACT Some very unusual fishes live in the pools and streams of underground caves. The blind cave fish, as its name suggests, has no eyes, for they would be useless in the pitch dark of a cave.

FACT Bats are common inhabitants of caves. In very damp caves, some bats cover their wings over their bodies to act as 'umbrellas'.

FACT Cave salamanders (found mostly in North America) hunt in underground streams, and catch their prey by smell, rather than by sight.

FACT Cave swiftlets are birds which live in parts of Asia and Oceania. The nests of some types of cave swiftlets are made of vegetable matter glued together with hardened saliva. They are considered a delicacy in some parts of the world, and are eaten as bird's nest soup!

FACT In caves which have a population of bats, there are also many insects, for these feed on the bats' droppings, and on dead bats which fall to the ground.

The unmistakable trail of a ▶
sidewinder adder in the desert.

ODD MOVER

How did the sidewinder get its name? The sidewinder is a kind of snake which lives in hot American deserts. The deserts are so hot that the sidewinder can't bear to slither along the ground as snakes usually do. Instead, it literally winds itself along in a looping corkscrew action, so that only part of its body is in contact with the hot ground at any one time.

SAFETY ZONE

Which plants are used by frogs to lay their eggs in? In certain parts of South America, the tropical forests contain trees with curious plants called bromeliads growing on them. Bromeliads are known as epiphytes: they are plants which attach themselves to other plants in order to obtain a better supply of sunlight.

However, just as the bromeliads take advantage of the trees on which they grow, so another living thing also takes advantage of the bromeliads – and in a most peculiar way.

Bromeliads are shaped like deep vases, with the long, thick leaves spiralling around each other. As it rains, water collects within the 'vase', making a permanent little pool. Here, tree frogs can lay their eggs and hatch their young in safety, far away from predators like fishes which inhabit the places where frogs normally lay their eggs. It must have been a very curious sight for the first naturalists who peered inside a tropical bromeliad, only to find tiny frogs swimming about!

◀ The leafy 'vase' of the bromeliad makes an ideal home for this frog.

FAKE FINERY

Why do some animals mimic others? If you study the insects that visit the flowers in your garden, you may notice that many of the flies have black and yellow bands and look like wasps. Many of the insects that you might think are bees will also be flies, such is the accuracy of their mimicry. Some of them even sound like bees and wasps, producing a loud buzzing.

But what can be the advantage? Many birds and other predators of insects, including man, have learned that if they interfere with a bee or a wasp, they will be stung. Therefore, if an insect can disguise itself and resemble something with a sting, there is a good chance that it will be passed over by a predator. Some mimicking flies go one stage further and even fool the bees. Several species of hoverfly can enter colonies of bees at will and lay their eggs inside.

WINGED WONDER

Do swifts sleep on the wing?
Swifts spend the vast majority of their lives on the wing, only landing to nest. Contrary to former belief that swifts landed at night, they are now known to remain on the wing, taking short naps in between bursts of flight. In addition to sleeping on the wing, swifts also feed on the wing, catching insects in their gaping mouths. They may even mate on the wing as well. All these pursuits must require considerable aerobatic precision!

A hover-fly mimicking a bee.
▼

AMAZONIAN MONSTER

Which is the largest freshwater fish? The River Amazon in Brazil is famous for its exotic animals and plants. It is home not only to some of the largest snakes, insects and flowers, but also to the largest freshwater fish, called the arapaima.

Its body is rather eel-like in appearance, and it may reach a length of 3 m (10 ft). The arapaima is an active carnivore and lurks in muddy waters waiting for prey. The male has the unusual habit among fish of guarding the eggs and young.

◀ A pike-like arapaima of South America lurking among the weeds.

▲
Camouflaged creatures: a female woodcock and chicks (above) and a stick insect (below).
▼

NOT WHAT THEY SEEM

Why are some animals camouflaged? Camouflage is generally used by animals so that they can avoid being seen by predators. A classic example is seen in the woodcock, an unusual wading bird which nests in woodland. Its feathers bear a remarkable resemblance to fallen bark and leaves, and consequently it can nest on the ground without fear of being spotted.

A bizarre example is found in a group of nocturnal birds called frogmouths that nest on the end of broken twigs and branches. Their plumage also closely resembles the bark of the branch, but the effect is enhanced when the bird stretches its body out and looks exactly like an extension of the branch. As their huge eyes would make them very conspicuous, frogmouths spend most of their time on the nest with their eyes clamped firmly shut.

STRANGE INSTRUMENTS

How do insects sing? Although they do not make use of vocal chords, many different insects throughout the world have developed the ability to sing. Among the most familiar are the grasshoppers. Their song is produced by rubbing their hind legs against their wings; rows of small pegs help produce the sound, acting rather like the teeth of a comb when rubbed. Crickets produce their song in a similar way, but in their case the wings are rubbed against each other.

Anybody who has visited the tropics or watched television programmes about the area, will be familiar with the nocturnal noises. Many of the contributors to this chorus will be cicadas. These strange-looking insects have large membranous wings which they rub together to produce the sound.

▲
Grasshoppers use the ratchets on their back legs to produce sounds.

CUSTOM MADE

Can limpets find their way back home? If you study the shoreline when the tide is out, some of the rocks may have clumps of conical limpets clustered on them. The limpets clamp themselves to the rocks to prevent them losing water, and to protect them from predators. It appears that limpets never move but, in fact, when they are covered by the sea, limpets travel some considerable distance whilst feeding.

How then do they find their way back? In fact, they leave a chemical trail as they walk and they simply follow this back. It is vital that the limpet finds its correct 'home', since its shell will have grown to fit a particular piece of rock. If it is in the wrong spot, it will not be able to clamp itself down properly.

OXYGEN MAKERS

Why are most plants green? Green is almost the universal colour found in the leaves of plants. The colour is due to a pigment called chlorophyll, which is contained within the cells in the leaf. Chlorophyll has some unique properties which enable plants to thrive.

The pigment is able to trap sunlight energy, and helps the plant use this energy in photosynthesis to convert carbon dioxide (a gas present in the atmosphere) and water into sugar. The sugar is used to help the plant grow, and a by-product of the reaction is the gas oxygen. This is the gas which all animals need for the process called respiration, so we should all be thankful for the abundance of plants.

Other colours Some plants' leaves are colours other than green, often red. In most cases, this is not because there is no chlorophyll present, but because they contain additional pigments which mask the green colour.

sun

oxygen

carbon dioxide   water

▲ When green plants trap light energy they take up carbon dioxide and release oxygen.

BATTLING BEETLES

Which beetle has antlers? Male stag beetles have remarkable antler-like projections on their heads which bear an uncanny resemblance to the antlers of deer. As with the deer, the beetles use their antlers to battle over possession of a female. It is rarely a fight to the death, but they can sometimes do considerable damage to each other. It is generally the stag beetle with the biggest antlers that wins the fight.

◀ Two battling male stag beetles. Fighting usually occurs only during the mating season.

MEANINGFUL MUSIC

Why do birds sing? All of us look forward to the coming of spring, at least partly because the birds start singing. The familiar 'dawn chorus' heralds the arrival of a new breeding season, but does the bird's song have any other significance?

Even though scientists concede that birds may sometimes sing for pleasure, in general, song has a more practical function. Male birds sing to attract a female and to announce their presence in a territory to a rival male. The song helps to define the boundaries of this territory.

Some birds sing throughout the year. The robin, for example, has a special winter song which is again used to announce his claim to a territory. However, during the winter, he guards this as a feeding area, and not for nesting purposes. Indeed, a male robin will even drive the female, with whom he nested in the previous spring, out of their territory.

ARTFUL DODGERS

How can a mongoose defeat a snake? The mongoose is a small, agile mammal with short legs and a long body ending in a pointed muzzle. There are several species in the world, found in Asia and Africa.

One of the best-known features of mongooses is their ability to overcome and kill snakes, even large, dangerous species like cobras. So how do they do this?

To begin with the mongoose is adept at dodging and weaving; it never keeps still, making it very difficult for the snake to strike with its fangs. Secondly, the mongoose's coarse, bristly fur makes it difficult for the snake's fangs to penetrate, even if it does succeed in striking its target. Thirdly, the mongoose has a great resistance to the snake's venom – ten times more resistance, in fact, than other mammals of a similar size.

◀ The mongoose is an expert snake killer, though snakes form only a small part of its diet.

QUIZ: AMPHIBIANS

1. Which is the world's largest amphibian?
2. How do you tell the difference between frogspawn and toadspawn?
3. What is an axolotl?
4. How far can a frog jump?
5. How many species of newt live in Britain?
6. Why is the midwife toad so called?

ANSWERS
1. The giant salamander, which grows to a length of 1.5 m (5 ft). 2. Frogspawn is usually laid in clumps, whereas toadspawn is usually laid in long strands. 3. A curious Mexican salamander which never reaches true adulthood, and even breeds while still in the larval stage. 4. The South African sharp-nosed frog has been recorded jumping a distance of 3 m (nearly 10 ft) in a single leap. 5. Three: common, palmate and crested. 6. Because it carries its eggs around on its back until they are ready to hatch.

MAMMOTH CRUISER

Which is the world's biggest fish? The world's biggest fish is the whale shark. Specimens of 18 m (60 ft) have been discovered. The whale shark is a rare creature, which swims sluggishly near the surface, taking in plankton through its huge mouth. Seen head-on, the whale shark resembles a huge frog, as it glides about, mouth open, in the warm waters of the Pacific, Atlantic and Indian Oceans.

KILLER SLUGS!

Do all slugs eat plants? Most slugs eat a mixture of living and dead vegetable material, but one group, the shelled slugs, are carnivores. Found throughout Europe, shelled slugs spend most of their lives underground, but come to the surface of the soil at night to hunt for earthworms. They have a large mouth, with rows of backward-pointing teeth, with which they engulf the unfortunate worm.

◀ The forest-dwelling banana slug, named after the fruit it resembles.

ONE GOOD TURN . . .

Why does the bitterling depend upon a freshwater mussel? Most fish species abandon their offspring as soon as the eggs have been laid. In a few instances, the parents guard the young until they are old enough to fend for themselves. However, in some European rivers there is a fish called the bitterling, which has developed an extraordinary way of looking after its young. Instead of tending them itself, it employs the help of a freshwater mussel – a mollusc found in stream beds.

Mussels feed by filtering food from the water around them through tubes called siphons. The female bitterling has an extremely long ovipositor (egg-laying apparatus), and with this she lays eggs inside the mussel by inserting her ovipositor through the siphon.

Hitching a lift The mussel, however, also benefits from this arrangement. While the bitterling is laying her eggs the mussel releases its young. These have small clamps with which they attach themselves to the side of the fish to 'hitch a lift' to a different part of the river.

A bitterling swimming near a bed ▶ of freshwater mussels.

FAR AND WIDE

How do plants disperse their seeds? Plants space themselves apart to avoid competing with each other for light, air and water. Consequently, most plants have developed ingenious ways of dispersing their seeds far away from the parent plant.

Perhaps the most familiar method is to use the wind. Dandelion seeds have an umbrella of fine hairs that catch the wind which can carry them for great distances. The seeds of sycamore are heavier, but with their 'wings' can also travel some distance. Even more extraordinary are the seeds of gorse. These are contained in pods which dry out as they mature. Eventually, when completely dry, they explode, scattering the seeds far and wide.

Animal carriers Animals and birds are more mobile than plants, and so it is not surprising that plants use them to transport their seeds. A succulent meal of berries and fruit also contains seeds which are usually resistant to digestion. They therefore pass out with the droppings of the animal, which by this time has usually moved some distance away, thereby helping to disperse the seeds.

Some plants such as burdock use animals in a different way. Their seeds have barbs and hooks which tangle in the fur of passing animals and are carried a considerable distance before being dislodged.

Floating seeds Many plants exploit the water to disperse their seeds. The seeds of water lilies, for example, are buoyant and are carried by currents to new stretches of water.

ALL ROUND KELP

What do seaweed, ice-cream and beer have in common? Although seaweed may appear to have little economic value, it is widely used, particularly in the food industry. Some seaweeds, such as carragheen, are eaten for their own sake. Others, such as the large kelps, produce a chemical called alginic acid.

Alginic acid is a remarkable substance having strong glue-like properties. The seaweed produces it naturally to hold fast to rocks, thus preventing it being dislodged by waves. When used in brewing, it helps keep the froth rigid on the top of beer. Alginic acid is added to ice-cream, helping to give it 'body'.

Such is the versatility of alginic acid, that it is now found in a large number of prepared foods in our shops.

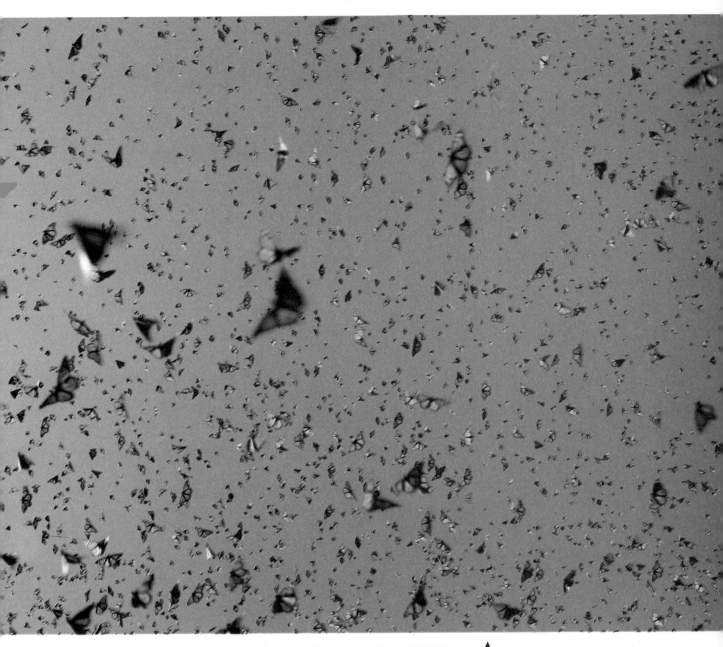

A host of migrating butterflies.

FOLLOWING THE SUN

Do insects migrate? Migration is normally something that we associate with birds. Many birds, such as swallows, spend the summer in Europe but return to warmer climates during the northern winter. However, many butterflies and moths also undergo lengthy travels across different parts of the world.

The most famous example is the monarch butterfly of North America. It spends the winter in the southern states of North America and Central America, but flies north across the States in vast numbers during spring.

During their southward migration in the autumn, some monarch butterflies are blown off course by the prevailing westerly winds and get carried out to sea. As a result, there are annual records of this species in Europe in September and October. Some of these butterflies may have had 'assisted passage' perhaps coming on transatlantic ships, but most are considered to be genuine un-assisted migrants.

TOWERING MAMMAL

Which is the world's tallest animal? The giraffe. It can browse on vegetation growing as high as 6m (19ft), and could easily look over the top of a double-decker bus. Because of the extreme length of the front legs and neck, the giraffe has to spread its legs wide and almost 'do the splits' to get low enough to reach down and drink from a water hole.

CUTTING BACK

Why do lemmings commit suicide? Lemmings are small rodent-like creatures which live in cold regions like the Norwegian tundra. Every few years a population 'explosion' occurs, and many more lemmings are born than can be supported by the available food resources. When this happens, some instinctive urge causes huge hordes of lemmings to migrate. These occurrences are so regular and frequent (they happen every three to five years) that they are called 'lemming years'.

Disaster For many lemmings this mass migration from the breeding ground ends in disaster. Thousands upon thousands are picked off by marauding predators, such as snowy owls and foxes. Others simply drown from exhaustion in rivers and oceans.

It was once thought that the lemmings were deliberately committing suicide, so reckless is the way in which they follow each other across hazardous roads, waterways and even over cliffs. But, in fact, it is nature's way of ensuring that the numbers are reduced to a level which can be maintained by natural resources.

▲
The lemming is a burrowing rodent which lives on mosses, sedges, grasses and bark.

The chameleon's unusual eyes and its tongue in action.
▼

STRANGE DESIGN

Which animal can look in two directions at once? The chameleon is a strange, slow-moving lizard which hunts mainly for insect prey among the trees. Its eyes are situated on the end of little conical-shaped turrets, and it can move them independently in any direction. One eye can be whirling around looking upwards for food, while the other keeps a watch out for things happening below.

Camouflaged hunter The chameleon has other peculiarities. The toes are modified to form effective clamps, which grip the twigs and branches very tightly. Then there is the ability of chameleons to change colour. The skin, and even the body markings, can alter colour to match the surroundings, making the chameleon much harder to spot as it stalks through the trees.

When the slow-moving chameleon spots prey, it shoots out a long, sticky tongue at the victim at incredible speed. The prey sticks to the tongue and is quickly pulled back into the chameleon's mouth. All this happens in about 1/25 of a second!

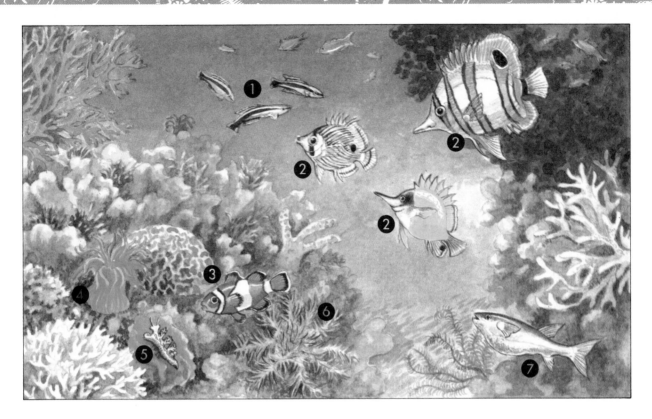

1 cleaner wrasse
2 false-eyed fish
3 clown anenome fish
4 sea anenome

5 sea slug
6 crown-of-thorns starfish
7 puffer fish

▲
Reefs are found only in the tropics, where the water is warm enough for reef-building corals to survive. Many corals are brilliantly coloured and reefs are usually populated by equally colourful inhabitants.

FACT FILE: CORAL REEFS

FACT Coral reefs are formed from the chalky skeletons of millions of coral polyps. These colonial animals are related to sea anemones and jellyfish.

FACT The pufferfish, an inhabitant of coral reefs, gets its name from its ability to puff itself up like a balloon when threatened. Few animals can then get this fat, spiky body into their mouths.

FACT The cleaner wrasse is a small, striped fish that feeds on the skin parasites of other, larger, coral reef fishes. It swims into their open mouths to clean their teeth. Fishes have even been seen queuing up for attention from a cleaner wrasse!

FACT Many coral reef fishes have bright colours, warning predators that they are distasteful or even poisonous to eat. Others have striped bodies which help to confuse predators by breaking up their outline.

FACT The crown-of-thorns starfish actually eats coral reefs. This destructive predator is now causing great damage to Australia's Great Barrier Reef, posing a serious threat to this habitat.

FACT Although sea slugs sound rather dull-looking creatures, the sea slugs of coral reefs are often brilliantly coloured, with elaborately shaped gills protruding from their bodies.

WISE EYES

Why do flatfish have both eyes on one side of their heads? If you examine a flounder or plaice in a fishmongers, you will notice that, unlike most animals, both eyes are on one side of the head. The result is a rather grizzly appearance, but it suits the life-style of the fish perfectly.

Flatfish live on the bottom of the seabed in estuaries and deeper water. As one side of the body will inevitably be facing the mud, there is little point in having an eye facing downwards.

Surprisingly, when the young flatfish hatches from the egg it looks just like any other fish, and has an eye on each side. However, during its development, the eye on the left side of its head gradually migrates to the right side! The fish then starts to swim on its side with the right side uppermost.

▲
A great water beetle diving.

THE DIVER

How do water beetles breathe under water? In order to survive, all animals need a supply of oxygen. This can present a problem if you live in water and many animals, such as fishes, have overcome this by using gills to extract the gas from the water.

Some aquatic animals still rely on oxygen from the air and have to come to the surface to breathe. Water beetles, however, have an ingenious way of staying submerged for long periods. In a similar way to subaqua divers, they take their air supply with them. Consequently, they only have to return to the surface periodically for a fresh supply.

All beetles have hard wing cases which protect the wings when not in use. In water beetles, the gap between the wing cases and the body is used to hold an air supply and, as a result, they can stay under for hours if necessary. (This method does have the unfortunate drawback of giving added buoyancy, and so, unless the beetle grasps something under water, it bobs to the surface.)

THE NAME OF THE SHAPE

How did lungwort get its name? In early times, herbal medicine was very popular, and was often the only hope of cure. Many herbalists considered that plants which resembled in some way a part of the human body, were designed to treat ailments or afflictions of that particular organ.

The leaves of lungwort are large and oval and covered in white blotches, which gives them a superficial resemblance to lung tissue – which is how the plant got its name. Whether or not it successfully cured ailments of this tissue is, however, open to speculation.

Another example in herbal folklore is toothwort. The curious flowers of this plant look like teeth, and were used as a cure for toothache.

This food chain would normally ▶ include alternative food sources, thus producing a 'food web'.

TANGLED WEBS

What is a foodchain? We all know that some animals eat plants while others eat other animals. Linking these animals and plants together in terms of what they eat, gives a foodchain.

A good place to start is with the wildlife in a field. There may be snails eating the grass. Some birds, such as thrushes, will eat the snails, and they in turn will be eaten by predators such as stoats. There might even be birds of prey in the field, which catch and eat the stoats, so already there is a long chain.

This is further complicated if you consider alternative diets. For example, the birds of prey would also eat the thrushes, and so the more closely you examine an environment, the more complex the foodchain becomes.

Because the items in any particular foodchain do, in fact, also 'link up' with items in other foodchains, it is best to think of the relationship between predators and prey in terms of food webs.

snail
thrush
stoat
hawk

PROTECTION RACKET

What is symbiosis? This is a term used to describe the relationship between members of two different species, in which each is dependent upon the other, and each partner benefits.

A good example of symbiosis can be found in the garden. During the summer months, many garden plants are attacked by aphids. If you study an affected stem you will see hundreds of aphids lined up side-by-side, feeding on the plant's sap. You may also be lucky enough to see ants running between the aphids.

Ants are normally fierce predators of other insects, so it is surprising that they do not kill the aphids. In fact, they are feeding on a substance called honeydew which the aphids exude. Honeydew is rich in sugar, and the ants feed on this themselves and also carry it to their nests for their larvae.

The ants benefit in an obvious way from this partnership, but so do the aphids. In return for the honeydew, the ants protect the aphids from attack by other insects often much larger than themselves.

EVER-WIDENING CIRCLE

How are fairy rings formed? Autumn is the time of year for mushrooms and toadstools. Many permanent pastures produce an abundance of fungi, and sometimes you come across groups growing in a perfect circle. These are popularly known as fairy rings and were thought to have magical properties, but unfortunately the truth is rather more straightforward.

As with all fungi, most of the tissues are composed of tiny threads called a mycelium, which in the case of these fungi grows underground. The toadstools are produced each year to distribute the spores of the fungus.

At first, toadstools appear in the middle of the ring, but by the end of the first year, the mycelium in the middle has died, and growth the following year occurs on the outside. As the years progress the new growth radiates outwards, and the toadstools produced on the growing edge form a ring.

MASKED KILLER

How do dragonfly nymphs catch their prey? Dragonfly nymphs are fierce predators, and some species, such as the emperor dragonfly, can catch prey as large as minnows.

Their mouthparts have evolved to form an odd-looking structure called the 'mask'. The mask is a hinged apparatus with two 'fangs' at the front end. When the nymph spots a fish it creeps slowly towards it until it is about 2 cm (1 in) away. It then catapults the mask forward and the prey is secured by the fangs. All this takes a fraction of a second and the unfortunate fish has no chance to escape.

A newly emerged dragonfly nymph.
▼

A typical 'fairy ring' of horse mushrooms in a meadow.
▼

IT'S YOUR WORLD

How can we conserve our environment? Nowadays, most of us are aware of the need for conservation. We all depend upon thriving plant and animal communities for our food, peace of mind and our very existence. But how can this be achieved?

Endangered forests Tropical rain forests are often in the news because of their widespread destruction. They provide useful timber, but do not easily regenerate. If the timber was harvested in a less destructive manner, and regrowth of the forests permitted, then all our needs, and the survival of the trees, could be ensured. A more sensible approach might be to use timber from less sensitive habitats and in a more economic way – for instance, by recycling paper.

Rubbish Pollution is also a newsworthy subject. Most problems from litter to oil pollution could be solved with a little more thought and care and, of course, more money.

Wild garden Nearer home, there are things which we can all do. Hedges and fields are fast disappearing in many countries, being turned over to houses and agriculture. However, a small area set aside in our gardens – where things can grow naturally – will attract an amazing variety of wildlife.

◀ Industrial pollution in the form of acid rain has destroyed these trees in Germany's Black Forest.

An otherwise ungainly swimmer, the squid will sometimes move along – backwards or forwards – at great speed by means of jet propulsion. ▼

WATER-POWERED MOLLUSCS

Which animal moves by jet propulsion? Several animals can move by jet propulsion, and they are all molluscs belonging to the class Cephalopoda. This group of molluscs includes the octopuses, squid and cuttlefishes.

Cephalopods draw in water from the sea by means of slits in the body wall. The water is then drawn over the gills so that the animals can breathe. When the water is pumped violently out of the body by means of a tube called the siphon, it causes the animal to shoot along by jet propulsion. By altering the direction of the siphon, the animal can move in any direction it wishes. It uses this method particularly to escape from predators.

Inflation This is not the only method these animals have for escaping. Anyone who has tried to prise an octopus from a rocky crevice will know how hard this is. The animal inflates its body to wedge itself in, and can also grip the rock with its powerful suckered tentacles.

Camouflage Cephalopods can also change their body colour to match their surroundings, and so remain undetected. Also, they can squirt a dark inky substance into the water while they make their 'jet-propelled' escape.

GROWING DOWN

Why is the paradoxical frog a paradox? The paradoxical frog is an unusual species found in South America. Unlike most animals, the size of the young – in the case of this frog it's a tadpole – far exceeds that of the adult frog. A fully grown tadpole may reach a size of 25 cm (10 in), but it turns into a frog which is only 7.5 cm (3 in) long!

The answer to this puzzle lies in the process of development called metamorphosis – when much of the tadpole's tissues are used to form new tissues and organs in the frog – a remarkable but apparently rather wasteful process.

The coffee-bean caterpillar shows ▶ warning *and* disruptive colouring.

HOUSE HUSBAND

Is it always the female bird that incubates the egg? In some species of birds, the male deserts the female after mating and she is left to look after the eggs. A fairer system has developed in many small birds, where the male and female share responsibilities of parenthood.

However, a curious twist to this story has evolved in a group of birds called phalaropes. These are wading birds that spend most of their lives at sea. On breeding grounds in the high arctic, you would notice a striking difference in the plumage of the sexes. One is brightly coloured, the other dull. Contrary to expectation, it is the female which is the brighter sex. She has taken over the task of courting the male, and after laying the eggs, he is left entirely in charge – an extraordinary example of the reversal of the role of the sexes.

MATES AND TASTES

What are warning colours? Many animals are brightly coloured, especially in the breeding season. In birds, the colours are often used to advertize the presence of a male to a female, and so are used in courtship.

Many insects are also brightly coloured, but here the markings often serve to advertize the presence of the insect to potential predators rather than to potential mates. This may seem rather unusual, since animals normally try to avoid being seen. However, the answer lies in the animals' taste, for these are 'warning colours'. Ladybirds, for example, are easy to spot even to our eyes, but they have a most unpleasant taste. Once a bird has eaten one and discovered its revolting flavour, it will seldom peck at another animal with the same markings.

Some animals, such as the black and orange caterpillars of the cinnabar moth, are poisonous. They acquire the poisons by eating their foodplant, ragwort, and a snack of a few caterpillars can kill a bird.

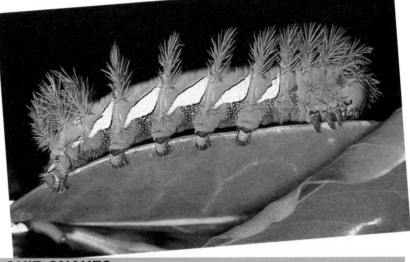

QUIZ: SNAKES

1. Name the most venomous snake in the world.
2. Can a snake blink?
3. Name the only venomous snake in the British Isles.
4. What is 'sloughing'?
5. What is the age of the oldest known snake: 30 years, 40 years, 50 years or 55 years?
6. Which is the shortest snake in the world?

ANSWERS
1. A seasnake of the genus *Hydrophis*. Its venom is 100 times more potent than any other snake's. 2. No. The eyelids form a fixed, transparent covering over the eye. 3. The adder. 4. Sloughing is the process by which the snake sheds its skin. 5. 40 years. 6. The thread snake, which is found on some islands in the West Indies. The longest measured was only 10.8 cm (4¼ in). A thread snake of this size can glide through a 3 mm hole – about the size of the hole in a pencil after the lead is removed.

BORING DIET

Which are the longest-lived insects? They are beetles called metallic wood-borers. Although they don't actually bore through metal, several cases are on record of adult beetles crawling out of woodwork 30 years old. This means they probably burrowed into the wood, as larvae, when the tree was still alive.

ANIMALS ONLY

Which snake eats plants? This is a trick question, as there is no living species of snake that eats plant material! All snakes are total carnivores, eating nothing but other animals. This is quite unusual, for among most groups of animals there are usually species which eat either meat or plant food, or sometimes both.

DIET OF KNOWLEDGE

Which animals learn by eating? This seems a strange question, but the explanation for the answer is just as strange.

Scientists have discovered that if they teach planarians (a kind of flatworm which lives in ditches) a simple trick – such as which way to swim up a maze in order to obtain a reward of food – this information can be passed on to other planarians in a remarkable way. Planarians that had not been taught the trick were fed on the chopped remains of planarians which *had* been taught the trick. These planarians now also swam the correct way up the maze!

LIGHT-FOOTED LIZARDS

What is a basilisk? Basilisks are lizards that can move about in a rather different way from other lizards. Most reptiles crawl about on all fours on short, stubby legs, with their bodies barely clear of the ground. But basilisks are slender, agile lizards that can run very fast on their back legs only.

Basilisk lizards in the jungle.
▼

INSECT TERRORIST

What is the world's most dangerous animal? Think of all the dangerous creatures you know, like sharks, snakes, tigers or even poisonous wasps or jellyfishes. None of them, however, ranks as 'public enemy number one'.

The most dangerous creature world-wide is, believe it or not, the common housefly. Through its habit of visiting animal waste and then transferring germs on to the food we eat, the housefly can transmit more diseases than any other animal, and is responsible for laying low more humans than all the other so-called dangerous animals put together.

A housefly feeding on sugar grains.

JUMPS FOR ITS LIFE

Which is the high-jumping champion of the animal world? The flea, a tiny wingless insect which lives as a parasite on vertebrate animals. In fact, there are several species of flea, all adapted to living on their particular host, although a few species aren't quite so fussy about who provides their meal of blood.

To survive, fleas must be able to jump on to a passing host, and so they have developed immensely powerful legs which enable them to leap effortlessly high into the air and land on their chosen victim. Fleas can jump 130 times higher than their own height. In human terms, this is the equivalent of a 1.8m (6ft) human leaping 237m (780ft) into the air!

COOL CAT

What cat likes to take a dip? Most domestic cats hate getting wet. If they get even their paws wet they usually stand and shake them until dry. However, one type of domestic cat, the van cat from Turkey, actually *likes* swimming and can often be seen paddling about in water.

The tiger is also fond of a dip, and many zoos now recognize this and provide a special pool in which the tigers can swim whenever they wish.

Unlike most cats, the tiger actually enjoys a swim.

FACT FILE: SLUGS AND SNAILS

FACT Slugs and snails belong to a group of animals called molluscs. This group also contains sea slugs, squids and octopuses.

FACT The largest terrestrial snail is the giant land snail of Africa, whose shell may reach a length of 15 cm (6 in) or more. Its body is so large that it cannot be withdrawn fully into the shell.

FACT Most slugs and snails breathe using a lung which opens through a small hole in the side of their bodies.

FACT Slugs and snails have a heart, a simple blood system and blood similar to our own. This helps transport oxygen around their bodies, although the pigment in their blood is slightly different from ours.

FACT The bodies of slugs and snails are covered in mucus. This prevents water loss from their bodies, and also helps them move along. It does this by providing a miniature pool of liquid through which the mollusc glides by the action of beating hairs on the soles of their feet, and also by muscular action of the foot.

FACT Most slugs and snails are hermaphrodites for at least part of their life. This means that they possess both male and female organs. Eggs are produced after cross-fertilization.

FACT Europe's largest slug is the ashy-grey slug, which may reach a size of 30 cm (12 in) when fully stretched out. If disturbed, it will contract into a ball 10 cm (4 in) in diameter.

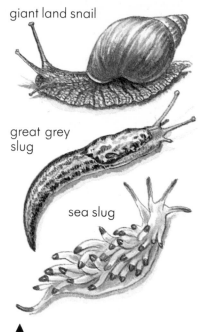

giant land snail

great grey slug

sea slug

▲ **Three contrasting members of the mollusc family.**

DAYLIGHT SAVING

Which bird migrates the longest distance? The arctic tern, a graceful seabird which nests in northerly latitudes, and often inside the arctic circle. It is a fish-eater and like many related species, moves south once the breeding season has finished.

However, the arctic tern is exceptional since it continues flying until it reaches the antarctic circle. This means that each year the birds are involved in a round trip of over 32,000 km (20,000 miles). Consequently, arctic terns probably see far more daylight than any other living creature. During their summer in the arctic, the sun never sets, and during the winter in the northern hemisphere it is summer in the antarctic – so they enjoy a sun-filled summer there, too.

DECAY AND GROWTH

Are all bacteria harmful? When we think of bacteria, the most popular image is of the diseases and infection that they cause. However, the vast majority of bacteria are beneficial to us. If it were not for bacterial decay, then the nutrients from decaying plants and animals would not be recycled into the soil in, for example, the form of compost.

Taste makers Bacteria are also responsible for many of the textures and flavours in our food. They are particularly important in milk products and are used in yoghurt- and cheese-making.

Mutual benefit If you uproot a bean plant you will discover a more surprising example of bacterial action. The roots of beans and many other plants in the pea family are covered in small nodules. These nodules contain colonies of special bacteria without which the plant would not grow properly. The bacteria have the ability to trap nitrogen from the surrounding soil, which is then used by the plant in growth. In return, the plant provides the bacteria with the nutrients that it requires, so both parties benefit.

Section through a nitrogen-trapping nodule

tissue containing bacteria

cortex

vascular cylinder

nodules

These nitrogen-trapping nodes ▶ help the bean plant to thrive.

▲
A colourful array of wild
woodland flowers.

USEFUL BEAUTY

Why are flowers so colourful?
When we see a beautiful, flower-
filled meadow, we may imagine
that the colours are there for our
benefit. There is a much more
practical reason for the brightly
coloured petals on display. They
are there to attract insects, which
in turn feed on nectar provided
by the plant.

In the process of feeding,
many insects, and in particular
bees, pick up pollen from the
flower. This is then carried by the
insect to the next flower, and
enables cross-fertilization of the
plants to occur. Some flowers
have special markings, called
pollen guides, often visible only
to the insect's eyes, which ensure
that the insects collect pollen as
well as nectar.

ROLL ON

How does the guillemot look after its eggs? Most people imagine
birds' nests as neatly formed structures made of twigs and feathers. This
is usually so, but some birds have developed methods for looking after
their eggs without the need for nests.

A striking example of this can be seen on cliffs round the British coast.
During the summer months, every available ledge and crevice is
occupied by breeding seabirds, and guillemots are commonly found
on the most precipitous of ledges.

No nest Guillemots lay only one egg a year and, instead of using a
nest, they place the egg between their large, webbed feet and sit on it.
This provides protection for the egg while the bird is present, but what
stops it rolling off the ledge when it is away feeding? The answer lies in
the shape of the egg. Its conical shape means that if it rolls, the egg
moves in a circle, so reducing its chances of falling off.

The one disadvantage to the guillemot's technique of incubation can
be seen if the birds are suddenly disturbed. If they take to the wing while
the egg is tucked between their feet, then it plunges into the sea.

These guillemots seem unaware ▶
how precariously their nests
are positioned.

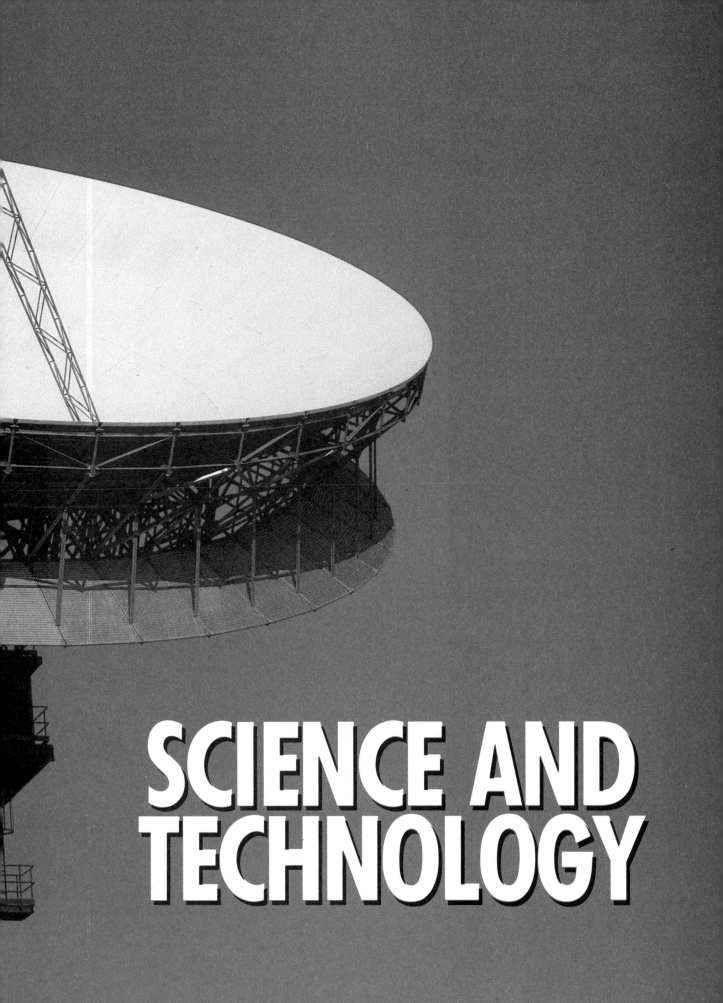

SCIENCE AND TECHNOLOGY

▲
A solar-powered glider.

SPACE PIONEER

Who was the first astronaut?
The first astronaut was Yuri
Gagarin, a Russian airman. He
made one orbit of the Earth
aboard the Vostok spacecraft on
12 April 1961. The whole
spaceflight lasted 89 minutes. (In
fact, Gagarin was really a
cosmonaut, which is what
Russians call people who fly in
space.)

▲
Pioneer cosmonaut Yuri Gagarin
before his first spaceflight.

FREE POWER!

How can we tap the Sun's power? The Sun shines constantly, bathing
the Earth in its heat and light. We can tap this power and put it to use.
Solar cells on spacecraft turn sunlight into electricity, and in hot regions
on Earth there are solar power stations that harness the heat of the Sun
to generate electricity. Solar panels in the roofs of houses can also
capture the Sun's heat rays to warm water.

Imitation The Sun produces heat by a process called nuclear fusion,
which scientists are trying to reproduce in experimental fusion reactors.
For fuel, it uses hydrogen, which occurs in vast quantities in water. If
nuclear fusion becomes a reality, it could give us unlimited power.

SCIENTIFIC UGLY DUCKLING

**Who was asked to leave school but went on to make one of the
greatest discoveries in science?** Albert Einstein, who was born in
Germany in 1879 and died in the United States in 1955, is revered as
one of the greatest scientists to have lived. Yet at school, he was so poor
at most of his studies that his teacher asked him to leave, saying that he
would never amount to anything.

Original thinker However, Einstein was good at one subject –
mathematics – and he soon became a government official. He began
to work out new theories in physics in his spare time, and in 1905
astounded the world with his special theory of relativity. This was
followed ten years later by the general theory of relativity. The two
theories revolutionized physics by presenting new ways of understanding such fundamental aspects as mass, energy, gravity and time.

Einstein's theories were later proved to be correct by scientific
observations and experiments, and they have led to many modern
developments in science, including nuclear power and much of our
understanding of black holes. It's clear that the so-called backward
schoolboy was, in fact, a genius.

NO HIDING PLACE

Which machines can see right through you? The one machine from which you can't keep any secrets is a scanner, a device that can see inside something and show what is there. For example, scanners are important in airport security for inspecting passengers' baggage. But their most important use is in medicine.

Safe screening Medical scanners are able to produce pictures of the interior of the body and show up anything that might be wrong. X-ray machines can do this to a limited extent, but large doses of X-rays are harmful. Scanners give better pictures and are safe.

Ultrasound scanners can produce pictures of an unborn baby inside its mother's womb and show that it is growing normally. Brain scanners can give pictures of the inside of the brain, showing any abnormality that may have to be removed. Whole-body scanners can look right into the interior of the body to find the cause of an illness.

Many scanners work by firing harmless rays into the body and picking up the rays that emerge. With others the patient first has to take a substance that produces the rays inside the body.

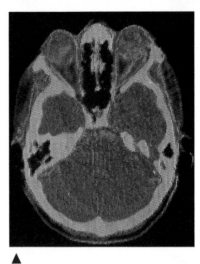

▲
Brainscans enable doctors safely to 'see' inside a patient's skull.

SIMPLE BEGINNING

Which form of transport was invented with a tin can? The hovercraft began life as a tin can! Its inventor, the British engineer Christopher Cockerell, had the idea in 1954 of a new form of transport that would rest on a cushion of air. To test it, he rigged up a vacuum cleaner to blow air into two empty tin cans, and used his kitchen scales to measure the force of air that emerged. From this simple beginning, he then developed the hovercraft.

▲
Moving over the water enables hovercraft to travel faster than ships.

FINANCIAL FLOP

Why did nobody want the first calculating machine? Blaise Pascal, the French scientist, invented the calculating machine in 1642 when he was only 19 years old. It could add or subtract numbers automatically using cog wheels. However, although it worked well, it was not a financial success.

At that time, employers used poorly paid clerks to do their calculations. Pascal's machine was expensive, and it would have put many clerks out of a job, so nobody wanted it.

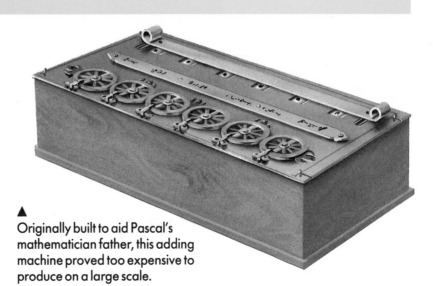

▲
Originally built to aid Pascal's mathematician father, this adding machine proved too expensive to produce on a large scale.

▲ Microwave communications apparatus.

▲ Microwave ovens have reduced cooking time for all kinds of food.

MICROWAVES IN ACTION

What do microwaves do?

Many people use microwaves in their homes. They are the kinds of rays that heat food in microwave ovens. Microwaves are also important in communications. They are used like radio waves to carry signals from one place to another. No need to worry, though – these microwaves don't roast birds or burn aircraft that fly through them.

Laser beam cutting through metal. ▶

SOLAR POWER

Did you know that we get almost all our energy from the Sun? The Sun sends us heat and light rays that keep us alive. However, we get extra energy by burning coal, oil and other fuels to drive power stations, and from falling water in hydroelectric power stations.

Nevertheless, most of this extra energy also comes from the Sun. Fuels such as coal, oil and wood are all made from living things, coal and oil being the remains of plants and animals that lived millions of years ago. All living things depend on the Sun, so these fuels are really stores of the Sun's energy.

The water in a dam or river feeding a hydroelectric station falls as rain on hills above. It gets there by rising through the air as water vapour from the land or sea below. To do this, the water needs warmth and this heat comes from – you've guessed it – the Sun. So the water also stores the Sun's energy.

One important source of energy does not originate in the Sun. This is nuclear energy, which is produced from nuclear fuels present in the Earth's crust.

GETTING IT TOGETHER

Why does a laser beam 'pack such a punch'? Laser light is incredibly powerful. A laser beam can burn a hole in steel plate. This is because laser light is basically different from normal light.

Light rays consist of waves of energy. Normally the waves overlap each other as the rays travel through the air. They tend to cancel each other out, so that the amount of energy in the rays is low. But in a laser beam, the waves of light energy are all in step. The waves arrive together, and the amount of energy in the light 'packs the punch'.

SEE AND KNOW

Which simple invention has improved the lives of millions of people? One invention that almost all of us will need sooner or later is a pair of spectacles or contact lenses. With them, failing eyesight is corrected, so that the wearer can see to read again or make out distant objects.

Before spectacles became common, millions of people were condemned to misery through their inability to see properly. Glasses with convex lenses that correct long sight came into use in the 1200s, and short sight was relieved with the invention of concave lenses in the 1400s.

FACT FILE: SCIENTIFIC UNITS

FACT There are only seven basic scientific units – those that measure length, mass, time, electric current, temperature, light and amount of substance. All other units are combinations of some of these basic units.
FACT Most scientific units are named after famous scientists. There's even a unit called a henry. It's an electrical unit named after the American physicist, Joseph Henry.
FACT Weight is often measured in kilograms, but it is actually correct to use newtons. One newton is the weight of a mass of 102 grams (3.6 ounces) – about the weight of an apple.
FACT In temperatures, °C correctly stands for degrees Celsius, not degrees Centigrade.
FACT The smallest unit of length is the attometre. There are a million million million attometres in a metre.

A CENTURY TOO SOON

Who first thought of computers? The idea of the computer first occurred to the British inventor Charles Babbage in about 1833. Others had made calculating machines before him. But Babbage was the first person to conceive of a machine that could be programmed to carry out different calculating operations, as a computer can.

Babbage designed a machine called the Analytical Engine that had the basic features of a modern computer. It was to be a mechanical computer, containing complex systems of shafts and gear wheels. However, only parts of the Analytical Engine were ever built. The engineering required to complete it was far beyond the techniques of the age, and Babbage died in 1871 without knowing whether his computer would work or not.

Later developments In fact, Babbage was far ahead of his time; the first computer – a British wartime decoder called Colossus – was not built until 1943. Like modern computers, it used electronics, as mechanical operations were too slow. Colossus and all other computers since are really the descendants of Babbage's Analytical Engine.

▲ ▶ Calculators old and new: a home computer (right) and Babbage's analytical engine (above).

ALL NUMBERS

Who believed that everything works by numbers? One of the earliest great scientists, Pythagoras, who lived in ancient Greece in the 500s BC. He was convinced that the entire universe is governed by numbers.

This theory is illustrated by a famous discovery made by Pythagoras. He found that musical notes which are in harmony are given by pipes or strings whose lengths are in simple numerical proportions, such as 3:2 or 4:3. This gave rise to the belief that simple mathematical relationships underlie everything and can explain everything. This idea is fundamental to science, even though the mathematics involved may often be complex.

▲
Greek philosopher Pythagoras lecturing to his students.

▲
Fibre optic cable like this is used in telecommunications.

FORCED LABOUR

What does 'robot' mean? The word 'robot' was coined by the Czech playwright, Karel Čapek, in a play called *R.U.R.*, which stood for Rossum's Universal Robots. In the play, people have mechanical servants which look like people and do manual work for them. Čapek called these machines robots from the Czech word *robota*, which means labour.

ON AUTOMATIC

What were the first robots? If we define a robot as a machine that works like a human being, then the first robots were automata: remarkable moving dolls that could copy human actions, sometimes with amazing facility. For example, one could write a whole sentence using a pen and ink.

Automata were made in the 1700s. They worked by clockwork and contained very complex systems of gears. They were made purely to astound and entertain people and could not do physical tasks like modern robots. These developed as machines became more and more automatic. However, only with the development of computers over the last 40 years have robots been able to perform complex tasks.

ON-OFF

What has the latest advance in communications in common with Morse code? The latest method of communications is fibre optics. Light signals are flashed by lasers along cables containing thin glass threads. The system gives communications of very high quality and in great quantity. Yet it is basically the same as the communications system developed by the American inventor Samuel Morse in the 1830s!

Morse invented a code in which letters, numbers and punctuation are changed into short and long signals called dots and dashes. The code was used for sending messages, either as electric signals along telegraph wires, or as light signals produced by flashing lamps. Today's fibre optics is like a combination of these two methods. Also, a code is used in which the light signals are sequences of on-off flashes, rather like Morse code. The signals are incredibly fast – up to 2,000 million on-off flashes in a second!

SPACE GAZERS

Why put a telescope into space? Many of the satellites in space carry telescopes and other instruments used in astronomy. They look at the stars and other heavenly bodies, sending pictures and information about them back to Earth by television and radio.

Astronomers like to use satellites in this way because the Earth's atmosphere blocks out some of the rays that come from stars and other bodies and also makes the images of stars seen in big telescopes rather indistinct. Space-based astronomy captures all the rays and gives sharp, clear pictures of everything to be seen out there.

MELT AND SKIM

Why do ice skates have such thin blades? The thin blades of ice skates help the skater to skim over the ice. As the skate moves on the ice, the whole weight of the skater presses down on the blade. This exerts a very high pressure on the ice and, as a result, the surface layer instantly melts. Friction with the ice may also serve to melt it.

The layer of water that is formed makes the ice slippery, enabling the skater to travel over the surface very quickly. The water freezes again as soon as the skater has passed.

◀ The Gamma Ray Observatory will enable scientists to investigate the electromagnetic spectrum in detail.

High fibre foods such as these are becoming increasingly popular with health-conscious consumers.
▼

ROUGH BUT RIGHT

Would eating roughage make you feel uncomfortable? No. You'd feel very uncomfortable without it, for it is an important part of a healthy diet. Roughage, also called fibre, is believed to speed the movement of food through the digestive system, so that bacteria may not, perhaps, have time to convert chemicals into compounds that might produce cancer. Fibre also seems to help the body to extract energy from food more efficiently. Fibre is present particularly in 'wholefoods' and vegetables.

▲
A typical computer chess game.

BREAK IT UP

***Why should marching soldiers
break step on bridges?*** A long
line of soldiers marching in step
across a bridge will set up a
vibration in the bridge. This
vibration could possibly build up
until it becomes strong enough
to damage the bridge. So,
soldiers may be ordered to
break step on bridges.

RIGHT TIME

***How accurate can we make
clocks?*** The best clocks in the
world are atomic clocks used by
scientists. They measure time so
accurately that, if they were to
work for a million years, they
would be less than a second out,
after all that time!

ARTIFICIAL INTELLIGENCE

Are computers intelligent? The answer depends on what you mean by
intelligent. It was once thought that any machine which could play
chess would be considered to be intelligent. Now chess-playing
computers are common, and they can play at a very high standard.
Even so, not everyone agrees that computers are intelligent. It's
arguable that the intelligence in the computer is only put there by the
programmer instructing the computer to play chess or perform any
other task.

Definitions If we define intelligence as the ability to remember things
and follow rules, then the computer is certainly intelligent. Many people
pride themselves on their good memory and their efficiency in
performing tasks, and they would be considered intelligent. But there's
more to people than being able to work well. If we define intelligence as
the ability also to be creative, then computers fail the intelligence test,
for they can only follow instructions and not produce new ideas or new
solutions to problems.

Artificial intelligence Computer engineers are, however, working
hard to produce artificial intelligence. This would be possessed by
advanced computers able to look at problems from different
viewpoints and to learn from their experience, as we do. They would be
able to understand human speech and talk in everyday language.
These computers could possess more knowledge about a subject than
any human being, and this could be used to help us make decisions.
    Such an ability certainly seems like intelligence, but so did playing
chess. Whether computers will ever be considered intelligent or not,
they are certainly making us explore the nature of intelligence.

rigid plastic or metal casing

flexible plastic tube

ink reservoir

rotating metal ball

ink flow

Section through a ball-point pen

▲

Lasalo Biro's invention is now a familiar part of everyday life.

BIONIC MAN?

Can machines take over from human transplants? If part of our bodies goes wrong, it is possible that a machine may be able to keep us alive. Kidney machines, for example, are used to help patients with kidney disease. Every few days, the patient's blood is passed through the machine, which purifies it and returns the clean blood to the body. Without this machine, the patient's only hope of life is a kidney transplant.

It is possible that artificial organs such as a mechanical heart may soon be developed. Unfortunately, it is difficult to make these organs small enough to fit inside the body.

QUIZ: FAMOUS INVENTIONS

1 What did Alessandro Volta invent in 1800?
2 Where and when was the telescope invented?
3 Which invention was first used to fasten boots and shoes?
4 When were stereo records first released?
5 What did Lasalo Biro invent in 1938?
6 Which invention did Mark Twain become the first famous author to use?
7 Who invented pneumatic (inflatable) tyres?
8 Where and when did the first colour television service begin?
9 Which invention was made by Joseph Swan and also by Thomas Edison?
10 What was invented solely for the use of King Louis XV of France?

ANSWERS
1 The electric battery. 2 Holland, 1608. 3 The zip fastener.
4 1958. 5 The ball-point pen. 6 The typewriter. 7 John Boyd Dunlop. 8 The United States, 1951. 9 The electric light bulb. 10 The lift or elevator.

SERVICE AT SEA

What form of transport is so big that 400 people could play tennis on it at the same time? Oil tankers, the biggest ships, are so large that their decks could accommodate a hundred tennis courts each with four players. They can exceed 450 m (1,500 ft) in length.

The contrasting sizes of this supertanker and 16th-century galleon show how shipbuilding has developed over the years.
▼

▲
The Maglev train will improve rail transport in many countries.

FLOATING TRAINS

Did you know that some trains run without wheels? The new *maglev* trains being developed in some countries have no wheels. Maglev is short for magnetic levitation, which means that the trains float just above a special track, suspended by strong magnetic forces. The trains are propelled along the track by a linear induction motor, which is a kind of magnetic motor powered by electricity. Permanent magnets and electromagnets in the track and on the train raise and propel it.

Speed and economy Maglev systems are under development in Britain, West Germany and Japan. When fully developed, streamlined maglev trains will be able to provide very fast (and silent) services reaching speeds of 500 km/h (300 mph). Because there are no wheels, train and track maintenance is minimal, and energy costs are also low – about a quarter of aircraft costs per passenger. Maglev services are likely to be cheaper than aircraft, and also quicker for intercity journeys of up to about 1,000 km (600 miles).

COMPACT PACKAGE

What's the best sound on record? The best sound you can get in your home is not from records or even tapes, but from compact discs. These small silvery discs are only 11 cm (4½ in) across, but may contain more than an hour's music on just one side. They need a special player which contains a laser and computer, and give superb sound without any background hiss or crackles.

The reason that compact discs are so good is that the sound is digital. This means that it is recorded on the disc in the form of computer codes which reproduce the recorded sound very accurately.

▲
Compact discs are easy to handle and provide excellent sound quality.

LIGHT FANTASTIC

How did the laser get its name? Invented by American physicist Theodore Maiman in 1960, laser works by a process called 'light amplification by stimulated emission of radiation'. The amazing new device got the name laser from the initial letters of this process.

A FRUITY NATION

Why are the British sometimes known as 'limeys'? In Australian and American slang, British sailors used to be called 'limeys' because of the practice of issuing lime juice on British ships to try and prevent a disease called scurvy. Scurvy is caused by insufficient vitamin C, or ascorbic acid, in the diet, and it was very common among sailors, causing many to die. When its cause was understood in 1795 it became the practice in the British Navy to issue fresh lime juice, which contains ascorbic acid, to the men. The nickname 'limey' came to apply to the British generally.

OUT OF THE BLUE?

Where does television come from? Wherever you live, television pictures come to you from broadcasting stations located in various cities around the country. But they may get to you in several different ways.

Many programmes are transmitted from a local television mast. They go to the mast from the broadcasting stations along cables or via radio links. Then from the mast, the programmes come to the home as radio signals that are picked up by the aerial connected to the television set.

Homes that have cable television get their programmes from a local television station through a cable connected to the set. It is also possible to receive television programmes broadcast from special satellites in space.

POWERFUL NAME

What's measured in watts? Power is measured in watts. This can mean either the power that something produces as it works, or the power that is needed to drive something.

A watt is not a very big unit of power. As you read this, your body is using about 100 watts of power – about the same as a light bulb. Powerful machines are therefore graded in kilowatts (kW) or megawatts (MW). A kilowatt is 1,000 watts and a megawatt 1,000,000 watts.

The watt is named after James Watt, the British engineer who developed the steam engine in the 1760s.

Thousands of watts of electricity ▶
are used to power illuminated
displays such as these.

EUREKA!

Who made a famous discovery in his bath? Archimedes, the renowned Greek scientist who lived from about 287 to about 212 BC, was asked to find out whether the king's crown was made of pure gold or of gold mixed with a less valuable metal. The story goes that one day, preoccupied with his seemingly impossible task, he filled his bath too full and the water overflowed as he got in. Immediately, Archimedes realized the solution and rushed naked into the street shouting 'Eureka', which is Greek for 'I've got it'. We still use this Greek word to signify an astounding discovery.

Comparative densities What Archimedes realized was that he could test the quality of the crown by immersing it in water. He measured how much water the crown displaced, and then checked to see if a piece of gold having the same weight as the crown displaced the same amount of water. If so, the crown would be pure gold. In fact, the king's crown displaced more water, proving that it was adulterated with a less dense metal. What ended in triumph for Archimedes ended in tragedy for the goldsmith, who was executed.

SHOCKING TIME

Who risked being struck by lightning to make a great discovery? Benjamin Franklin, the famous American scientist and statesman, must be the bravest scientist to have lived. In 1752, to prove that lightning is electricity, he flew a kite up into the clouds of a thunderstorm. The string of the kite was connected to an electricity detector, which showed that electricity was flowing down the string towards the ground.

Franklin's dangerous experiment saved many lives, for he went on to invent the lightning conductor.

AT RISK?

Should we all have constant health checks? Some people need constant health checks. Diabetics, for example, have to make sure that the level of sugar in their blood stays just right. They tend to do this by experience, but new devices called biosensors can check their blood automatically and make life much easier.

Health checks can also help to prevent disease. In future, biosensors may be used to make frequent checks on people's health and warn them of any illness that might be developing, or to identify diseases from which they might be at risk.

▲
Franklin's experimentation proved that lightning is an electrical force.

OLD OR YOUNG?

Does all wine get better as it grows older? Not necessarily. Although many types of wine, particularly red ones, improve with age, there are some which do not keep so well, and may become unpleasant if kept for too long. Also, it has become fashionable recently to drink some wines when they are 'new' – this means that the wine has been made from grapes harvested in the same year. In the wine-making industry, experiments continue to speed up artificially the ageing process in fine wines.

FACT FILE: PIONEERS OF MEDICINE

FACT Vaccination was discovered by the British doctor, Edward Jenner in 1796. He injected people with cowpox germs to stop them getting smallpox.

FACT The first anaesthetic was laughing gas. It was discovered by the British chemist, Humphry Davy in 1799, and it is still used in dentistry.

FACT The Hungarian doctor, Ignaz Semmelweiss showed in 1847 that uncleanliness spreads diseases. However this important discovery was not believed until 1867, when the British surgeon, Joseph Lister began to use antiseptics to prevent infection.

FACT The need for vitamins in our diet was discovered by the Dutch doctor, Christiaan Eijkman in 1896.

FACT The first antibiotic drug, penicillin, was discovered by accident. The British scientist, Alexander Fleming found it in a fungal mould in 1928.

ROUND THE BEND

How can we see round corners? We can see round corners with a mirror or a periscope, which uses mirrors, but neither are very convenient to handle. With an optical instrument called an endoscope, we can look around and into virtually anything, even ourselves.

The endoscope is basically a flexible tube containing two bundles of thin glass fibres and a lens at each end. Doctors insert an endoscope into the body so that they can actually see what is wrong with their patients. Light is shone into one end and passes down one bundle of fibres to the other end. There it illuminates a part of the body. The light rays then travel back up the second bundle of fibres, forming an image of the interior in an eyepiece at the top end of the endoscope.

This use of glass fibres to carry light rays is called fibre optics.

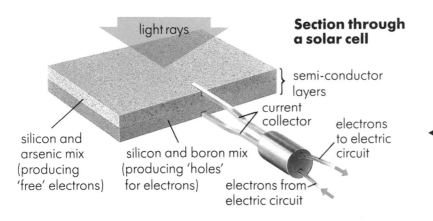

light rays

Section through a solar cell

semi-conductor layers

current collector

electrons to electric circuit

silicon and arsenic mix (producing 'free' electrons)

silicon and boron mix (producing 'holes' for electrons)

electrons from electric circuit

PORTABLE POWER

Where do spacecraft get their power? Spacecraft cannot carry large supplies of fuel and there aren't any filling stations in space. Instead, many have large panels of solar cells. These capture sunlight and turn it into electricity. The Sun always shines in space, so there is always electricity to power the spacecraft.

Some space probes travel to the outer planets far from the Sun. There the sunlight is too weak for solar cells, and the probes have small nuclear power plants instead. These plants produce electricity from a small amount of a long-lasting nuclear fuel such as plutonium.

◀ In a solar cell, a voltage is created as light causes electrons to move from the top to the bottom layer of semi-conductor crystals. Dozens of cells have to be joined to produce a worthwhile output.

FROG OR FISH?

Which invention has enabled people to swim freely underwater? With a little training, we can all swim underwater as freely as a fish. All we need is an aqualung, which consists of portable breathing equipment carried by the diver. The aqualung supplies air naturally as the diver breathes in and out. Wearing froglike fins, aqualung divers can swim quickly with little effort.

Before the aqualung was developed, divers had to wear bulky suits – which restricted movement – tethered by cables to boats on the surface. Jacques Cousteau, the famous French diver, invented the aqualung during World War II while fighting with the French resistance.

▲
The aqualung gives divers great freedom in underwater exploration.

RESTORATION JOB

Where is London Bridge not in London? The answer is Arizona in the United States. In 1971, the famous old London Bridge across the River Thames in London, England, was replaced by a wider bridge. But instead of being demolished, the blocks of stone were carefully dismantled and shipped to Arizona. There, at Lake Havasu, London Bridge was rebuilt.

▲ Two weightless space shuttle crew members in orbit around the Earth.

LIGHTER THAN A FEATHER

Did you know that space travel makes you lose weight – yet grow? During a space mission all the astronauts become effectively 'weightless'. As a result, instead of standing firmly on the floor of the spacecraft, they float about in mid-air.

Weightlessness happens because the orbit or path of a spacecraft through space is totally controlled by a field of gravity, usually that of the Earth. The spacecraft and the astronauts inside are both moved by gravity. They are not pulled to the floor of the spacecraft because it is moving in just the same way as they are moving.

Because the astronauts are weightless, the muscles in their bodies act to stretch them slightly so that they grow in height a little. However, they shrink to normal height very soon after returning to Earth.

PRIMARY PICTURES

How many colours does a colour television produce? No matter how brilliant and colourful the picture on a colour television set, it consists of only three colours – red, green and blue. The picture on the screen is actually made up of tiny strips or dots of these colours. When you see the screen from normal viewing distance, the strips or dots merge together to form a full-colour picture.

The reason is that all possible colours can be made by mixing three primary colours together in various proportions. In colour television, and also in colour photography, the three primary colours are red, green and blue.

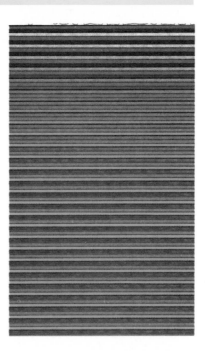

SYNTHETIC SOURCES

Where do plastics come from? Strange as it may seem, many familiar things like telephones and carpets may be made from coal and oil! Many household objects are not made from natural materials such as wood and wool, but from plastics or from artificial fibres, which are kinds of plastics. These are synthetic or artificial products that are formed from chemicals – mostly made from coal and oil – in factories.

◄ An enlarged view of the vertical 'sandwich' of coloured lines which create the picture on a television screen.

NOTHING MATTERS

Where is nothing important? Nothing is vital in arithmetic or in any branch of mathematics that involves numbers. By this, we mean 0 – the symbol of the numeral zero. Without it, we would not be able to make calculations – not even simple ones that we can do in our heads.

Ancient origins The number systems used in ancient times, such as Roman numerals, did not have a symbol for zero. It didn't seem necessary. But this made calculating almost impossible: imagine trying to multiply VII by XL and eventually – you hope – getting CCLXXX. We can do this instantly – it's simply 7 times 40.

The reason is that we use a place value system with a symbol for zero. Invented in India about 2,000 years ago it's a decimal system, having ten numerals – 1 to 9 and 0 (or Ø in computers). In any number, the position of each digit or numeral from the right shows how many ones, tens, hundreds, thousands and so on there are in the number, and a symbol for zero is essential.

Computer calculations Computers use a place value system too, though not the decimal system. They do calculations using a binary system, which has two numerals – 0 (or Ø) and 1. Computer programmers may also use the hexadecimal system, which has 16 numerals – Ø to 9 and A to F. The reason for this is that a binary number having four digits (or bits in computer jargon) can be represented by a single digit in hexadecimal, which greatly simplifies the computer programmer's task.

The radiation warning symbol.

HEALING RAYS

When is radiation good for you? Radiation consists of the rays that come from nuclear products and processes. Normally, it is harmful because the rays can kill the living cells in the body.

In some cases, however, controlled radiation is used for treating cancer. This is a disease in which cells go 'out of order' and grow abnormally. The radiation is able to destroy these abnormal cells.

STEAM TRAIN

Who saw immense power in a kettle of water? The story goes that when James Watt was a child, he noticed that the steam in a boiling kettle repeatedly lifted the lid. Perhaps it was this memory that inspired him to improve the steam engine in the 1760s, making it a really effective source of power. Certainly, it was the work of this great British engineer that made the industrial revolution and modern technology possible.

An early drawing of 'Old Bess', ▶ James Watt's prototype steam engine.

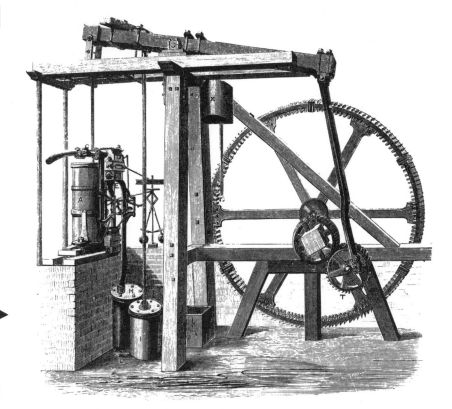

UP AND AWAY

Why do balloons fly? Balloons rise into the air because they contain a gas that is less dense or lighter than air. They actually float in the same way that a piece of wood floats on water.

Many balloons contain the light gas helium. Hot-air balloons contain air heated by a gas burner. They fly because hot air is less dense than cool air.

Hot-air balloons descend by allowing the air in the balloon to cool. Airships, which contain helium, admit air to the balloon to descend.

◀ Hot air balloons competing in a race make a colourful and spectacular sight.

ROBOT SURGEONS?

Could robots ever perform surgical operations? It is possible that robots may begin to perform some surgical operations on people. The robot would be directed with great precision by a computer working from pictures of the inside of the patient's body taken with scanners. The computer would be controlled by human surgeons, who would check the progress of the operation on video screens.

Robot surgery could use laser beams instead of knives. The beam would be projected by the robot down a tube into the patient's body to remove or destroy diseased tissues. This kind of surgery would cause patients less distress than conventional operations.

A PRECIOUS GIFT

How much blood can you give to others? A blood donor can give about half a litre of blood. The blood is kept for blood transfusions to help save people's lives. The body then makes more blood, but the donor should not give blood again for at least two months.

The life-saving process of giving blood is simple and relatively painless. ▶

QUIZ: GENERAL SCIENCE

1 Which is the odd one out: salt, oxygen, gold, mercury?
2 What's measured in volts and amps?
3 Why does ice float on water?
4 What's the common name for iron oxide?
5 How many millimetres are there in a metre?
6 Electricity flows from positive to negative in a circuit – true or false?
7 Where would you find a nucleus?
8 What's the next number – 1 . . 2 . . 3 . . 5 . . 7 . . ?
9 Infrared, ultraviolet, X and gamma – what are they?

ANSWERS
1 Salt – it's a chemical compound and the others are all chemical elements. 2 Electricity. 3 Because water expands and becomes less dense when it freezes. 4 Rust. 5 1,000. 6 False; it goes from negative to positive. 7 Inside an atom or a living cell. 8 11 (they are all prime numbers – numbers that can be divided only by themselves and 1). 9 Kinds of invisible rays.

BALL GAMES

Which kind of ball – rubber or steel – will bounce higher? If the balls are the same size, and are thrown with equal force on a pavement, then the steel ball will bounce higher.

What determines the bounce of a ball is the speed with which it returns to its shape after it has been compressed on impact. This return to shape is what forces the ball up into the air. Rubber compresses very easily, but it is fairly slow in returning to shape. Steel compresses quickly, and returns to its shape very rapidly.

NO RESISTANCE

What's super about superconductivity? Superconductivity is a complete lack of electrical resistance. This means that a wire of superconducting metal can carry an electric current without losing energy – which in turn means that it can carry a strong current and not overheat. This strong current can generate a powerful magnetic field, so superconducting metals are capable of producing very strong magnetic forces without consuming much electric current.

This quality would make superconductivity very useful in technology, for example, in powering magnetic trains. However, there's a problem. Metals become superconducting only at very low temperatures close to absolute zero (−273°C or −460°F). Because keeping them at such an intensely cold temperature is tricky, superconductivity so far has been used mainly in laboratories.

ON THE LINE

What are the uses of the telephone? Most of us find telephones extremely useful for talking to others, but the telephone has several other uses. The telephone network sends voices around the world in the form of electric signals. It can also send other kinds of electric signals that are not voice signals – for example, computer signals.

Computer networks are groups of computers connected together by telephone lines. They link computers in business, but you can link your home computer into networks to get information and computer programs of all kinds, and to send messages to other computer users. It's also possible to send pictures over the telephone with special machines that convert the pictures into easily transmitted electric signals.

levitation magnets   guideway

▲
Trains of the future may use superconducting magnets for levitation, guidance and propulsion.

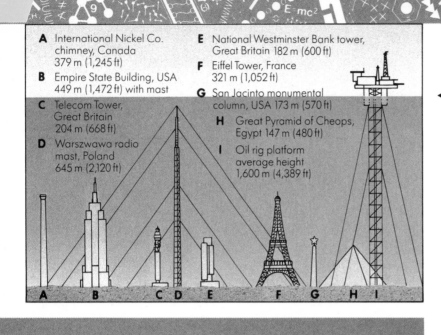

A International Nickel Co. chimney, Canada 379 m (1,245 ft)

B Empire State Building, USA 449 m (1,472 ft) with mast

C Telecom Tower, Great Britain 204 m (668 ft)

D Warszwawa radio mast, Poland 645 m (2,120 ft)

E National Westminster Bank tower, Great Britain 182 m (600 ft)

F Eiffel Tower, France 321 m (1,052 ft)

G San Jacinto monumental column, USA 173 m (570 ft)

H Great Pyramid of Cheops, Egypt 147 m (480 ft)

I Oil rig platform average height 1,600 m (4,389 ft)

◀ Drawn to scale, the size of a modern oil rig can be fully appreciated when it is compared with other massive structures from around the world.

OUT OF SIGHT

Which is the most massive steel structure? Many people would vote for the Eiffel Tower in Paris, which tops 300 metres (325 yds) in height. Then there are the towering television masts, some of which are higher than the Eiffel Tower.

But to find the answer you have to go to sea, for oil rigs are more massive than any steel structure on land. Some of them may contain five times as much steel as the Eiffel Tower, and match it in height, even though most of it is hidden – underwater.

SEEING'S NOT BELIEVING

How does a mirage trick the eye? A mirage is a kind of optical illusion that occurs in hot, still weather. A pool of water suddenly appears in the distance. But on approaching, it seems to evaporate and there's actually no water at all. You may see these mirages on roads in summer. They also occur in deserts, sometimes complete with trees, and may trick a thirsty traveller into thinking that an oasis lies ahead.

What you really see is simply a reflection, usually of the sky. The reason is that a layer of hot air near the ground acts like a mirror.

The expanse of water in this desert is, in fact, a mirage.
▼

RANGE OF RAYS

Who predicted that radio and other waves and rays exist? Radio and radar waves, microwaves, infrared rays, light rays, ultraviolet rays, X-rays and gamma rays all form what is called the electromagnetic spectrum. They are all various kinds of radiant energy and they differ only in their wavelength or frequency. Those with long wavelengths are generally called waves and the shorter ones rays.

Early research Before 1800, only light was known, as all the other rays and waves are invisible. Infrared and ultraviolet rays were discovered in 1800 and 1801, but no one was aware of any other waves and rays. Then in the 1860s, the British physicist, James Clerk Maxwell, worked out the nature of light rays. He showed that they consist of electric and magnetic fields, and so he called light an electromagnetic radiation.

Maxwell then went on to predict that other kinds of electromagnetic radiation must exist. He was proved correct when, inspired by his teachings, the German scientist, Heinrich Hertz, first generated radio waves in 1881. Other waves and rays were discovered later.

FISH OR FOWL

Does a Bombay duck go quack-quack? No – because it is actually a fish. Its Indian name is *bommaloe machee*. It is similar in size to a herring and it is caught off the west coast of India, especially near Bombay. The name probably derives from the fish's habit of skimming the surface of the water. After it has been caught, the fish is cut open and cleaned and heavily salted. It is then left to dry in the sun until often it resembles wood. It is usually fried before being served, but it may be baked in the oven.

All electromagnetic waves travel through space at the speed of light, but they differ in frequency and wavelength (as shown below).

▼

Electromagnetic spectrum

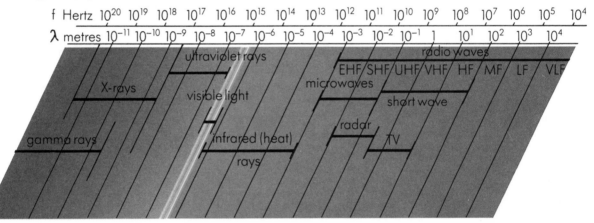

POWER WITHOUT AIR

Why do all spacecraft have rocket engines? Because space is completely empty. The only way a spacecraft can move is to produce a powerful stream of gas that thrusts the spacecraft forward. Rocket engines drive spacecraft by burning fuels to give hot gases.

There is no oxygen in space to support the combustion of fuels as there is in the air on Earth. So, to power its rocket engines, a spacecraft carries liquid oxygen, or uses fuels that burn without oxygen.

COMPUTER PILOT

Who really flies an airliner? A modern jet airliner, such as the Boeing 747 jumbo jet, has automatic guidance systems that can control its flight. This is more than an autopilot, which keeps the aircraft flying in a set direction. It is a fully computerized system that can take the aircraft anywhere in the world.

Before take-off, the crew tell the guidance computers their present position and that of their destination, as well as the route that they wish to take. Soon after take-off, the pilot switches in the computers and they guide the plane to the airport. The pilot then lands the aircraft, though computers may also be able to control landing, especially when bad weather causes poor visibility.

The computers are connected to sensors that detect every movement of the aircraft. If it departs slightly from the planned route, the computers operate the aircraft controls to bring it back on course. Guidance systems may also be linked to navigation satellites that can give any form of transport its exact location.

NUMBERS FOR QUALITY

What's so wonderful about digital? You often hear how much better digital systems are than others. Digital watches keep good time and digital recordings give very good sound or video quality. Computers are digital machines. But what does digital mean?

Basically, a digital system is one that works with numbers. A digital watch displays the time in changing numbers rather than the movement of hands over a dial. The other main kind of system is called analog, and analog systems work by using things to *represent* numbers or quantities. As a watch may use hands to show the time, a thermometer uses the movement of a column of liquid to indicate temperatures and a gramophone record uses the wiggles of a groove to preserve sound waves. These are all analog systems.

Number codes Digital systems work first by measuring a changing quantity – for example sound waves in digital recording – and then converting the measurements into strings of numbers. These numbers are in the form of codes and are usually handled by computers, which can deal with numbers very fast.

The numbers are then processed in some way; they may be recorded, for example. The system then takes the numbers and changes them back into the required form, such as sound waves. Now, in all the processes that take place, the value of the numbers does not change, so that when they are changed back, the sound or whatever is produced is virtually identical to the original. Using a digital system the quality does not deteriorate.

Distorted originals Analog systems change quantities into other quantities. In analog recording and broadcasting, for example, sound waves are changed into varying electric currents in wires, radio signals transmitted through the air, magnetic patterns on tape or wiggles in the grooves of a record, and then back into sound. All these changes degrade the sound, so that it is not as good as the original.

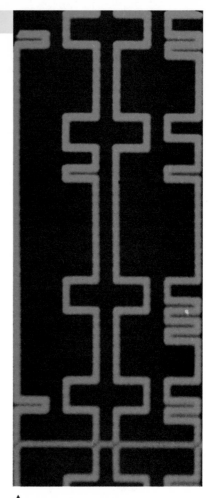

▲
A digital recording pulse displayed on a screen.

REAL COLD

How cold can things get? You might think that winter is cold enough, until you compare it with absolute zero, the coldest possible temperature. Absolute zero is −273°C or −460°F.

Nothing can get colder than this temperature. The reason is that everything has to lose heat energy to get colder. At absolute zero, an object has no heat energy left, so it can't get any colder.

FACT FILE: ENERGY

FACT Heat, light, radio waves, sound, movement and electricity are all different kinds of energy.
FACT Petrol is such a powerful fuel that a small cup of it contains enough energy to raise you to the top of the highest mountain in the world.
FACT The amount of heat energy that we get from the Sun is the same as having a one-bar electric fire on *every* square metre (square yard) of the Earth's surface.
FACT The foods that contain the most energy are foods made of animal fat, such as butter. Vegetables have the least energy.
FACT The people of the United States are the world's greatest energy users. Each American uses up about twice as much energy as people in Europe, and a thousand times as much energy as people in the poorest countries.

LIVE IN ACTION

What's new in news gathering?
When you see 'live' pictures of
events on the television news
from around the world, they may
be produced by electronic news
gathering. This is a system in
which a television camera at the
scene sends pictures back to the
television station by a radio link.
The pictures are then either
recorded on videotape or
broadcast live. This way, you are
able to see the very latest news.

The fastest method of electronic ▶
news gathering is to use a one-
man crew to transmit images by
microwave to base for live
broadcasting.

FORCEFUL

***How can you easily increase
your strength?*** You don't need
to go on a muscle-building
course to get more strength. In
fact, you increase your muscle
power every time you use a tool
like a screwdriver, nutcrackers,
spanner or pliers.

The very reason you use
such tools is that they increase
the force you exert with your
muscles, enabling you to
perform tasks that would
otherwise need great strength.
Such tools are called simple
machines, and they work by the
principle of levers. This means
that they allow you to exert your
muscle power at some distance
from the point at which it is
needed – say to crack a nut or
free a bolt. The distance
increases the force that you
exert on them.

The use of this spanner increases ▶
the effort which is applied to the
load (the resistance acting on the
nut that is being turned).

SKY DRIVER

***Who made his coachman a
reluctant pioneer of flight?*** The
first flight of a full-size flying
machine that was heavier than
air took place in England in
1853. The aircraft was a glider
built by Sir George Cayley, who
persuaded his coachman to fly it
for him. The coachman, having
made the first true aircraft flight in
history, was less than impressed
with the honour, and said: 'I wish
to give notice: I was hired to
drive, not to fly.'

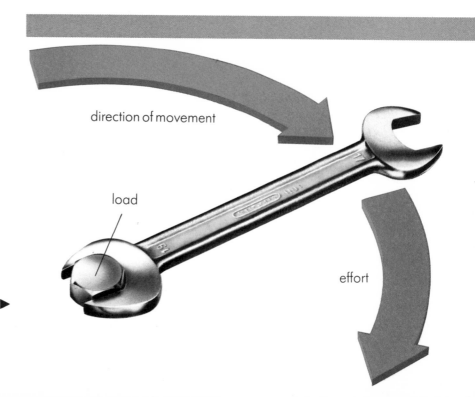

direction of movement

load

effort

EASY RULES

Where do metres, kilograms and other metric measurements come from? You may not enjoy doing calculations with metric units like centimetres and grams, but at least they all work the same way. There are 100 centimetres to the metre and 1,000 grams to a kilogram. Metric units and their subdivisions are all related by a factor of ten, a hundred, a thousand and so on, which greatly simplifies measurements and calculations. The old imperial units were very inconsistent, with 16 ounces to a pound and 2,240 pounds in a ton (2,000 in the USA), or 36 inches to a yard and 1,760 yards in a mile, and so on.

The metric system This was devised in France in 1795. The actual size of each of the basic units, such as the metre and kilogram, could have been anything. The metre was, in fact, defined as one ten-millionth of the distance from the Equator to the North Pole, and the kilogram as the mass of a particular lump of metal. It is the simple relationship between the units and their various subdivisions that makes the metric system so valuable and easy to use.

A HELPING MOUTH

How does the 'kiss of life' save life? If someone is badly injured, they may stop breathing. They do not die right away, but they will live only a few more minutes unless their breathing starts again.

It is possible to save people in this condition by giving the 'kiss of life'. This is a method in which one person uses their own mouth to force air into the injured person's mouth. Its proper name is mouth-to-mouth ventilation. It may help to keep the person alive until proper medical help arrives.

SEEING THE LIGHT

Who made an important discovery by feeling his pulse? The great Italian scientist, Galileo, made a famous discovery in 1581, while still a teenager. While attending services in Pisa Cathedral, a chandelier swinging in the air caught his eye. It seemed that the chandelier always took the same time to swing first one way and then the other, regardless of how far it swung each time. As there were no accurate clocks in those days, Galileo measured the time of each swing by feeling his pulse and counting the beats. The answer was always the same.

What Galileo had discovered was the pendulum. Using this, it proved possible at long last to build clocks which kept time accurately.

HUSH-HUSH DECODER

Why was the first electronic computer kept a secret? The invention of the first electronic computer was kept strictly secret for several years. The reason—it was invented in wartime.

This computer was called Colossus, and it was invented in Britain in 1943. It was developed in total secrecy because Colossus was built to crack enemy code messages. It did this with great success, playing an important part in the defeat of Germany in World War II. The existence of Colossus was not revealed until after the war ended in 1945.

COLOSSUS

COUNTERS

FIG. 4

▲
Modern computers occupy a fraction of the space needed to house Colossus.

GUIDANCE FROM ABOVE

How can satellites in space improve transport on Earth? Transport, both public and private, could become much better because of advances in space technology. The Navstar satellites being placed in orbit around the Earth will provide a world-wide navigation system by 1990. Any vehicle will be able to receive radio signals from the satellite that will give the vehicle's exact position. Aircraft and ships will be able to navigate precisely throughout the world, and land transport will benefit too.

Computer display Using a computer in a car linked by radio to the satellites, it will be possible for drivers to see their position on a moving map displayed by the computer. Railway train drivers will be able to see the track ahead on a similar display. In this way, car drivers could find their way easily and train drivers could spot any trouble ahead.

The system will really come into its own as the computer guides or even controls the vehicle. The computer will be able to tell a car driver which way to go, and drive a train automatically. Also, a central computer could show the positions of buses in a city, or trains in a rail network, and so help to improve services.

THE *TURTLE*

Did you know that the first submarine was powered by just one man? The first submarine to go into action was an American vessel called the *Turtle*. It tried to attack a British warship in 1776, during the American War of Independence. The *Turtle* was an egg-shaped craft powered by one man, who sat inside and turned two handles connected to screw propellers outside.

Manned by Sergeant Ezra Lee, the *Turtle*'s mission was to attach a mine to the warship's hull. The submarine worked well, but the bottom of the ship was lined with metal, preventing Sergeant Lee from fixing the mine.

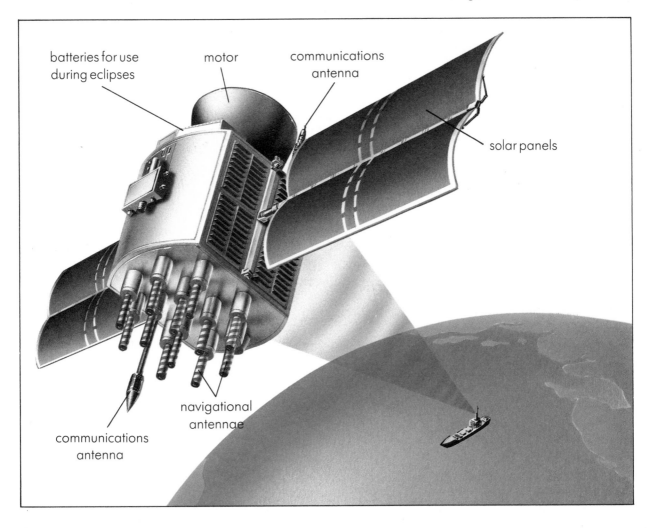

▲
Navstar satellites will be used in research, navigation and defence.

JUST JAVELINS

Did you know that javelins are designed for throwing different distances? Modern javelins are described as 'distance-rated', which means that you can use a javelin that is designed to travel about the distance you are likely to throw.

Improvement Javelin is one of the sports which has benefited most from modern technology. Early wooden javelins vibrated in flight and were subject to a great deal of aerodynamic drag, but steel javelins, developed in the 1940s and 1950s, helped to eliminate this problem.

More recently, an air-powered javelin gun has permitted scientific study of the sport. The speed and height at which the javelin leaves the hand, the angle at which it is thrown, and its flight path have all been studied. These experiments have produced the highly sophisticated javelins, made of steel and aluminium, that are used today.

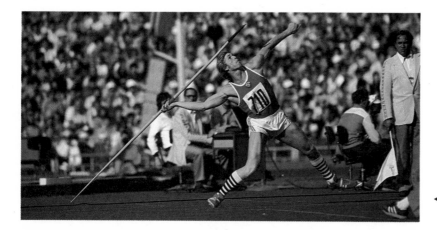

SOUND PICTURES

Is television going to get bigger and better? A good colour television set can give a fine picture right now, but one thing that's not so good about it is the sound. The quality is poor compared with that produced by a high-fidelity sound system, but high-quality stereophonic TV sound is on the way. In fact, it's already available on hi-fi video recorders and it makes watching music videos really exciting.

The television picture is going to get better, too. New high-definition systems having double the present number of lines will soon appear, giving pictures that are as sharp and detailed as the best colour photographs. The picture will be bigger and wider that in today's sets, and it is likely to appear on a flat screen that can be hung on the wall.

◀ Design modifications have created highly efficient modern javelins.

QUIZ: MEDICINE

1 Which operation was pioneered by Christiaan Barnard in 1967?
2 Who discovered that blood circulates round the body?
3 What is an analgesic?
4 Which kind of surgery can restore or improve a patient's appearance?
5 What is the common name of the disease that doctors call rubella?
6 A, B, AB and O – what are they?
7 Which kind of people are treated by pediatricians?
8 Which part of the body is affected by conjunctivitis?
9 What does a pharmacist do?
10 Which French scientist showed that germs cause disease?
11 What is flu?

ANSWERS
1 Heart transplant. 2 William Harvey. 3 A painkiller, such as aspirin. 4 Plastic surgery. 5 German measles. 6 Blood groups. 7 Children. 8 The eye. 9 Prepares and dispenses drugs. 10 Louis Pasteur. 11 Short for influenza, a serious virus illness of the respiratory tract.

ALL WORK AND NO PLAY?

Who considered genius to be '99 per cent perspiration'?
It was the prolific inventor, Thomas Edison, who lived in the United States from 1847 to 1931. Best-known as the pioneer of sound recording, Edison, in fact, made over a thousand inventions. He approached inventing as a business, and was the first person to assemble a team of scientists to carry out research work.

Edison did not believe that scientists and inventors must wait for an idea to strike them. He considered that discoveries could be made by hard work, and summed up his attitude in the immortal saying: 'Genius is one per cent inspiration and 99 per cent perspiration.'

SHIP ALOFT!

Where do boats take a lift?
Most canals have locks to raise or lower boats to different levels. However, some canals have lifts as well. Basically, the lift is a huge box filled with water that carries boats or barges from one canal to another. It may travel vertically or more gradually up and down a slope. The highest canal lift is in Belgium. It is 68 m (223 ft) high.

RODENT OPERATIVE

How can a mouse help us to operate a computer? In computer jargon, a mouse is not a small furry animal but a simple device that helps people to use a computer. It consists of a box that can roll around on a table top, and one or more press buttons. A wire leads from the mouse to the computer, and as you move the mouse, an arrow shifts around the screen. You move the arrow to a picture of some kind on the screen – such as a clock – and press a button. The computer responds in a way indicated by the picture, for example, by telling you the time.

The screen normally has a whole set of small pictures or diagrams called icons that you can select with the mouse. Each one produces a different operation. The system is very easy to use as it requires no knowledge of the computer.

▲
Canal lifts may be used instead of locks to raise barges up very steep inclines.

METAL MONSTERS

When did tanks first go into action? The first tanks to fight in a war were British tanks in 1916. They went into action in France during World War I.

Originally known as 'landships', the name 'tank' was adopted as a deliberately misleading cover name for the early armoured vehicles.
▼

ONCE BITTEN . . .

Why do some countries control the entry of animals? In several countries, people cannot bring in animals freely from abroad. Any animal that does arrive must go into quarantine and spend several months in a cage before being allowed to mix freely with other animals and people.

There is a very good reason for this law. It is to prevent the spread of a terrible disease called rabies. People can get rabies from the bite of an infected animal such as a dog or cat. But not all countries have rabies, and quarantine regulations are meant to stop it entering the country by making sure that the arriving animals are free of rabies.

However, quarantine can only succeed where a country is surrounded by water. In countries with land borders, rabies can be brought in by wild animals such as foxes, bats and mongooses.

Countries that are free of rabies include Britain, Australia, Japan and New Zealand, as well as a number of smaller island nations.

▲
Warning notices play a vital role in preventing the spread of rabies.

KICK BACK

Can objects push back when you push them? Strange as it may seem, the answer is yes. When you push or exert any kind of force on something, it always exerts the same force back. You can demonstrate this by standing on a trolley or a boat and throwing something heavy away from you. The trolley or boat will move backwards. As you push on the object to throw it away, it pushes back on you and moves you backwards if you are free to move. These two forces are called action and reaction.

CHIP CHAT

How are computers able to talk and listen to us? Computers can address us in electronic voices and recognize spoken words. They are able to handle speech by changing the sounds in words into electronic code signals and back again. They can process these signals very fast to respond to and produce words. As they are developed, the ability of computers to talk and listen becomes ever more lifelike.

Better talkers At the moment, computers are better at talking than listening. This is because speech synthesis, the artificial production of spoken sounds, is more advanced than voice recognition.

When a computer talks, a stream of code signals goes to a special voice chip which turns the codes into electric signals that drive a loudspeaker to speak words. Each code signal produces a *phoneme,* a separate sound in a word. The word 'garden' for example, has five phonemes – g, ar, d, eh, n. The phonemes are strung together to give words. Intelligible English speech can be produced with 44 phonemes, but the computer also has to be programmed to vary the intonation to make the words sound lifelike.

Listening and learning To recognize speech, the computer needs a microphone to convert sounds into electric signals. A chip then converts the signals into codes that the computer can process. However, as people do not speak exactly alike: vowel sounds can vary greatly. The word 'paper', for example, could easily be mistaken for 'piper' or 'pepper'.

The computer gets round this problem by learning the speech of the person using it. If it is to understand certain commands, such as 'start' and 'stop', the computer first asks the person to pronounce these words. It then stores all the commands, as codes, in its memory. Every time it has to recognize a word, the computer changes the sound into a code and checks its memory to see if this code is there. If so, the computer recognizes the command and responds to it.

▲
This talk-writer computer interprets and acts upon human voice patterns.

SAFETY MARK

Could you travel by the Plimsoll line? The Plimsoll line is to do with ships, but it's not a shipping line. Named after the British politician, Samuel Plimsoll, it's a line that's marked on the side of a ship and shows the level to which the ship can be safely loaded. The water must not come above the Plimsoll line.

The international legal load line ▶ for shipping, the Plimsoll line, was introduced in 1876 and is now used by all seafaring countries.

Plimsoll line markings

Key

TF	Tropical Fresh Water
F	Fresh Water
T	Tropical
S	Summer
W	Winter
WNA	Winter North Atlantic
LR	Lloyd's Register (organization responsible for enforcing loading regulations)

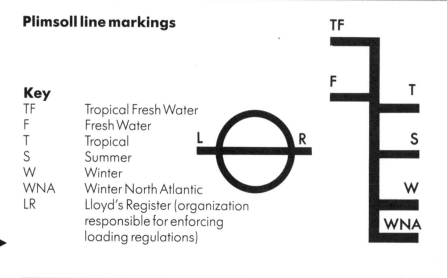

THE BIG PULL

Who was inspired by a falling apple? Several great discoveries in science have been made by asking simple or obvious questions. In about 1665, the great English physicist, Isaac Newton, watched an apple fall from a tree to the ground. He asked himself why the apple should fall, and reasoned that a force must pull it to the ground. Newton then told himself that the same force must keep the Moon in orbit around the Earth.

The force is, of course, the force of gravity, and Newton's daring to say that the Earth's gravity would affect both a little apple in his garden and a distant world like the Moon was a stroke of genius. It was not for another twenty years, when the size of the Earth had been correctly calculated, that Newton could prove he was right. He was then able to show that gravity is a force that is universal.

pulp (blood vessels and nerves)

enamel

gum

dentine

bone

Section through a tooth

▲
Pain is caused when the inner layers of a tooth are exposed.

OPEN WIDE

Could we do away with the dentist's drill? A dentist uses a drill to remove the decayed part of a tooth before filling the hole left in the tooth. It's not a pleasant experience, and it may involve an anaesthetic as well as the drilling.

In future, the dentist's drill may well disappear. Teeth could possibly be treated with a liquid that would dissolve the decay, or laser beams could take the place of drills. Of course, it would be better to do away with tooth decay altogether. It may soon be possible to prevent it with vaccines that would stop bacteria attacking the teeth, or alternatively, laser beams could seal the teeth against invasion by bacteria.

DOTS OR DAISIES

How do computer printers work? Computer printers print the results calculated by computers on paper. They are also used in word processors to type letters and documents automatically. There are two main kinds of printers used with home computers and word processors. They are dot matrix printers and daisy wheel printers.

Dot matrix printers These produce characters (letters, numbers and signs) that are each made up of a different pattern of dots in a matrix (a rectangle consisting of several columns of dots). The printer has one vertical column of needles, which are fired at an inked ribbon above the paper. The computer sends code signals to the printer, which operates the needles to produce the patterns of dots on the paper. Dot matrix printers work fast, but the quality may not be very high.

Daisy wheel printers These are slower but give excellent quality, because each character is formed by a separate type bar striking the ribbon, as in a typewriter. The type bars are arranged in a wheel similar to the petals of a daisy. The daisy wheel revolves rapidly, and the computer causes a hammer to strike the correct type bar as it passes.

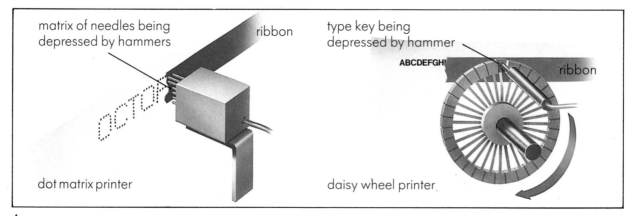

matrix of needles being depressed by hammers

ribbon

type key being depressed by hammer

ABCDEFGHI

ribbon

dot matrix printer

daisy wheel printer

▲
This enlarged view of the two computer printers shows their different type characteristics.

▲
Natural forces influencing the shape of these raindrops would have also determined the shape of the Earth.

TROUBLE BUBBLE

Why is a bubble like the Earth? Pessimists might say that it's because they're both likely to be blown up. However, this is not really a riddle. The answer's fairly obvious – they're both round. But why?

Usually gravity forces a liquid to take the shape of its container. But any liquid naturally forms itself into a round sphere if it is free to do so. Raindrops do as they fall to the ground. A bubble – which is a thin film of soapy water – forms itself into a ball as it floats through the air. The Earth was liquid when it formed and took the shape of a globe because it was floating in space.

Liquids behave like this because of surface tension, a force in the surface of the liquid that acts to pull the liquid into a sphere. Gravity, being stronger, normally stops this happening, though surface tension may curve the liquid's surface.

ON THE MAT

How did judo begin? Judo was devised in 1882 by Dr Jigoro Kano in Japan. It was developed from *ju-jitsu*, an ancient method of self-defence without weapons, in which the strength and weight of the opponent are used against him. The highest efficiency award in judo, called *Shihan*, has never been awarded, and fewer than ten men have ever been awarded the red belt *Judan* or 10th dan!

Judo champions in combat.
▼

FACT FILE: DISCOVERIES IN COMMUNICATIONS

FACT The telephone was invented by the American engineer, Alexander Graham Bell in 1876.
FACT Radio was first used for communications by the Italian engineer, Guglielmo Marconi in 1894.
FACT Magnetic sound recording was invented by the Danish engineer, Valdemar Poulsen in 1898. He used wire, not tape.
FACT The first television picture was transmitted by the British inventor, John Logie Baird in 1924. However, the kind of electronic television we have today was invented later in the United States.
FACT The first communications satellite was *Score*, launched by the United States in 1958.

RETURN TRIP

What have we bounced off the Moon and back again? A laser beam has been bounced off the Moon. The American astronauts who landed on the Moon placed a mirror on the surface. This was then used to reflect a laser beam sent from Earth to the Moon. By detecting the reflected beam, scientists have been able to measure the distance to the Moon with great accuracy.

PLANETARY PROBES

What did Pioneer pioneer and where has Voyager voyaged? *Pioneer* and *Voyager* are the names of two kinds of American space probes that have made important discoveries about the solar system. The first *Pioneer* probes investigated conditions in space. *Pioneer 10* became the first space probe to fly past Jupiter in 1973, and *Pioneer 11* first visited Saturn in 1979.

The two *Voyager* probes left Earth in 1977 and flew on past Jupiter and Saturn. *Voyager 2* then went on to pass Uranus in 1986, and is now making its way to Neptune, where it is due in 1989.

Other ventures Other American space probes have been the *Mariner* probes to Mars, Venus and Mercury, and the *Viking* probes that have landed on Mars. Russian probes have concentrated on Venus.

New space probes have been given names of famous people. There is the European probe *Giotto*, which intercepted Halley's comet in 1986, and the American probe *Galileo*, which is to orbit Jupiter and send instruments down into the giant planet's atmosphere.

NOBEL MONSTER

Which inventor was dismayed by his most famous invention? Handling high explosives was once very dangerous, even for experts. They were liable to go off without warning and injure or kill the people using them. Nowadays, in trained hands, they are safe to use. The man who 'tamed' explosives was the Swedish inventor Alfred Nobel. In 1866, he invented dynamite, the first safe high explosive.

Although dynamite has many peaceful uses, many people saw Nobel as a monster bent on destruction. Dismayed at the reception of his discovery, he endowed the Nobel Prizes. These awards – in chemistry, physics, medicine, literature and peace – have become the most prestigious of all prizes, and Nobel's name is now highly respected.

Saturn's rings as seen by *Voyager 2*.
▼

▲
The twin towers of the World Trade Center dominate the New York City skyline.

GLASS SKIN

How do skyscrapers stay up?
Many modern skyscrapers
appear to be made mainly of
glass, but how can flimsy glass
walls support such an enormous
structure?

The answer is that they don't
support it. Inside the skyscraper
there may be a steel or concrete
frame to which all the walls and
floors are fixed. The frame
supports the whole structure,
and the walls can be made of
any material that is attractive.
Some skyscrapers are built
around a concrete core instead
of a frame.

The skyscraper rests on
foundations that may extend
deep into the ground to take the
building's weight.

VIDEO VALUE

Tape or disc – what's best in video? With video, you decide what to
watch. You can use your television set to provide you with the films,
shows, music – virtually any visual entertainment or information – of
your choice. There are two systems: videotape recorders and videodisc
players, each with their own particular advantages.

Videotape and videocassette recorders play tapes and you can
record television programmes on them as well as watch films or other
pre-recorded material.

Videodisc players play special discs containing films and shows. You
cannot record on the discs, but the picture quality produced by the discs
is much better than that given by tapes. The reason for this is that discs
are digital whereas tapes are analog.

One advantage that discs have over tapes is that any part of the disc
can be played immediately. This means that computers can be linked to
videodisc players and allow people to interact with them. Computer
games with real pictures are one development now taking place, and
the system is likely to have tremendous potential in education.

THE BOUNCERS

***Millions of them have just struck
you – what are they?*** Unless
you are reading this book in your
bath, they are molecules of air. If
you are immersed in water, then
they would mostly be molecules
of water.

Everything is made up of
tiny atoms, which in many
substances are linked in groups
to form molecules. Air mainly
contains molecules of the gases
oxygen and nitrogen. In a litre of
air, there are about 30,000

million million million molecules,
and they are all in constant
movement, bouncing off one
another and any surface they
meet. Water contains millions of
molecules too, which are also in
ceaseless motion.

▲
Specially cultivated bacteria can be invaluable to man.

MICRO-WORKERS

Did you know that many products we use are made by microscopic living creatures? There's something you use everyday that is made by creatures so small that you need a microscope to see them. It's bread. All bread that is made to rise depends on a process called fermentation. It employs yeasts, which are tiny living things that make the dough rise by producing tiny bubbles of carbon dioxide gas. Fermentation is also used in brewing and wine-making to form alcohol. Similar biological processes using bacteria produce antibiotics, such as penicillin, and other drugs.

   This field of science is called biotechnology, and it's also used to produce various kinds of chemicals, fuels and animal feeds. Special new kinds of bacteria·that give better products or improve production can now actually be made by genetic engineering. This development is very important in biotechnology, especially in the production of drugs and vaccines that treat dangerous diseases.

CHIPS ON YOUR WRIST

Did you know that you may be carrying a computer on you? You may not be aware of it, but if you're wearing a digital watch, then you've a tiny computer on your person.

   A digital watch contains a device called an oscillator that produces an exact number of electric signals every second. A miniature computer in the watch counts the signals and every time they reach this number, it sends another signal to change the display. The oscillator and computer are very accurate, so the watch keeps good time. The watch's computer can also work out the date and display it.

Automatic sensitivity Another portable machine that contains a computer is the compact camera, which operates automatically. The camera has sensors that measure the light and the distance of the subject. A computer in the camera then works out the correct settings for the lens and shutter and operates them to take a perfect photograph.

BEWARE GRAVITY!

Where is your centre of gravity? The centre of gravity of an object is a point at which all its weight can be considered to be located. This point is usually inside the object. However, your centre of gravity may be inside or outside your body, depending on whether you're standing, sitting, bending or falling over.

   If your centre of gravity is over your feet, then you remain upright. But if it is not above your feet, then you will fall over – unless, of course, you've taken the precaution of having a chair or stool under you.

An inside view of a digital watch

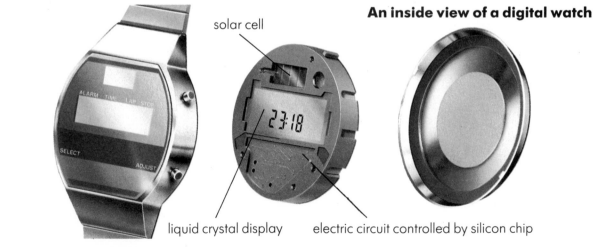

solar cell

liquid crystal display   electric circuit controlled by silicon chip

▲
Solar powered digital watches do not use the springs and cogs of conventional analog watches.

UP THE POLE

Why can some athletes vault 1 m (39 in) higher than 50 years ago? Because vaulting poles have improved in design. In the sport of pole vaulting great changes to the material from which the pole is made have enabled athletes to jump much higher. In the 19th century, the poles were heavy wooden ones with a steel spike. At the very beginning of the 20th century a much lighter, more flexible bamboo pole was introduced. In the 1940s, a steel pole was used, but the sport was revolutionized by the introduction of the glass-fibre pole. At first these poles were rather heavy and stiff, but in the 1960s lighter, more flexible glass-fibre poles helped athletes to achieve great heights. The record has risen by more than a metre in just 50 years.

◀ The flexibility of a glass-fibre vaulting pole can be seen clearly in this high-speed photograph.

HEAT AND BEATS

What do your temperature and your pulse tell a doctor?
If you feel ill, the doctor will often check your temperature with a thermometer. This indicates the amount of heat being produced by your body. Your pulse may also be taken. This tells the doctor how fast your heart is beating.

Normally, these remain steady, your temperature at about 37°C or 98°F and your pulse at approximately 60 to 80 beats a minute when resting. If they are too high or too low, it tells the doctor that you are not just trying to get out of going to school.

QUIZ: SPACEFLIGHT

1 Who was the first American astronaut to orbit the Earth?
2 What was the first animal to make a spaceflight?
3 Where did the *Viking* space probes land?
4 How far away does space begin?
5 What is *Intelsat*?
6 What was unlucky about *Apollo 13*?
7 What are *Columbia, Discovery, Challenger* and *Atlantis*?
8 American astronauts have spent the longest time in space – true or false?

ANSWERS
1 John Glenn. 2 A Russian dog called Laika. 3 On Mars.
4 About 160 km (100 miles) above your head. 5 The International Telecommunications Satellite Consortium, and the name of satellites launched by it. 6 It was a Moon mission that went wrong – the astronauts had to abandon their Moon landing but returned safely to Earth. 7 Names of space shuttles.
8 False; Russian cosmonauts have spent about four times as long.

APPLIED IMAGINATION

Which great scientist was useless at maths? During the last 400 years, most inventions and discoveries have been made by scientists using mathematics or applying scientific laws. However, one great British scientist, Michael Faraday, who lived from 1791 to 1867, did not make use of mathematics. Faraday was the son of a poor blacksmith and received no education beyond reading and writing.

Inquisitive Fortunately, Faraday was very inquisitive and taught himself all about science. He was also imaginative, which enabled him later to gain great fame for his immensely popular lectures on science. His inquisitiveness led him to investigate electric current, which was new to science in the early 1800s, and its uses.

Electricity Although unable to express his work in mathematical terms, Faraday used his imagination to picture how electricity works. He visualized that a wire carrying an electric current is surrounded by lines of magnetic force produced by the flow of the current. He used this idea to find out how electricity and magnetism are linked. This led him to build the first working model of an electric motor in 1821, and, ten years later, the first electric generator. He then went on to show how electricity affects chemical substances.

These discoveries enable us to generate and use electric current, and are among the most important ever made. Yet they were made by a man who today would not be able to pass science examinations.

Chemist and physicist Michael Faraday was a pioneer of much important scientific experimentation.
▼

▲
Cells used to make monoclonal antibodies are carefully refined.

RIGHT ON TARGET

How do 'magic bullets' fight disease? New drugs, popularly called 'magic bullets', are being developed to cure illnesses that doctors have found difficult to treat. They use substances called monoclonal antibodies.

Antibodies are natural substances in our bodies that give us immunity to many diseases. Vaccination helps to produce antibodies that may prevent us getting specific diseases. Monoclonal antibodies are very pure kinds of antibodies. When taken, they go only to the part of the body that is affected.

If drugs are attached to these antibodies, they can be delivered by them to the very place where they are needed to deal with the illness. Normally, drugs spread throughout the body and can produce severe side-effects, limiting the dose that can be given. Monoclonal antibodies can enable doctors to target the drugs so that they are much more effective. It is hoped that cancer may be cured in this way.

DENTAL DUMMY

Could you ever hurt a robot? We think of robots as perfect machines that never do anything wrong, let alone get hurt. However, there are some robots whose whole purpose is to get hurt and to say 'ouch'.

These robots are dummy patients for dentists. They have a model human head, and student dentists practise doing fillings and other kinds of dental work on the robot's teeth. If the student does anything that

would hurt a human patient, the robot indicates the mistake. Dental robots can even be programmed to squirm about in the chair, as some children — and adults — do when they visit the dentist.

▲
The massive cutting head of a mechanical mole in a tunnel.

MOLES FOR HOLES

How fast can tunnels be dug? Many tunnels are now dug by tunnelling machines, called mechanical moles. Some of them are totally automatic, guided underground by lasers and controlled by computers from the surface. The mole digs out the soil or rock underground, which is then conveyed away, or mixed with water and piped to the surface. The machine then puts curved linings into place so that the tunnel will not collapse.

The speed at which mechanical moles burrow through the ground depends on the kind of rock or soil and the size of the tunnel. But they are capable of burrowing at the rate of 150 m (500 ft) a day!

SKIP IT!

When is a leap year not a leap year? Usually a leap year occurs every four years – when the year is divisible by four, as in 1988 and 2000. However, even though they obey this rule, century years divisible by 100 like 1800 and 1900 are *not* leap years. The year 2000 is an exception because century years divisible by 400 *are* leap years!

WRONG END

Did you know that potatoes can be poisonous? Potatoes belong to the same plant family as deadly nightshade, and there is a poison called solanine in their leaves. Although they do not contain enough poison to be really harmful, it is said that when potatoes were first eaten in Elizabethan times, people were ill because they ate the leaves and stems and threw away the tubers, instead of the other way round.

SHUTTLE CREW

How many people can fly in the space shuttle? As many as eight people can fly aboard the space shuttle. One of them is the commander and another the pilot who flies the shuttle. The other members of the crew are called mission specialists and payload specialists. They operate the equipment taken into space by the shuttle.

▲
Part of shuttle 51A's mission included the retrieval of this satellite.

The double-stranded DNA structure.
▼

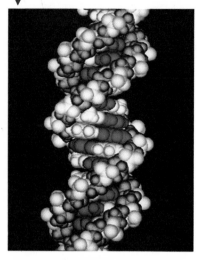

JUST LIKE HIS DAD

What is DNA? DNA stands for deoxyribonucleic acid. It's a very important substance in biology, but people always use the initials because the full name is such a mouthful.

DNA is important because it is the main substance in living things that governs heredity. Different living things have different kinds of DNA, which they get from their parents. Your kind of DNA ensures, firstly, that you are a human being as your parents are and not, say, a potato or a centipede. Secondly, it causes your body to possess many of the features of your parents, giving you blue eyes or red hair, for example.

LIGHT LIGHT

What is the smallest thing ever discovered? The smallest object known is not an atom, nor even the particles such as electrons, protons and neutrons that make up atoms. Much smaller still is the photon, which is a particle of light. Its mass is about 3×10^{-50} grams — a decimal point followed by 49 zeros and then 3!

SONAR SEARCH

How are deep-sea wrecks discovered? The wrecks of ships, and sometimes crashed aircraft, may lie several kilometres or miles deep at the bottom of the ocean. It is often necessary to find these wrecks, perhaps to recover valuable cargo, or to examine the wreckage to discover the cause of a disaster. There are also famous wrecks, like the *Titanic*, which in 1985 was found at a depth of 3,600 m (12,000 ft) in the Atlantic Ocean.

Wrecks at such a depth lie far below the limits to which divers or submarines can descend. They are located by sonar, a system that bounces pulses of sound off the seabed. A receiver on a ship above produces a profile of the seabed on which wrecks may stand out.

To inspect a deep-sea wreck, unmanned submersibles are used. These are underwater craft equipped with lights, television cameras and claws that can grip objects.

▲
Now being salvaged, this wrecked barge was located underwater by sonar.

FACT FILE: COMPUTER TERMS

FACT Booting a computer means to load a program automatically.
FACT A bug is a fault in a computer, usually in a computer program.
FACT The cursor is the point on the screen at which a letter or number next appears. It is often indicated by a flashing square or line.
FACT A file is a collection of information that can be held in a computer, such as a list of names.
FACT Hardware means the actual machinery used in a computer system.
FACT An interface is a unit that connects two other units together.
FACT A modem is a unit that enables a computer to be linked to other computers over a telephone line.
FACT Software means any kind of computer program that makes the computer perform a particular task.

DETECTION, DISTANCE AND DIRECTION

What is radar used for? A radar system is a kind of radio transmitter and receiver that bounces radio waves off objects. The object could be a car speeding along a road, a boat or aircraft, or even a distant planet. The radio signals that return to the receiver from the object give us information about the target.

Radar stands for radio detection and ranging, which means that the radio signals can detect an object and then measure its range, or distance, and possibly its direction and speed. Police use radar to check the speed of passing vehicles. Air traffic controllers depend on radar to give the positions of the aircraft they are directing, and ships and boats carry radar to aid navigation.

Radar is also used in the automatic guidance systems of aircraft, spacecraft and weapons such as missiles. Space probes landing on other planets use radar to control their descent to the surface. Radar waves from orbiting space probes or from Earth can be bounced off the surfaces of other planets, such as the cloud-enveloped Venus, to give information about them.

◄ Flight controllers use radar to keep track of nearby aircraft (left). A row of radar tracking dishes (below).
▼

SUGAR CONTROL

Why are some people diabetic? Diabetics are people who suffer from diabetes. The main kind of diabetes affects the pancreas, which is a gland that produces a hormone called insulin. This hormone controls the amount of sugar in the blood, which provides energy for the body. In diabetes, insufficient insulin is produced and the sugar level is uncontrolled, resulting in illness.

Diabetes usually cannot be cured. But by taking insulin and following strict rules for diet and exercise, the effects can be prevented. In the future, doctors hope that a method of automatic sugar control will be developed so that diabetics need no longer be concerned with their condition. This method could involve biosensors to monitor blood sugar levels and release insulin when it is needed.

ALL IN WHITE

Who captured the rainbow?
The British scientist Isaac Newton first demonstrated that sunlight, which is white light, contains all the colours of the rainbow. In about 1665, he placed a glass prism in a beam of sunlight and saw that it produced a rainbow-like pattern of colours. This pattern is called a spectrum. A rainbow is formed in a similar way by raindrops splitting up sunlight.

In order to prove that the colours came from the beam of sunlight, Newton placed another prism in the path of the spectrum. This prism combined all the colours together to give white light again.

▲
The spectrum can be seen in a rainbow (above) or by using a prism to split white light (below).
▼

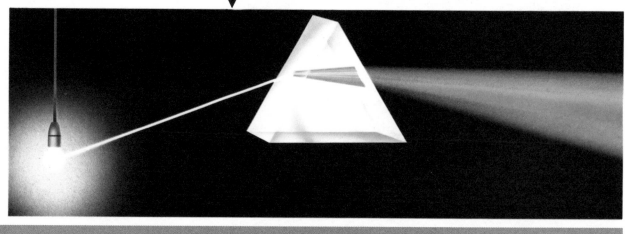

ASK THE COMPUTER

Database and data processing – what's the difference? These two terms are both computer jargon. They are both methods of handling data, which is information of any kind that can be put in a computer.

Information store A database is rather like an electronic library. It's a collection of information of a particular kind that is held in the computer's memory. Such information could be aircraft flights or the titles of books. The advantage of a database is that you can, for example, ask the computer to search through the database and find out all the flights that leave for a particular airport on a certain day or at a stated price. In a library you might select the titles of all books on a particular subject, or just those by a certain author.

Data processing This is the application of computers to business. It deals with the use of computers to calculate wages and salaries, produce sales figures and so on.

HOLD YOUR BREATH

What happens when you hiccup? Hiccups or hiccoughs are caused by sudden movements of your diaphragm, which is a large muscle beneath your chest. The diaphragm controls breathing, and the movement causes a sudden intake of air. This is the hiccup.

Hiccups can start for many reasons, but they usually soon go away. Sometimes the attack lasts for a long time and it can be exhausting. In very rare cases, it lasts for years!

FAST MOVERS

How fast do spacecraft fly?
A spacecraft like the space
shuttle that flies in an orbit
around the Earth has to reach a
speed of about 28,000 km/h
(17,500 mph). If it does not reach
this speed after being launched,
the spacecraft falls back
towards the Earth. If the
spacecraft has to fly out to
another world like the Moon or
Mars, then it must go even faster
and reach a speed of 40,000
km/h (25,000 mph).

Space probes travelling far
from the Earth may speed up as
the Sun's gravity, or the strong
gravity of other worlds, pulls
them. They can reach speeds of
more than 200,000 km/h
(125,000 mph).

CRYSTAL CLEAR

***Why do crystals form in such
beautiful shapes?*** Pure crystals
always form in regular shapes of
particular kinds. Salt forms tiny
cubes, and many crystalline
minerals consist of beautiful
formations of smaller identical
crystals.

Crystals take these shapes
because the tiny atoms inside
them are lined up in particular
patterns of rows. When the
crystal forms, its atoms link
together at certain angles. The
crystal enlarges as more and
more atoms link to those in the
crystal at the same angles. In this
way, the whole crystal grows in a
specific shape.

This greatly magnified view of ▶
the crystals of a pain-killing
drug reveals its intricate
crystalline structure.

▲
Factory robots welding a car on an automated production line.

MECHANICAL SLAVES

Will robots ever be like mechanical people? A robot is really any
machine that is able to control its own actions. It does this by checking
its own performance. If necessary, the machine automatically makes
adjustments so that it continues to work correctly. An important
example of automatic control is the navigation and guidance system in
an airliner.

Computer controlled We usually think of robots as being machines
that can do all kinds of physical tasks for us. Such robots are used in
factories to build products such as cars. They are controlled by
computers, which are programmed to make the robot carry out
particular movements and actions. The robot is simply an arm that can
grip a tool and apply it to any position required.

Versatility Robots will become more and more versatile as they are
equipped with sensing systems that enable them to see and feel things.
But it's unlikely that they will actually look like mechanical people.
Keeping a machine balanced on two legs is difficult, and robot eyes
should be capable of seeing all round instead of just ahead like human
eyes. But there is one way in which robots are very likely to become
more like people – they should soon be able to talk *and* listen to us.

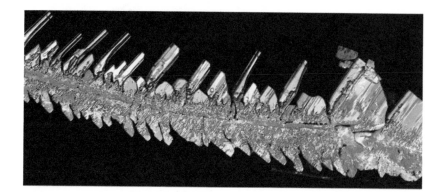

▲
Scanning can help detect cancerous cells (top right).

WITHOUT END

Which number can never be finally calculated? Pi or π, the ratio of the circumference of a circle to its diameter, is a number that can never be absolutely known. It begins as 3.141592, but the number of decimal places continues indefinitely. A computer has calculated pi to more than 16 million decimal places!

NON-STOP TRAVEL

How do satellites stay in space? Satellites are launched into space by rockets. The rocket sends the satellite speeding into space high above the Earth's atmosphere. The rocket then cuts out and the satellite moves on, no longer under any power. It takes up a curved path called an orbit in which it keeps moving around the Earth.

Why does the satellite not slow down and fall back to Earth? The reason is that space is totally empty. There is no air, nor anything else to slow the satellite. The satellite moves too fast to be pulled back to Earth by the Earth's field of gravity, but it doesn't keep on flying straight ahead. Gravity pulls it into an orbit around the Earth.

DREAD DISEASES

Why are cancer and AIDS so feared? Cancer and AIDS are two of the most dreaded diseases. They are not highly infectious diseases like the plagues of centuries past, so that people who are with sufferers are not necessarily at risk. But they can be difficult to treat, and there is little hope for patients who have either disease in its advanced stages.

The two diseases may seem to be alike in that they both invade the body. However, they are basically very different. Cancer is a condition in which some body cells suddenly begin to behave abnormally. They may start to produce growths called tumours either inside or outside the body. If the tumours cannot be controlled, they can interfere severely with the body and eventually cause death. But there are several ways in which doctors can treat cancer and many patients are cured.

AIDS stands for 'acquired immune deficiency syndrome'. This means it is a disease in which the body's immunity – its natural defence to diseases – fails. The person becomes susceptible to diseases that would normally be resisted, and may die from them.

Intensive research is being carried out in many countries to find effective ways of fighting both cancer and AIDS.

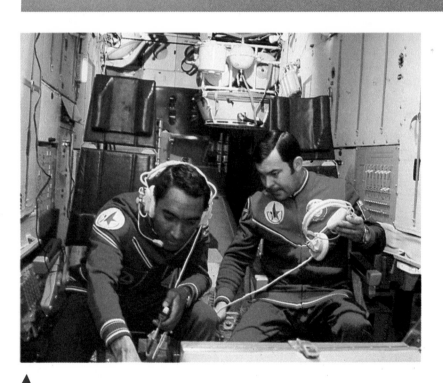

▲
Cuban cosmonauts in training for a Salyut space mission.

TIME IN SPACE

How long can space missions last? The longest space missions have lasted more than nine months. Several Russian cosmonauts have spent long periods aboard the *Salyut* space station in orbit around the Earth. It is possible that these missions may be preparations for a manned spaceflight to Mars.

▲
A prototype Harrier II jump jet engaged in vertical manoeuvres.

STRAIGHT UP

Do jump jets really jump into the air? Jump jet is the popular name for a VTOL aircraft, which is a fighter plane capable of vertical take off and landing. It can rise straight up into the air without speeding along a runway to become airborne.

The aircraft can also descend vertically to land.

As the jump jet requires no runway, and can land and take off again virtually anywhere, it is particularly useful for military forces based on aircraft carriers.

GEAR CHANGE

What is an automatic car?
An automatic car sounds as if it's a car that drives itself. In fact, it's one in which the gears change automatically. The driver has to steer the car and operate the other controls such as the accelerator and brakes.

The gears change as the car speeds up or slows down, and when it has to climb or descend a hill. This enables the engine to drive the wheels with more power when it is needed. In a car without an automatic gearbox, the driver chooses when to change gear. This gives the driver more control over the car, but an automatic car is easier to drive.

QUIZ: FOOD

1. What is a Welsh rabbit or rarebit made from?
2. How long does your body take to digest an apple?
3. What do you add to food when you season it?
4. What is the general name for foods such as spaghetti, macaroni and ravioli?
5. What does vinaigrette sauce contain?
6. If you garnish a dish, what do you do to it?
7. Which expensive food consists of fish eggs?
8. How hot should oil be to cook chips or french fries?
9. What is sauerkraut?
10. What part of a lemon or orange is the zest?
11. What kind of cooking is named from a Spanish word meaning a framework of sticks?

ANSWERS
1 Cheese and toasted bread. 2 About an hour and a half. 3 Pepper and salt, plus other flavourings. 4 Pasta. 5 A mixture of oil, vinegar and spices. 6 Decorate it. 7 Caviare. 8 About 180°F (82°C). 9 Pickled cabbage. 10 The rind. 11 Barbecue.

JAWS IN 3-D

How does a dentist use holograms? A dentist may take an impression of your teeth to make a plaster model of your jaws. The dentist's technician can then make false teeth or a brace that will fit exactly.

However, the dentist needs to keep the plaster jaws to see how the mouth changes as the patient grows. And storing thousands of plaster jaws and finding the right set years later can be a problem.

Dentists have found a solution in holograms. A hologram is a pattern, usually made on photographic film, that can produce a three-dimensional image of an object or scene. Dentists can store a hologram of each jaw in the patient's file. They can then look at the hologram whenever necessary and view the jaw from any angle.

BODY BITS

Which body organs can we do without? Your body is able to withstand a lot of punishment. You can actually lose several of your organs and stay alive. Some of these organs may have little or no use, such as your appendix and tonsils. If they become infected, surgeons can simply remove them.

Several other organs come in pairs – for example, your kidneys and lungs – and one of them can be removed if it becomes diseased and threatens your health. The remaining organ will keep you alive. However, several organs, such as your heart and liver, are vital to life and do not come in pairs. But not all is lost if they are diseased. They can possibly be replaced with organs transplanted from people who have died as a result of an accident.

COLOSSAL ENERGY

Who first unleashed the power of the atom? Nuclear reactors provide immense amounts of power because they split the nuclei (centres) of atoms of uranium and other nuclear fuels in a process called nuclear fission. The first scientist to produce nuclear fission was the Italian physicist, Enrico Fermi, in 1934. He did this on a very small scale in his laboratory, but it was clear that fission could produce energy on a colossal scale.

Fermi later went to the United States and built the first nuclear reactor, which can produce heat energy by nuclear fission. It began operation on 2 December, 1942 at Chicago, introducing nuclear power to the world.

The first nuclear weapon, which was a bomb that worked by nuclear fission, was tested by the United States on 16 July, 1945. Two bombs were dropped on Japan in the following month. Although he had worked on earlier atomic bomb projects, Fermi did not build these bombs.

SUPERTRAINS

How fast are high-speed trains? The fastest rail service in the world is the TGV (*Train Grande Vitesse*) line from Paris to Lyons in France. These trains can reach almost 400 km/h (250 mph), and their average speed is about 250 km/h (150 mph). Japan's 'bullet' trains and Britain's high-speed trains can reach 200 km/h (125 mph). The fastest trains are the experimental maglev trains, which have exceeded 500 km/h (300 mph) in trials.

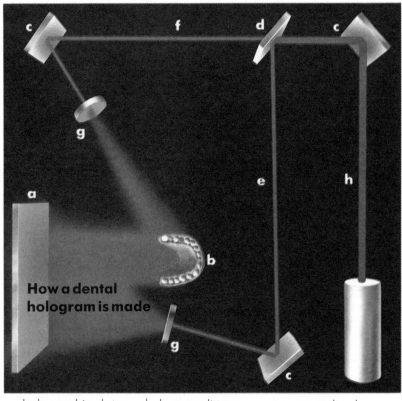

How a dental hologram is made

a	holographic plate	d	beam splitter	g	expanding lens
b	dental cast	e	reference beam	h	laser beam
c	mirror	f	object beam		

◀ A reconstruction beam (identical to the reference beam) is needed to view a hologram.

HOT WELCOME HOME

What is the most dangerous part of spaceflight? The end of a spaceflight is the time when the astronauts aboard are in the most danger. Just before landing, the spacecraft has to re-enter the Earth's atmosphere from space. At this point, the spacecraft is travelling very fast. As it rushes into the upper atmosphere, friction with the air heats the outside of the spacecraft so much that it glows red-hot.

The base of the spacecraft has a heat-resistant shield that enables it to withstand this intense heat. Of course, the spacecraft must be in the right position so that the heat shield strikes the air. If not, the whole spacecraft could burn up.

▲
A flotation collar being inflated around Apollo 14 following its successful re-entry and splashdown.

SILENT SOUND

Which machines are silent but make use of sound? Ultrasound is a kind of sound that we cannot hear. It is too high-pitched for our ears to pick up, though animals such as bats make use of ultrasound. Even though we cannot hear ultrasound, we have machines that can utilize it.

Reflected sound Many ultrasonic machines work in similar ways to bats, which listen to the echoes of their ultrasound squeaks to find their way in the dark. Sonar is a system that measures the depth of water or a shoal of fish beneath a boat. A beam of ultrasound emitted from the boat is reflected by the seabed or the shoal and picked up by a receiver. The time taken for the ultrasound signals to return to the boat is used to calculate the depth.

Inside story Ultrasound scanners are used in medicine to examine the interior of the body, particularly unborn babies inside their mothers. In this case, the ultrasound signals are used to produce a picture, making it possible to check that all is well and, sometimes, to show whether the baby is a boy or a girl. Ultrasound is used not just because it is silent, but because it gives better results than would ordinary sound.

▲
An ultrasound picture of a human foetus in the womb.

THE WHOLE TRUTH?

Do computers have to be so logical? Computers work by obeying the instructions in their programs. These instructions have to be very precise because the computer is totally logical. It follows a program exactly, making decisions on the basis of the information it receives. At each point, it finds out whether something is true or false, and decides to follow one of two possible paths – the yes path or the no path. The computer cannot in one decision determine a state that is *between* true and false and act accordingly.

Precise programs A computer, for example, can easily decide if a number is bigger than a certain value or not. But it could not decide if the number is *much* bigger or just *slightly* bigger. To make this decision the computer would need further very precise instructions. We would have to tell it that a number is much bigger than another if it is more than twice the other number, for example, and then tell it what to do if the number is more than twice as big or less than twice as big, and so on. All that computers can at present decide is true or false.

Fuzzy logic We do not think in such a totally logical way. We assess things, using such concepts as 'high', 'low' and 'probably'. We often say that something is not *completely* true. Computer engineers who are working towards advanced computers that can think more like human beings are investigating a new kind of logic called fuzzy logic. In this kind of logic, statements can be graded so that they have a certain degree of truth but are not necessarily totally true or totally false.

Fuzzy logic will be important in the computers of the future. One field in which it will be necessary will be in medical computers that diagnose illness. They will be able to ask patients questions like '*How much* pain do you feel?' and act on the answer. Another useful field is weather forecasting, in which many different possibilities of weather conditions have to be assessed.

A bank of keyboards and display units linked to a master computer.
▼

CLAY OVEN

What kind of food might be cooked in a hole in the ground? Indian *tandoori* food. The *tandoor*, or *tandur*, is a clay oven which is often sunk neck deep in the ground. Or it can be a tall cylindrical clay oven which was used originally in northern India to cook meat dishes and bread. *Tandoori* food is usually marinated in yoghurt and spices before being cooked in the pre-heated oven. It is possible to cook food that will taste very like *tandoori* dishes in a normal oven at home.

THE LONG SLEEP

What puts people in a coma? A coma is a medical condition in which a person remains unconscious for a long time, possibly for years. There are several causes, including strokes, head injuries and drug overdoses.

One possible reason for continued unconsciousness is brain damage. If this has occurred, then the person may never wake up. However, in many cases patients do come out of a coma and begin life again.

PIONEER FLIGHT

Why was* Flyer 1 *such a good name? *Flyer 1* was the name of the first powered aircraft to take to the air. It was built by the American inventors, Orville and Wilbur Wright, and made its first flight at Kitti Hawk, North Carolina, on 17 December, 1903.

Although *Flyer 1* never made a flight lasting longer than a minute, its design was very sound. Its successors outshone all other early aeroplanes for several years.

BACK IN EIGHT HOURS

How long did it take to take the first photograph? The first photograph was taken by the French inventor, Joseph Niepce, in 1826. It showed the courtyard of his home and it took eight hours to make the exposure! Fortunately, photography soon improved and exposures became short enough to take pictures of people.

The world's first photograph was ▶ taken using a specially treated light sensitive metal plate.

SUPER SPARK

How powerful is lightning? A flash of lightning is a giant spark of electricity with a power of as much as 30 million volts. Its temperature is about 30,000°C or 54,000°F, which is five times as hot as the surface of the Sun.

Lightning is caused by huge electrical sparks during thunderstorms.
▼

FACT FILE: SPACEFLIGHT

FACT The first satellite was the Russian *Sputnik 1*. It was launched on 4 October, 1957.
FACT The first spacecraft to reach another world was the Russian space probe *Luna 2*. It crashed on the Moon on 13 September, 1959.
FACT The first woman to fly in space was the Russian cosmonaut, Valentina Tereshkova. She orbited the Earth aboard the spacecraft *Vostok 6* in 1963.
FACT The first space shuttle, called *Columbia*, began its maiden flight on 12 April 1981 — exactly 20 years to the day after the first manned spaceflight.
FACT In 1983, the American space probe *Pioneer 10* became the first spacecraft to leave the solar system and head for the stars.

▲
Mist is caused by water vapour condensing into water droplets in the air.

BONDS OF FORCE

Why are some things solid and others liquid or gas? All substances consist of atoms, which are tiny particles that are linked to each other by forces called bonds. The atoms may link together to form groups called molecules, which are similarly bound together by forces.

The strength of the forces between atoms and molecules varies from one substance to another. In a solid, the forces are strong and they hold the atoms and molecules together in rows. This makes a solid tough. In a liquid, the forces are less strong and the atoms and molecules can move about sufficiently to allow the liquid to flow. In a gas, the atoms and molecules are linked very weakly, and they move about a lot. This is why a gas behaves in the way it does.

Heating a substance makes the forces between the atoms and molecules weaker, while cooling makes them stronger. As a result all substances freeze, melt, condense or boil at certain temperatures.

CURVED STRENGTH

What do dams have in common with eggs? High dams often consist of a slim arch of concrete. The dam curves into the water so that as the water pushes against the dam, it compresses the whole structure. Compressed concrete is very strong, and the dam remains standing even though it is so thin.

Similarly, a bird's egg has to be sufficiently strong to protect the growing bird inside, yet weak enough to allow the bird to break out and hatch. Eggs are curved for this reason. A force applied to the outside compresses the egg, making the shell strong and preventing it from breaking (unless the force is very strong). The growing bird is likely to remain safe inside. However, as the shell is not compressed when force is applied from the inside, the chick finds it easy to force its way out into the world.

◄ The curved construction of these dams — clearly seen from above.

TRUE TARTAN

What subject was chosen for the first colour photograph? The first colour photograph required a very colourful subject, so a tartan ribbon was chosen. It was produced under the direction of the British physicist, James Clerk Maxwell, in 1861. He took and superimposed separate red, green and blue photographs of the ribbon to produce a full-colour picture. The same basic process is used in colour photography and television today.

RADIUM PIONEER

Who was the first woman to become a great scientist?
Marie Curie, a French physicist, was the first woman to achieve great fame in science. She was born in Poland in 1867 and married the French scientist, Pierre Curie, in 1895. Her main interest was radioactivity, which she showed to be caused by radioactive elements such as uranium.

Investigating a source of very intense radioactivity in uranium ore, Marie Curie identified radium in 1898. Four years later, she managed to prepare the element itself, having extracted less than a gram of radium metal from several tons of ore. In 1934, she died of leukaemia, a form of cancer probably caused by her lengthy exposure to radioactivity in her work.

▲
Pioneer physicist Marie Curie in her laboratory.

SPACE WAR

How do antisatellite weapons work? Antisatellite weapons could take war into space, for they are intended to destroy enemy satellites, especially communications satellites. One form of antisatellite weapon is a missile fired from an aircraft flying very high in the Earth's atmosphere. The missile streaks off up into space, homes in on the satellite and destroys it.

A future space weapon may consist of a satellite armed with a laser that could instantly destroy any other satellite within reach of its beam.

TAMING THE THAMES

How is London protected from flooding? The whole of Britain is slowly tilting, so that the south-east corner is sinking at about 30 cm (1 ft) per century. Also, tides in the North Sea have been increasing in height. These two things have combined so that, over the past century, the level of the River Thames has risen by about 60 cm (2 ft) where it flows through London. This rise is likely to continue, threatening London with a major disaster when heavy rain and flood tides produce a sudden increase in water surging up from the sea.

Engineers have now tamed London's river so that it is no longer a danger. The Thames Barrier has been constructed across the mouth of the river and the banks built up at dangerous points. If a surge should occur, the barrier will hold it back. Massive gates 20 m (65 ft) high will rise from the riverbed to seal off the river while the surge lasts.

▲
The Thames Barrier — the largest tidal river barrier in the world — has ten hydraulically operated gates to hold back any tidal surges. ▶

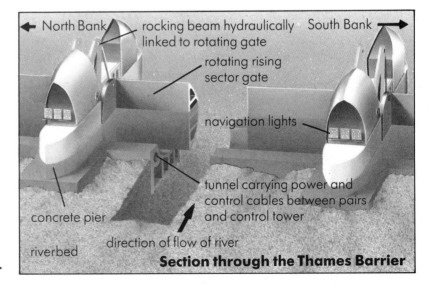

← North Bank   rocking beam hydraulically linked to rotating gate   South Bank →

rotating rising sector gate

navigation lights

tunnel carrying power and control cables between pairs and control tower

concrete pier

direction of flow of river

riverbed

Section through the Thames Barrier

FINE WORK

How do surgeons sew on severed limbs? There is now less fear of losing a limb or a finger in an accident. Surgeons can reattach the missing part by sewing it back on again.

The method, which is called microsurgery, is highly intricate.

The surgeon has to connect up tiny blood vessels and nerves, using minute needles and nylon thread so fine that it is almost invisible. The operation is performed using a microscope to magnify the surgical instruments and tissues.

◄ Blood vessels being connected artificially during microsurgery.

FOOLING RADAR

How can warplanes avoid being detected by the enemy? Defences against modern fighter bomber aircraft depend greatly on radar. The radar systems bounce signals off the aircraft, picking up the reflected signals so that aircraft can be located and tracked. If an aircraft is to get through defences, it needs to make itself invisible to radar.

There are two ways to do this. One is to fly very low – at tree-top height or just above the waves. The radar systems are then confused by signals reflected by the land or water, and cannot detect the aircraft. The second is to design the aircraft so that it does not reflect radar signals. This is done by using radar-absorbent coatings on the aircraft and smoothing its surfaces.

LOW BOWS

When do archers lie on their backs to shoot an arrow? There are several forms of the sport of archery. They include bow hunting, target archery, field archery and flight shooting. In flight shooting the object is to shoot the arrow as far as possible.

Special bows with a draw weight of up to 91 kg (200 lb) are used, and small, lightweight arrows. In ordinary flight shooting, archers shoot while standing. But in free-style flight shooting, archers lie on their backs with the bow strapped to their feet. This enables them to use both hands to draw the bow. In this way, expert archers can shoot farther than 640 m (700 yds).

QUIZ: FAMOUS STRUCTURES

1. How many spectators can cram into the world's largest stadium?
2. How high is the world's tallest structure?
3. Where is the Eiffel Tower?
4. How many rooms are there in the world's biggest hotel?
5. What is crossed by the world's longest bridge?
6. Where would you find the Empire State Building?
7. Which famous structure stretches from the Atlantic Ocean to the Pacific Ocean?
8. Where is the tallest tower in the world?
9. Which city has the world's highest monument?

ANSWERS
1 240,000 – in the Strahov Stadium, Prague, Czechoslovakia.
2 646 m (2,121 ft) – it's a radio mast in Poland. 3 Paris, France. 4 3,200 – at the Hotel Rossiya, Moscow. 5 Lake Pontchartrain, Louisiana, USA; it's 38.4 km (nearly 24 miles) long. 6 New York City. 7 Panama Canal. 8 Toronto, Canada. 9 St Louis, Missouri, USA – it's an arch 192 m (630 ft) high.

GOOD AND EVIL

What's so special about nuclear power? Nuclear power, or atomic energy as it is also called, is extremely powerful. It produces energy in far greater amounts than any other source of power. Nuclear power stations generate electricity using only small quantities of nuclear fuels such as uranium, instead of the huge amounts of coal and oil burned by ordinary power stations.

But as well as providing us with useful power in the form of electricity, nuclear power also threatens us. Nuclear weapons use the immense strength of nuclear power for destruction. They also produce dangerous radiation, as does the waste from nuclear power stations.

COMPUTER KNOW-ALL

How can systems be expert? Expert systems are computer programs that make a computer into an expert on a subject. You can ask the computer any question on a subject and it should give you the answer. This is not just like looking up a book to get some information. An expert system may ask *you* questions to find out exactly what you want to know, and then give you advice if necessary. Expert systems are produced by feeding the computer with as much knowledge as possible about a subject. The program is then written so that people can usefully quiz the computer.

Practical applications Expert systems are becoming an increasingly important field of computing. Two areas in which they have made headway are geological prospecting and medical diagnosis. Geologists can tell the computer about the rocks in a particular location. The computer can then predict whether valuable minerals are likely to be found there or not. In medicine, doctors can give the computer facts about a patient's condition, and it will reply with the likely causes.

Fuel rod entry point of a power plant reactor (right) and the radioactive 'mushroom' cloud caused by an atomic bomb test. ▼

▲
Many plants flourish in the warm conditions of a greenhouse.

TRAPPED RAYS

Why is it warm in a greenhouse? Even without heating, it's warmer in a greenhouse than it is outside. The same increase of air temperature also occurs behind closed windows – for example, in a car.

The reason is not that a cold wind might be blowing outside. It's because invisible heat rays from the Sun bombard us, even on cloudy days. They pass through the panes of glass but cannot get out again. Once inside, the rays warm the interior.

The keyboard of a professional assembly language computer.
▼

BINARY BYPASSES

What kind of language does a computer really understand? To program a computer for a certain task, you have to write a computer program. This is a list of instructions that is fed into the computer. The program is written by using the keyboard of the computer. When it is complete, the program can be recorded on a magnetic tape or disc.

High-level language A program is written in a computer language. Often this is a high-level language, such as BASIC. It contains special keywords that are English words, such as PRINT, AND, NEXT, REPEAT and so on. The computer obeys instructions containing these words, just as we do. PRINT causes the computer to print or display something, while REPEAT tells it to repeat something, and so on.

Using a high-level computer language makes programming possible for many people, as well as enabling programmers to understand other people's programs. Also, a program written in a particular language for one computer will generally work on another kind of computer that uses the same language.

Binary code However, a computer contains a high-level computer language only for our convenience. The computer does not really understand it. It turns the various instructions in the language into electric signals in binary code, which consists of rapid on-off pulses of electricity. Each instruction has a particular code and causes the computer to carry out a particular operation.

Binary code is the language that the computer really understands. It would be impossible for people to use binary code to program computers, which is why computer languages have been developed. However, the translation process by which the computer turns the language into binary code can take some time, and programs written in high-level languages may run slowly and also take up a lot of memory space in the computer.

Assembly language To overcome this problem, programmers can instead use assembly language, which is a low-level language. In this language, instructions are given as initials, such as LDA, meaning 'load the accumulator' (a section of the central processing unit). The computer translates assembly language into binary code very quickly, and programs using it run fast. They also take up little memory. However, to use assembly language, a good knowledge of the workings of the particular computer is required. Many computer games are written in assembly language, which is also known as machine code.

MANNED KITES

Did you know that people first took to the air in China many centuries ago? The first people to be carried aloft were lifted into the air by huge kites. The explorer Marco Polo witnessed man-carrying kites in China in the 1200s – and they may have been invented long before that.

These pioneers of flight did not do it for pleasure. The kites were used to lift people in order to spy on enemy positions, and also as an unusual means of punishing criminals!

SPACE FLOAT

Can astronauts really walk in space? A space 'walk' is performed when an astronaut leaves a spacecraft during a mission. Wearing a spacesuit, the astronaut floats in space, moving with the aid of gas-powered thrusters that work like miniature rocket engines. But the astronaut does not use his or her legs to walk. The suit and manoeuvring unit act like a personal spacecraft that carries the astronaut through space.

PHANTOM FINN

Why is Paavo Nurmi regarded as one of the greatest distance runners ever? Known as the 'Phantom' or 'Flying Finn', Nurmi held more than twenty world records. He used to run carrying a stopwatch in order to check his own speed. At the Olympic Games in Paris in 1924, he won seven races in six days!

BARGING ALONG

Where can you see trains on water? You can see trains on large rivers like the Rhine and Mississippi. They're not railway trains, of course, but 'trains' of barges. These are long lines of unpowered barges hauled or pushed by a powered barge. There may be as many as 40 barges in a train.

AMPLE FLOW

How many electrons are there in an electric current? When an electric current flows through a wire, tiny particles called electrons move along the wire. For every amp of current, about 6 million million million electrons pass every second.

◀ An astronaut floats above Earth with the aid of a manoeuvring unit.

▲
This windmill generates electricity for use in the home.

BREEZING ALONG

Has the windmill a future?
Windmills are coming back, though not the beautiful old buildings with great whirling sails. Modern windmills are called wind generators, and they look like enormous propellors. They are built in windy places and generate electricity.

Boats may also sprout windmills. Experimental boats have been built that capture the wind with a large propellor called a wind turbine. This turns a screw to drive the boat through the water. The advantage of a wind turbine over sails is that the turbine can be turned to face the wind, enabling the boat to proceed in any direction.

SNAPS ON DISC

Photographs without film – how do they work? A new system of taking photographs does not use film at all. It is electronic and the camera is rather like a television camera and video recorder rolled into one. It converts the scene into electric signals that are recorded on a magnetic disc in the camera. To see the pictures, the disc can be placed in a viewer unit that is plugged into a television set. It is then possible to record the pictures on video tape and have prints made of those you like.

One great advantage of this system is that when you have finished with a disc, you can wipe it clean and take new pictures on the same disc. Unlike film, you don't waste your money on poor or unwanted pictures.

This prototype 'video still' camera ▶ uses a traditional lens system to record images on a magnetic disc.

FACT FILE: TRANSPORT FEATS

FACT The first vessel to sail around the world was the Spanish ship *Vittoria*. The voyage took almost three years from 1519 to 1522.
FACT The deepest undersea voyage was made in 1960 to the bottom of the Pacific Ocean, a depth of nearly 11 km (7 miles).
FACT The fastest car is the British jet-engined vehicle *Thrust 2*. It reached a speed of 1,019 km/h (633 mph) in 1983.
FACT The fastest bicycles can exceed 150 km/h (93 mph).
FACT The fastest form of passenger transport is the supersonic airliner *Concorde*. It has a cruising speed of about 2,300 km/h (1,430 mph), and can fly from New York to London in less than three hours.
FACT A new aerospace vehicle planned by the US for the 1990s will be able to fly anywhere in the world in no more than 90 minutes.

IN TOUCH

How can we not get away from it all? Some people like to be in touch with others at all times, even when they are travelling. For them, there are now cellular telephones. These are telephones that you carry with you wherever you go. They ring if anyone wants to contact you, and can be used just like an ordinary telephone.

Cellular telephones work by radio and do not have wires. They link up with local radio communications centres that are scattered in a network of radio 'cells' throughout the country.

▲
Keeping in touch with the home or office is easy with a cellular phone.

HEALTHY GLOW

How much energy have you got? We say that we have a lot of energy when we're lively and no energy when we're tired. In fact, we all possess energy all the time, for we need it to stay alive.

Your energy is in the form of your body heat, the movement of your muscles, and the electrical currents in your brain and nerves. It comes from your food and drink. You use up more of this energy when you are lively and less when you rest. But, on average, you have about the same amount of energy as a glowing electric light bulb.

DO AS I DO

How does a robot perform actions? A robot has an arm which contains hydraulic or electric motors that move it in three basic directions. The arm can move up and down, to either side, and in and out. A computer controls the motors, combining all three movements so that the end of the arm can be directed to any position within reach.

At the end of the robot's arm is a gripping unit. This has its own motors which, also under computer control, enable the unit to move like a human wrist. It holds a tool such as a welding torch, and the gripping unit and robot arm move so that the tool follows a particular routine.

The computer is programmed with all the movements that the robot must perform. These may be 'taught' to the robot first. A human operator handles the robot, moving the tool through all the actions required. The computer memorizes the movements so that the robot can perform them exactly whenever required.

Robot arms like this are invaluable in many industrial processes.
▼

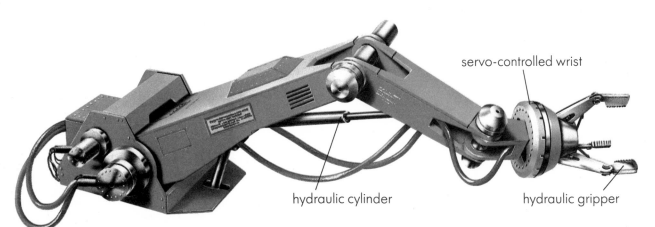

servo-controlled wrist

hydraulic cylinder

hydraulic gripper

FLIGHT FANTASTIC

How can you learn to fly without leaving the ground? Many aircraft pilots are trained in flight simulators on the ground. These are computer-controlled machines that resemble the flight deck of an aircraft. As the pilot operates the controls, the simulator twists and turns to produce the same kind of movements as a real aircraft. The pilot sees moving pictures, so that a ride in the simulator not only feels like a real flight, but also looks real.

In fact, flight simulators are so realistic that trainee pilots cannot bring themselves to 'crash', even for fun. There are also car simulators that help people learning to drive.

▲
The computerized control panels of a flight simulator used in research.

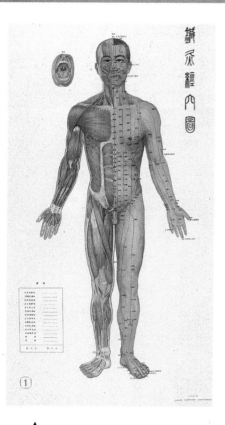

▲
A traditional acupuncture chart showing lines of body 'energy'.

GETTING THE NEEDLE

How does acupuncture treat people? The ancient Chinese medical practice of acupuncture treats people by sticking needles into them. This is not done to give injections. The needles are lightly inserted into the skin at selected places on the body, and twirled or vibrated for a certain period of time. While it may not always effect a cure, it appears that acupuncture does relieve pain.

The reason that acupuncture works seems to be that the insertion and movement of the needles affect the nervous system and brain, stimulating the release of natural pain-killing substances and so preventing pain. The needles must be placed at the right points (which may be anywhere on the body) to treat a particular condition.

Applied technology Two developments of traditional acupuncture employ modern technology – electro-acupuncture and laser therapy. In electro-acupuncture, electric currents are fed to the needles to stimulate them. Laser therapy uses low-power laser beams instead of needles at the acupuncture points.

QUICKSILVER

Are all metals solid? At everyday temperatures, all metals except one are solid. The exception is mercury, which is a silvery liquid – hence its other name of quicksilver. Mercury only becomes solid at −39°C (−38°F), a temperature that is reached in very cold regions.

If heated sufficiently, all metals melt to liquids and then boil to become gases.

LASERS FOR LIFE

Cutting without knives and welding without torches – how's it done? Surgeons can cut tissues without using knives. They use a laser beam which delivers intense heat to the tissue. The beam cuts effortlessly and with total cleanliness. It also seals blood vessels so that the cut does not bleed.

Eye surgery can also be carried out by laser – without cutting open the eye! The retina at the back of the eye can become detached, which causes blindness. Firing a laser beam into the eye can weld the retina back into place and thus restore sight.

DOING THE DIRTY WORK

Where do robots really come into their own? Robots can help us greatly by doing work that is too dangerous for us. They can go into places that we dare not or cannot enter and carry out essential repair work. These places include parts of nuclear power stations, chemical processing plants and coal mines. It's quite possible that in this way, robots will prevent disasters from happening. And if an accident does occur, robots might be able to rescue people.

Robots may also become astronauts. Instead of sending people into space, much work in space is likely to be performed by robots controlled by radio and television signals from transmitters on the ground.

Col. Edwin 'Buzz' Aldrin stepping ▶ onto the surface of the moon on 20 July 1969.

THE APOLLO PROJECT

How did the first astronauts get to the Moon? The first people to fly to the Moon were the American astronauts Neil Armstrong and Edwin Aldrin, who landed there on 20 July 1969.

The spacecraft The *Apollo* spacecraft was launched by the huge Saturn 5 rocket towards the Moon. It contained three modules, or sections. The conical command module was the main cabin for the three astronauts aboard *Apollo*. Behind it was the cylindrical service module, which contained the main engine, fuel and oxygen supplies. In front of the command module was the lunar module, a strange spider-shaped craft with legs for landing on the Moon.

Landing and returning When *Apollo* neared its destination, the main engine fired so that it went into orbit around the Moon. Then two of the astronauts entered the lunar module, separated it from the rest of the spacecraft and flew it down to the Moon's surface.

After exploring the Moon, the two astronauts flew back to *Apollo* in the lunar module. The main engine fired again to send the spacecraft back to Earth. Only the command module landed, splashing down into the sea beneath parachutes. The other two modules were abandoned.

BUBBLES UP

What gives the rise in self-raising flour? Self-raising flour contains baking powder which is usually made from a mixture of sodium bicarbonate and tartaric acid. When this mixture is heated or made wet it produces carbon dioxide gas, causing the formation of bubbles in the dough or cake mixture. It is these bubbles of gas that cause the mixture to rise when it is cooked.

A scene of devastation resulting from the use of defoliant weapons during the Vietnam War.
▼

AUTOMATIC TYPIST

What does a word processor do? Word processor is rather a grand name for a machine that is a combination of computer and typewriter. It processes words, meaning that it can handle words in several useful ways, and helps people to produce high quality letters and documents, and to save time.

'Keying-in' To operate a word processor, you type words on its keyboard. The words appear on the machine's screen and also go into its memory. At any time, you can change any word or words that you have typed. You can correct mistakes, repeat sections or insert particular words, for example, often at the press of a single key. The word processor will also automatically count the words and lines in a letter or document, and set the margins. It may even check the spelling and warn the operator if a word is not spelt correctly!

Storage and retrieval When the letter or document is finished and corrected, the word processor's printer will print it out on paper at the touch of a key. The contents can be stored on magnetic disc and fed back into the word processor later if required. Any part of the document can be changed. In this way, copies and changes can be made later without having to type the whole document again.

POISON WAR

How do chemical weapons strike? Chemical weapons contain poisons that are directed against an enemy. They can be placed in shells and bombs that are fired or dropped on enemy positions. Some of the most dangerous include nerve gases, which affect the nervous system and are deadly even in minute amounts. Several countries have stocks of chemical weapons.

Poison gases were used in World War I, causing more than a million casualties. No chemical weapons were used in World War II, but substances which destroyed crops and trees that could hide troops were used in the Vietnam War. These also affected many people.

CHUTE PROOF

Which life-saving invention was inspired by the umbrella? The invention was the parachute which was invented by the French scientist, Louis Lenormand, in 1783. His first jump was an experimental descent from a tree-top, suspended beneath two parasols. (The parasol is so-named because it gives protection against the sun, and the parachute gives protection against a chute or fall.)

The parachute is an example of an invention that came at just the right time, for the first flights in balloons were made in the very same year. The first true parachute jump was made from a balloon in 1797, when André-Jacques Garnerin safely descended 680 m (2,230 ft) beneath an enormous umbrella-shaped canopy.

◀ Parachutes enable these sky divers to float gently to the ground.

SPACE FOLK

Could people be born in space? It is possible that people will be born in space and live their whole lives there. These space people will be human beings who have left Earth to live in space colonies. The colonies will be gigantic spacecraft, many kilometres across, in which there could be whole cities, together with fields and lakes.

The colonies would grow their own food to support a human population of thousands of people. They could make special space products to trade with Earth, or maybe offer space holidays to Earth tourists. It all sounds like science fiction, but scientists have actually designed viable space colonies that may one day exist.

QUIZ: SPORTS

1. What is the real name of Pelé, the Brazilian footballer?
2. How long is a marathon?
3. What is the maximum break in snooker?
4. What is the Cresta Run?
5. What sport is associated with the Queensbury Rules?
6. Which country has won the greatest number of medals in the Olympics?
7. What is a clean and jerk?
8. How often does the Ryder Cup professional golf match take place?
9. In lugeing, does the rider lie on his front or back?
10. In international gymnastic competitions, how many events are there in men's contests?
11. In which game is play started by a bully?

ANSWERS
1 Edson Arantes do Nascimento. 2 42.95 km (26 miles 385 yds). 3 147. 4 Toboggan course in Switzerland. 5 Boxing. 6 USA. 7 Type of lift in weightlifting. 8 Every two years. 9 Back. 10 Seven. 11 Hockey.

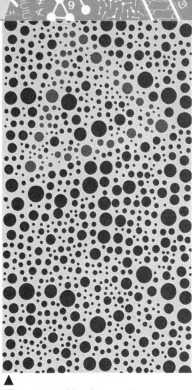

Illustrations like this can be used to detect colour blindness.

RAYS AND RAINBOWS

Why are colours different to each other? Unless you are colour blind, you can see things in all the colours of the rainbow. Objects have different colours because the light rays that come from them to our eyes have different frequencies.

Varying frequencies A light ray consists of magnetic and electric fields that vibrate at a certain rate which is called the frequency. The vibration is very fast — from about 400 million million times a second for deep red light, up to about 750 million million times a second for blue light, with the other colours of the rainbow in between. When a light ray strikes your eye, small structures called cones in the retina at the back of the eye respond to the frequency of the light and you see a colour. In colour-blind people, the cones are abnormal. They may respond differently, so that another colour is seen.

What makes a colour? But why does a red object, say, produce red light and a yellow object yellow light? The answer lies in the surface of the object, which sends light rays towards the eye. As the rays leave the surface, the atoms in the surface emit the light rays at a particular frequency. This frequency depends on the movement of electrons in the atoms. The light that comes from the surface has, therefore, a certain colour, which is determined by the kinds of atoms in the surface.

DO NOT BEND

Why are floppy discs floppy?
Floppy discs are magnetic discs on which computer programs and data (information) are stored in the form of code signals. They fit into a disc drive connected to a computer. The discs revolve rapidly inside the drive, and a head records or picks up the computer code signals.

Floppy discs are flexible rather than floppy. This is so that the discs can be handled without risk of permanently bending them, which would make them useless.

POLES APART

What can't you split in two?
No matter how hard you tried, there is one thing that you could not divide in two. It is a magnet. If you cut any magnet in half, no matter how large or small, you would not get two *separate* halves of the magnet. You would get two new smaller magnets.

The reason is that every magnet has two poles — a north pole at one end and a south pole at the other. It is impossible to have one kind of magnetic pole without the other. So, if a magnet is cut in half, new poles form at the ends of the two pieces.

◀ A floppy disc in position. Because a disc can store so much data, it is divided into a number of tracks which simplifies the location of specific pieces of information.

TWITCH ON

Who made a famous discovery using a frog's legs? Electric current was first produced in the legs of a dead frog! The Italian anatomist, Luigi Galvani, made this momentous discovery by accident in about 1790.

Galvani hung the legs on some brass hooks against some iron railings, and noticed that they began to twitch. He thought that the frog's body contained electricity that made the muscles in the legs twitch. In fact, the electricity was produced by connecting up the brass and iron metals in the hooks and railings with the damp tissue in the legs.

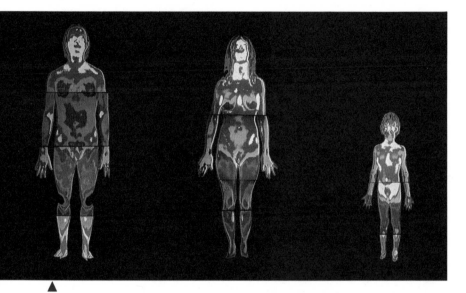

▲
Doctors can use heat pictures to identify different body temperatures.

HEAT SEEKERS

How can we see heat? You may not know it, but your body is giving off heat rays. So is everything else around you. The strength of these rays, which are also known as infrared rays, depends on how warm or cold things are.

Special cameras and instruments can pick up these heat rays and turn them into pictures. In this way, it is possible to detect and see things in complete darkness. Some burglar alarms work in this way, and so do night sights used on guns. It's also possible to take heat pictures of objects that show how hot or cold various parts of them are. This is very useful in finding out where heat is escaping from a building, for example, or if a part of the body is unusually hot or cold.

After the earthquake in Mexico City in 1985, these special instruments were used to locate survivors buried in the rubble.

WING-SWINGER

Why do fighter planes swing their wings? Many modern fighter aircraft take off and land with their wings at right angles to the fuselage. Then, once in the air, the wings swing back.

The reason for this is that swept-back wings work best at high speeds, particularly supersonic speeds. However, they do not give much lift at the slow speeds of take off and landing. So, as the plane slows down to land, the wings swing forward to maintain lift and keep the aircraft flying.

With wings swept back, this bomber ▶ can fly at twice the speed of sound.

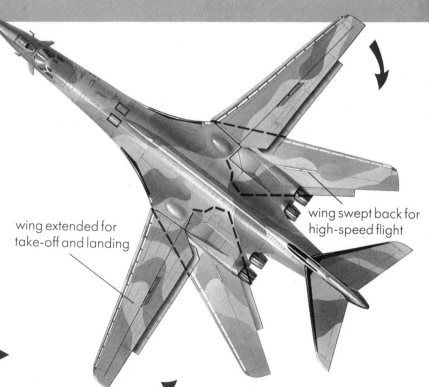

wing extended for take-off and landing

wing swept back for high-speed flight

PICTURES IN DEPTH

Pictures in which you can look round corners – how are holograms made? A hologram of an object is made on a piece of photographic film by using a laser. The object is lit by the laser, and this light is reflected by the object on to the film. Light from the laser also strikes the film directly. The light from the object and from the laser combine to produce a pattern, which shows when the film is developed.

The pattern does not resemble the object – until the film is illuminated. Then the object appears, and this is the hologram. The image is three-dimensional, having depth like the real object. By moving your head, you can see round any corners in the image.

Each part of the film actually contains a slightly different image of the object. When you look at a hologram, each eye therefore receives a separate image, and these images combine to give the realistic three-dimensional effect.

Holograms can also be made in which very different images can be seen when you move your head. The image may appear to move, or it may change completely.

▲ A holographic plate of the keys of St Petersburg in the USSR.

▲ A good sense of balance is essential for a racing cyclist.

BALANCING ACT

How do we manage to stay upright on bicycles? If you try to balance on a bicycle that is not moving, you simply fall over. But once the wheels start turning, you can do it. Why should this be?

The answer lies in a strange property possessed by a rotating wheel. It's called precession. Take a bicycle wheel from the frame, hold it by the axle and spin it. Then try to turn the axle and the wheel will twist violently. This is precession. What happens is that the wheel twists at a right angle to the direction in which you try to turn the axle.

Without realizing it, you constantly wobble the front wheel slightly as you ride a bicycle. The bicycle tilts to left or right as you ride, and you turn the front wheel to correct the tilt. Precession occurs and moves the wheel – and bicycle – upright, so that you balance.

NIGHT SHIFT

What do power stations do at night? Power stations do not need to produce so much electricity during the night, but they do not all take a rest. At night, many stations use their power to pump water up to a reservoir above the power station. Then during the day, they use this water to generate electricity. In this way, the power generated at night is stored in the water so that it can be used during the day.

SOFT LANDING

At what speed are skydivers travelling when they hit the ground? Provided the parachute opens, at about 40 km/h (25 mph). During free-fall they reach speeds of more than 160 km/h (100 mph). They usually open their parachutes at a height of about 700 m (2,300 ft).

Free-falling skydivers (right) ▶ before their parachutes open.

ALL CLEAR

Why are 'rip-offs' so important to a Grand Prix racing driver? During a race the driver's visor becomes obscured by oil and dirt thrown up from the track. Attached to the front of the visor are a number of thin, transparent plastic strips, one placed over the other. These are the 'rip-offs'. The strips are torn off by the driver and thrown away during the race as they become hard to see through. This ensures clear vision for the driver.

▲ Visor 'rip-offs' enable a racing driver to maintain clear vision.

NUMBER CRUNCHER

How fast do computers work? Although computers perform amazing tasks, they do them by breaking everything down into many simple calculations. But these calculations are done at lightning speed. The most powerful computers can carry out as many as 800 million calculations a second.

LIKE TWO PEAS IN A POD

Who made the great discovery by growing peas? The laws of heredity, which explain why children are like their parents, were discovered by an Austrian monk called Gregor Mendel. He did this by growing peas in his monastery garden. For eight years from 1857, Mendel observed traits in successive generations of peas and deduced the laws of heredity. Yet his discovery was ignored at the time. It was not until 1900, sixteen years after Mendel died, that scientists realized the importance of his work.

FACT FILE: WORLD'S GREATEST STRUCTURES

FACT The world's biggest structure is the Great Wall of China. Built in the 200s BC, it originally had a total length of almost 10,000 km (6,200 miles).

FACT The tallest skyscraper, the Sears Tower in Chicago, USA, has 110 floors and rises 443 m (1,454 ft), discounting the television masts on top.

FACT The bridge with the longest single span is the Humber Bridge in Britain. The span measures 1,410 m (4,626 ft).

FACT The highest dam, under construction in Russia, is to rise 325 m (1,066 ft).

FACT The longest tunnel used for transport is an undersea rail tunnel in Japan almost 54 km (33½ miles) long.

FACT The largest monument is the Quetzalcoatl Pyramid in Mexico. Built about 1,500 years ago, it has a volume of more than 3 million cubic metres (over 4 million cubic yards).

FACT The deepest shaft, bored in Russia, is about 12 km (7½ miles) deep.

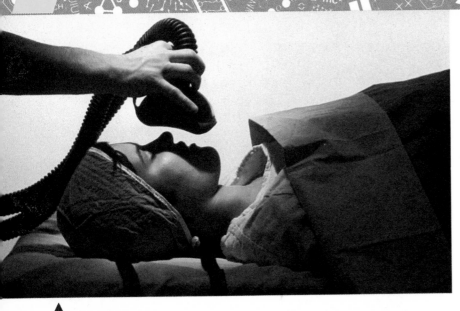

▲
A patient being given an anaesthetic before undergoing surgery.

ROM AND RAM

In what ways does a computer use its memory? A computer has three kinds of memory – ROM, RAM and storage. They hold information and instructions, either permanently or only when required. This is rather like the way in which we can remember things so deeply that we never forget them, like our names, or so lightly that we forget them as soon as we no longer need them, such as a telephone number.

Microchip memories Inside a computer are two kinds of memory chips – ROM (read-only memory) and RAM (random-access memory). ROM chips contain the instructions that operate the computer; these are permanent. RAM chips are fed with programs and data, which they hold only as long as they are required. New programs and data can be fed into RAM to make the computer perform different tasks.

Storage systems The programs and data are stored permanently on magnetic discs or tapes. These are connected to the computer and fed into RAM whenever particular programs and data are needed.

Instant picture film allows you to see a finished print seconds after pressing the shutter release button.
▼

THIS WON'T HURT

How do anaesthetics work? Having a tooth extracted or drilled may not be pleasant but – thanks to anaesthetics – at least it's not painful. These drugs also prevent pain in surgical operations.

We feel pain because electrical signals flash along the nerves in our body from the part that hurts to the brain. Anaesthetics interfere with the nerves so that these pain signals are blocked. A general anaesthetic renders the whole body painless (and temporarily unconscious), while a local anaesthetic affects only the part that hurts and leaves the patient conscious.

SNAP AND DELIVER

How do instant cameras take instant pictures? Today's cameras can really make photography foolproof. They have electric motors to wind the film, automatic light sensors that measure the light in a scene, autofocus mechanisms that detect the distance of a subject, and miniature computers that work out the correct exposure. All you need do is point the camera in the right direction and press the button.

Some cameras then go on to deliver colour prints instantly. The print is a sheet of plastic on which the picture rapidly appears. It contains several layers of dyes and chemicals, over which a white top layer forms immediately the print leaves the camera. This top layer prevents light reaching the lower layers, while the picture develops there. The top layer clears when the picture is ready to be seen.

A GIANT LEAP

Why is the 1968 long jump record so difficult to beat? The Olympic Games were held in Mexico in 1968 and some athletes set spectacular records. Robert Beamon (USA) jumped an incredible 55.25 cm (1 ft 9¾ in) further than anyone had ever jumped before! He added a greater amount to the long jump record than all the additions of the previous forty years added together. The main reason for such an enormous jump is that Mexico City is at high altitude and the force of gravity is slightly less. The record-breaking achievements at Mexico were also helped by the introduction of smooth artificial surfaces.

▲
Bob Beamon's medal-winning jump at the Mexico Olympics in 1972.

FAST LIVING!

Why did people once believe that astronomers were shortening their lives? In 1582, on the advice of astronomers, Pope Gregory XIII decided to reform the calendar. He introduced the calendar we have now with its use of leap years. However, to get the calendar in step with the seasons, it was necessary to change the date. The Pope decreed that Thursday, 4 October would be followed by Friday, 15 October!

Many people thought that this change would shorten their lives by ten days. They rioted, demanding that their lost days be given back to them.

A FISHY BUSINESS

Why do some Japanese fishmongers have a licence not to kill? Because they are the special fishmongers in Japan with a licence to prepare *fugu*, a species of blowfish which has certain parts that are deadly poisonous. If the fish is not cleaned properly, it is said that the poison can kill within five minutes. In spite of very careful precautions, some 200 Japanese people a year die from *fugu* poisoning!

FLYING LEVIATHANS

Which are the largest aircraft? The largest airliner is the Boeing 747 jumbo jet, which can carry as many as 600 passengers. The aircraft with the biggest capacity is the Aero Spacelines Super Guppy cargo aircraft. Its hold measures more than 1,000 cubic metres (35,000 cubic feet) in volume, the size of a house.

But these monsters of the air are not the biggest machines ever to have flown. The airships of the past would dwarf today's aircraft, being more than three times as long as a jumbo jet.

The nose of one of the largest airliners—the 747 Jumbo jet.
▶

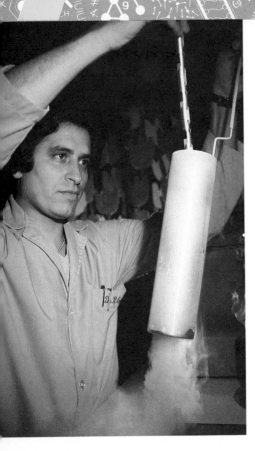

▲
A doctor stores sperm to be used in test-tube conception.

HEAT FLOW

Why are some materials colder to the touch than others?
Provided it has not been heated, a metal object normally feels quite cold. Something made of wood feels less chilly and cloth doesn't feel cold at all. Yet all these objects have the same temperature!

The reason is that your fingertips are warmer than the objects. Heat therefore flows into the metal from your fingertips, sharply lowering their temperature, so that they feel cold. Most metals are good conductors of heat. Wood is not such a good conductor, while cloth is a poor conductor. So less heat leaves your fingertips as you touch them, and they do not feel so cold.

HELPING NATURE

Can babies really be born in test-tubes? We hear a lot about 'test-tube' babies. These babies are not, in fact, born in a test-tube, but they do *begin* life in one.

Medicine can sometimes help people who cannot have children. Normally, a new life begins in the mother's womb when a sperm cell from the father fertilizes an egg cell from the mother. The two cells fuse together into one human cell, and this cell begins to grow into a baby.

If normal fertilization does not occur, doctors can now carry out fertilization outside the mother's body. They take the cells and unite them in suitable equipment, which is popularly called a test-tube. The fertilized cell is then placed in the mother's womb to grow normally.

The first 'test-tube' baby was Louise Brown, who was born perfectly healthy and normal in Britain in 1978. Many more such babies have been born since then.

BITS IN A BYTE

Binary, bits and bytes – what's the difference? These three terms are all computer jargon, and they refer to the way in which the computer works.

All computers work by changing everything they handle into electric code signals. These are in binary code, which means that they consist of sequences of on-off pulses of electricity. These code signals flash to and fro between the computer's electronic components to make it work. The code is called binary code because there are only two different states used – on and off.

Each on or off pulse in binary code is called a bit, which stands for binary digit. A byte is a set of eight bits. Kilobytes are used to indicate the size of the memory in a computer and give the number of different code signals it can hold. One kilobyte or 1K is equal to 1,024 bytes or 8,192 bits.

QUIZ: MACHINES AND INDUSTRY

1. When was the first practical steam engine invented?
2. Which organization employs the most people in the world?
3. Where and when was the first nuclear power station built?
4. Which machine was the first to have automatic control?
5. Where was the first hydroelectric power station?
6. Which country produces the most cars?
7. What goods were first manufactured by mass production and when?
8. Which is the world's largest computer company?
9. What was first manufactured by the Bessemer process?
10. Where and when was the first oil well drilled?

ANSWERS
1 In 1700. 2 Indian Railways. 3 Russia, 1954. 4 The windmill – with the invention of the fantail in 1745. 5 At Niagara Falls in the United States. 6 Japan. 7 Muskets, 1801. 8 International Business Machines Corporation (IBM). 9 Steel. 10 Pennsylvania, USA, 1859.

Flying microlight aircraft is becoming an increasingly popular sport.
▼

FLYING LIGHT

Did you know that some aircraft weigh less than their pilots?
Aircraft that are low-powered and do not fly very fast must be light in weight if they are to get off the ground. These specialized aircraft include hang-gliders, microlights, pedal-powered and solar-powered planes, and they may weigh less than their pilots. The first pedal-powered plane, the *Gossamer Condor*, weighed only 32 kg (70 lb).

TELLY GET-TOGETHER

What is teleconferencing?
Teleconferencing is a system of holding conferences by television. People who need to get together for discussions need no longer all travel to the same place to hold a conference. They can now communicate with each other by a form of television sent over telephone lines or via satellites.

The system is not like television in the home. The people can see each other on a large screen in their own rooms and talk easily to anyone taking part. Computers handle the transmission of the sound and pictures, using a very clever system. A computer at each end holds the picture in its memory. But after initially transmitting the whole picture, the sending computer only transmits the parts that move. The receiving computer mixes the still and moving parts so that a complete picture is always shown on the screen.

Teleconferencing enables these ▶ company executives to hold simultaneous 'face-to-public' conferences with people in several cities.

ELECTRONS IN MOTION

Why are only a few metals magnetic? Only the metals iron, nickel, cobalt and some of their alloys can be made into strong magnets. However, an electric current also gives a strong magnetic field when it flows through a coil. The Earth has a magnetic field too, probably because of electric currents circulating in its core.

There is a connection here. The atoms of which all substances are made contain electrons in motion. This movement produces a magnetic field, as do the moving electrons in an electric current. But in most substances, the magnetic fields of the electrons in their atoms cancel each other out, and the substances are not magnetic. In magnetic metals, the fields reinforce each other.

PASSING SOUND

What important discovery was made by putting trumpeters on a train? This discovery was the Doppler effect, which explains why a moving sound, such as an ambulance siren, drops in pitch when it passes you. The effect has been long known, but it was not until 1842 that the Austrian scientist, Christian Doppler, explained that it happens because the sound waves reach the ear less quickly as the source moves away and, as the frequency decreases, so the pitch drops. The effect was therefore named after him.

To test his explanation, Doppler placed a group of trumpeters on a train and had it driven to and fro past several musicians, who wrote down the note that they heard as the trumpeters passed. The results showed that Doppler's theory was correct.

Experiencing the Doppler effect is ▶ common in busy towns and cities.

TIDAL POWER

How do we get energy from the Moon? The Moon's force of gravity pulls on the Earth's surface. It's not strong enough to lift us off the ground, but it is powerful enough to raise the tides. The Sun's force of gravity helps to raise the tides too.

At the mouth of the River Rance in northern France, a power station harnesses the tides. As the water in the river rises and falls, it flows through turbines in the power station. The turbines drive generators that produce electricity.

This energy therefore comes to us from the Moon and the Sun. And it's very economical – apart from the cost of building and maintaining the power station, it's totally free.

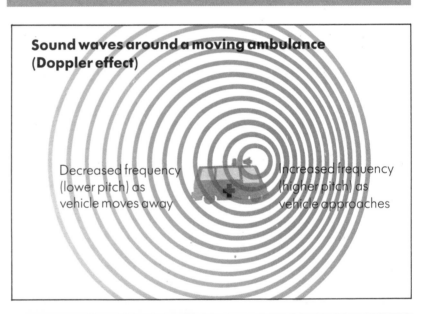

Sound waves around a moving ambulance (Doppler effect)

Decreased frequency (lower pitch) as vehicle moves away

Increased frequency (higher pitch) as vehicle approaches

GETTING NOWHERE FAST

Are geostationary satellites really stationary? Most communications satellites are geostationary satellites. This means that the satellite always remains in the same position above the Earth, enabling ground stations and radio dishes to keep in permanent contact with it.

However, the satellite does move. It takes exactly 24 hours to travel the equivalent of one orbit of the Earth. As the Earth takes this time to rotate once, the satellite remains above the same spot on the Earth's surface. Seen from the ground, its position in the sky does not change.

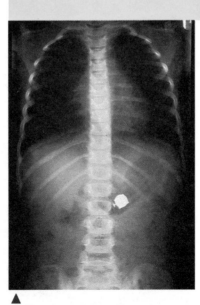

▲
This X-ray has revealed a watch in the patient's stomach.

X = ?

How did X-rays get their name? X-rays were discovered by the German physicist, Wilhelm Roentgen, in 1895. He was astonished by the way in which the rays could penetrate things and had no idea what they could be. He therefore called them X-rays, because in science X is often used to represent something that is unknown.

X-rays were also called Roentgen rays for a time, but the name X-rays stuck. Roentgen's name is commemorated in science in the unit of X-ray dosage, which is the roentgen.

IMAGE OR REALITY?

Did you know that valuable objects can be exhibited in several places at once? In the future, you may be able to go to a museum and see all the most valuable and important objects in the world. But it won't be a special exhibition: every museum could be showing the same objects!

The reason is that the objects will not be there. Instead, you will be looking at holograms of them. With holograms, you see an image that looks completely real. You can walk around it and view it from different angles, just as you could the object itself.

AT YOUR SERVICE

How can computers help disabled people? Computers can be of great help to people who have a physical handicap such as blindness as they can control such varied machines as wheelchairs and domestic appliances. To operate the computer, the person speaks commands. The computer recognizes the voice and springs into action to work the machine. If the person cannot speak, then a system that detects eye movements can be used. The person simply has to look at a point on the computer screen.

Computers can aid blind people by reading books to them. The computer scans the printed page and turns the words into sounds. The words have to be in the computer's memory for it to speak them. If the word is unknown to the computer, then it can spell out the word letter-by-letter instead.

MATHS OF DESTRUCTION

How powerful were the first nuclear weapons? The first nuclear weapons used in war were two atomic bombs dropped on the cities of Hiroshima and Nagasaki in Japan by the United States in 1945. The two bombs killed a total of more than 200,000 people. No nuclear weapons have been used in warfare since then.

The two atomic bombs each had a power of 20 kilotons. This means that their explosive power was equal to that of 20,000 tons of the high explosive TNT. The most powerful of today's nuclear weapons have powers measured in megatons (millions of tons of TNT), and are about a thousand times more powerful.

This aerial view of Hiroshima, Japan, shows the devastation from by one atomic bomb dropped on the city on 6 August 1945.
▼

▲
Skylab in orbit in 1974.

FACT FILE: SPORT

FACT FIFA (Fedération Internationale de Football Association) was founded in 1904 and started the World Cup in 1930.

FACT The Tour de France cycle race is about 4,000 km (about 2,500 miles) long.

FACT A super-heavyweight boxer must weigh more than 91 kg (about 200 lb).

FACT A Formula One racing car is one designed especially for Grand Prix races.

FACT The America's Cup in yachting is named after the schooner *America* that won it in 1851.

FACT A period of play in polo is called a chukka, from a Hindi word *chakkar*, meaning a round.

FACT The biathlon is a combination of skiing and rifle-shooting.

FACT An individual medley event in swimming consists of butterfly, backstroke, breast stroke and freestyle.

FACT In motorcycling, moto-cross is another name for scrambling.

SPACE SCIENCE

Skylab and spacelab – what's the difference? These are both laboratories that fly in space. Skylab was an American space station that contained much scientific equipment. It was used in 1973 and 1974. Spacelab is the name of a series of space laboratories taken into space by the space shuttle. Astronauts aboard the shuttle use them to do scientific experiments in space.

COLD DEATH

What would happen in a nuclear winter? Many scientists believe that a nuclear winter will occur if there is a nuclear war. The great power of the weapons and the immense destruction will cause a vast amount of smoke and dirt to rise into the atmosphere. The winds will blow this material around the world high in the air, and it will screen the Sun's rays from the ground.

The result will be a savage winter extending possibly over the whole world. Crops will die and farming will become impossible. There will be little hope for the survivors of the war – if there are any!

SHARP CAMERA

How can a camera know how far away you are? If an autofocus camera is used to take your picture, it automatically measures the distance to you, and adjusts the focus of the lens to give a sharp picture. It does this by shooting a beam of invisible infrared rays at you and picking up the rays that bounce back. The time it takes is a measure of the distance.

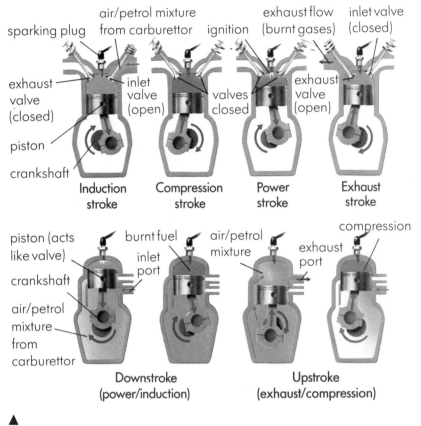

Petrol engine cycles: four-stroke (top) and two-stroke (bottom).

STROKES OF POWER

What's the difference between a two-stroke and a four-stroke engine? Two-stroke and four-stroke engines are the two basic kinds of petrol or diesel engines. Inside these engines, there are one or more cylinders in which a piston moves up and down. The stroke is each up or down movement of the piston.

In the engine, fuel goes to the cylinder and explodes to power the piston. In a two-stroke engine, this happens every time the piston reaches the top of the cylinder. In a four-stroke engine, the piston goes up and down twice before the fuel explodes again.

Each piston is connected to a crankshaft that changes the reciprocal (up-and-down) movement of the piston into rotary or circular motion, which goes through gears to the wheels of a vehicle.

BITS OF EVERYTHING

How long ago were atoms discovered? People first realized that everything is made of tiny, invisible particles called atoms 2,400 years ago in ancient Greece. The philosophers Leucippus and Democritus put this idea forward because they believed it explained why things are different from one another. Different things are made of different kinds of tiny particles. The particles could not be divided into smaller particles, and so were called atoms, which comes from a Greek word meaning 'uncuttable'.

Although scientists can now split atoms, this idea is basically correct. It's amazing that the Greeks came to this conclusion more than 2,000 years before atoms were proved to exist.

WATER WINGS

Which kind of boat really flies through the water? Most boats cannot travel very fast because they have to force their hulls through the water. Hydrofoils, which can carry people at speeds of 80 km/h (50 mph) an hour or more, overcome this problem. At rest, a hydrofoil looks much like any other boat. But beneath the hull are winglike foils, which rise as the hydrofoil begins to move through the water. As the speed increases, the foils lift the hull of the boat clear above the surface, and it can then quickly accelerate to a high speed.

At speed, the hydrofoil moves with its hull lifted clear of the water.

▲
Uranus's ring system as seen by cameras on the *Voyager 2* probe.

DESTINATION NEPTUNE

How far can we communicate by radio? The American *Voyager 2* space probe that is now flying on a mission to the outer planets is controlled by radio. Directions go to the probe by radio and it sends pictures back by radio. In January 1986, it made the most distant radio communication when it sent back pictures over a distance of about 3,000 million km. Having taken pictures of the planet Uranus and its moons, *Voyager* is now on its way to the planet Neptune, which it should reach in 1989.

Nuclear submarines can stay on patrol for months without surfacing.
▼

LOOK – NO DRIVER!

Why have a computer in a car? More and more cars have computers that improve the car's performance and make it easier and more pleasant to drive. Computers and electronic controls can look after the engine and other parts, helping them to work efficiently and safely.

Driving aid A car computer linked to a display screen can also give the driver all kinds of information, such as the distance to the destination and the amount of fuel being used, as well as standard items like the speed and time. The driver can operate many controls, such as heating and lights, simply by touching different parts of the screen. The computer may also speak to the driver to give warnings or reminders, and in the future the driver may be able to operate controls simply by talking to the computer.

Informed navigation Another feature that the computer is bringing to the car is navigation. Navigation systems can display the car's position moving over a map on a screen. They will also be able to guide the driver, if necessary. These systems may in time link up to radio networks, so that the driver is guided around hazards or diversions ahead. Ultimately, it's possible that the computer may actually take over the driving of the car!

SUBMERGED KILLERS

How do nuclear submarines use nuclear power? Nuclear submarines use nuclear power in two ways. They have nuclear engines and they carry nuclear missiles.

A nuclear reactor at the heart of the submarine's engine uses nuclear fuel such as uranium to generate great heat and raise steam in a boiler. The steam powers a steam turbine that drives the submarine's propellers as well as its electricity generators.

A nuclear engine does not need air to work, so the submarine can remain below the surface for as long as its fuel lasts, which can be several months.

Underwater weaponry The missiles that the submarine carries are armed with nuclear warheads. These missiles can be launched underwater. They rise to the surface and then fly to their targets, which may be in distant countries. Because nuclear submarines are very hard to locate underwater and are constantly on the move, it is virtually impossible to mount an effective defence against them.

WHIRLYBIRDS

How can helicopters hover in the air? The whirling blades of a helicopter act like spinning wings. They lift the helicopter into the air. The pilot can adjust the blades so that they produce enough lift to equal the helicopter's weight. The helicopter then hovers in the air.

To move, the pilot adjusts the blades so that they also push air to one side of the blades, rather like a whirling fan. The helicopter then moves in the opposite direction.

▲
Oil rig workers depend on highly manoeuvrable helicopters for transport.

IT'S ELEMENTARY

There are less than 100 of them, but they're everywhere and in everything – what are they? They are the elements – not the weather, nor the ancient Greek elements of earth, fire, air and water, but the chemical elements. They include metals like iron, gold, copper and aluminium; gases like oxygen, hydrogen and chlorine; and other substances such as iodine, carbon and sulphur. Just under 100 of these elements exist naturally in the whole Universe, though scientists have made a few artificial elements.

Most substances are not made of pure elements, but of combinations of elements called chemical compounds. Water is a compound of hydrogen and oxygen. Sugar contains these elements and also carbon. Because the elements can link in different combinations, there are very many different compounds.

WINNING SPIN

How does the spin of a ball affect its flight? People who are good at ball games like cricket and tennis often put a spin on the ball. The ball spins as it moves through the air, causing it to swerve unexpectedly to one side. A good player can control the spin to great advantage.

As the ball spins, it causes the layer of air in contact with its surface to move too. But because the ball is also travelling forward, the layers on each side of the ball move at different speeds. This causes a difference in air pressure that makes the ball swerve.

INSECT CAKE

Why would you want to put crushed insects into food? You probably wouldn't, but older people have done so in order to colour it. Pink and red food colouring was at one time made from the dried, crushed bodies of female cochineal insects, and the colouring itself was called cochineal. These insects are found chiefly in Mexico where they live on cactus. Nowadays food colours are generally obtained from a variety of artificial substances.

CATCH THIS

How fast can a ball travel? In the ball game Pelota Vasca, or Jaï Alaï, the ball speed has been measured as high as 302 km/h (188 mph)! The game, which is popular in Latin America, is played with a wooden bat strapped to the arm, and the ball is hurled against a wall. It is said to be the fastest of all ball games.

Cricketer John Embury, an ▶ off-spin bowler, in action.

VERSATILE CERAMICS

Why is the shuttle like a saucer? You could say because they are both spacecraft. However, the right answer is that they are both made of ceramics. Saucers are made of ceramic material called porcelain, and the space shuttle is covered with ceramic tiles that resist the intense heat of re-entry into the Earth's atmosphere.

Ceramics are materials like pottery. They are made of substances such as clay that can first be shaped and then heated to high temperatures to make them rigid. This is a simple way of producing plates, cups and saucers, but ceramics have other useful features. Although brittle, they strongly resist heat, which is why ceramic tiles line furnaces as well as space shuttles. They also resist electricity, and so are used to make insulators and sparking plugs.

◄ Space shuttle Columbia touching down in California, USA, following a 54½-hour mission.

HORSE FAILURE

Who first demonstrated the power of air pressure? In 1654 in the town of Magdeburg, Germany, an extraordinary experiment took place. Otto von Guericke, an inventor, constructed two large metal hemispheres and fitted them together to form a sphere. He next pumped all the air out of the sphere through a valve, and then hitched a team of horses to each half.

Guericke drove the horses to pull the hemispheres apart – without success. The vacuum inside caused the air outside to exert such enormous pressure on the hemispheres, that even the horses could not overcome it. But when Guericke admitted air through the valve, the pressure was removed and the two hemispheres fell apart instantly!

NO WRONG NUMBERS

What's a smart telephone?
A smart telephone is one that can do things for you, such as remembering telephone numbers. It contains memory chips that hold the telephone numbers of friends or the number you last dialled. To call one of these numbers, you simply press a button instead of dialling the whole number.

In future, the telephones themselves are likely to be able to talk to you and receive spoken orders. To call someone, you will simply ask the telephone to get the person for you! And instead of ringing, it could announce an incoming call.

QUIZ: HISTORY OF TRANSPORT

1. Where and when was the first city bus service?
2. What was the name of the biggest ocean liner ever built?
3. In which country were the first railways built?
4. Where and when did the first helicopter fly?
5. Who invented the petrol-driven motorcar and when?
6. In which city was the first underground railway constructed?
7. What was the first self-propelled transport?
8. Which is the most popular car in history?
9. Which was the first country to have a motorway?

ANSWERS
1 Paris, France, in 1662 (horse-drawn). 2 *Queen Elizabeth* (destroyed by fire in 1972). 3 Britain. 4 France, 1907. 5 Karl Benz in Germany, 1885. 6 London, in 1863. 7 A paddle steamer built in France in 1783. 8 The Volkswagen *Beetle*, of which more than 20 million have been built. 9 Germany, in 1921.

▲
Innovative high jumping won Dick Fosbury the 1972 Olympic gold medal.

AN ABSOLUTE FLOP

When is it better to land on your back than on your feet? In high-jumping. Over many years various techniques have been developed in high-jumping, such as the Eastern Cut Off, the Western Roll and the Straddle, all of which involve landing on one foot or on one foot followed by a shoulder. The introduction of soft, foam rubber landing beds in the late 1960s allowed the development of the Fosbury Flop, named after its inventor, in which the jumper lands on the upper part of his back. This enabled jumpers to set better records than had been achieved using other styles.

DRY IN THE WET

How can you avoid getting soggy when jogging? One of the problems people have when they go jogging, or take any form of exercise in wet weather, is that material that keeps water out usually stops the body from breathing properly. Recently a Scottish company has revolutionized tracksuits by producing a rainproof suit that allows the skin to breathe, and reduces the overheating caused by ordinary waterproof garments. The fabric is designed in such a way that the holes or pores in it are larger than particles of water vapour, which can pass freely in or out. But the pores still act as a barrier to liquid water, such as rain.

MULTIPLYING MAGNIFICATION

Is there a limit to what microscopes can make visible? An optical microscope – one that uses light rays – can magnify up to about 2,000 times. This is enough to make invisible things like bacteria visible. An electron microscope can use electron beams to magnify objects up to about 200,000 times.

This limit is not set by the construction of the microscopes. It is imposed by the nature of light waves and electron beams. Special microscopes that work in other ways can magnify millions of times, and even make individual atoms visible.

▲
A human hair seen through a false colour scanning electron microscope.

NIGHT LIGHT

Which invention improved both cookery and education? An important development in the history of education was the spread of gas lighting in the early 1800s. This followed the invention of coal gas by the British engineer, William Murdock, in 1792. Gas lights were much brighter than oil lamps. They illuminated whole rooms adequately at night and evening classes sprang up. As education for most people at this time was very limited, studying after work was the only way to improve their learning.

At the same time, gas burners and ovens gave people a powerful and reliable source of heat for cooking.

SPRING FLAVOUR

Which flavouring comes from crocuses? Saffron – the dried stamens of the saffron crocus – is used both as a flavouring and to colour food. It is very expensive to buy because a great many crocuses are needed to produce a small amount of saffron. The saffron crocus is a different species to the common garden one, so don't try to eat that!

A Trident cruise missile on test run.
▼

NOT A MOVE

Do all machines have moving parts? You might think that most machines have moving parts – but do they? What about a radio, a television set, a telephone, a digital watch, a computer? Apart from their controls, these machines do not have any moving parts. They all work quite happily without anything moving at all.

These machines do have one thing in common – they all work by electronics. Electric signals flow along wires between electronic components, such as transistors. The components change the signals so that they can operate a device, such as a loudspeaker or screen.

JUST RELAX . . .

Can hypnotism cure illness? A person who is hypnotised is placed in a state in which a suggestion made to them is carried out involuntarily. The hypnotist asks them to do something and they do it.

This can be of use in medicine. A doctor or dentist can hypnotise the patient, and then suggest to them that they will not feel pain. In some cases, it works – though hypnotism may have to be combined with a local anaesthetic for treatment. Although hypnotism cannot really cure illness, it can reduce pain, tension and anxiety, and thus relieve symptoms. However, not everyone can be hypnotised.

MAP-READING MISSILE

How do cruise missiles navigate? Cruise missiles are slow-flying missiles that keep close to the ground or sea. They do this to escape detection by radar defence systems.

A cruise missile is a nuclear weapon designed to penetrate a country's defences and deliver a warhead to a particular target. It has a map of the route in the memory of its guidance computer. The missile uses its own radar to survey the ground below, and can follow the map to find its way to the target.

PLAIN LANGUAGE

What's basic about BASIC?

BASIC is the name of the computer language used in most home computers. The name actually stands for Beginners' All-purpose Symbolic Instruction Code. However, the language is basic in that it is among the easiest of computer languages to use and understand.

One reason for this is that BASIC uses English words, such as IF, THEN, PRINT, AND, OR, INPUT, NEXT. These words are used in writing programs, and the computer 'understands' them in much the same way as we do.

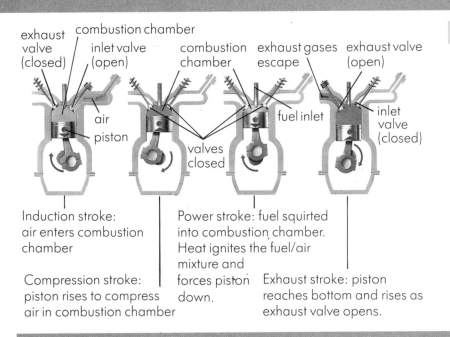

exhaust valve (closed)
combustion chamber
inlet valve (open)
combustion chamber
exhaust gases escape
exhaust valve (open)
air
piston
valves closed
fuel inlet
inlet valve (closed)

Induction stroke: air enters combustion chamber

Compression stroke: piston rises to compress air in combustion chamber

Power stroke: fuel squirted into combustion chamber. Heat ignites the fuel/air mixture and forces piston down.

Exhaust stroke: piston reaches bottom and rises as exhaust valve opens.

SPARKLESS

What's different about diesel?

Trains and some road vehicles are often called diesels, and this is because they have a diesel engine. This is a kind of petrol engine that does not have sparking plugs to ignite the fuel. Instead, the fuel is heated so that it ignites automatically.

The diesel engine is a hard-working and rugged engine. It was invented by the German engineer, Rudolf Diesel, in 1897.

◄ The cycle of a four-stroke diesel engine.

MIGHTY MIDGET

What are incredibly small and hard, have enormous power, yet are mostly made of space?
Give up? The answer is atoms, the tiny invisible particles of which everything is made. An atom is about a millionth of a millimetre across. But if you think that's small, then you haven't heard about the nucleus, another particle at the centre of every atom. This is 10,000 times smaller than the atom!

Between the nucleus and the outside of the atom is mostly empty space. The rest of the atom is not solid, but consists of one or more electrons moving around the nucleus. They're even smaller still – a tenth the size of the nucleus!

Immense force So how can an atom be hard and have enormous power? The electrons have an electric charge, and their electric force pushes away the electrons in any other atom that comes near. So it's difficult to penetrate the atom. However, in nuclear power, this does happen and the nucleus is affected, either splitting apart or fusing with another nucleus. There are tiny particles called protons and neutrons in the nucleus, and these are held together by an extremely strong force. So when the nucleus is disrupted, this force is released, producing great energy. This is why nuclear power is called nuclear, and why it's so immensely powerful.

Simplified structure of an atom

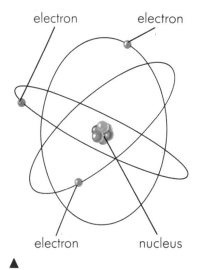

electron
electron
electron
nucleus

▲

An atom is the smallest particle into which a chemical can be divided without losing its chemical properties.

EARLY HANGER-ON

Who pioneered hang-gliding?
The hang-glider is not a modern
invention. It was pioneered a
century ago by the German
inventor, Otto Lilienthal. He built
several different kinds of hang-
gliders to test aircraft design,
managing to fly as far as 250 m
(820 ft). Lilienthal was killed in a
crash in 1896.

FLOOD BARRIERS

**Which country wages a life and
death struggle against the
sea?** Large parts of the
Netherlands are below sea level
and at risk from flooding. The
airports at Amsterdam and
Rotterdam are both about 4 m
(14 ft) below sea level. Following
disastrous flooding of the south-
west of the country in 1953, the
Delta Project was set up to
protect the land at whatever
cost.

The scale of construction of
sea defences has been
enormous. Great sea walls, or
dykes, have been built, and the
mouths of four major rivers have
been sealed with dams or fitted
with barriers that can close to
hold back the high tides. The
main barrier is 9 km (6 miles) long
and contains 66 massive steel
gates.

▲
The thrilling sport of hang-gliding is older than one might imagine.

SHARP OR CHUNKY

**What is the resolution of a
computer?** The resolution of a
computer is usually said to be
low, medium or high. It indicates
the quality of the picture on the
computer screen. A high-
resolution computer can show
pictures in sharp detail, whereas
a low-resolution machine
produces chunky pictures made
up of patterns of square blocks.

Medium resolution comes in
between.

Many computers can show
pictures with different grades of
resolution. This is because high-
resolution pictures — especially in
full colour — take up a lot of
memory space, leaving less
room for programs. It is often
better to have low resolution and
plenty of memory available.

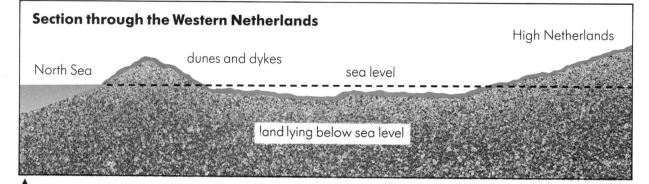

Section through the Western Netherlands

High Netherlands

North Sea

dunes and dykes

sea level

land lying below sea level

▲
The Dutch use dykes and dunes to protect or reclaim low-lying land from the sea.

SPEED LIMIT

What is the fastest possible speed? You might think that if you had enough power, you could make a machine like a spaceship travel as fast as you like. Use more power and it would always get faster and faster.

This is true at normal speeds, and at the high speeds at which spacecraft now travel. But there is a limit to the speed at which any object can travel, regardless of its power. The fastest possible speed is the speed of light, which is 300,000 km (187,500 miles) a second.

The faster an object moves, the more energy it needs. For us to reach the speed of light would require an infinite amount of energy – more energy than exists in the entire Universe.

BUMPER NUMBERS

What is the biggest possible number? What's the biggest number you can think of? A million million million million perhaps, or maybe a billion billions. You could go on for ever in this way, for there's no actual limit. We speak of something that is immeasurably large or endless as being infinite, and we can say that the greatest possible number is infinity minus one. But it cannot be given an actual magnitude.

One of the largest numbers that is named is a centillion, which is the hundredth term in the series million, billion, trillion and so on. It is 1 followed by 600 zeros. There's also a googol, which is 1 followed by 100 zeros, and a googolplex, 1 followed by a googol zeros.

MICROBRAIN

How big is the brain of a home computer? The brain of a home computer is its central processing unit, which controls all its operations. If you could look inside the computer, you would find that this is a microchip unit no bigger than your thumb.

The actual chip itself is hidden inside the casing of the microchip for protection. And it's very small indeed – about the size of your little fingernail! Nevertheless, it is packed with thousands of miniature electronic components.

FACT FILE: COOKING TERMS

FACT Poached eggs are not stolen, but named from the French word *poche*, meaning pocket, because the white forms a pocket around the yolk.

FACT Condensed milk is made by removing some of the water from cow's milk and adding sugar.

FACT Truffles are tasty round fungi which grow underground. They are dug out by dogs or pigs.

FACT The American term 'broil' and the British term 'grill' mean the same thing.

FACT Yeast used in baking bread and brewing beer consists of tiny living things.

FACT Chewing gum was originally made from chicle, the gum of the sapodilla plum tree.

FACT Stock is a liquid made by boiling bones or vegetables with flavourings. It is often used in making soups.

FACT To baste meat means to pour fat or stock over it in order to keep it moist as it cooks.

▲
A greatly magnified view of a computer micro-chip.

PLANET HOPPERS

How do space probes get to other worlds? Space probes are automatic spacecraft that fly to other planets in the solar system. Some fly there directly. They are launched on a path that takes them straight to the planet. They may go into orbit round the planet or land on its surface.

Often a space probe flies past a planet, taking pictures of it and its moons. In many cases, the probe uses the planet's field of gravity to speed its flight and send it off towards another planet. *Voyager 2* is using this method to visit four planets during a 12-year mission.

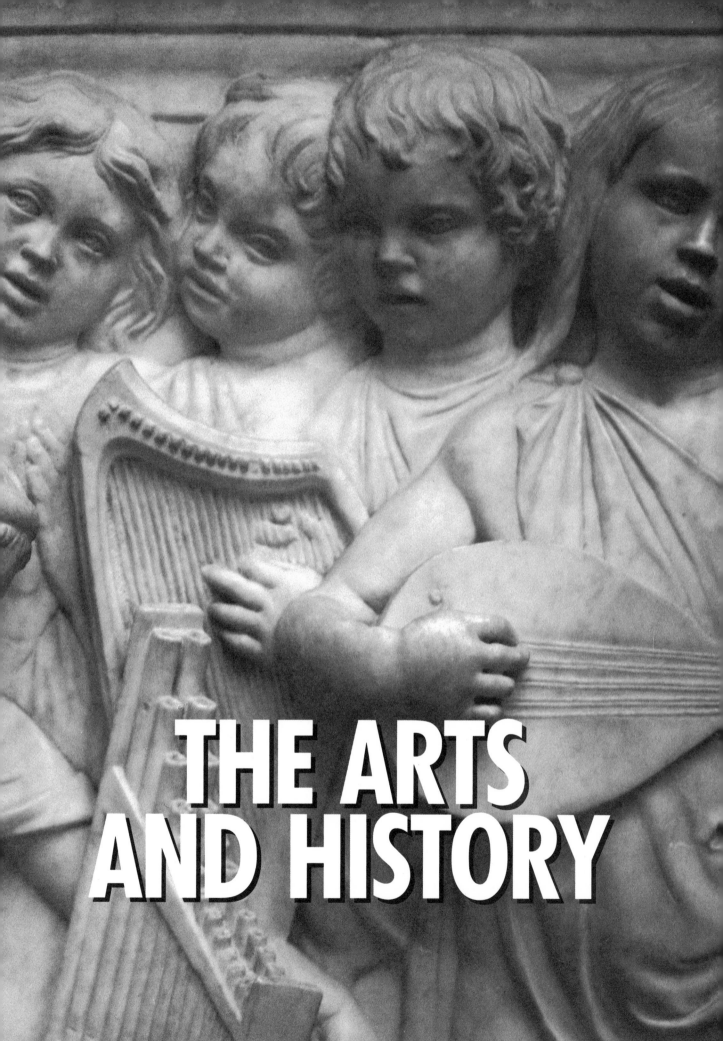

THE ARTS AND HISTORY

SHOCK TACTICS

What was Dadaism? It was an artistic movement started in Switzerland during World War I. A group of artists and writers decided to rebel against what they felt was the smug attitude to art at the time, and they set out deliberately to shock people. A similar movement was begun in New York, led by the French artist, Marcel Duchamp.

The kind of thing the Dadaists did was to exhibit a bicycle wheel (signed by Duchamp), or a version of the Mona Lisa with a moustache and a vulgar caption (Duchamp again). Duchamp liked to produce what he called 'ready-mades', and call them art.

▲
Bride stripped bare painted by Marcel Duchamp (1887-1963).

The Boston Tea Party. Afterwards ▶ the British hardened their policy towards the American colonies and war broke out in 1775.

A STAKE IN HISTORY

Was there a real Dracula? Yes and no. *Dracula* is a book by the Irish author, Bram Stoker (1847-1912), about an evil count living in Transylvania (now part of Romania) who could turn into a vampire bat and suck people's blood.

Count Dracula was a figment of Stoker's vivid imagination, but

FREEDOM FIGHTERS

Who were the Sons of Liberty? They were a group of secret societies that came into being in North America before the American War of Independence. They were particularly active in New York City and Boston, Massachusetts.

The Sons of Liberty led the fight against what Americans saw as British interference in their affairs, and in particular the levying of taxes to pay for an army. It was the Boston Sons of Liberty who took part in the Boston Tea Party of 1773, when a group of Americans disguised as Red Indians boarded tea ships in Boston Harbour and threw their (taxed) cargoes into the sea.

The Sons of Liberty played a major part in the campaign that led to the War of Independence and the American colonies' break with Britain.

in the 1400s there was a ruler of Transylvania who was every bit as nasty. He was known as Vlad the Impaler, and he got his nickname because of his habit of driving stakes through the bodies of his enemies and leaving them to die. No doubt Stoker had Vlad in mind when he wrote his book.

BIBLE STORY

What were Mystery Plays?
They were religious dramas, also called Miracle Plays, performed by amateur actors in the late Middle Ages and into the 1500s. At first they were presented by the clergy, but later they became the responsibility of the various craft guilds in the small medieval towns.

The purpose of the plays was to bring the Bible stories, especially those of the trial and crucifixion of Christ, to the mass of people who could not read or write. The texts of many of these plays have survived. Some contain a good deal of rustic humour and by-play, as well as the traditional message of the New Testament.

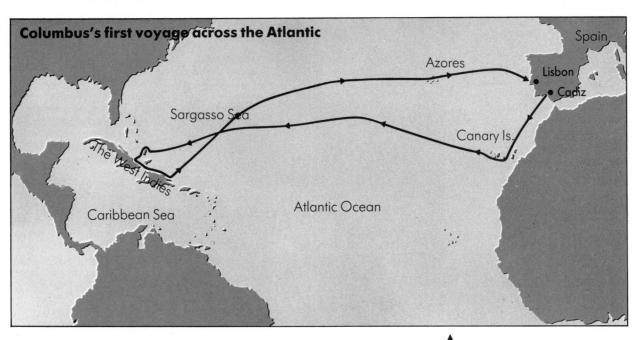

Columbus's first voyage across the Atlantic

▲
Columbus's first voyage in 1492.

FAR OUT

Why did Columbus sail west? That was the question many of his contemporaries asked, because Italian explorer Christopher Columbus's destination was Japan, which lies far to the east of Europe. Although many people thought the world was flat, scholars – and Columbus – were convinced it was a globe.

Miscalculation After studying old maps and consulting so-called experts, Columbus came to the conclusion that Japan lay about 4,400 km (2,750 miles) west of the Canary Islands, and so it would be a fairly simple voyage to travel west to it. But he underestimated the size of the Earth by about 16,000 km (10,000 miles) because the direct route from the Canaries to Japan is about 20,000 km (12,500 miles).

Not what he thought Columbus persuaded the rulers of Spain, Queen Isabella of Castile and Ferdinand of Aragon to back him. They gave him three small ships and 90 men, and he set off in August 1492. After three weeks the fleet sighted land, one of the islands of the Bahamas. Columbus named it San Salvador, but it is now known as Watling's Island.

Columbus was convinced he had found the Indies (south-eastern Asia), which is why the Caribbean islands – which he did find – are known as the West Indies to this day.

A NAME DEFAMED

What is a quisling? It's another term for a traitor. The word comes from the name of Vidkun Quisling, a Norwegian Fascist who served as an army officer, a diplomat and a government minister in the years before World War II. He collaborated with the Nazis who invaded Norway in 1940, becoming the puppet ruler of Norway under German occupation.

When the war ended with the defeat of Germany, the Norwegians tried Quisling for treason, and he was shot in October 1945.

RADIO PANIC STATIONS

Have Martians ever landed?
Not to our knowledge, but on the 31st October, 1938 millions of Americans thought they had.

They were listening to a radio adaptation of H. G. Wells's science-fiction novel, *The War of the Worlds*. Its producer, a young actor named Orson Welles, made the whole story sound so realistic, with fake news bulletins and government statements, that all over the United States listeners panicked, and many fled from the towns into the countryside to escape what they feared was an attack by alien forces. The radio station had broadcast an announcement just before the play to say that what followed was pure fiction!

Acclaim The play made Welles' reputation and he then went to Hollywood where he wrote and produced *Citizen Kane*, still acclaimed as one of the finest films ever made. His later work in cinema was mainly as an actor. He died in 1985, aged 70.

MATTER OF DESIGN

How much furniture did Sheraton make? Probably none, except when he was a young man learning his trade. Thomas Sheraton was born in 1751 and, when he set up in business in London in about 1790, it was as a drawing master.

Between 1791 and 1794 he published *The Cabinet-maker and Upholsterer's Drawing Book*, in four parts. It contained many designs for furniture which were copied and used by other craftsmen. Sheraton himself seems not to have had a work-shop. He died in poverty in 1806.

▲
A newspaper headline tells of the panic caused by Welles's radio play.

FACT FILE: FOOD

FACT The potato was introduced into Europe in 1539 from South America – as an ornamental plant!

FACT Dormice were highly esteemed by the Romans, who ate them as an hors d'oeuvre cooked with honey and poppy seed.

FACT The sandwich is said to have been invented by John Montagu, fourth Earl of Sandwich (1718-1792), who wanted a 'convenience food' he could eat easily while playing cards.

FACT Hippolyte Mège-Mouriès, a French chemist, invented margarine in the 1860s as an inexpensive substitute for butter. Its name comes from the Greek *margaron*, meaning pearl, because it was formed in pearl-like flakes.

FACT Some ancient Egyptians refused to eat eels because they worshipped them as gods – and others because they thought eels were indigestible.

FACT North American Indians used to make a cake of dried and powdered meat mixed with hot fat, which they called pemmican. It kept for months and was much used by travellers because it was light to carry.

FACT The main food of ancient Babylonia was flat, unleavened bread eaten with onions.

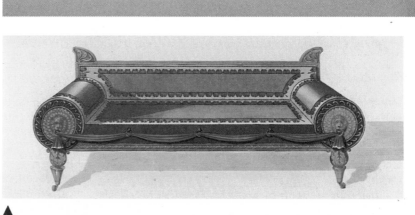

▲
A Sheraton sofa. Sheraton used rectangles to emphasize lightness.

FREEDOM FIGHTERS

Who were the Red Shirts? They were the irregular troops led by the patriot Giuseppe Garibaldi (1807-1882) during the struggle for Italy's independence.

Garibaldi formed his first regiment of Red Shirts in Uruguay in 1843, when as an exile he was helping the government of that country in a war against Argentina. The government gave Garibaldi a large consignment of red flannel shirts for the Italian Legion he was forming.

On his return to Italy in 1848, Garibaldi brought a few loyal followers and their red shirts with him. They wore red shirts in 1860 when Garibaldi and a force of less than a thousand men conquered Sicily.

MAN-MADE DESERT

What was **The Plow That Broke the Plains?** It was a propaganda film produced in 1936 for a US government agency trying to cope with a drought that had hit the Great Plains. The theme was that ploughing up the plains to grow wheat had removed the plant cover from the soil, allowing it to dry out and blow away.

During the 1930s, unsuitable farming techniques and over-grazing of grasslands in the Great Plains produced what became known as the Dust Bowl. As the soil dried out, storms blew it away in great curtains of dust, which hung in the air and were then carried south to the Gulf of Mexico and out to sea.

Pit girls and boys of the 1800s. ▶
They had to work long hours.

WOMEN UNDERGROUND

Were women ever coal miners? Yes. It was not until the 1800s that coal mining was considered 'unsuitable' work for women. Until that time whole families worked underground, women generally being responsible for hauling coal. With the coming of the Industrial Revolution in the 1700s, the demand for coal increased enormously. It is estimated that in the early 1800s, there were over 5,000 women working in the mines in Britain alone, and women also worked in mines in France, Germany and Russia.

'A woman's place' Britain was first to introduce a ban. In 1841 a Royal Commission investigated conditions in British mines. The findings shocked the nation and, saying that 'a woman's place is in the home', the government banned women from working underground. Similar acts were later passed in France, Germany and the Soviet Union.

Continued employment For the women who were thrown out of the mines there was no other work, and some disguised themselves as men in order to keep their jobs. Women also resisted attempts to ban 'pit brow' work, and continued to work on the pit surface for many years. In Britain, for instance, in Wigan, Lancashire, women continued to work on the pit top, preparing coal brought from below until as late as the 1950s.

Recently, however, women have demanded their right to be coal miners, and in the early 1980s women in the United States began work underground in the mines.

▲ Johannes Gutenberg (above) studies the first page of his Bible.

An example of Gutenberg's work. ▶

NOBEL NUN

Who is Mother Teresa? She is a Roman Catholic nun who was awarded the Nobel peace prize in 1979 for her selfless work among the poor of Calcutta in India. She was born in 1910 in Albania, and her name before she took the veil was Agnes Ganxha Bojaxhiu. She went to India as a teacher in 1928. After twenty years she decided to devote her life to caring for the poor, and has been working for them ever since.

EARLY IMPRESSIONS

Who invented printing? Like so many things, printing had many 'inventors'. The Chinese, Japanese and Koreans were the first people to print, sometime before AD 800. Early printing was done by the laborious and slow process of carving a design in reverse on a block of wood, inking the surface and pressing a piece of paper on it.

Movable type The Koreans and Chinese both experimented with type – that is, separate characters for each letter which can be used over and over again. In about 1050 a Chinese scientist, Pi Sheng, made pottery type, and some years later wooden type was also made in China. But the Chinese system of writing, which requires thousands of different characters, made the work difficult.

Gutenberg Printing as we know it today was invented by a German goldsmith, Johannes Gutenberg, who lived in Mainz. By 1450 he had made his system capable of being used commercially.

The essence of Gutenberg's invention was three-fold: the casting of standard-sized metal type from moulds; the development of a suitably sticky ink; and the adaptation of a winepress to make a printing press.

Gutenberg produced his first book – an edition of the Bible – between 1452 and 1455. He had enough type to be able to set up a few pages at a time, then distribute the type and start again. This Bible had two columns to the page, each of 42 lines, and is known to collectors as the '42-line Bible'.

Progress The earliest books were made to look as much as possible like the hand-written books of the time, but soon printers began to make changes and the modern style of book came into being. Printing enabled more people to have books and thus revolutionized the spread of learning.

◀ Mother Teresa cradles a baby named after her.

NO BREECHES

Who were the Sans Culottes?
At the time of the French
Revolution, which began in
1789, the wealthy aristocrats
who supported the king wore
fashionable knee-breeches – in
French, *culottes*. The working
classes who formed the bulk of
the revolutionaries were *sans*
(without) *culottes*; they wore
ordinary long trousers instead.

WARRING WORDS

**Which book helped to start a
civil war?** Written by Harriet
Beecher Stowe, a staunch
opponent of slavery, it was
Uncle Tom's Cabin. The book
tells the story of a dignified old
Black slave and his experiences
at the hands of a brutal
slaveholder. It was a bitter
exposure of the evils of slavery
and helped to harden the
feelings of Northerners in the
United States against this
practice. The slave-owners of
the Southern States considered
it an insult, and the feelings it
aroused there helped to bring
about the US Civil War of
1861-1865.

WAR DEAD

**Which country suffered most in
World War II?** About 55 million
people lost their lives in World
War II. Except in countries where
no ground fighting took place,
such as Britain and the United
States, more civilians died than
members of the armed forces.

The country that suffered the
greatest loss of life was Russia,
where about 20 million died. This
death toll was greater than the
numbers of all who died in World
War I, which was 17 million.

HE CAME, HE SAWED, HE CONQUERED

Which emperor became a carpenter? He was Tsar Peter I, known as
'the Great', who was emperor of Russia from 1689 to 1725. As a boy
Peter became interested in technical subjects and he learned such
crafts as carpentry and printing. When he met some Germans, he soon
realized that his country was very backward compared with the
countries of western Europe.

In 1697 Peter sent a party of 250 people, led by some Russian
noblemen, to tour the countries of the west. With them went one
Sergeant Peter Mikhailov, who was actually the tsar in disguise.

The role of Sergeant Mikhailov gave Peter the chance to gain some
practical experience he would not have been able to get as tsar. He
worked for four months as a ship's carpenter in a Dutch shipyard, and
for a while in the British Royal Navy shipyard at Deptford. He visited
factories and schools. When he returned to Russia in 1698, he began to
modernize his country, and later set up the Russian navy.

▲
A portrait of Peter the Great as a ship's carpenter.

MODEL ARMY

Who was the 'First Emperor'? He was Cheng Ying, who adopted the title of Shih Huang-ti (meaning the 'First Emperor') when he became ruler of the whole of China in 221 BC.

Shih Huang-ti was by no means the first emperor of China, but he was probably the first really powerful one. He reorganized the country's economy, standardizing its coinage and its weights and measures, which helped to speed up trade and so make people more prosperous.

Standardization One reform that helped trade perhaps more than any other measure was the regulating of the width of carts and wagons. The soft ground of the roads wore into deep ruts, which exactly fitted the carts of each region. With standardization, goods no longer had to be off-loaded from one cart on to another when they reached a frontier between one state and another.

Terracotta retinue When the 'First Emperor' died he was buried in great state. Earlier rulers of China went to their graves accompanied by a large entourage of courtiers, wives and servants (who either voluntarily committed suicide or were put to death). In an ingenious way, Shih Huang-ti went as close as he dared to reviving this ancient custom.

He, too, was buried with a huge retinue – an army of 6,000 soldiers. But these soldiers were modelled lifesize in terracotta, a kind of pottery. Each one has an individual face; they were not mass-produced.

The huge tomb which contains the remains of the emperor and his model army was found in 1974, and is still being excavated.

▲ Winchester Cathedral, which has the longest nave in Britain.

SWAMP BEATER

Which building was saved by a diver? It was Winchester Cathedral, in southern England. This huge building stands on swampy ground, and the men who constructed it between 600 and 800 years ago laid great logs of oak and beech to spread the load of the stone resting on top of them. However, by 1905 some of the walls were cracking and leaning dangerously.

The walls were shored up, and then the builders slowly excavated the foundations. The hole promptly filled with water. Down into the water, which was black with peat, went the diver, William Walker. Working in complete darkness – for no light could penetrate the murk – he finished digging out the old foundations, then laid sacks of cement, concrete blocks and bricks to provide solid new foundations for the cathedral. The work took him from 1906 to 1912. A memorial to him now stands in the cathedral.

◄ Some of the life-size warriors and horses found in the tomb of the First Emperor.

MAGIC WINDOWS

Who invented the land of Oz?
This mythical country was the brainchild of a newspaperman, Lyman Frank Baum (1856-1919). At the time the idea for Oz came to him, Baum was editing a trade magazine for window-dressers, especially aimed at the dry-goods (drapery) stores. In 1900 he published two books. One was *The Art of Decorating Dry Goods Windows*; the other was the now famous *The Wonderful Wizard of Oz*.

Altogether Baum wrote 14 Oz books, and a great many other books for children, some of them under pen-names. Another 26 books about Oz were written by various authors after he died.

ADMIRAL 'BUBBLES'

Which admiral appeared on soap posters? It sounds ridiculous doesn't it? Actually he didn't appear as an admiral, but as a little boy. His portrait was painted by his grandfather, the popular and highly-respected artist Sir John Millais. Millais was a very fine artist, but some of his pictures were decidedly sentimental. This one, titled *Bubbles*, showed his small grandson, a curly headed boy, blowing bubbles.

The picture was bought by a leading soap firm, which then used it on posters and in other advertisements to advertize the lathering quality of its soap! 'Bubbles' went on to become Admiral Sir William James, serving in both World Wars and for three years as an English Member of Parliament.

Bubbles painted by Sir John Everett Millais (1826-96). ▶

QUIZ: FAMOUS EXPLORERS

1. In order to attract settlers, what name did Eric the Red give the island he discovered in 980?
2. Which 13th-century Italian explorer travelled through Persia, Ceylon, India and China?
3. What continent did Christopher Columbus think he had reached when he crossed the Atlantic Ocean?
4. What did Vasco Nunez de Balboa discover when he crossed the Panama in 1513?
5. Who was the first explorer to sail round the world?
6. Who discovered Tasmania and New Zealand in 1642?
7. Who discovered Africa's Victoria Falls in 1855?
8. Which American explored the perilous Gobi Desert and Tibet between 1910 and 1930?

ANSWERS
1. Greenland. 2. Marco Polo. 3. Asia; it was actually the West Indies. 4. The Pacific Ocean. 5. Ferdinand Magellan. 6. Abel Tasman. 7. David Livingstone. 8. Roy Chapman Andrews.

◀ Cones of lava which were made into dwelling places in the Goreme district of Turkey. The caves can be seen clearly.

CONE HOMES

Where do people live in volcanic cones? In Cappadocia, a region of eastern Turkey. There, millions of years ago, the now-extinct volcano, Erciyaş Daği, spewed out vast quantities of lava and ash, which over the years have been worn away by wind and rain. The soft rock formed by the ash is easily eroded, but where it is protected by a capstone of hard lava, a cone-shaped hill has survived. There are hundreds of these tower-like structures, which are gradually wearing away.

Unusual dwellings About 1600 years ago a group of Christians under the leadership of St Basil, Bishop of Caesarea, made their homes in this desolate landscape. They hollowed out caves in the soft rock, some of them as much as ten storeys high. By the 1200s up to 30,000 people lived in this region, and 300 of their churches have been discovered.

A few of these volcanic dwellings are still used by Turkish farmers, some as barns, others as homes.

ENERGETIC EMPRESS

Who was Catherine the Great? She was a German princess who became Empress of Russia. Born in 1729, she was the daughter of Prince Christian of Anhalt-Zerbst, ruler of a tiny German state. In 1745 she married the Grand Duke Peter, heir to the Russian throne. It was not a happy marriage, because Peter was mentally and physically sub-normal.

In 1762 Peter became emperor but, because of his increasingly strange behaviour, a group of army officers staged a coup, and proclaimed Catherine II empress in his place. Peter, who died a few weeks later in mysterious circumstances, was not mourned.

Industrious Catherine proved to be a good ruler, hard-working, strong-minded and capable. Her diplomacy and her armies enlarged Russia's territory at the expense of Poland and Turkey. She had schools built, and improved medical care.

In her spare time Catherine collected works of art and wrote plays, stories and history. When she died in 1796, her people gave her a title she had refused: 'The Great'.

TIMBER TIME

Can clocks be made with wooden works? Indeed they can – and in the early colonial days in America some actually were. In the 1700s brass, the main material used in making the works of clocks, was both scarce and expensive in America.

About 1745 two brothers, Benjamin and Timothy Cheyney, decided to find a way of making cheap clocks to sell to the pioneers. They were working in East Hartford, Connecticut, then the heart of the American clock industry. They used hard black cherrywood to make the gears, and oak for the plates in which the mechanism was mounted.

The idea quickly spread, and thousands of these clocks were made in North America. Eli Terry of Plymouth, Connecticut, had such large orders for wooden clocks that he started making standard parts, and had an assembly line very much like that of a modern factory. It seems that no wooden clocks were made after about 1840.

SOMETHING "LOOMS IN THE FUTURE."

▲
A cartoon of Benjamin Disraeli which appeared in *Punch* in July 1852.

BARGAIN BUYS

Which country bought much of its land? The United States did just that, in three bargain lots.

Expansion The first was the Louisiana Purchase, which doubled the country's size overnight. The Louisiana Territory belonged to France and lay beyond the Mississippi River, which then formed the United States' western frontier. In 1803 Napoleon Bonaparte, faced with a major war in Europe, accepted an offer of about $15 million for the land from the United States, which borrowed the money from British and Dutch banks.

Mexican deal The second bargain was the Gadsden Purchase of 1853. It was negotiated by the US Ambassador to Mexico, James Gadsden. Mexico sold a strip of land south of the Gila River for $10 million.

Hidden resources The third, and biggest, bargain was Alaska. US Secretary of State, William H. Seward, bought it from Russia for $7,200,000 – about 5 cents a hectare – in 1867. Many people sneered at what they called 'Seward's Folly', but the subsequent discovery of gold and then oil made it a real 'best buy'.

A map of North America showing the three areas of land bought by the United States. ▶

The 19-century USA Land Purchases

Canada

USA

Mexico

■ Louisiana
■ Gadsden
■ Alaska

PICTORIAL FUN

Why are cartoons so called?
The word comes from the Italian *cartone*, which means thin card or stiff paper. Originally a cartoon was a full-sized drawing used as a preliminary to making a finished painting or tapestry. It got its present meaning through the British comic magazine *Punch*.

In 1841 there was a competition for wall paintings to decorate the new Houses of Parliament, then being rebuilt after a fire. When the various artists submitted their cartoons, some of their designs were unsuitable. *Punch* made fun of them in a series of humorous drawings which it called 'Punch's cartoons' – and the name stuck. Now any comic drawing, especially one with a political message, is called a cartoon.

NOW YOU SEE IT . . .

What is a magic mirror? Magic mirrors have been made in China and Japan for centuries. When you look into one of these highly polished bronze mirrors you see, as you might expect, your reflection – and nothing more.

However, if you hold the mirror towards the sun and reflect the light on to a white surface, the reflection shows a design, such as a picture of the Buddha.

Over the years, the construction of magic mirrors has remained a closely guarded secret and even today few people know exactly how they work.

FACT FILE: PAINTING

FACT Impressionism gets its name from a painting by Claude Monet in 1872 called *Impression: Sunrise*, which was in this style.

FACT Art Nouveau – literally 'New Art' – was a style that became fashionable in the 1890s. It was based on long curving lines inspired by climbing plants.

FACT Gouache is an opaque form of watercolour paint, which most people know as poster paint. It produces effects similar to those of oils.

FACT Fresco is a kind of wall-painting or mural which is done on fresh (Italian, *fresco*) wet plaster. The paint sinks into the plaster and bonds with it.

FACT The Blue Rider (German, *der Blaue Reiter*) was the name given to a group of Munich artists in the early 1900s. The group's leaders, Wassily Kandinsky and Franz Marc, chose the name because Kandinsky liked riders, Marc liked horses, and they both liked blue.

FISH WITH EVERYTHING

What was the Romans' favourite seasoning? It was a fish-sauce called *garum* or *liquamen*, which was made in factories and used lavishly in cooking savoury dishes. There were several ways of making it, but the simplest was to put small fish, such as sprats and anchovies, into a mixture of salt and water (brine), boiling it until it reduced.

A Roman cookery book has survived, apparently written by Marcus Gavius Apicius more than 1,900 years ago. *Liquamen* occurs in nearly all the savoury recipes.

MUSIC MATTER

What are violin bows made of? The best bows are made of pernambuco wood, which comes from the area around Recife in north-eastern Brazil. Pernambuco is a superior quality of brazilwood, *Caesalpinia echinata* which is hard and heavy, but when worked to a bow stick is both strong and flexible.

One of the first woods to be used for bows for viols and early violins was snakewood, another South American timber. The value of brazilwood was recognized as early as 1630, though it did not come into general use until François Tourte the Younger (1747-1835) standardized the violin bow at its present shape and dimensions. One of the earliest pernambuco bows is dated about 1700, and was probably made by Antonio Stradivari, the greatest of all violin makers.

HARD FACTS

Who invented concrete? The Romans, more than 2,100 years ago. They began by making a cement that was very similar to the cement used today. It set very hard, which is why so many Roman buildings are still standing. Then they mixed the cement with small stones to make concrete, and used it to build walls. The platform-like base of the Second Temple of Concord, built in Rome in 121 BC, is the earliest known example of true concrete.

One of the finest examples of the Roman use of concrete is the dome of the Pantheon in Rome, completed in AD 126. This dome is 44 m (144 ft) across.

◀ The dome of the Pantheon.

GLAMOUR GIRL

Who was Norma Jean Mortenson? That was the real name of the film star, Marilyn Monroe, who died from an overdose of sleeping pills in 1962 at the age of 36. She was born in Los Angeles, and brought up in an orphanage and several foster homes.

She began her working life as a photographer's model, and went into films in 1948. Marilyn's beauty made her a great success, but as she was aware that it could not last, she tried to train as a serious actress.

She was married to baseball star Joe DiMaggio, and later to the playwright Arthur Miller. Neither marriage proved successful, and her life ended in unhappiness.

◄ Marilyn Monroe, star of many films including *Some Like it Hot*, *Gentlemen Prefer Blondes* and *The Seven Year Itch*.

BIG COVER-UP

What was Watergate? It was a political scandal which rocked the United States in the early 1970s. It got its name from a block of offices and homes in Washington, DC.

The story began during the campaign for the presidential election of 1972. Five men broke into the offices of the Democratic Party in the Watergate building. They turned out to be supporters of the rival Republican Party, anxious to secure the re-election of their candidate, President Richard M. Nixon, by spying operations against his political opponents.

Nixon's staff denied that anyone close to Nixon was involved. But in time more evidence was found, that not only linked staff at the White House – the official residence of the President – but also suggested that there had been a conspiracy to conceal the involvement of Nixon himself.

The tapes It was then discovered that Nixon had made tape recordings of his conversations at the White House with his staff about the affair. He was forced to provide a committee of the Senate with written transcripts of the tapes, and people became convinced that the president knew all about the break-in and had tried to cover it up. Faced with being brought to trial on charges of concealing the truth and obstructing justice, Nixon resigned in August 1974.

▲ Richard Nixon makes a TV broadcast just prior to the publication of the Watergate transcripts.

FANTASTIC MATHEMATICIAN

Who really was Lewis Carroll?
He was a lecturer in mathematics at Oxford University, and his real name was Charles Lutwidge Dodgson. His story of *Alice's Adventures in Wonderland*, a children's favourite ever since it was first published in 1865, was first told to three small daughters of a friend whom he took boating on the river near Oxford.

His two careers, as a writer of nonsense and a university don, rarely overlapped – except on the famous occasion when Queen Victoria asked Lewis Carroll to send her a copy of his next book – she received a dull volume on higher mathematics by C. L. Dodgson!

▲ An illustration by John Tenniel from *Alice's Adventures in Wonderland*.

CRISS-CROSS-ROW

What were hornbooks? For hundreds of years they were the early readers for schoolchildren in Britain and North America. They were made and used by the million at a time when books were expensive.

A hornbook consisted of a flat wooden board, about 230 mm by 130 mm (9 in by 5 in), with a handle to hold it. A sheet of printed paper carrying the lessons was pasted on the board and protected by a thin sheet of virtually transparent horn – hence the name.

The lesson This generally began with a large cross, and from this came another name for the hornbook, 'Criss-cross-row' (a corruption of 'Christ's Cross row'). Then followed the alphabet and the Lord's prayer, and Roman and Arabic numerals. Although many hornbooks were made, they wore out easily, so they are now quite rare.

HOLIDAY TASK

Why did Vivaldi write so many concertos? Because he was under contract to do so. Antonio Vivaldi lived from about 1675 to 1741, a period when people expected to hear fresh music all the time, not to have old music revived.

For more than 30 years he held the post of concert master at a girls' orphanage in Venice where he was expected to write two new concertos a month. If he was away he still had to produce the music and send it back to Venice, carriage paid. So it is not surprising to find that Vivaldi wrote altogether 447 concertos.

▲ A hornbook showing the alphabet and the Lord's Prayer.

STERLING SILVER

What is a hallmark? It is one of several marks stamped on a piece of silver that tells you that the silver is of a certain quality. 'Hallmark' is strictly a British term, and refers to the mark used by a particular 'hall', or assay (testing) office.

Mixed metals Silver is too soft to use by itself, so it is mixed with another metal, generally copper, to make it harder. For hundreds of years governments in all countries where silverware is made have controlled the amount of copper that can be added. It varies from 65 to 200 g in every 1,000 g of metal.

Governments insist that every piece should be tested and marked by an official assayer. Nowhere are these controls more strictly maintained than in Britain, for years acknowledged as the world's leading maker of silverware.

The markings On a piece of British silver you will find the following marks:

Mark of origin: This shows the assay office. For example, Birmingham has an anchor, Edinburgh a castle, London a leopard's face, and Sheffield a crown.

Date letter: Each assay office uses a different letter of the alphabet each year.

Assay mark: This indicates that the silver is of sterling quality – that is, at least 92.5 per cent silver. English silver bears a lion, Scottish silver a thistle.

Maker's mark: This is a personal mark, and usually consists of the maker's initials.

Similar marks are used in many countries of continental Europe, but American silver does not carry assay marks.

A silver hallmark, with the four different marks. ▶

▲
Jean Bernadotte (1764-1844) as Marshal of France.

GENERAL'S POST

Who was the French soldier who became King of Sweden? He was a French lawyer's son, Jean Bernadotte, an ancestor of the present royal family of Sweden.

He had an amazing career. He joined the French army in 1780, under the monarchy, rose to be a general in the republican régime following the French Revolution that began in 1789, and became minister of war in the republican government.

Under Napoleon I, Bernadotte became military governor of Hanover, then occupied by France, and returned to his military career with the rank of Marshal of France. Napoleon then created him Prince of Pontecorvo.

An amazing invitation In the meantime news of his capabilities had reached the Swedes whose elderly king, Charles XIII, had no son to succeed him. They invited him to become crown prince and Charles XIII adopted him as a son with the name of Karl Johan. The new crown prince immediately acted as regent for the king, and when the old man died in 1818 he became King Charles XIV. He died in 1844, revered by his new countrymen.

▲
A Viking stone picture showing a scene in Valhalla, the home of the gods.

ROLLING WRITING

Who invented the ball-point pen? The ball-point pen was 'invented' several times, at first as early as 1888.

The earliest workable ball-point pen, and the ancestor of the millions that are used today, was the brainchild of a Hungarian-born inventor, José Ladislao Biró.

Biró was invited to go to Argentina by a former president, and he settled there in 1940. In 1942 he patented his pen, which cost much more than its modern equivalent. Biró sold his patent rights to an American company and spent the rest of his life inventing. He died in 1985 at the age of 86.

The house in Eyam, Derbyshire ▶ where the first plague victim died in 1665.

LUCKY VOYAGER

Who discovered America? Most people would say Christopher Columbus, but a Viking adventurer named Leif Ericsson has an earlier claim. Ericsson, who was nicknamed 'the Lucky' because of his good fortune in life, heard that a fellow Viking, Biarni Heriulfsson, had been driven off-course on a voyage from Iceland to Greenland and had sighted a new land far to the west.

Landfall With 35 brave companions Ericsson set off in a longship, in about the year 1002. They first came to a land of stony coastline, which was probably Labrador. From there they moved along the coast to what they called 'Woodland', believed to be Newfoundland, and further south reached a land where grapes grew, which they called Vinland. This may have been as far south as Maryland, or even Virginia.

No legend Ericsson's story was preserved in a Norse saga, and for a time it was assumed to be legend. But in 1963 remains of a Viking settlement were found at L'Anse au Meadow, on the northern tip of Newfoundland.

HEROIC STORY

Where is the Plague Village? It is Eyam in Derbyshire, England. This tiny place fell victim to the Great Plague of 1665, which devastated London. A local tailor received a bundle of cloth from London, which carried with it the fleas that bore the dreaded disease. Within a few days the tailor was dead and several of his neighbours were ill.

Isolation The rector, William Mompesson, persuaded the villagers to isolate themselves to stop the plague spreading further in the neighbourhood. So for 13 months nobody stirred out of Eyam. Food, clothing and medicine were supplied by people from nearby villages. They were left at various collecting points on the village boundary, and money to pay for them – disinfected with vinegar and spring water – was left by the villagers.

Remembrance When the outbreak came to an end, 262 of the 350 people of Eyam were dead. The village keeps the last Sunday in August every year as Plague Sunday, when a religious service is held in the open air, just as services were during the epidemic.

CLASHING STEEL

Which was the longest sword fight in the history of cinema? There have been many spectacular sword fights on screen. One of the most memorable was that performed by the dancer Gene Kelly in *The Three Musketeers* (1948). It lasted five minutes. Even longer was the thrilling sword fight between Mel Ferrer and Stewart Granger, in the swashbuckling cinema classic, *Scaramouche* (1952), which lasted a full six and a half minutes!

▲
Stewart Granger (facing) and Mel Ferrer in the film, *Scaramouche*.

QUIZ: PEOPLE AND PLACES

1. What event does France celebrate on July 14?
2. America was named after an explorer. What was his name?
3. Which American film star became a princess by marrying the ruler of Monaco?
4. Ireland is divided into four provinces. What are they?
5. Of which country was Juan Perón twice president?
6. By what name was the Communist leader Josip Broz better known?
7. Which famous city was burned in 1666?
8. Which French palace is famous for its Hall of Mirrors?
9. What were the former names of these African countries: Burkina Faso, Ghana, Zambia, Malawi?

ANSWERS
1. The Fall of the Bastille. 2. Amerigo Vespucci. 3. Grace Kelly. 4. Ulster, Munster, Leinster, Connacht. 5. Argentina. 6. Tito (he ruled Yugoslavia 1945-1980) 7. London. 8. Versailles. 9. Upper Volta, Gold Coast, Northern Rhodesia, Nyasaland.

ABSENT ROYALTY

What was Jacobite glass? After the Stuarts were chased off the British throne in 1689, their few faithful followers had to be very careful how they expressed their loyalty to the banished royal family. They became known as Jacobites, from the Latin form of the exiled king's name, James II (Jacobus).

They used to drink the health of the absent king by passing their glasses across a bowl of water before they drank, so toasting 'the king over the water'. Special glasses were made, with symbols such as a red rose, symbolizing the throne, with two buds, standing for James II's son and grandson, James Edward and Charles Edward, the Old and Young Pretenders. Others had a star, signifying 'Hope'.

DOLLAR DISASTER

What was the Wall Street Crash? It was the biggest financial crisis of the century, and it happened in 1929.

Financial optimism For several years before the crash more and more Americans had been buying shares, and the economy seemed to be booming. By 1928 people were speculating wildly, borrowing money to buy shares, confident of making fortunes overnight.

Unfortunately, the industries on which the United States' prosperity depended were not continuing to expand as expected. They were producing more goods than they could sell, the banking system was poorly organized, and some companies were in the hands of inept businessmen.

Selling In September 1929 there were signs of a loss of confidence. Some investors started selling their shares and taking what profits they could. But business on Wall Street – the popular name for the New York Stock Exchange which stands on that street – stayed fairly steady for a few weeks longer.

On the morning of Thursday, 24 October, business on the Stock Exchange started normally, with people buying and selling shares in the ordinary way. Suddenly, after an hour of trading, there were no more buyers, only sellers. On that one day 12,894,650 shares were sold, many of them at huge losses.

The following week, dealers who had bought shares cheaply on what had come to be called 'Black Thursday', were forced to sell them again, at further heavy losses. On Tuesday, 29 October, 16,410,030 shares changed hands.

Unemployment The Wall Street Crash led inevitably to the Great Depression, which affected every country in the world and lasted until World War II. Many US banks found that they had invested their customers' money in now worthless shares. By 1932 more than 5,000 banks had closed, with the loss of people's savings. As a result, many businesses also had to close, and unemployment rocketed in the United States to 25 per cent by 1933.

RELIGIOUS PERSUASION

Who said 'Paris is well worth a Mass'? The Mass is the Catholic form of the communion service, and this remark is said to have been made by the protestant Huguenot leader, Henry of Navarre, when he inherited the throne of France in 1589. It was made clear to Henry that he would win more support in the country if he allowed himself to be converted to Roman Catholicism, the religion of the majority of the French. Henry agreed, became Henry IV, and brought prosperity to France.

MONSTROUS SUCCESS

Who was the 'Modern Prometheus'? That's the sub-title of *Frankenstein*, a science fiction book written by Mary Wollstonecraft Shelley and published in 1818. Contrary to popular belief, Frankenstein was not the monster, but the scientist who made one, using human bones from a graveyard. The monster looked fairly human, and had some kind of life.

Mary was the second wife of the poet Percy Bysshe Shelley. Together with the poet Lord Byron they once spent some weeks writing ghost stories to pass the time, and *Frankenstein* was developed into a book from one of Mary's stories. She was only 19 when she wrote it.

And Prometheus? He was a Greek god, said to have made men from clay.

◀ A scene taken from Universal Pictures' film, *Frankenstein*, starring Boris Karloff (right), as the monster.

DAZZLING TALENT

What is Op Art? It is a form of abstract art – that is, art that does not pretend to show an actual scene – which tries to produce optical illusions. The contemporary artist, Victor Vasarely, was one of the first painters to produce this kind of work, in 1935.

In Op Art painters use lines and colours in such a way that they dazzle the eyes and make the design appear to move. Sculptors make three-dimensional patterns of string and coloured plastic which have the same effect. Op Art became fashionable in the 1950s.

Turquoise, Cerise, Mustard Twist ▶
with Black, by Bridget Riley.

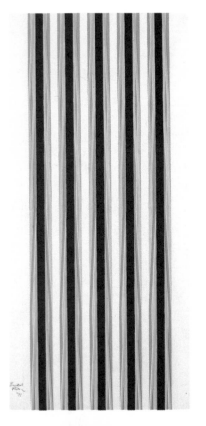

FAMILY FUN

How many Marx Brothers were there? Altogether there were five, but only four ever appeared in their 13 films.

The five were Chico (real name Leonard, 1891-1961), who played the piano and spoke with an Italian accent; Harpo (real name Adolph, later called Arthur, 1893-1964), who played the harp and never spoke; Groucho (real name Julius, 1895-1977), who smoked a cigar and had a heavy painted moustache); Zeppo (real name Herbert, 1900-1979), who always played a romantic 'straight' rôle; and Gummo (real name Milton, 1901-1977), who never appeared in films. He is reputed to have said: 'I attribute their success entirely to me – I quit the act.'

▲
The Marx brothers with their director, Sam Wood. From left to right: Gummo, Groucho, Harpo, Sam Wood, Chico and Zeppo.

SEWING HISTORY

What is the Bayeux Tapestry?
Despite its name, it is not a tapestry: it is needlework with the design embroidered on the fabric. A true tapestry has the design woven in when the material is made.

The Bayeux Tapestry is a band of linen 500 mm (about 19 in) wide and 70 m (almost 76 yd) long. It tells the story of the Norman Conquest of England in 1066, in 72 scenes – it's really a medieval strip cartoon. The embroidery is done in eight different colours of wool.

Unfortunately some of the fabric is missing and we do not know how much more there originally was. This picture story ends with the flight of the English forces at the end of the Battle of Hastings. The tapestry is kept at Bayeux, in north-western France.

◄ Part of the Bayeaux Tapestry. It shows William the Conqueror's ship sailing to England.

SSSH!

Who wrote silent music? The American composer, John Cage, who was born in 1912. He had been experimenting with *aleatoric* music – that is, music that owes its form and nature to chance. Believing that even the act of casting dice implied interference on the part of the composer, Cage in 1952 wrote a piece for piano which he called simply 4' 33".

For the four minutes and thirty-three seconds of the title, the pianist sits at the piano, sheets of blank paper in front of him. By arm movements he indicates the three movements of which the work consists. The 'music' is the random sounds the audience hears within the hall and coming from outside.

THE WORMS' TURN

Who discovered silk? According to an old Chinese legend, silk was discovered by the Empress Hsi Ling-shi, about 2700 BC. Trying to find out what was eating the imperial mulberry trees, she found a fat worm-like creature munching the leaves and spinning shiny cocoons. She accidentally dropped a cocoon into hot water, and at once a long, shiny mass of threads began to unravel from the cocoon. The creatures were silkworms – actually the larvae of the silkworm moth, *Bombyx mori*.

Chinese secret For the next 3,000 years only the Chinese knew how to spin and use silk. Other countries asked for the secret, but the Chinese refused to divulge it. Wealthy Europeans imported silk from China via Persia (modern Iran). It travelled by a winding route that lay to the north of the Himalayas, and became known as the Silk Road.

Cunning monks Eventually the Chinese monopoly was broken by the cunning of two Christian monks, sent by the Byzantine Emperor Justinian about AD 550. The monks used heavy bamboo sticks as staffs, and inside these they hid samples of the silkworm moth's eggs and some seeds of the mulberry trees on which they fed.

As a result, the silk industry became established in Europe.

▲
A 19th-century picture of silk manufacturing in China.

STEPS TO FAME

Who built the first pyramid? It was the work of a versatile man, Imhotep – priest, astronomer, writer, physician, and chief minister to Pharaoh Djoser of Egypt, who reigned about 2,600 BC. Like all the later pyramids, this first pyramid was designed to crown a tomb, in this case Djoser's own.

Mastabas Before that time Egyptian royal tombs were built as *mastabas*: flat, rectangular slab-like constructions containing the burial-chamber and a group of rooms to hold treasures that were buried with the king. These treasures were to accompany the dead man into the afterlife.

Imhotep built a tomb that consisted of a series of six mastabas of decreasing size, one on top of the other. This tomb, known as the Step Pyramid, survives to this day at Saqqara, in Egypt.

▲ Taglioni in *La Sylphide*.

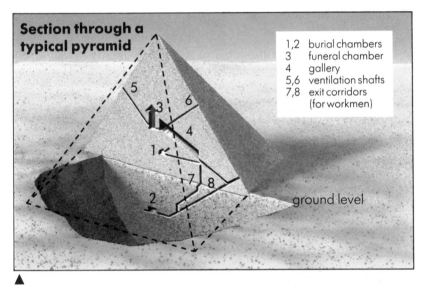

Section through a typical pyramid

1,2	burial chambers
3	funeral chamber
4	gallery
5,6	ventilation shafts
7,8	exit corridors (for workmen)

ground level

▲ Burial chambers of a pyramid could be in the body of it, or underground.

FACT FILE: THE ROMAN ARMY

FACT The average size of the Roman army was 150,000 Roman soldiers, plus about the same number of auxiliary troops recruited from conquered peoples.

FACT Each of the legions (equivalent to regiments) that made up the army contained about 5,000 infantrymen and 120 cavalrymen.

FACT The main weapons of a Roman legionary were a two-edged sword and a spear.

FACT Service for a legionary was 20 years, plus five years in the reserve; he then retired with a gratuity equivalent to 13 years' pay.

FACT Roman soldiers were not allowed to marry.

FACT During sieges Roman soldiers held their shields over their heads for protection against missiles, forming a plate-like covering called a *testudo* (tortoise).

FACT Artillery consisted of the scorpion, which was like a gigantic crossbow firing a spear, and the ballista, a catapult which hurled huge rocks.

FACT A centurion was a junior officer in command of a *century*, originally 100 men.

TUTU DARING!

What is a tutu? The light, short ballet skirt known as the tutu was introduced by the ballerina Marie Taglioni at the first performance of her father's ballet *La Sylphide* in 1832. Her skirt came to mid-calf, whereas before then ballerinas wore full-length skirts.

The very short, almost horizontal form of the tutu was introduced in the late 1800s. The word *tutu* comes from a childish word for 'bottom' in French.

MEN ONLY

Did women act on the Greek stage? No, they didn't: *all* the parts were taken by men, who wore masks that showed the type of person they were supposed to portray. The tradition that women were not allowed on stage lasted for hundreds of years.

In England, all the female rôles in Shakespeare's plays were originally taken by boys. Women did not appear in the theatre until the Restoration of Charles II in 1660, when the use of female actors was introduced from Continental Europe.

The capture of Parma by ▶ Tintoretto. It is typical of his compositions which are full of figures in violent movement.

QUICK STARTER

How did Tintoretto astonish the Venetians? Tintoretto was a Venetian painter who lived from 1518 to 1594. His real name was Jacopo Robusti, but he was always called *Il Tintoretto*, which means the little dyer, because his father was a dyer. He was both a fine artist and a shrewd businessman who knew how to get commissions.

When the Guild of S. Rocco wanted a painting for the ceiling of their hall they asked four leading painters – including Tintoretto – to submit designs. Tintoretto quietly slipped into the hall and measured the ceiling. Then he went back to his workshop and prepared a canvas to fit the space.

In place The day when the Guild met to examine the designs arrived. The other three painters exhibited their cartoons (preliminary sketches). Then Tintoretto had some plain canvas which was masking the ceiling removed – and there was his finished picture in place, where it remains to this day.

When the members of the Guild began to protest at his 'jumping the gun', Tintoretto promptly told them the painting was a gift. He knew that under their own rules the Guild had to accept all gifts. As a result of this bold move, Tintoretto became a member of the guild and agreed, in return for a regular salary, to complete the decoration of the hall. He finished the work in 1588.

SINGING STRINGS

Why does a violin bridge have holes in it? The graceful twirls and curls of the holes in a violin bridge add to the beauty of the instrument – but they also have a practical purpose. The bridge transmits the vibration of the four strings to the belly of the instrument, which is the sounding board, just like the sounding board of a piano.

If the bridge were solid, when one string was vibrating the others would limit the vibration of the bridge and the result would be a strangled, quiet sound. That's just the sound you hear when a violinist puts a mute on, because the mute clamps the bridge and makes it, in effect, solid.

The bridge of a violin.
▼

WORDS OF WINSTON

Which statesman was awarded the Nobel Prize for literature? He was Sir Winston Churchill (1874-1965), famous as Britain's prime minister and leader during World War II. Churchill had an amazing career as a soldier, journalist, statesman, painter, orator *and* writer. The citation for the Nobel Prize, awarded in 1953, referred to Churchill's 'mastery of historical and biographical presentation and for his brilliant oratory'.

The books which helped to win Churchill this honour included *The World Crisis*, a history of World War I; *The Second World War*; *Marlborough, His Life and Times*, a study of his ancestor, the soldier John Churchill; and *Lord Randolph Churchill*, a study of his father.

INFANT QUEEN

Who was Margaret the Maid of Norway? She was a three-year-old girl who became Queen of Scots in 1286. Margaret was the grand-daughter of King Alexander III, and she was called the Maid of Norway because her mother was married to the King of Norway.

The Scots lords agreed to acknowledge her as queen, and in 1290 she set out by ship to travel to her new country. But on the way she fell ill, some say with sea-sickness, and died. Her death began a 20-year civil war over who should succeed to the throne.

TASTY AWARD

What is the origin of the cakewalk? This was a dance performed by American Blacks in the days of slavery. It was accompanied by strongly syncopated (offbeat) music. The dance was a high-stepping strut, mimicking the Southern plantation owners and their haughty, aristocratic ways.

The dancers improvised most of the time, and were watched by judges, who gave the couple who performed the most intricate steps a highly decorated cake as a prize – hence the name. The cakewalk, and dances derived from it, became popular in show business in the early 1900s.

MYSTERIOUS RUINS

What was the original Zimbabwe? It was a group of ruins in the south-eastern part of the modern country of Zimbabwe. The word, meaning 'stone houses', comes from the Shona language. The Shona peoples had a number of locations known as zimbabwe, which were used for tribal religious ceremonies.

The ruins at Great Zimbabwe, as it is now called, consist of a cone-shaped stone tower inside a temple. The temple is within a stone wall, which in places is as much as 10 m (32 ft) high. The stones, large slabs of granite, are built up without cement. Great Zimbabwe may have been the capital of the Shona Empire.

The buildings were probably erected from about AD 1100 onwards until the 1400s. They were abandoned when Zulu bands from the south conquered the Shona in the early 1800s.

The ruined wall and towers of Great Zimbabwe.
▼

▲
An etching depicting Paul Revere's Ride.

ARTISTIC CAVEMEN

Which are the oldest pictures? They are cave paintings made by hunters of the Stone Age in southern France. About 35,000 to 40,000 years ago groups of Stone Age people settled in the Pyrenees between France and Spain, where there are many caves which they used as shelter from the bitter winters. (For the Ice Age still gripped northern Europe.)

Dating methods The cave paintings are 10,000 to 30,000 years old. Approximate datings have been confirmed by two main methods. Years of use have left debris thickly strewn on the floors of some of the caves, covering the bottom of the paintings. By radiocarbon tests on organic debris, such as bones, a date can be estimated for the accumulation of the rubbish.

The second method is based on the rate at which a mineral deposit — calcium carbonate — leaching out of the limestone rock with centuries of percolating water has built up over the pictures. By measuring the thickness of the flow, it is possible to calculate how long it has taken to build up.

▲
A cave-painting of a black cow from the famous Lascaux caves in France.

MIDNIGHT RIDER

Who was Paul Revere? He was an American silversmith who worked in his father's business in Boston, Massachusetts. He was a versatile craftsman who deserves to be remembered for his skill — yet he is best known for a courageous exploit in the early days of the American War of Independence.

Revere was a leading member of the independence movement for which he acted as a special messenger. In April 1775 he made a dramatic, and now famous, midnight ride to warn other revolutionaries that a British force was on its way to arrest them.

Later Revere served as a lieutenant colonel in the revolutionary army. He also built and operated a gunpowder factory and cast bronze cannon.

After the war, Revere returned to silversmithing and, as well as casting hundreds of church bells, built the first North American machine for rolling out sheet copper.

HISTORY IN THE MAKING

What was the Anglo Saxon Chronicle? It was an account of events compiled by monks from some time in the AD 800s until the coronation of Henry II in 1154. The chronicle was begun by the monks at Winchester, then the capital of England. They started by drawing on earlier histories from the year 1, and taking the story up to their own times. Thereafter they kept it up to date every year.

The chronicle was written in Old English, although most scholarly works at the time were in Latin. Historians value it as an important source of information.

◀ Harold Lloyd performs his own stunt on the top of a skyscraper in *Safety Last*.

ARCTIC ANTICS

Who reached the North Pole first? It's generally accepted that the American naval engineer, Robert E. Peary (1856-1920), accomplished this feat,on April 6, 1909. But another explorer, an American surgeon named Frederick A. Cook, claimed that he had reached the Pole a year earlier.

Disputed claims Enquiries, including one by the University of Copenhagen and another by the US Congress, decided that Cook's claim did not stand up, and Cook did not appear to question their findings.

Although Peary was honoured all over the world for his achievement, his triumph was spoiled by the dispute over Cook's claims.

STUNT STARS

Did Harold Lloyd, the film comedian, do his own stunts?
Cinema stunting is dangerous and usually performed by professional stuntpeople – anonymous women and men who double for the stars when the going gets tough.

Some stars have always insisted on doing their own stunts, and Harold Lloyd was certainly one of those brave actors. He directed and performed all his own stunts, including a terrifying climb up a skyscraper in a film called *Safety Last* (1923). Other stars who performed and directed their own stunts include Buster Keaton, Sean Connery and Steve McQueen.

QUIZ: FICTIONAL CHARACTERS

1. What is the name of the villainous pirate in *Treasure Island* by Robert Louis Stevenson?
2. Who are Meg, Jo, Beth and Amy?
3. What is the name of the fairy in J. M. Barrie's story, *Peter Pan*?
4. In Rudyard Kipling's *The Jungle Book*, who was the boy who was brought up by wolves?
5. What are the names of *The Three Musketeers* in Alexander Dumas's book?
6. What do the main characters of these books have in common: *National Velvet* by Enid Bagnold, *Black Beauty* by Anna Sewell, and *My Friend Flicka* by Mary O'Hara?
7. What is the first name of Gulliver in Swift's book, *Gulliver's Travels*?
8. Who is the miserly hero of Charles Dickens's book, *A Christmas Carol*?

ANSWERS
1 Long John Silver. 2 Characters in *Little Women* by Louisa May Alcott. 3 Tinker Bell. 4 Mowgli. 5 Athos, Porthos and Aramis. 6 They are all horses. 7 Lemuel. 8 Ebeneezer Scrooge.

LAND OF BABEL

Which country has the most languages? The leading contender is probably India, where the people speak 15 major languages and 857 other languages and dialects! This country of more than 700 million people has one official language, Hindi, but only half the people can speak it. Almost as many have English as a second language.

A smaller country with a similar language problem is Papua New Guinea, whose population of just over 3 million speak more than 700 different languages.

ANCIENT DETERRENT

Who built the Great Wall of China? Like so many major structures, the Great Wall of China was built over a long period. Over many years, several short walls were built in northern China to keep out the raiding Mongols from the desert lands. During the brief period of the Ch'in Empire (221-206 BC), these short lengths were linked to form a large part of the Great Wall as it exists today.

For this work thousands of men, mostly discharged soldiers, toiled in appalling conditions to build the wall.

The Great Wall was expanded in the late AD 500s, and was repaired under the rule of the Ming emperors (1368-1644).

The Great Wall is more than 2,400 km (1,500 miles) long and in recent years the Communist government has set about repairing it as a tourist attraction.

CHILDREN'S BOOKMAN

What is the Newbery Medal? A prize given every year to the author of the best American book for children. The award was set up in 1922, and it takes its name from one of the most important people in the history of children's books.

John Newbery was an English printer and publisher who lived from 1713 to 1767. His shop, at the sign of the 'Bible and Sun' in St Paul's Churchyard, London, sold not only books but also patent medicines. Newbery was the friend of many famous writers, including Samuel Johnson and Oliver Goldsmith, both of whom wrote books for him.

Newbery's books were designed to entertain children, rather than to be 'improving' or educational. So he may be said to have started children's literature as we know it.

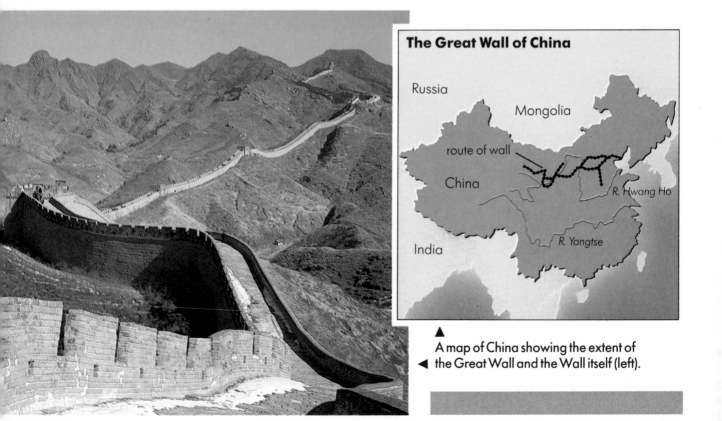

The Great Wall of China

Russia

Mongolia

route of wall

China

R. Hwang Ho

India

R. Yangtse

▲
◀ A map of China showing the extent of the Great Wall and the Wall itself (left).

DIPLOMATIC POET

Which poet was also a diplomat? He was England's first great poet, Geoffrey Chaucer, who lived from 1340 to 1400. Although he is well known today as the author of *The Canterbury Tales*, official records show that he was 'pensioned' as an employee of King Edward III in 1367. He was then only 27 years old, but the pension was a kind that was more like a regular salary, for past and future services.

Chaucer was employed on diplomatic missions on at least seven occasions that we know of. One trip was apparently to take part in peace negotiations with France. For the rest of his life he was generally in the employment of the court, though with the changes of king (Richard II in 1377 and Henry IV in 1399) he had some periods of unemployment and hardship.

▲ A portrait of Geoffrey Chaucer painted in the early 15th century to illustrate a manuscript.

MAN OF DREAMS

Who was Sigmund Freud? A physician who founded the practice of psychoanalysis. He was born in 1856 and lived for most of his life in Vienna. After qualifying he set up in practice as a neurologist, treating disorders of the nervous system. From this work came his gradual evolvement of psychoanalysis, persuading patients to talk freely about their problems and experiences.

Freud was particularly interested in dreams and what they reveal of a person's mind and subconscious. His book *The Interpretation of Dreams* (1900) is now considered a classic in the field. In 1938 he moved to London, following the annexation of Austria by the Nazis under Adolf Hitler, and he died there a year later.

TRAVELLING LIGHT

What was the* Kon-Tiki *? It was a balsawood raft, with a sail, on which six men sailed across the Pacific Ocean from Callao in Peru to the Raroia Reef in the Polynesian islands, in 1947. The leader of the expedition, Thor Heyerdahl, a Norwegian ethnologist (studying races of people), organized the voyage to test a theory that some of the Polynesian islands had been colonized from South America.

The voyage proved that the theory *could* be right, but did not prove conclusively that it *was*. During the 101-day voyage, the *Kon-Tiki* drifted with the wind and current a distance equal to that from Chicago to Moscow by the most direct route.

◄ The *Kon-Tiki* on its voyage across the Pacific.

FAILING FOUNDATIONS

Why does Pisa's Tower lean?
Because the ground beneath the
foundations began to subside in
1173, soon after work on the
tower began, and has been
giving way gradually ever since.

The foundations are only 3 m
(10 ft) deep, which is not much
for a building 55 m (180 ft 6 in)
tall. The tower – the campanile
(bell-tower) of the city's
cathedral – was already leaning
when it was completed in 1372,
and part of the upper works
were 'straightened' during
construction in order to
counteract the lean.

The amount of lean has been
gradually increasing over the
years, until in the mid-1900s it
was about 4 m (13 ft) out of line.
Work has since been undertaken
to prevent the tower collapsing.

SHADY HISTORY

Who invented the umbrella?
Believe it or not, this useful item
was probably first used by the
Assyrians. The name umbrella
comes from the Latin *umbra*,
meaning 'shade', and it's likely
that the earliest umbrellas were
sunshades. They are pictured in
Egyptian tomb paintings and
Assyrian and ancient Persian
sculptures.

Although umbrellas were
known to the Saxons, they did
not become popular in the West
until the 1700s. The umbrella was
then introduced to London by a
traveller and philanthropist,
Jonas Hanway, who came
across it in his travels to Persia.

◄ The leaning tower of Pisa.

PLAGUE PROMISE

***When did the Oberammergau
Passion Play begin?*** It was first
planned in 1633. The plague had
struck the German village of
Oberammergau, and in
thankfulness for the ending of the
outbreak the villagers vowed to
perform a Passion Play (a
dramatized account of Christ's
betrayal, trial and crucifixion)
every ten years.

The first performance was
given in 1634. From 1680 the
date was changed so that the
play always falls on decimal
years. The only break was
caused by World War II: there
was no play in 1940.

All the inhabitants of the
village of Oberammergau are
involved in the play, either
acting, singing, or backstage.
During the season several
performances a week are given,
each lasting more than seven
hours.

▲
A potter from Oberammergau as Christ in the Passion Play.

FEMALE FIGHTERS

Which country first gave women the vote? Even as early as the 1500s, a few women were demanding the right to vote. But it was not until the 19th century that women's suffrage (voting rights) became a major issue. The struggle was intense, particularly in the United States and Britain.

Thousands of women, led by Elizabeth Cady Stanton and Susan B. Anthony in the USA, and the Pankhursts and Millicent Fawcett in Britain, marched, petitioned, and were imprisoned as part of their fight for the vote.

Although the suffrage movement began in the USA and Britain, it was New Zealand that, in 1893, first granted women the right to vote in national elections, followed by Australia (1902), Finland (1906), and Norway (1913). Women did not get the vote in Britain and the USA until 1918 and 1920 respectively.

One of the first women to vote in Britain in an election on 14 December 1918.
▼

FACT FILE: THE INDUSTRIAL REVOLUTION

FACT The first practical steam engine was a pumping engine built in 1698 by Thomas Savery, a Cornish military engineer.

FACT John Kay's flying shuttle, patented in 1733, marks the real beginning of the Industrial Revolution. The flying shuttle doubled the amount of cloth weavers could make.

FACT Belgium was the second European country after Britain to become industrialized.

FACT An Anglican clergyman, Edmund Cartwright, invented the first steam-powered loom.

FACT The first person to use coke rather than charcoal to smelt iron was Abraham Darby II of Shropshire, in the early 1700s.

FACT The first commercially successful steamboat was built in 1807 by the American inventor, Robert Fulton.

FABRIC OF STATE

Why does the Lord Chancellor of the United Kingdom sit on the Woolsack? This ancient custom was originally designed to underline the importance of the wool trade in England's economy. All through the Middle Ages this was the mainstay of British trade, a position it held until the Industrial Revolution that began in the 1700s. Woolsacks were first used as seats in the House of Lords in the reign of Edward III (1327-1377), to whom Parliament had to vote a grant of 20,000 sacks of wool to pay his debts, incurred in war with France.

Four seats Originally there were four woolsacks, which were arranged facing one another in an open square in front of the throne. One held the Barons of the Exchequer (a sort of court of appeal); another held High Court judges; the third held Serjeants-at-law (equivalent to senior barristers); and the fourth was for the Masters in Chancery (officers of the High Court).

Today The present-day Woolsack is a large square cushion of wool, covered with red cloth. When seated on the Woolsack, the Chancellor presides over the debates in the House of Lords. If he wishes to take part in a debate, the Chancellor rises from the Woolsack and stands beside it to speak.

▲
A 19th-century print of a chancellor on the Woolsack.

SCANT COVER

When was the bikini invented?
Much longer ago than you might think! Girls in Roman times wore garments that were very close in style (and brevity) to the modern bikini. The Emperor Maximian had a palace near Piazza Armerina, in Sicily in the late AD 200s, where one room was decorated with mosaics of girl athletes, all wearing bikinis.

Similar mosaics have been found in other Roman ruins, while in the volcano-devastated town of Pompeii a statue of Venus with a gilded bikini was found. A Roman leather bikini was discovered preserved in the mud of a well in London.

The name was coined from Bikini Atoll, a group of tiny islands in the Pacific Ocean where atomic bomb tests were carried out shortly after the end of World War II. The implication was that the sight of a bikini on a pretty girl was likely to be as devastating as the atomic tests!

BUNDLE OF LOVE

What were love spoons?
They're part of an old Welsh custom, which flourished in the 1700s. A young man who was in love with a girl would carve one of these wooden spoons as a token that he wanted to court her. The bowls of the spoons were fairly plain, but the handles were elaborate, often with designs of hearts, anchors and flowers.

The spoon as a love token arose from the old custom of 'bundling'. In the days when many families lived in just one room, the only place for a courting couple was the bed. The couple lay on the bed, fully clothed, with a blanket between them. If the bed had curtains they were drawn around them. As the easiest way to lie comfortably in such circumstances is to fit together like a pair of spoons, the wooden love spoons were really a plea to be allowed to 'bundle'.

A craftsman carves a love spoon.

▲ A Delftware tulip pot.

POTTERY TOWN

Is all Delftware Dutch? Far from it – much of this pottery was actually made in England! Delftware is a lightweight earthenware, coated with a glaze that contains tin, which makes it white and opaque. Typically it is decorated in blue designs, in imitation of Chinese blue-and-white porcelain.

Delft, in the Netherlands, became a major European centre for this kind of pottery during the 1600s, and the ware is still made there. Because of the popularity of Delft pottery, the name came to be applied to similar ceramic wares made in England, and the real Delft was called 'Dutch Delft'.

A Pony Express rider in hostile country. ▲

GALLOPING POSTMEN

What was the Pony Express? It was a postal service linking the eastern United States with the far West. It began on April 3, 1860, at a time when no railway went farther west than the Mississippi and Missouri rivers. All mail for the West had to travel by stage-coach, on a long, slow route.

The Pony Express used a shorter, more northerly route starting at St Joseph, on the Missouri River. It followed an immigrant trail for part of the way, and then ran across the salt desert of Nevada and Utah.

Relay stations A series of relay stations was set up, between 16 and 24 km (10 and 15 miles) apart all along the route, where horses were kept. Riders were stationed at bases about 120 km (75 miles) apart.

The mail was carried by riders galloping at top speed between relay stations. They changed horses at each station, changeover time being two minutes. The mail took about nine days to travel from St Joseph to Sacramento, California, a saving of nearly two weeks on the mail coach route.

Short-lived However the service lasted only 18 months. It ended on October 24, 1861, when the electric telegraph cable across the United States was completed, enabling messages to be sent in minutes instead of days.

GETTING IT TAPED

Who invented video-taping? Like so many inventions these days, video-tape recording was the work of *many* technologists. Probably the first demonstration of a practical video-tape recording was in 1956. Soon after that producers began making programmes on tape for screening later: before then programmes were either broadcast live, or were on film, which sometimes led to less than the best quality. Video recordings are now available on both tapes and discs.

RUSSIAN RULERS

Who were the boyars? They were the ruling class, the aristocracy, in Russia during the Middle Ages. They consisted of army officers and large landowners. From the 900s onwards the boyars ruled the land, controlling each of the small princedoms into which Russia was then divided.

By the 1400s, Muscovy, the princedom with Moscow as its capital, had become the most important state in Russia. Its boyars were members of only about 200 families who controlled the way the country was run.

Defeat The first tsar, ruler of all Russia, was Ivan IV, the Terrible. He determined to break the power of the boyars. He organized a band of faithful followers called the Oprichnina, which included special police. With their aid he crushed the power of the boyars, and had many of them arrested and murdered.

Peter the Great, who ruled from 1689-1725, abolished the title of boyar, though he created a new aristocracy subordinate to himself.

▲ The Copernican system of the Universe. The figure in the bottom right-hand corner is Copernicus.

ROYAL RÔLE

Which actor played the same part 4,625 times? Yul Brynner, and the rôle was that of the King of Siam in the musical, *The King and I.*

Brynner's real name was Taidje Khan. He was born in the Soviet Union, the son of a Swiss-born Mongolian mining engineer. His father took the name of Brynner when he became a Swiss citizen.

In the United States Brynner worked first as an actor, then as a TV producer. In 1951 he was offered the part of the King of Siam in a Broadway production, and shaved his head for it. He kept it shaved ever after.

The first run of *The King and I* was 1,246 performances, and Brynner played the part in an Oscar-winning film in 1956 and in a TV series in the 1970s. He was appearing in a revival of the show until a few weeks before his death in 1985.

A scene from 20th-Century Fox's film, *The King and I*, starring Yul Brynner and Deborah Kerr. ▶

CONFUSED ORBITS

Who first realized that the Earth goes round the Sun? Because the Sun rises in the East and appears to travel across the sky to set in the West, it was natural for people to believe that it went round the Earth. However, as early as the 200s BC, a Greek philosopher called Aristarchus of Samos suggested that perhaps the Earth revolved around the Sun, but few people took his theories seriously.

Revived theory Centuries later the Polish astronomer and mathematician, Nicolaus Copernicus (1473-1543) put forward the same theory in a book published a few weeks after his death. He explained that the Earth revolves on its own axis, and orbits the Sun.

For many years there was opposition to the Copernican theory, not for any scientific reason, but because leaders of the Christian Church thought it was foolish and contradicted the Bible.

Galileo The opposition of the Church to Copernicus's theory came to a head in 1632, when the Italian astronomer, Galileo Galilei (1564-1642) published *A Dialogue of the Two Principal Systems of the World*, supporting Copernicus's work with his own researches using the newly-invented telescope. This was totally against the views of a body of theologians in Rome who thought that Earth was at the centre of the universe and that everything else must be revolving around it.

On the instructions of Pope Urban VIII Galileo was immediately arrested and put on trial before the Inquisition. Under threat of torture the aged Galileo was forced to renounce his belief that the Earth went round the Sun. However, it is said that, as he solemnly agreed that the Earth stays still, he muttered under his breath, 'But it does move, all the same!'

FIRST SIGHTING

Which European first saw the Pacific Ocean? Vasco Núñez de Balboa, who was a Spanish *conquistador* (conqueror, but actually an adventurer). He went to the recently-discovered New World in 1501 to make his fortune. In 1510 he became governor of Darien, the narrow part of what is now Panama.

Hearing from some American Indians that there was another sea not far to the west, Balboa set out in 1513 to find it – and from a hilltop he saw the Pacific. It took him four further days to reach the shore, where he promptly rushed into the sea in full armour, regardless of the rust, to claim its waters for his master the King of Spain.

El Cid at the head of his troops. ▶

DIY

What is a Grangerized book? It is a book with some blank pages which can be illustrated with prints or pictures cut out of other books. The first one was the brainchild of an English clergyman, the Reverend James Granger, who, in 1769, produced a book with the snappy title: *A Biographical History of England, from Egbert the Great to the Revolution . . . Adapted to a Methodical Catalogue of Engraved British Heads*. This tome contained a number of blank pages so that purchasers could illustratè it themselves. It was an instant success.

Some books exist in the form suitable for grangerizing, and some collectors have other books pulled to pieces and rebound with blank pages to allow for the inclusion of whatever illustrations they like.

SPANISH HERO

Who was El Cid? He was a Spanish warrior named Rodrigo Díaz de Vivar, and he lived from about 1043 to 1099. The name 'El Cid' comes from the Arabic *sid*, meaning 'lord'. Díaz was also known as El Campeador, 'the champion'.

Although there are many fantastic stories about his exploits, it is clear that El Cid was involved in plenty of real adventures. His greatest achievement was to conquer Valencia, a province then held by the Moors. Earlier he was exiled by Alfonso, the king of Léon and Castile, and took service with the Moorish rulers of Saragossa.

Both in legend and in reality El Cid was a brave warrior and a clever and successful general. With his sword he won both fame and fortune.

QUIZ: POT LUCK!

① Which artist produced the series of paintings known as *The Rake's Progress*?
② Which city is famous for its shell-like opera house?
③ In what sport was Don Bradman famous?
④ Which country won the Russo-Japanese War of 1904-1905?
⑤ What and where is Big Ben?
⑥ What famous battle began on October 23, 1942?
⑦ The cor anglais is neither English nor a horn. What is it?
⑧ For 123 years British rulers were also rulers of a German state. What was its name?
⑨ To what country did Bangladesh belong before it became independent in 1971?

ANSWERS
① William Hogarth. ② Sydney, Australia. ③ Cricket.
④ Japan. ⑤ Big Ben is the bell in the Clock Tower of London's Houses of Parliament (and not the whole clock). ⑥ The Battle of Alamein, in North Africa. ⑦ An alto oboe. ⑧ Hanover.
⑨ Pakistan – it was the eastern province.

▲
Nazi soldiers enter a Stalingrad factory. It had been deliberately destroyed by the Russians to make it useless to the Germans.

HEROIC DEFENCE

Why did a British king award a ceremonial sword to a Russian city?
The Battle of Stalingrad was one of the most heroic defences of World War II. Stalingrad was the name from 1925 to 1961 of Volgograd, a city on the banks of the River Volga in the southern part of the Soviet Union.

The German invasion of Russia, which began in June 1941, drove deep into Soviet territory. By August 1942 the German armies were approaching the Volga; they aimed to capture Stalingrad because it was an oil-distribution centre and a key place to cross the river.

Demolition The attack on Stalingrad began on August 21. The German troops and tanks fought their way into the city, but its defences held firm. For months there was bitter hand-to-hand fighting in the streets, during which much of the city was pounded into rubble.

Surrender On November 19 two Russian armies counterattacked, and the Germans were surrounded. Hard fighting went on until January 31, 1943, when the German commander surrendered. The 350,000 soldiers with which he started the attack had been reduced to 90,000, who became prisoners.

Royal recognition Britain's King George VI sent the city a special ceremonial sword, the Sword of Stalingrad, to commemorate its brave defence.

The Prince and ▶
Princess of Wales kiss on the balcony of Buckingham Palace on their wedding day in July 1981.

OPERATIC EPILOGUE

Which composers fought a duel? They were George Frederick Handel and Johann Mattheson, who fought outside the opera house in Hamburg, Germany in 1704.

Mattheson, a versatile musician, had written an opera *Cleopatra*, in which he sang the part of Antony. Handel directed the orchestra from the harpsichord, as was the usual practice. After Antony 'died' on stage, Mattheson normally took over from Handel for the rest of the performance.

One night Handel decided he was tired of this arrangement, and refused to hand over the baton. A fierce quarrel broke out, the performance was concluded, and the two musicians went outside and drew their swords. In the ensuing duel, Handel was saved by one of his waistcoat buttons which deflected and broke Mattheson's blade. Fortunately the quarrel between the fiery tempered friends was resolved without much more ado.

ROYAL RATINGS

Which TV programme had the biggest audience? This statistic is constantly changing as worldwide TV links are increased. One of the biggest audiences ever was for the royal wedding of Britain's Prince of Wales and Lady Diana Spencer in 1981. It was seen by 750 million viewers.

However, an estimated 1,000 million viewers watched – either live or recorded broadcasts – the 1972 and 1976 Olympic Games. Boycotts by some countries resulted in smaller audiences for the 1980 and 1984 Olympics.

LITTLE BOOT

What was the real name of the infamous Emperor Caligula? It was Gaius Julius Caesar Germanicus, and he reigned as the Emperor Gaius. He got his nickname, which means 'Bootikin' or 'Little Boot' when he was a very small boy. His father, Germanicus, was commanding Roman troops on the River Rhine, then the northern frontier of the Roman Empire. Accompanying him, young Gaius was dressed in a miniature version of a soldier's uniform, which included the *caliga*, a boot reaching to mid-calf.

FASHION NOTE

What were bloomers? They were a form of trousers for women, named after an American campaigner for women's rights, Mrs Amelia Jenks Bloomer. Although trousers have been commonly worn by women in the Muslim world for hundreds of years, in the 1800s people in the Western world thought they were shocking.

Mrs Bloomer adopted bloomers in 1851. They were like baggy Turkish trousers, worn under a skirt which reached to below the knees. For about eight years Amelia Bloomer wore these garments when giving lectures on temperance and women's rights, but later she abandoned the idea. It was not until about 40 years later that trousers for women finally became fashionable in the West.

DYNASTY

Who were the Medici? They were a family who played a leading part in ruling Florence, in Italy, from the 1400s until 1737. They were bankers (although their name suggests that they were originally doctors), and among the richest people of their day. Florence was then a city-state, small, independent and powerful.

Power and wealth The family fortunes were founded by Giovanni di Bicci (1360-1429). His son Cosimo the Elder (1389-1464), one of the richest men in the world, was imprisoned by rival Florentine families, but escaped and became ruler of the city. Giovanni and Cosimo began the family tradition of employing the leading artists of the day to beautify their own homes and the churches and public buildings of the city.

Cosimo was succeeded by his son, Piero the Gouty (1416-1469), a quiet, shy man. He was followed by the most famous Medici of all, Lorenzo the Magnificent (1449-1492), who spent his wealth making the city of Florence one of the most beautiful in the land.

Famous names Other notable members of the Medici family included three popes, Leo X, Clement VII and Leo XI; two queens of France, Catherine de Médicis (the French spelling of the name), wife of Henry II, and Marie de Médicis, wife of Henry IV; and Cosimo I (1519-1574), who became the first Grand Duke of Tuscany.

The monument by Michelangelo to ▶ Lorenzo Medici, in the Medici Chapel in Florence.

ROMANTIC STATE

What was the Golden Horde? It was the romantic-sounding name given by the Russians to a Mongol state that was set up on the steppes of southern Russia, after the break-up of the great Mongol empire of Kublai Khan. Its real name was the Khanate of Kipchak, *khan* being the Mongol equivalent of lord or prince. The khanate's wealth and power earned it its Russian name.

We don't know the exact area under the rule of the Golden Horde, but the khans exerted their authority over all the Russian princes, and levied taxes and recruited soldiers from the Russian princedoms.

Civil war For a hundred years from the mid-1200s the Golden Horde had a busy trade with the Byzantine Empire, Egypt, and countries of Europe. Civil warfare within the khanate weakened it in the later 1300s, and after that the Russian princes gradually grew more independent. Its power was broken when it was attacked by another Mongol khan, Tamerlane, in 1395, and though a Mongol khanate survived in the Crimea until the late 1700s, it was no longer the illustrious Golden Horde.

BIG VALUE

Which island was bought for $24? That was the value of the trade goods – beads, trinkets and cloth – with which Peter Minuit, governor of the Dutch West India Company, bought Manhattan Island from an Indian tribe in 1626. He founded a settlement there called New Amsterdam.

Today, Manhattan Island is the heart of New York City, and its value would be reckoned in billions of dollars.

Manhattan Island today, on which hundreds of skyscrapers have been built.
▼

TRAVEL AGENT

How did Greenland gets its name? This unlikely name for an island which has a permanent icecap averaging 1.6 km (1 mile) thick, was the brainwave of a Viking explorer, Eric the Red. Born in Norway about AD 950 he was brought up in the more appropriately named Iceland.

A rough, tough Viking, Eric was exiled for some misdeeds in 981. He decided to spend his years of banishment in foreign travel, so he sailed westwards in his longship with a band of faithful followers. On the western coast of what we now know as Greenland he found a landing place which was free from ice.

After three years Eric's sentence of exile ended, so he returned to Iceland to recruit more settlers. To induce them to come, he gave his newly-found land the glamorous name of Greenland, and persuaded several hundred people to join him.

PASSIONATE PRINCESS

Which queen married two kings? Eleanor of Aquitaine, daughter of Duke William X of Aquitaine. When her father died, she inherited his lands as Duchess of Aquitaine at the age of 15. In the same year she married Louis, the dauphin (crown prince) of France, who succeeded his father as Louis VII a month later.

Unfaithful? Eleanor bore her husband two daughters. Louis was a pious man and his apparent coldness towards her led to trouble. When she accompanied him to Palestine on the Second Crusade in 1147-1149, her conduct was such that Louis became certain she had been unfaithful to him. He persuaded the pope to annul the marriage (on the grounds that they were distantly related).

Future king Eleanor, a beautiful and spirited woman, had many offers for her hand. She accepted young Henry, Count of Anjou, whose main attraction was that he was a likely heir to the throne of England. Within two years Henry was king.

Eleanor brought her husband vast estates in France which, with those he already ruled, meant that he controlled more than half of France, though nominally as a vassal (inferior) of Louis VII.

FACT FILE: NEWSPAPERS

FACT The first English news-sheet – a one-off – was *The Trewe Encounter* of the Battle of Flodden Field, published in 1513.

FACT The first crossword puzzle was published in the *New York Sunday World* in 1913.

FACT *The Times* of London had the name the *Daily Universal Register* when it was founded in 1785. It changed its name in 1788.

FACT There are more than 1,700 daily newspapers in the United States – more than in any other country.

FACT The oldest continuously published newspaper in the world is the *Post och Inrikes Tidningar*, an official journal issued in Sweden since 1645. It has been a daily publication since 1820.

FACT Reuter's, one of the world's biggest international news agencies, supplying news to more than 100 countries, was founded in England by Paul Reuter, a German, in 1851.

CREATION CORRECTION

What was the Scopes trial? It was one of the most dramatic legal cases in the United States. John Thomas Scopes, who taught science at Dayton, Tennessee, was charged in 1925 with violating a law which prohibited the teaching in State schools of any theory that contradicted the Bible account of the Divine creation of mankind. Scopes had been teaching Charles Darwin's theory of evolution.

Two leading lawyers of the day appeared, Clarence S. Darrow for the defence, and William Jennings Bryan for the prosecution. After a hearing followed by readers all over the world, Scopes was convicted and fined $100, but this verdict was later reversed. The law under which Scopes was brought to trial was repealed in 1967.

▲
Eleanor of Aquitaine, queen of Louis VII of France and Henry II of England.

PAPER PORTRAITS

How did silhouettes get their name? These outline portraits, usually cut out of black paper, are named after a French Statesman, Etienne de Silhouette (1709-1767), who served as finance minister to King Louis XV. Silhouette was faced with the need to make savings, partly to pay for the Seven Years' War against Britain and Prussia. He tried to cut pensions and privileges, and so incurred the wrath and contempt of the French aristocracy.

The *aristos* used the phrase *á la Silhouette* to mean 'on the cheap', and the term came to be applied to the outline portraits, which were inexpensive compared with paintings. The unfortunate Silhouette had nothing to do with the invention of the portraits that bear his name, which were being made probably as early as the 1600s.

▲
A picture of Theodore Roosevelt which was in *The Tatler* in 1902.

STATIONARY EXPLORER

Who was Henry the Navigator? He was a Portuguese prince, the third son of King John I and a grandson of the English prince, John of Gaunt. Henry earned his title because he was the driving force behind Portuguese exploration of the African coast and the sea route to India. His aim was to make Portugal stronger in its fight against the Arabs, who dominated North Africa and held part of Spain.

Henry himself made no voyages of exploration, but he set up a school of navigation at Sagres in south-western Portugal to train seamen for long ocean voyages, had ships built for such voyages, and sent out a series of expeditions. By the time he died in 1460 his sailors had reached as far as what is now Sierra Leone. To achieve this he had to overcome the superstitions of his crews, who believed that if they travelled far south they would either fry in the torrid conditions, or fall off the edge of the world.

Sergei Diaghilev (centre) with the famous dancers, Tamara Karsavina and Vaslav Nijinsky. ▶

ADVENTUROUS 'TEDDY'

Which US President explored Brazil? Theodore ('Teddy') Roosevelt was, in fact, an ex-president by the time he did his exploring. (He held office from 1901 to 1909.) In 1913 he set out on his expedition, which was to explore rivers in South America. He started from Asunción, the capital of Paraguay, up the Paraguay River. Once across the border into Brazil, the party crossed the Matto Grosso, a

BALLET MAN

Who was Sergei Diaghilev? Although he was neither a dancer nor a composer nor even a choreographer, Sergei Diaghilev was one of the most important figures in ballet in the early part of the 20th century. He was perhaps the greatest *impressario* (organizer) that ballet has ever seen.

Born in Russia in 1872 he began presenting opera and ballet in Paris in 1908. He founded his own company, the *Ballets Russes*, in 1911, which he directed until his death in 1929. His skill lay in persuading the finest dancers, composers and choreographers to work for him, and using such talented artists as Pablo Picasso, Henri Matisse and Georges Braque to design his sets.

region of grassland with scattered trees, and came across a hitherto unknown river. They named it the River of Doubt.

The party travelled slowly downstream in dugout canoes, and after some adventures and much hard work came into the Amazon, having added some 1,500 km (937 miles) of river to the Brazilian map. It is now known as the Roosevelt River or Teodoro River.

ROLLING ALONG

When was the wheel invented? Although the wheel was probably the world's most important invention, with the exception of how to make fire, nobody really knows when it came about.

We have evidence that primitive people used rollers to move huge stones. Stone rollers have been found under some of the megaliths (giant stones) in temples built in Malta more than 4,000 years ago. Wooden rollers were probably used much earlier, but they have long since rotted away.

The oldest wheels found were made about 5,000 years ago. They were discovered in graves in Mesopotamia (now part of southern Iraq). Wheeled carts were in use in many parts of Asia by a thousand years later.

The American Indians seem to have made little use of the wheel (although wheeled toys have been found in some Aztec graves in Mexico). This may be because they had no large domesticated animals such as horses or oxen capable of pulling carts before colonial settlers came along.

HEAR THIS

Which was the first talkie? It was *The Jazz Singer*, made by Warner Brothers in Hollywood in 1927. This film starred Al Jolson, who sang accompanied by an orchestra. The only dialogue spoken was an aside to the cameras by Jolson in the middle of the film. He said, 'You ain't heard nothin' yet!'

He was quite right. *The Jazz Singer* marked the end of silent films. Within two years, thousands of cinemas were equipped to show films with sound tracks, and dozens of 'talkies' had been issued.

ARTISTS' LICENCE

Who invented Cubism? The Spanish artist Pablo Picasso (1881-1973) and the Frenchman Georges Braque (1882-1963). They were greatly influenced by Black African art, with its vigour and simplicity.

Aims and developments The object of Cubism was to express the idea of something rather than create a likeness of it, and to give an idea of movement in time and space. The result was often to present several superimposed views of the same subject. The Cubists were intent on finding the basic shape behind the apparent shape of an object.

The earliest Cubist painting is believed to be Picasso's *Les Desmoiselles d'Avignon*, which he painted in 1907. A later form, called Analytical Cubism, broke down shapes into fragments and planes, in which the original subject, as defined in the title of the picture, is often hard to detect.

Portrait of Uhde by Picasso. ▶

SKIRTS ASWING

What was the New Look? It was the name given to a 'new look' in women's clothes that appeared in the late 1940s. After the hardships of the war years, the emphasis was on luxury. Skirts were full, sweeping almost to ankle length, 280 mm (11 in) above the ground. Waists were tightly nipped in, and jackets were figure-hugging with long, narrow sleeves.

The New Look was created by the Frenchman, Christian Dior, who launched the new fashion in Paris in 1947, New York in 1948, and later in London.

▲ A model shows off a 'New Look' dress and jacket.

TALL STORY

What happened to the Colossus of Rhodes? This huge bronze statue of Helios, the Sun-god, and one of the Seven Wonders of the World, was sold for scrap. It stood at the entrance to the harbour on the Greek island of Rhodes about 300 BC. It was 32 m (105 ft) tall, which compares with the 46 m (151 ft) height of the Statue of Liberty in New York Harbour (measured from the top of the torch to the feet).

Earthquake Like the Statue of Liberty, the Colossus of Rhodes had an iron framework to support it, and the lower part was ballasted with stones to hold it down. But the iron of Rhodes was not as strong as modern steel, and after only half a century an earthquake toppled the Colossus. The ruins lay untouched for nearly 900 years until the Muslim Arabs captured Rhodes in AD 653. They sold the scrap metal to a merchant, who carted it away in 980 camel-loads.

◄ Artist, Mario Larringa's own idea of the Colossus of Rhodes.

BUILDER'S NIGHTMARE

Who was Antonio Gaudi? He was Spain's most original and eccentric architect and he lived from 1852 to 1926. His *art nouveau* designs are a wild mixure of Gothic and Moorish ideas, producing a riot of curves and carved stonework that looks as though it is made of melted wax.

In 1905-1910 he built a block of flats in Barcelona, the Casa Milá. It has an undulating exterior, and inside is a maze of multi-sided rooms, none with straight walls or right-angles. Unfortunately his most remarkable design, the Church of the Holy Family in Barcelona, is unfinished. Its four towers resemble elongated termites' nests.

The church of the Holy Family in ▶ Barcelona, designed by Antonio Gaudi.

THEY PROTESTED

Who were the Huguenots? French Protestants, a minority in a predominantly Roman Catholic country. Historians don't agree on the origin of the name, but it may have had some connection with a Protestant leader named Hughes or Hugo.

For a time the Huguenots had a reasonable amount of religious freedom, but in 1685 Louis XIV removed their rights to worship as they pleased, and about 400,000 fled to other countries. Many skilled textile workers went to England, where they soon helped to build up the British textile industry. Other Huguenots went to live in the Netherlands, Germany and North America. The French Revolution finally brought religious toleration in 1789.

QUIZ: MUSICAL MATTERS

1. Who was Robin Hood's minstrel?
2. How many symphonies did Johannes Brahms write?
3. What song did Bill Haley and the Comets make famous?
4. What song did Claude Joseph Rouget de Lisle write in 1792?
5. In which film and stage musical did the song 'Gee, Officer Krupke' occur?
6. What is the difference between the reeds of an oboe and a clarinet?
7. Who wrote the music of *The Beggar's Opera*?
8. Which popular composer wrote *Rhapsody in Blue*?
9. Their first names are Paul and Art; they split up in 1970 and came together again in 1981. Who are they?

ANSWERS
1. Alan A'Dale. 2. Four. 3. 'Rock Around the Clock'. 4. *The Marseillaise*, the national anthem of France. 5. *West Side Story*. 6. Oboe has double reeds, clarinet a single reed. 7. No one person: in 1728 the organist Dr John Pepusch arranged English and Scottish folk tunes, popular songs of the day, and a few tunes by Purcell and Handel. 8. George Gershwin. 9. Simon and Garfunkel.

LADY IN THE HOUSE

Who was the first woman to take her seat as a Member of Parliament in Britain's House of Commons? Nancy, Viscountess Astor, who was elected in November 1919 as the Conservative MP for Plymouth, which she served as until 1945.

Slow progress It was not until 1918 (following more than 50 years of struggle) that British women won the right to vote, let alone to sit in Parliament. In 1919 the vote was granted to propertied women over the age of 30, and for the first time 17 women stood for Parliament. Lady Constance Markievicz, a Sinn Fein (Irish Republican) candidate, was actually the first woman to be elected, but did not take her seat.

▲
Lady Astor campaigns in Plymouth in 1924.

RING OF FAME

Who organized the first circus of modern times? Individual circus acts such as trick riding, juggling, and acrobatics go back thousands of years. Even so, most people agree that the modern circus began with the Englishman, Philip Astley.

Born in 1742, Astley was an accomplished horseman and showman, who invented the modern circus ring when he discovered that it is easier to balance on the back of a horse when it is travelling in a circle. He opened his first circus in 1768, featuring his own trick riding. Soon he added other, now traditional, acts such as clowns, acrobats and rope walkers. The modern circus was born.

STREET SCENE

Where did break dancing begin? On the streets of the Bronx, New York City, USA, spreading across the world like wildfire in 1984 and 1985. It gets its name from being a break in fighting between rival gangs of young people. Each gang would send its best dancers to compete — which is perhaps why a break-dance competition is known as a 'battle'.

Mixed movements It combines elements of disco dancing, gymnastics, the martial arts, and mime. Some of its movements, such as spinning round on one shoulder or the head, can cause injury unless they are practised carefully.

◄ A crowd watches a demonstration of break dancing.

▲
A painting of the slave deck on the ship, *Albany*. It shows the terrible conditions that the slaves had to put up with.

HUMAN CARGOES

What was the Middle Voyage? It was the second leg of a three-part journey for ships engaged in the slave trade. They set out from European ports, sailed to the West Coast of Africa, where they bought slaves for trade goods such as cloth, trinkets and guns, then took the slaves across the Atlantic Ocean to America on the Middle Voyage. The slaves were sold there, often by auction, and the ships returned to Europe laden with American goods.

Economic necessity American slaves were imported into the Americas because the native Amerindians proved unsuitable for the hard labour needed on the new plantations. The Spaniards began the trade in 1517, soon followed by other countries, notably England, France, the Netherlands and Portugal. England had the biggest share, and the ports of Bristol and Liverpool owed much of their growth and prosperity to the slave trade.

For many years people ignored the evils of the slave trade because they believed it to be an economic necessity – the plantations couldn't be run without slaves, and British export trade depended largely on it.

Abolition In fact, Britain eventually led the way in the abolition of the slave trade. Trading was banned in 1811, but the liberation of all slaves in British possessions came only slowly after an Act was passed in 1833. Other European and some American countries followed suit. The United States maintained slavery in some Southern States until the Civil War of 1861-1865, which was fought on the slavery issue.

The campaign against slavery was led in Britain by a group of Christian politicians – known as the 'Clapham Sect' – headed by a wealthy Yorkshireman, William Wilberforce. Their name came from the place, now part of London, where several of them lived.

DEAF BUT UNDAUNTED

Which famous composer couldn't hear his own music?
Deafness, the cruellest handicap for a musician, has attacked many composers, usually in old age. The outstanding sufferer was Ludwig van Beethoven (1770-1827), who began to lose his hearing when he was about 30. He battled against it, and was able to play the piano in public for another 12 years. In 1814 he gave his last public performance.

Six years later he was so deaf that even shouting could not get through to him, so he carried 'conversation books' in which his friends would write what they wanted to say to him.

Beethoven was able to 'hear' music in his mind, and so he was able to continue composing. He wrote many of his finest works while he was deaf.

CLIFF FACES

Who carved Mount Rushmore?
Several people did, but to the
design of one man, sculptor
Gutzon Borglum. Mount
Rushmore is a granite cliff in
South Dakota, USA. The idea of
carving a national memorial on it
was conceived by Jonah L.
Robinson, of the State Historical
Society. The cliff carries the
heads of four US presidents –
George Washington, Thomas
Jefferson, Abraham Lincoln, and
Theodore Roosevelt –
representing the country's
founding, expansion,
preservation and unification.

Work began in 1927. Men with
drills and explosives carved the
faces, working from scale
models made by Borglum, and
supervised by him. Borglum died
in 1941, at the age of 70, but the
work was completed under the
watchful eye of his son, Lincoln.

Heads of the four US presidents ▶
carved out of Mount Rushmore.
From left to right: Washington,
Jefferson, Roosevelt, Lincoln.

SUBTERRANEAN MYSTERY

What is Malta's Hypogeum? This is one of the world's most mysterious
Stone Age monuments. It appears to be a temple, but it has been cut
three storeys down into the soft solid rock of this Mediterranean island.
There is a maze of rooms going down more than 10 m (33 ft) below the
surface. Its name, Hypogeum, is Greek for 'below the earth'.

The Hypogeum, constructed about 4,500 years ago, is similar to
temples built above-ground elsewhere in Malta at about the same time.
It contains an oracle chamber, in which there is a cavity for a man to
speak into. The sound is carried clearly all around the chamber – but
only male voices carry in this way!

Speculation The real mystery is the 7,000 sets of human bones found in
one of the rooms when archaeologists excavated the site in 1902.
Nobody is sure whether the Hypogeum was a temple which was later
used as a form of mausoleum, or whether it was a burial place with a
part set aside for worship.

FACT FILE: GLASS

FACT The oldest glass known was made in Egypt about 4400 years
ago, in the form of beads; the first glass vessels, also from Egypt, were
made in the 1400s BC.
FACT Aleyards, trumpet-shaped drinking glasses about 1 m (3 ft 3 in)
long, have been made since the 1600s.
FACT Stained glass was used in medieval churches to help tell the
Bible stories to a largely illiterate congregation, and to create a
religious 'atmosphere'.
FACT The blowpipe for blowing glass, still used for hand-made
vessels, was invented in the eastern Mediterranean area about 30 BC.
FACT Glass rolling-pins were first made in the early 1800s in England
as a container for selling salt, which then carried a tax of 3,000 per cent
on its value.
FACT Friggers are small, purely decorative articles made in glass,
often to show off a glassmaker's skill.
FACT The first cut-glass was made at Alexandria in Egypt in the first
century BC.

ELECTION SPECIAL

***Does television affect election
results?*** Nobody knows for
sure, but it's widely thought so.
The first time that television was
thought to have a major impact
was in the 1960 US Presidential
election.

The two candidates, John F.
Kennedy (Democrat) and
Richard M. Nixon (Republican),
took part in a series of debates on
television. Nixon, who had been
Vice-President since 1953, was
better known, but the debates
helped to bring Kennedy before
the public eye, and he won by a
very narrow margin.

SISTER'S SHIP

▲
Mary Rose with Charles Brandon.

Who was Mary Rose? The name has been familiar since Henry VIII's flagship *Mary Rose* was raised from the seabed off Portsmouth, England, in 1982, 437 years after she sank. But the real Mary Rose was Henry's favourite sister, Princess Mary, after whom he named the ship when she was launched in 1509. The 'Rose' was almost certainly an allusion to England's national flower.

Mary was married in 1514 to Louis XII of France. He was 52 and ailing; she was a beautiful 18-year-old girl. Fortunately for Mary, her elderly husband died within two months, and she then married the man she had secretly set her heart on, Charles Brandon, first Duke of Suffolk. Henry was furious, because he had other plans for Mary, but she and Suffolk were forgiven on payment of a hefty fine. Their granddaughter was Lady Jane Grey, for nine days Queen of England following the death of Henry's daughter, Mary I.

The *Mary Rose* was lost in a battle off Portsmouth against a French fleet – not through enemy action, but because she suddenly keeled over, filled with water and sank.

GOLD RUSH

What was a 'Forty-niner'? A person who took part in the great California Gold Rush.

Gold was discovered at Sutter's Mill, in California, USA on January 24, 1848. The news spread, and a great rush of prospectors took place the following year, 1849. Some idea of the effects of the rush can be gauged by the fact that in 1848 San Francisco had a population of 820. Within a year it had grown to a city of 25,000 people, many of them living in tents.

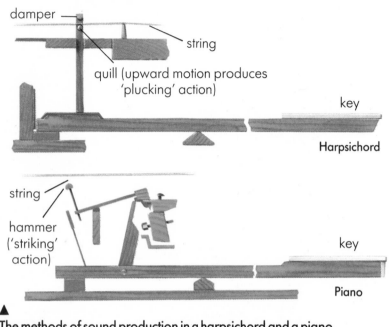

damper

string

quill (upward motion produces 'plucking' action)

key

Harpsichord

string

hammer ('striking' action)

key

Piano

▲ The methods of sound production in a harpsichord and a piano.

KEY MAN

Who invented the piano? The inventor was Bartolomeo Cristofori (1655-1731), an Italian maker of harpsichords. He built his first pianos some time before 1711. Two of his instruments, one dated 1720 and the other 1726, still survive in museums.

In the harpsichord the strings are plucked, and the notes are always of the same loudness. The piano's strings are struck by hammers, and the amount of sound can be varied by the player. Cristofori's instruments were therefore described as *gravicembali col piano e forté*, which means 'harpsichords with soft and loud'.

REVOLUTIONARY HEROINE

Who was Madame Roland? She was Jeanne, wife of one of the leaders of the French Revolution, Jean Roland de la Platière. They were members of a group of revolutionaries who were known as Girondins. Madame Roland played hostess to many meetings of the Girondin leaders, and her charm and wit made her a leader in her own right.

But in 1793 the Girondins' rivals, the Jacobins, gained power and decided to liquidate their opponents. Madame Roland had a brief trial and was condemned to die. As she went to the guillotine, she was heard to say: 'O Liberty, what crimes are committed in thy name!'

SINISTER SYMBOL

What was the origin of the swastika? This symbol, which was feared and hated as the emblem of the Nazi Party from 1920 to 1945, is a very ancient one. Originally it was a sign of good luck. The name swastika comes from the Sanskrit, and means 'well-being'. It has been found on European pottery of the New Stone Age, in the Minoan ruins of Crete, and in the ruins of Troy.

It was common in India, and was taken by Buddhists from there to China and Japan. The swastika is also found among the ancient cultures of North and South America. The usual form was with the arms pointing anticlockwise; the Nazis had the arms pointing the other way, and the symbol standing on one corner.

Examples of the use of swastikas: ▶ a mosaic floor in Herculaneum, buried when Vesuvius erupted in AD 79; a Cretan jug of 1000 BC.

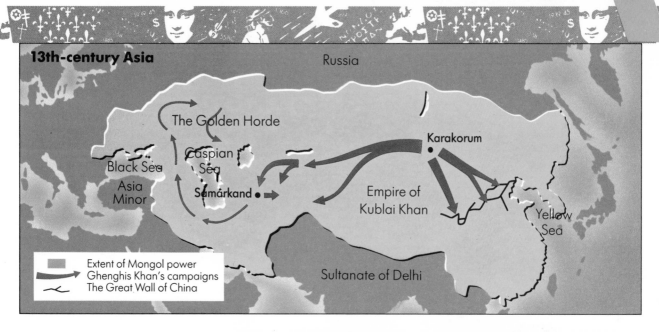

13th-century Asia

Russia

The Golden Horde

Karakorum

Caspian Sea

Black Sea

Asia Minor

Samarkand

Empire of Kublai Khan

Yellow Sea

Extent of Mongol power
Ghenghis Khan's campaigns
The Great Wall of China

Sultanate of Delhi

▲
Genghis Khan's empire.

GRACIOUS LIVING

What is a nef? It's a model boat, usually made of silver or gold and used as a table ornament. The earliest nefs were made in the Middle Ages to hold the knife, spoon and napkin of a great lord.

Later nefs were mounted on wheels, and some were used to carry sweetmeats. Some models were elaborate and detailed, with small figures of sailors and all the rigging in fine gold or silver wire.

MONGOL MENACE

Who was Genghis Khan? He was a Mongol chieftain, and his original name was Temujin. He was born in 1162 in a tent in the Gobi Desert, in central Asia. His tribe, like all the Mongols in those days, was nomadic, wandering over the land with their herds, and raiding and fighting. He became the leader of his tribe at the age of only 13, when his father died.

Expanding empire By winning many battles over the years, he gathered more and more of the Mongol tribes under his leadership. About 1202 his followers gave him the title of Genghis Khan, which means 'Ruler of the Oceans'. Four years later he was elected as ruler of all the Mongols, with the title of Great Khan.

Ghengis Khan then decided to conquer the whole world! He began by breaking through the Great Wall of China and conquering the whole of northern China. Next, he turned west, overran Afghanistan, Persia (Iran) and southern Russia. He died in 1227, leaving a large empire which was divided among his four sons.

TALE OF HEADS

Which sculptor defied a city? Andrea del Verrocchio, and the city he defied was Venice, at that time an independent state as well as a city. In 1479 the city leaders commissioned Verrocchio to make an equestrian statue of Bartolomeo Colleoni, a redoubtable soldier who had led the Venetian armies to many victories.

Verrocchio began work, and had completed a full-sized model of the sculpture of the horse, when the city fathers told him that someone else would make the rider. Incensed, Verrocchio smashed the head off the horse and returned to his own city, Florence. The Venetians wrote to tell him never to return on pain of losing his own head.

To this Verrocchio replied that though they could remove heads they couldn't replace them, but in the case of his model horse he could. This so pleased the Venetians that they asked him to return to finish the whole statue. Verrocchio completed the model but died before it could be cast. Another artist completed the casting.

▲
Verocchio's statue of Colleoni.

ARIA THERESIA   VON ÖSTERREICH
Gemahlin Franz I   Kaisers v. Deutschland

TIME FOR THOUGHT

Why did Leonardo's 'Last Supper' crumble? Leonardo da Vinci's painting of the 'Last Supper' is on one wall of the dining hall at the monastery of Santa Maria delle Grazie, in Milan, Italy. The normal way of making such a wall painting was quickly and bit by bit, on wet plaster, with which the paint bonded.

But Leonardo wanted time to think about this solemn subject of the Christian religion. So he had the wall plastered completely, and then covered with a lead-white priming paint. On this surface he worked as inspiration came to him. The painting was finished some time after 1497, but within a few years some of the paint was already flaking off.

Dry years Critics suggest that Leonardo was experimenting with new, untried techniques, but it seems he was using well-known methods. Latest research suggests that a succession of very dry years when he was painting may have caused the plaster to dry too quickly, cracking the priming coat and so loosening the paint on it.

Restoration During the past 200 years the picture has been badly restored and overpainted many times. During the early 1970s work began to remove the handiwork of other artists and bring to light what still remains of Leonardo's own work – a task that is expected to take many years.

◀ A portrait of Maria Theresa, Empress of Austria.

YEAR OF THE THALER

What's special about the Maria Theresa dollar? This Austrian coin was first minted during the reign of the Empress Maria Theresa (1740-1780). It became popular as a form of universal currency in Arab countries, and along the east coast of Africa facing the Red Sea. To meet the demand for it, mints continued to produce these coins long after the Empress's death, always bearing the same year – 1780.

British and Austrian mints struck the coins, which were still being made (in silver) in the middle of the 20th century.

Originally made from silver mined at Joachims*thal*, once part of Austria and now the town of Jachymov in Czechoslovakia, they became known as Joachims*thaler*s. The word *dollar* is a corruption of the short form *thaler*.

QUIZ: SPORTS

1. Who ran the first mile in less than four minutes, and in which year?
2. What are the five events in the women's pentathlon?
3. An eight is a boat used in rowing races. How many people are in it?
4. In boxing, which is lighter, featherweight or bantamweight?
5. What sport was derived from an Iroquois Indian game called baggataway?
6. If you had a birdie, a bogey and an eagle, what game would you be playing?
7. What is a chukker, and in which game would you encounter it?
8. A swimmer broke more than 50 records in the 1920s, and then became famous as a film star. His name?
9. In what sport is the Tour de France an event?

ANSWERS
1 Roger Bannister in 1954. 2 Long jump, high jump, shot-put, 80-m hurdle race, 200-m race. 3 Nine, including the cox. 4 Bantamweight. 5 Lacrosse. 6 Golf. 7 A period of play in polo. 8 Johnny Weissmuller. 9 Cycling.

◄ Start of the Burke and Wills expedition. Wills is standing on the left holding a surveying instrument. Burke is riding the horse in front.

ONE WAY TRIP

What happened to Burke and Wills? Robert O'Hara Burke and William John Wills led the first expedition to cross Australia from south to north. They died on the return journey.

The expedition was organized in 1860 by the Royal Society of Australia. No expense was spared: 26 camels were imported from India, there were 28 horses, and a party of 18 men.

They set out from Melbourne. Burke, Wills and seven others rode north to Cooper's Creek in Western Queensland, leaving the other nine men to follow with supplies. After waiting six weeks for the support party, Burke, Wills and two others decided to continue, plodding through the heat with six camels and a horse for 119 days. At last they sighted tidal waters on the Gulf of Carpentaria, and decided to turn back, their mission as good as accomplished.

The way back The return trip, now through heavy rain, was a nightmare. One of the men died. Burke, Wills, and the fourth man, John King, arrived at Cooper's Creek to find no one there, and no supplies. They decided to march across country to Adelaide. On the journey Burke and Wills died. King, however, survived with the aid of a party of Aborigines, who looked after him until a rescue party from Melbourne finally arrived.

JUNGLE TEMPLE

Who built Angkor Wat? This vast temple, which covers an area of about 2.5 square km (0.96 square miles), was the work of the Khmer, who had a mighty empire in what is now Kampuchea (Cambodia) from the 800s to the 1400s AD.

Inscriptions show that the man mainly responsible for Angkor Wat was King Suryavaran II, who became king of the Khmer in 1113. It was an elaborate building, its walls thickly covered with carvings portraying scenes from the Hindu religious texts. The temple itself was dedicated to the Hindu god, Vishnu.

Jungle city Together with the capital city of Angkor Thom, the temple was abandoned in the 1400s, and was gradually swallowed up by the jungle. It was rediscovered by a French naturalist, Henri Mouhot, in 1860.

Over the next century Cambodian and French archaeologists cleared the jungle growth and restored the ruins to show a little of their former glory. But the civil war that has been raging for some years in Kampuchea has undone all their work, and the latest reports are that looting and the return of the jungle have undone the restoration work.

◄ A view of Angkor Wat from across the moat.

WORLD'S END

What was Ultima Thule? It was a mysterious northern land discovered by Pytheas of Massilia, who lived at the time of Alexander the Great and was the first Greek sailor to venture beyond the confines of the Mediterranean Sea.

Bold explorer On his memorable voyage he sailed up the Atlantic coasts of Portugal, Spain and France to the English Channel. He reached 'Brettania', where he visited Kent and the Cornish tin mines. Then he sailed six days to the north of Britain where he found the Island of Thule, surrounded by a mass of freezing fog. He was told that beyond Thule lay the sleeping place of the Sun.

Pytheas's stories were widely disbelieved in his own day, but he was obviously reporting factually. Thule gained its name of Ultima, because it seemed to be the ends of the Earth. Historians cannot agree whether Pytheas had found Scandinavia or Iceland.

MASSIVE REMOVAL

Why was the Abu Simbel temple moved? The temple, in southern Egypt on the banks of the River Nile, was cut deep into the solid rock of a cliff. It was constructed at the order of Rameses II, who was pharaoh (king) from 1304 to 1237 BC.

The entrance to the temple consists of a porch flanked on each side by two colossal statues of Rameses, carved from the cliff face. The interior includes two halls and three chapels. One of the chapels contains some more huge statues, also cut from the rock.

Rescue operation When the Aswan High Dam was planned in the 1950s to trap the waters of the Nile in a huge reservoir (now called Lake Nasser), the Abu Simbel temple seemed doomed to vanish beneath the waters. So a huge rescue operation funded by 50 countries, and costing more than $17,000,000, was mounted. Craftsmen cut the temple out of the cliff face and removed it to higher ground nearby. This gigantic jigsaw puzzle operation was completed in 1968.

NO SURRENDER

Who were the Free French? They were a group of French soldiers who continued the fight in 1940 when France surrendered to Germany during World War II. They were led by General Charles de Gaulle, who had been appointed under-secretary of state for war in the French government at the height of the German attack.

Escape Ten days after his appointment the French government fell. De Gaulle escaped to England and broadcast to the French people, putting himself at the head of a Free French movement. The Free French organized their own forces, which were armed by the British and Americans, and fought with British and American armies in North Africa. Many of the French colonies also came under Free French control.

Success The success of the Free French was due largely to the inflexible will of de Gaulle, whose patriotism encouraged many Frenchmen to join him and carry on the fight. A Free French division played a large part in the invasion of France in 1944, and marched into Paris to liberate it on August 24.

▲
The huge statues of Abu Simbel on their higher site.

MAN OF LETTERS

Was Caxton always a printer?
No, indeed, although that is his main claim to fame. William Caxton, who was born about 1422, was a dealer in silk and other fine fabrics. In 1441 he set up a business at Bruges, in Belgium (then the centre of the wool trade), where he remained for 30 years and eventually became governor of the English merchants.

New craft Caxton was also well educated and knew several languages. In 1469 he began to translate into English a French romance, *The Recuyell of the Historyes of Troye*. However, he found copying it out so much of a chore that he went to learn the new craft of printing in Cologne, Germany. There he set up his own printing press and produced five books before returning to England in 1476 to establish the first English press in the precincts of Westminster Abbey.

Altogether Caxton printed about 90 books, 74 of them in English, a score of which were his own translations. The two most important were Geoffrey Chaucer's *Canterbury Tales* and Sir Thomas Malory's *Le Morte d'Arthur*.

▲ Part of a page from *The Royal Book* printed by William Caxton in 1484.

FACT OR FICTION?

Who found the ruins of Troy? They were discovered in 1873 by Heinrich Schliemann, a German merchant who had become a millionaire by the age of 36. Since childhood he had been fascinated by the story of Troy and its war, as told by the Greek poet, Homer, in the *Iliad*. ('Ilium' was another name for Troy.)

In the mid 1800s many scholars thought the *Iliad* was fiction; Schliemann believed it was basically true. By studying the text he came to the conclusion that the site of Troy was a mound in north-western Turkey, now known as Hissarlik. Months of digging on this site revealed the ruins not of one city, but of many, each built on the ruins of the previous one. Right at the end of his excavations, Schliemann found hidden treasures of gold, silver and jewellery.

Too far back However, later scholars and archaeologists discovered that Schliemann has been too enthusiastic. He had gone through too many layers, too far back into the past. The Troy he uncovered was destroyed in about 2200 BC, long before the time of the *Iliad*, which is believed to refer to events that happened about 1200 BC.

Altogether nine cities have been found on the site. Homer's Troy was layer VII, a small fortified city that showed every sign of destruction by fire and violence, just as the *Iliad* recounts.

◄ Heinrich Schliemann's wife wearing ornaments of Helen of Troy.

MEDIUM DEVELOPMENT

Who invented oil painting?
The use of oil as a medium for colours in paints was known at least a thousand years ago, but its use in the paints used for pictures came much later. Some pictures were painted in oil-paints from the 1200s onwards, but their use was not common until the time of the Flemish brothers, Hubert and Jan van Eyck, who developed their skills in the early 1400s.

For some time it was thought that Jan van Eyck actually invented oil painting, because from his time onwards Flemish painters used oils. Certainly he led the way in the general use of these adaptable paints. Earlier artists used tempera – in which powdered colours were mixed with egg – a medium which is still in use today.

Virgin and Child with the Chancellor Rolin by Jan van Eyck (1390-1441).
▼

PETTICOAT PIRATES

Who were Anne Bonney and Mary Read?
Believe it or not, they were pirates, and very successful and bloodthirsty ones, too. Sailing with 'Calico Jack' (Captain John Rackham), they flourished in the West Indies seas in the early 1700s. They were both caught and convicted of piracy – which then carried the death penalty – in Jamaica in 1720.

PUSS IN VAULTS

Which nation revered cats?
Some 3,000 years ago the people of ancient Egypt worshipped cats. One of their goddesses, Bast, had a cat's head, as can be seen on statues of her.

Archaeologists have found underground cat cemeteries, where the mummified bodies of cats have been reverently laid to rest, each with a saucer of milk and mummified rats or mice to sustain them in the afterlife.

▲
A mummified cat from Egypt.

FACT FILE: WORLD WAR I

FACT The incident that sparked off World War I was the assassination of Archduke Franz Ferdinand of Austria at Sarajevo (now in Yugoslavia) on June 28, 1914.

FACT The worst battle of the war was Third Ypres, also called Passchendaele, July-November 1917; it cost up to 400,000 British lives and was fought in a sea of mud and torrential rain.

FACT King Albert I of the Belgians commanded his army in the field all through the war.

FACT The biggest naval battle of the war was Jutland, May 31-June 1, 1916, between British and German fleets.

FACT A German U-boat (submarine) sank the British passenger liner *Lusitania* in 1915 with the loss of 1,198 lives.

FACT Further sinkings of ships, including US vessels, brought the United States into the war in April 1917.

FACT The Italians fought five Battles of the Isonzo along the river of that name between May 1915 and May 1917.

SUMERIAN JUSTICE

Who made the first known laws? The ancient Sumerians, who flourished in what is now southern Iraq, between 4,000 and 6,000 years ago.

The most famous *complete* code of laws known to us was based on those Sumerian laws; it was compiled and written down by King Hammurabi of Babylon who reigned from 1728 to 1686 BC. These laws were inscribed on a *stele* (an upright stone tablet) found at Susa in Iran in 1897. The stele was made of black diorite, a hard rock which has clearly preserved almost all the inscription. One section was polished away in antiquity, but the laws it contained have mostly been recovered from clay tablets found in Babylonian archives.

Penalties The 282 laws conclude with a comprehensive curse on anyone who tried to change the law. This curse is hardly more fearful than some of the punishments that Hammurabi laid down for various offences. For example, Law 21 states that a housebreaker shall be put to death and buried at the point where he broke in. Law 195 says that a son striking his father shall have his hands cut off.

Wise laws In general, however, this system of laws is designed to protect property, safeguard the rights of married people, settle the proper fees to be charged for professional services and to regulate trade.

The stele of Hammurabi. At the top Hammurabi is receiving the code of laws from the seated god, Shamash.
▼

WITCH HUNT

What was the Spanish Inquisition? The Inquisition was set up by the Roman Catholic Church to preserve the purity of the faith as taught by the Church – in other words, to combat heresy (ideas that conflicted with Church teachings). It operated in several countries in Europe during the Middle Ages.

The rulers who united Spain, King Ferdinand of Aragon and his wife Isabella of Castile, felt that their religion and power were threatened by the presence in Spain of *marranos* – Jews who had nominally adopted Christianity. In 1478 the king obtained permission from the Pope to set up an Inquisition in Spain.

Torture and death The Spanish inquisitors were more ruthless in their work than almost any others. They dealt with *marranos*, with Moorish Muslims, and later with Protestants, with great severity. People were imprisoned and tortured, and those found guilty of heresy were burned at the stake. The Spanish Inquisition was finally suppressed in the 1800s.

▲
A painting by Berruguette, court painter to the Catholic kings of the Spanish Inquisition, of St Dominic watching books burn.

▲
Benjamin Franklin (1706-90) working in his laboratory.

WORDS OF WISDOM

Which great statesman was also an inventor? Benjamin Franklin, and he was the only man to sign all four of the key documents that helped to make the United States: The Declaration of Independence in 1776, the Constitution of the United States in 1787, a treaty of alliance with France in 1778, and the Treaty of Paris of 1783 that ended the American War of Independence.

Besides his many activities in the service of his country, Franklin found time to be an inventor. His inventions included the lightning conductor and bifocal lenses.

PERFORATED PRIDE

Which stamps started a war? It's generally thought that stamps issued by Bolivia and Paraguay in the 1930s triggered off a war between the two countries. For some years each had been claiming a region called the Gran Chaco, and there had been odd skirmishes.

In 1930 Bolivia issued three stamps with maps showing the area prominently labelled 'Chaco Boliviano'. In 1932 Paraguay retorted with stamps of one value showing the same territory labelled 'Chaco Paraguayo', with the further inscription *Ha sido, es y sera* ('Has been, is and will be').

Bolivia began hostilities almost at once, and the fighting went on with varying ferocity until a truce was signed in 1935. By the Chaco Peace of 1938 (celebrated by Paraguay with yet more stamps!) Paraguay had gained 90 per cent of the disputed territory, but over 100,000 soldiers had been killed in the war.

A Fabergé egg given to Empress Alexandra by Nicholas II in 1897. Inside was this working model of the coronation coach. ▶

INLAID WORK

What are Fabergé's eggs? The court of the tsars, the Russian emperors, was a rich and glittering place. Wealth abounded, while thousands of Russians went hungry, which is why the Russian Revolution of 1917 overthrew the tsars.

One of the people who supplied the court with costly treasures was the talented goldsmith, Peter Carl Fabergé. He employed more than 500 craftsmen in his workshops in Moscow and St Petersburg (now Leningrad).

Every year he designed and produced an Easter egg for the tsar to give to his wife. These eggs, which are made of gold, silver and precious stones, open to reveal delicate models or miniature paintings.

FASHIONABLE CIRCLES

What was a farthingale? A hooped framework to support a very wide skirt – and the name had nothing to do with the old coin, the farthing, but comes from the Spanish *verdugádo*. The fashion was introduced into England from Spain during the reign of Elizabeth I.

The frame, made of willow rods, whalebone or wire, was worn at waist level and held the skirt well away from the body. Some women used a sort of long, thick bolster instead. The fashion lasted until the middle of the 1600s. It was revived in the early 1700s in a hooped bell-shaped form.

SONG TIME

Who wrote the first opera? Plays with music have been performed for hundreds of years, but the first opera in the modern sense is generally agreed to be *Dafne*, by the Florentine composer, Jacopo Peri. It was first produced in 1597. The music has long been lost. It was such a success that Peri followed it up with *Euridice* (1600), the earliest opera of which the music survives.

Other composers immediately began writing operas, one of the greatest of them being the Venetian, Claudio Monteverdi. His first opera, *La Favola d'Orfeo* (1607), and his last, *L'Incoronazione di Poppea* (1642), are still performed.

WAR WEARY

Who was Asoka? An emperor of India who ruled more than 2,000 years ago. Asoka's grandfather, Chandragupta Maurya, founded an empire in India soon after the country was invaded by Alexander the Great in 325 BC. Asoka was the third and greatest of the Maurya emperors. He came to the throne on the death of his father, Bindusara, in about 274 BC.

His first years as emperor were spent in warfare and enlarging his realm. Suddenly he sickened of war, abandoning the Hindu religion of his family to become a peace-loving Buddhist. He spent the rest of his life spreading Buddhism and trying to raise the moral standards of his people. He died about 232 BC.

Spanish farthingale c. 1550 French farthingale c. 1580 English hoop c. 1750

▲ The farthingale was concealed beneath a floor-length skirt.

SPY SCANDAL

Who were Burgess and Maclean? They were two British diplomats who spied for the Russians. They were among a group of young men who became Communists while studying at Cambridge University in the 1930s.

Donald Maclean (1913-1978) joined the Foreign Office in 1934 where he had access to secret information on atomic development. Guy Burgess (1911-1963) began his career as a BBC correspondent, and joined the Foreign Office in 1944. He was for a time attached to MI6, part of the British secret service.

In 1951 Burgess and Maclean were tipped off by another Russian agent, Kim Philby (born 1912), that they were in danger of arrest. They fled the country, and nothing more was heard of them until they surfaced in Moscow five years later. Philby, his activities also detected, fled to Moscow in 1963.

The fourth man For years there were rumours that a fourth man had been involved. In 1979 a book about Philby's activities led the Prime Minister, Margaret Thatcher, to reveal that the fourth man was the art historian, Professor Sir Anthony Blunt. He had confessed his involvement to the Secret Service in 1964, but the matter had been hushed up.

Blunt, who was born in 1907, had had a distinguished career in the world of art. He was a world authority on 17th-century art, was Keeper of the Royal Pictures from 1945 to 1972, and was knighted in 1956. When the scandal broke he was stripped of his knighthood. He lived the remainder of his days in obscurity, dying in 1983.

ROMAN JIG-SAW

What is the Portland Vase? It's the most famous example of Roman glass, made nearly 2,000 years ago. It is decorated in what is called the cameo technique. The basic vase is blue glass, coated with opaque white glass. The white glass is cut away to leave a design which represents the story of Achilles' mother, the sea-goddess Thetis.

The vase was bought in Italy in 1783 by the Duchess of Portland. Her son lent it to the potter, Josiah Wedgwood, who made 50 copies in fine earthenware. It was as well he did so. The original was put on exhibition in the British Museum in 1810, and 35 years later was smashed into 200 fragments by a madman. One of the Wedgwood copies was used to help reassemble the pieces.

QUIZ: FAMOUS WRITERS

1. Who were the three sisters who became famous English novelists?
2. William Sydney Porter was a famous American short-story writer. What pen-name did he use?
3. Who wrote the *Just So Stories*?
4. Who invented the fictional detective, Hercule Poirot?
5. Which English dramatist and poet was born at Stratford-upon-Avon in 1564?
6. What was the name of the nine-year-old girl who wrote *The Young Visiters*?
7. The author of *Black Beauty* was a campaigner against cruelty to horses. What was her name?
8. Who wrote *The Hobbit*?
9. The Italian poet Alighieri is better known by his first name. What is it?

ANSWERS
1 The Brontë sisters. 2 O. Henry. 3 Rudyard Kipling. 4 Agatha Christie. 5 William Shakespeare. 6 Daisy Ashford. 7 Anna Sewell. 8 J. R. R. Tolkien. 9 Dante.

The Portland vase. It is now in the British Museum in London. ▶

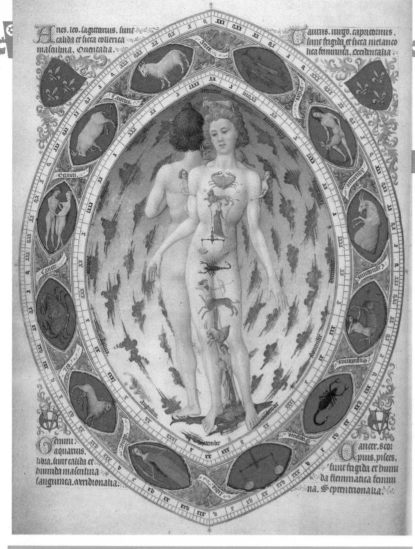

◀ A page from the illuminated manuscript *Les Très Riches Heures de Duc de Berri.*

ANIMATED MAGIC

Which was the first full-length cartoon film? Released in 1937, it was Walt Disney's *Snow White and the Seven Dwarfs.* This colour film lasts 90 minutes and is based on a traditional fairy tale retold by the German Brothers Grimm.

SELL-OUT

What is the slowest-selling book? Publishers used to keep an extensive 'back-list' of titles, especially of textbooks and scholarly works of reference. The Oxford University Press in England had a considerable stock of such works for many years, but their slowest seller was a translation of the New Testament of the Bible from Coptic into Latin.

It was published in 1716 when 500 copies were printed. The last one was sold in 1907!

SCREEN SCARE

Which was the first public cinema show? Although accounts differ slightly, it's generally held to be one given by the French brothers, Auguste and Louis Lumière, in Paris on December 28, 1895. The programme lasted 20 minutes, and consisted of ten short films. One film showed a train arriving at a station: as the engine puffed its way towards the camera the audience, it is said, was terrified!

PICTURE BOOKS

What is an illuminated manuscript? This is the name given to a handwritten book which is decorated with illustrations, fancy initial capital letters, highly decorative borders and a profusion of gold leaf.

Monastic labour The oldest surviving illuminated manuscripts are the decorated papyrus rolls of Ancient Egypt, but most of the finest illuminated manuscripts date from the Middle Ages. Nearly all of them were produced in monasteries, which were the places where scholarship and craftsmanship were preserved at a time when most people were illiterate.

Every large monastery had its *scriptorium,* where monks skilled at penmanship laboriously made copies of the Gospels, other religious texts and early music books. Copies were made to send to other monasteries, which in turn lent their books to be copied.

Works of art Some of the monks were artists, so spaces were left by the manuscript writers for them to decorate. The Irish monks were especially skilled at this work, so it is not surprising that one of the finest illuminated manuscripts, the *Book of Kells,* is an Irish product.

Not all illuminated manuscripts were produced in the cloister. Some were made to the orders of kings and noblemen. One of the most beautiful is the *Très Riches Heures du Duc de Berri,* produced sometime between 1411 and 1416 for a son of King John II of France. This was a book of prayers and services to be used at the canonical hours (set times for prayer) by three artist brothers, Pol, Hennequin and Herman de Limbourg.

▲
◀ Elvis Presley and his home, Graceland.

FLOATING A LOAN

How did Britain come to control the Suez Canal in Egypt? It was all due to the business acumen of the Prime Minister, Benjamin Disraeli, in 1875. When the canal was opened in 1869 Britain owned no part of it: the shares were held by the French and by the Khedive, who ruled Egypt for the Ottoman (Turkish) Empire.

The Khedive owned nearly half the shares. In 1875 Disraeli heard that he was broke and wanted to dispose of his holdings. He was asking £4,000,000 and needed the money at once.

A problem Parliament was not in session, and a sum that size – a huge one in those days – could not be raised without the vote of the two Houses. But Disraeli knew a way round the problem. He sent his private secretary, Montagu Corry, to see Lionel Rothschild, head of the British branch of the great banking firm, to ask for an immediate loan. This was granted as Rothschild accepted the unusual offer of 'the British Government' as security against the loan. From then on, until Egypt nationalized the canal in 1956, Britain had a controlling interest in it.

ROYAL SHAKES

Which king held court at Graceland? Elvis Presley, often described as the King of rock 'n' roll; Graceland was the plush, colonial-style mansion in Whiteland, Memphis, Tennessee, which he bought in 1957, turned into a near-palace, and lived in until his death there in 1977.

Elvis was born in Mississippi in 1935, the son of poor farmworkers. By the late 1950s he had become possibly the biggest rock 'n' roll idol of all time. Elvis's records sold in millions.

COLD TURKEY

Who was the Sick Man of Europe? It wasn't a person, it was a country – Turkey. More precisely it was the Ottoman Empire, of which modern Turkey was the heart. The phrase was coined in 1844 by Tsar Nicholas I

of Russia, who said of Turkey; 'We have on our hands a sick man – a very sick man'.

The Ottoman Empire was at its height in the 1500s, when it included most of North Africa and the Middle East, plus south-

eastern Europe as far as Hungary and the Crimea. It lost territory steadily during the 1800s, and by the time World War I broke out Turkey's stake in Europe was the same as it is today.

An aerial view of the ruins of ▶
the Masada fortress in Israel.

FAMILY MAN

Who was Dr Barnardo? He
founded the series of Dr
Barnado's Homes that brought
new hope and opportunity to
thousands of destitute children.
Thomas Barnardo was born in
Dublin, Ireland, and after being
'converted' at an evangelistic
meeting went to London to train
as a medical missionary.

In London he was appalled at
the conditions in which many
homeless orphans lived, and the
dreadful slum homes of many
families. He founded a mission
to help them, and in 1870
opened the first of his Homes.

By the time he died in 1905 at
the age of 60, he had admitted
59,384 children to his Homes,
helped more than 20,000 others
to emigrate to Canada, and had
assisted a further 250,000 waifs
in one way or another. He had
founded 35 Homes in England
and two in Canada.

Today there are more than a
hundred Dr Barnardo's Homes,
helping more than 9,000 boys
and girls every year.

COTTONING ON

Who invented the cotton gin?
An ingenious 28-year-old
American law student, Eli
Whitney, who produced it in
1793. The machine – gin is a
contraction of 'engine' –
separates cotton fibres from the
seed. Whitney's device could do
this task as quickly as 50 people
working by hand and it soon
revolutionized the American
cotton industry.

A cotton gin manufactured in 1863, ▶
modified from Whitney's machine.

COMMUNAL SUICIDE

What happened at Masada? This huge rock standing on the edge of
the Judean desert in eastern Israel, close to the Dead Sea, was the
scene of one of the most dramatic events in Jewish history.

Masada was a fortress, its defences having been built by Herod the
Great as a bolt-hole in the event of rebellion. In AD 70, long after
Herod's death, the Romans conquered Palestine and drove most of its
Jewish inhabitants out. But for three years a group of Jewish zealots
held Masada and kept the flame of independence alight.

No surrender A Roman legion laid siege to the fortress. They built a
ramp up to the top of the rock and prepared to launch a final assault.

The 960 Jews left, men, women and children, decided to take their
own lives rather than surrender. Ten men were chosen by lot to slay the
rest, and one of the ten killed his fellow executioners and then himself.
The only survivors were two women and five children, who hid in a
water tank hollowed out of the rock.

Excavations The ruins of Masada were excavated and restored
between 1963 and 1965 under the direction of Professor Yigael Yadin.
It is now both a tourist attraction and an Israeli shrine.

BLIND POET

Who dictated many of his works to his daughters? Tradition has it that John Milton, the famous English poet, did this after he became blind in 1652, at the age of 43. In fact he used some paid help, as well as friends and colleagues. His eldest daughter, Deborah, born in 1646, seems to have helped with the work when she grew old enough.

In 22 years of his blindness, before he died in 1674, Milton composed several of his greatest poems, including, *Paradise Lost, Paradise Regained,* and *Samson Agonistes.*

▲ A portrait of Queen Victoria.

SAD SECLUSION

Who was the Widow at Windsor? That was the slightly irreverent name that Rudyard Kipling (1865-1936) applied to Queen Victoria in one of his *Barrack-Room Ballads,* published in 1892. The ballad was written as if spoken by a British soldier, serving in India, and it may be that Kipling did not invent the phrase.

When Queen Victoria's husband, Prince Albert, died in 1861, she allowed her grief to overcome her so much that she spent most of the rest of her long reign in virtual seclusion – 39 years out of the 63 she was on the throne.

BLACK NOTES

Who invented jazz? Jazz wasn't invented – it evolved. Its origin lies in the traditional music of the Black African slaves who had been transported to America in their thousands. The basic form of this music persisted in the work songs that the slaves sang on the plantations.

In the late 1800s many American musicians developed an off-beat kind of music called 'ragtime'. The most celebrated of these musicians was the composer-pianist, Scott Joplin. From ragtime, jazz came into being, in several parts of the Southern States, but principally in New Orleans.

Music city New Orleans contained many bands, which played at parades, carnivals, funerals, dance halls and cabarets. Jazz as we know it began sometime between 1895 and 1917, when the first jazz record was made. That record was the work of a white group called the Original Dixieland Jazz Band.

Most of the great jazz players of the succeeding years, and in particular the 1920s and 1930s which were the key years for jazz, were Blacks. They included players who are now household names, such as Duke Ellington, Count Basie, Louis Armstrong, Jelly Roll Morton and King Oliver.

▲
Louis Armstrong and his band playing with African musicians in Ghana.

DRIP TOCK

What is a clepsydra? It's the Greek name for a water clock, an ancient device for recording the passage of time. There were several versions of the clepsydra.

The Egyptian water clocks of 3,400 years ago were pots filled with water, which could escape a drop at a time through a hole in the bottom. A scale marked on the inside of the pots showed how much time had elapsed.

Later, more accurate water clocks reversed the process. Water dripped into a vessel at a controlled rate, thus raising a float. A system of levers attached to the float operated a pointer on a dial. Such clocks were used by the Romans, the Chinese and the Arabs.

▲
The inside of a water clock (left) and a water clock with an alarm.

FIGHTING FISTS

Who were the Boxers? This was the European version of the name of a Chinese secret society, the Righteous Harmony Fists, who were violently opposed to everything European, because of alleged exploitation by Western traders and their governments.

In 1900 the Boxers rose in rebellion, broke into the houses of foreign missionaries and Chinese Christians and massacred them. Western inventions such as railways, post offices, and electric cables were ruthlessly destroyed. Potential victims fled to take refuge in the various foreign legations, where the Boxers besieged them.

The sieges went on for two months until armies of the eight countries involved – Austria, Britain, France, Germany, Italy, Japan, Russia and the United States – marched into Peking, China's capital, and relieved them.

QUIZ TIME

What is the sixty-four dollar question? The phrase has come to mean the most difficult part of a problem – the key to a final solution. The phrase arose from an American radio quiz game, 'Take it or Leave It', in which the top prize was $64. Later the idea was transferred to television, and multiplied considerably to become 'The Sixty-four Thousand Dollar Question'!

FACT FILE: WORLD WAR II

FACT About 16,000,000 soldiers, sailors and airmen died in the war, and at least the same number of civilians also died.

FACT More than 350,000 British, Belgian and French troops, cut off by German forces in May 1940, were rescued from the beach at Dunkirk, France, by a fleet of little ships.

FACT D-Day was the date of the Allied invasion of Normandy, June 6, 1944; the operation had the codename Overlord.

FACT The Battle of Britain in 1940 was the attempt by the Luftwaffe (the German air force) to defeat the Royal Air Force and so clear the way for an invasion.

FACT Pearl Harbor, Hawaii, the US Pacific naval base, was attacked by carrier-based Japanese planes on December 7, 1941, while the Japanese envoys were still negotiating in Washington.

FACT Adolf Hitler, the German dictator whose actions started World War II, committed suicide in the ruins of Berlin on April 30, 1945.

FACT The atomic bombs dropped on the two Japanese cities, Hiroshima and Nagasaki, in August, 1945, ended the war, without the necessity for an invasion of mainland Japan.

▲
The opening ceremony of the Los
Angeles Olympics in 1984.

SPORTING REVIVAL

When did the Olympic Games start? According to Greek tradition, in
776 BC. They were the oldest of the four major Games held in Greece,
the others being the Pythian, Nemean and Isthmian.

They began as amateur contests, but in time became professional.
Towns supported their own athletes, and winners could be sure of a life
pension, as well as a triumphal procession and a banquet.

Banned Eventually the Games declined in quality, so much so, that in
AD 394 the Emperor Theodosius I of Rome banned them (as indeed he
prohibited all other pagan practices). He might well have banned them
sooner had they been conducted as in ancient Greece, when all the
competitors (males only) were naked.

Revival In 1875, when archaeologists discovered the ruins of the
Olympic Stadium in Greece, interest in the Games was renewed. Baron
Pierre de Coubertin, a French scholar and educator, proposed that they
should be revived as an international competition to encourage both
sport and world peace.

The first of the modern Olympic series was held in Athens in 1896. Like
their classical predecessors, the athletes were men only, but women
were admitted to the following Games in 1900. (The Winter Olympics
began in 1924.)

Ever since, the Games have been held at four-yearly intervals, just
like those of ancient Greece. However, since de Coubertin's dream of
world peace has not been realized, the two World Wars prevented
those of 1916, 1940 and 1944 being held.

So far, the Olympic Games are confined to amateur athletes, but few
competitors can now pay for their training and expenses without some
form of sponsorship.

SAME NAME

***What did George Eliot and
George Sand have in
common?*** Both were novelists—
and both were women! George
Eliot (1819-1880) was originally
called Mary Ann Evans. Under
her pen name she wrote a
number of novels, including *The
Mill on the Floss* (1860), and
Middlemarch (1871-1872),
considered her masterpiece.

George Sand's original name
was Amandine Aurore Lucile
Dupin. She was born in Paris in
1804 and lived until 1876. She
rebelled completely against the
feminine image of the day,
adopted men's clothes and lived
a highly unconventional life.
Divorced in 1836, she supported
herself and her two children by
her writing, having adopted the
pen-name George Sand in 1832.

CAN DO

What is Pop Art? It is an art form related closely to the materialistic, brash, throw-away world of the late 20th century. It developed in the 1950s and 1960s in Britain and America. Pop artists use strip cartoon techniques, photographs, and packagings as the source of inspiration. The American pop artist, Andy Warhol, uses items such as Campbell's soup cans and the boxes in which Brillo pads are packed.

Swedish-born Claes Oldenberg reproduces everyday objects blown up to enormous size and reproduced in unlikely materials – such as plaster hamburgers.

Perhaps the best definition of pop art comes from Richard Hamilton, one of the British pioneers of the form. He said, 'It's intended for a mass audience, transient, expendable, mass-produced and cheap, young, witty, sexy, gimmicky, glamorous and deeply involved in big business.'

▲ Karl Marx (1818-1883).

CAPITAL FAILURE

Who was Karl Marx? A German freelance journalist, revolutionary and philosopher. He lived for a time in France and Belgium, then returned to Germany to help ferment the revolution of 1848. This failed and Marx fled to London, where he spent the rest of his life, helped financially by his great friend, fellow philosopher and revolutionary, Friedrich Engels.

Unfinished work Together Marx and Engels wrote *The Manifesto of the Communist Party* (1848), which sets out the political ideas now known as Marxism. Published in three volumes (two posthumously), Marx's main work was *Das Kapital*, which took him 30 years to write and was still unfinished when he died, in 1883.

Das Kapital (Capital) is an analysis of the free enterprise (capitalist) system, which he described as efficient, but thought would lead only to misery.

◀ Andy Warhol's *Campbell's Soup Can* exhibited in 1971.

QUIZ: INVENTIONS

1. Who was 'the Wizard of Menlo Park'?
2. King Camp Gillette made an important invention in 1895. What was it?
3. Who made the first working television set?
4. Hero of Alexandria invented the aeolipile in about AD 100. What was it?
5. Who had the first central heating systems?
6. Who invented the telephone, and in which year?
7. In which country was paper first made?
8. What important invention did Whitcomb L. Judson first demonstrate in 1893? (A clue: it's to do with clothes.)

ANSWERS
1. Thomas Alva Edison, who produced more than 1,000 inventions. 2. The safety razor. 3. John Logie Baird. 4. The first known steam engine. 5. The Romans. 6. Alexander Graham Bell in 1876. 7. China, in about AD 105. 8. The zip fastener.

REWARD FOR VILLAINY!

Who stole the Crown Jewels of England? An Irish adventurer, Colonel Thomas Blood. He fought on the Parliamentary side during the English Civil War, and was rewarded with estates in Ireland. When Charles II was restored to the throne in 1660, Blood lost his estates and thereafter indulged in various plots against the throne.

Alarm On May 9, 1671, Blood made his way into the Tower of London, contrived to grab the crown and the orb, and tried to get away with them under his cloak. Before he could reach his horse, the alarm was raised and he was captured.

With great presence of mind he insisted on seeing the king. Charles was so struck by Blood's courage and his honest replies to questioning, that he could not bring himself to award punishment. Instead, to everyone's surprise, the king pardoned Blood. Thereafter the gallant colonel was employed by the government to keep an eye on his old parliamentary friends, *and* his Irish estates were returned to him!

▲
Horses in a recent ploughing competition (top) wear collars to pull against instead of yokes as worn by the oxen (above).

HARNESSING HORSE POWER

Why did the horse-collar revolutionize farming in Europe? In the Middle Ages farmers in Europe used oxen to pull their ploughs and their wagons. The yoke, by which the oxen were linked to plough or cart, did not suit the horse. The straps which held it lay across the windpipe – the harder the horse pulled the more it cut off its supply of air.

In the AD 800s the horse-collar, which sits on the animal's shoulders, was introduced into Europe. It immediately gave the horse up to five times more pulling power. Over the centuries (until most farming became mechanized) the horse replaced the ox as the farmer's major power supply.

▲
Mao Tse-tung (left) and Chou en-Lai on the Long March.

RED VICTORY

What was the Long March?

A feat of endurance by the Chinese Communists, during the civil war that raged between them and the Chinese Nationalists, led by Chiang Kai-shek. Chiang attacked the Communists in a series of offensives, beginning in 1930. By the time the fifth offensive began in 1934, the Communists were encircled and facing utter defeat. Their only hope was to break out and march to safety.

To safety The Long March began on October 16, 1934, when 80,000 Communists, led by Mao Tse-tung, broke out of the Nationalist trap in south-eastern China. It lasted for 370 days and covered more than 9,500 km (5,900 miles). They travelled due west, and then due north to safety in Yenan in the north-west. Only 20,000 people survived the march.

From there the Communists convinced Chiang Kai-shek that a more pressing need than subduing them was to fight the Japanese, who were also threatening China. The two groups formed an uneasy alliance that lasted until after the end of World War II, in 1945.

Civil war broke out again in 1947, and this time it was the Communists who won. Chiang and the remains of his forces withdrew to the island of Taiwan.

FAMOUS FOUR

Who were the Beatles? They were an immensely popular rock music group who had more influence than any other group before or since.

The group The driving force in the group was John Lennon (1940-1980), a writer whose poetry came to express the feelings of a whole generation of young people. He formed his first group, the Quarrymen, in 1956. By 1960 the group had become the Beatles, and in 1962 its members were the four young men who rose to worldwide fame.

The four were Lennon, Paul McCartney (born 1942), George Harrison (born 1943), and Ringo Starr (real name Richard Starkey, born 1940). Starr played the drums, the others electric guitars, and they all sang.

The songs Lennon and McCartney wrote most of the Beatles' songs, from the time when they performed in youth clubs in Liverpool until the group split up. Their early songs were love ballads, which combined good melodies with the strong beat that had already become the dominant feature of rock music.

Later songs were an expression of social awareness, which endeared them even more to young people who could feel in the music the thoughts they themselves felt so deeply. 'Eleanor Rigby' (1966) had a meaning that was far more intense than the simple 'Love Me Do' which they produced in 1962, the year they shot to fame in Britain.

Break-up Success was engineered partly by their business manager, Brian Epstein, and after their first US tour in 1964 it was world wide. But it brought its problems and eventually contributed to the end of the Beatles in 1970. By that time they were very rich and each then made a new career for himself.

Lennon's career came to a tragic end on December 8, 1980, when a young man in a confused state of mind shot him dead in a street in New York City. Millions all over the world mourned him.

▲
The Beatles. From left to right: Starr, Harrison, McCartney, Lennon.

▲
Ché Guevara.

REVOLUTIONARY ROVER

Who was Ché Guevara? An Argentinian physician who became a revolutionary. He believed that violence was the only way to dispose of oppressive governments.

Guevara's real name was Ernesto Guevara; Ché was a nickname. In 1954 he held a post in the basically Communist government of Guatemala, but it was overthrown and he fled to Cuba. There he met the Communist revolutionary, Fidel Castro, and joined his movement. After Castro won power he appointed Guevara to high government office.

But seven years as a minister were long enough for Guevara and one day he vanished! He was next heard of in Bolivia – assisting a band of revolutionary guerrillas – where he was killed in 1967, aged 39. His striking personality, writings on revolutionary warfare and the manner of his death have since made him a legendary figure.

Women anti-strike demonstrators. ▶

NINE DAYS' WONDER

What was the British General Strike of 1926? It was a partial strike called in support of the mineworkers. In those days the mines were privately owned and the industry was in financial trouble. So the owners proposed a cut in wages and an increase in hours. A commission which was appointed to look into the problem also recommended a pay cut. The miners went on strike and appealed to the Trades Union Congress for help.

Negotiations The TUC negotiated with the Conservative government (led by Stanley Baldwin as Prime Minister) for several weeks without result, and threatened to call a General Strike in support of the miners. During the talks, printers at the *Daily Mail* refused to print an editorial that included what they regarded as misstatements. The Government took this as the start of a strike and broke off negotiations.

All out The General Strike began on May 4. All transport workers, printers, workers in the iron and steel, heavy chemicals, building, electricity and gas industries were called out, while food and health services were specifically ordered not to strike. The TUC also forbade violence. Altogether 3,000,000 people – three-fifths of the total trade union membership, and one-fifth of the total working population – went on strike.

Back to work Further negotiations produced a compromise proposal which the miners refused to accept, at which point the TUC felt it had no alternative but to call off the strike, which ended on May 12, after just nine days.

The miners continued with their strike until November 19, when they had to give in through lack of funds.

▲
Howard Jones in a recording studio, uses a synthesized keyboard.

SYNTHESIZED SOUND

How do electronic musical instruments work? All musical instruments work by the generation of sound waves, which are then modified and amplified by the shape and construction of the instruments. For example, violins and pianos work by the vibration of strings, and clarinets and organs by the vibration of a column of air in a pipe or pipes. When these sounds are recorded, they are changed electronically, through the action of microphones, into electrical impulses, which in turn cause a loudspeaker to vibrate and so reproduce the original sound.

Electronic instruments cut out the first stage – the physical production of sounds by instruments – and with the help of a silicon chip produce their sounds by creating frequencies electronically.

Sound production In the electronic organ, the sound is produced by a single oscillator, and from this sound (one note) a bank of capacitors, resistors and transistors produces the 12 notes of the normal western scale. The sound produced is the top octave that will be required, starting six octaves above middle C. Because all the notes are derived from one source, they will always be in tune with one another.

Electronic devices called frequency dividers then halve the frequencies of the notes, producing lower and lower octaves down to the lowest notes required. All these devices are now carried on silicon chips.

Harmonics Few notes in music consist of pure tone but they contain other notes, called harmonics, in various strengths and degrees. All these harmonics can be added to the notes to imitate organs, pianos, violins – any instrument of the modern orchestra. Also, modern synthesizers can produce new sounds, thus offering composers opportunities their predecessors never had.

RAIL CHARACTER

Who invented Paddington Bear? The man behind the bear is Michael Bond, a former television cameraman. Bond, born in 1926, wrote the first book in the series, *A Bear Called Paddington*, in 1958. The bear got his name from Paddington Station, in London, England where he was found in the first story. Paddington books have now been translated into over 20 languages and the bear has become the hero of a television series.

SURPRISE, SURPRISE!

Why are military tanks so called? The tank was developed in Britain during World War I. To keep this new weapon secret, it was referred to in all official communications as a tank or water-carrier, rather than by the earlier name 'landships'. Although thousands of people knew the secret, it was so well kept that when tanks were first used in battle in 1916, they terrified the German troops.

▲
A scene from *The Red Shoes*.

RECORD BREAKER

What was the longest single shot in a film? It's always difficult to pinpoint record breakers of this kind, but probably *The Red Shoes* holds the record. Filmed in 1948, this contained the full-length ballet of the same name, first produced in 1898. The whole ballet was filmed as one continuous shot. The film starred four leading ballet dancers: Moira Shearer, Leonide Massine, Ludmilla Tcherina and Robert Helpmann.

FACT FILE: SPORTS AND GAMES

FACT Badminton, adapted from a children's game called battledore and shuttlecock, takes its name from Badminton, England, where it was first played in 1873.
FACT The longest boxing match between two gloved fighters, Andy Bowen and Jack Burke, lasted more than 7 hours and 110 rounds in New Orleans in 1893.
FACT The oldest board game known is about 4,500 years old and was found in the ruins of Ur, in Iraq; the rules have not survived.
FACT The legendary English cricketer, Dr W. G. Grace, began playing at the age of nine, and carried on until he was 61.
FACT Playing cards were invented in China during or before the AD 100s, and were based on paper money then in circulation.
FACT In 1365, Edward III of England tried to ban football because it distracted people from archery practice, needed as war training.
FACT The world's first motor race was held in France in 1894 – only nine years after the first petrol-driven cars were built.

▲
A Barbary ape with a young one riding on her back.

MONKEY BUSINESS

What is the legend of Gibraltar's apes? The legend is that if the colony of Barbary apes on the Rock, the last monkeys in Europe, ever leave, then so will the British. Even if the legend is not taken seriously, the fact remains that the apes – about 30 of them – are on the official strength of the Gibraltar Regiment! They get a daily allowance of a few pence, which buys food for them. When the apes multiply beyond the 'establishment strength', some are sent to zoos elsewhere, officially recorded as 'posted overseas'.

Reinforcements During World War II, when the possession of Gibraltar was vital to Britain's war effort, the apes dwindled to a dangerously low number. The British Prime Minister, Winston Churchill, therefore ordered that a replenishment detachment should be imported from Morocco.

Despite their name, these Barbary Apes are not true apes, but monkeys of the group known as macaques.

WILLS'S CIGARETTES.

THE "MERRIMAC" & THE MONITOR

▲
The engagement between *Merrimac* (right) and *Monitor*.

BEAD COUNTING

What was the first calculator?

It was the abacus or counting board, still used in some Asian countries, particularly China, to make calculations. Nobody knows for sure how old the abacus is, but examples have survived from ancient Greece and Rome. The surviving Greek abacus was a counting board, made of white marble, on which counters were moved, just as the beads of a modern abacus are today.

Scholars think the symbol for zero may have come from the abacus. In calculations, the absence of a bead, or a space, would be used to indicate zero. Because the abacus has no memory, the results of any calculations have to be written down – and mathematicians almost certainly had to evolve some symbol to represent the empty space.

NAUTICAL ARMOUR

What were the **Monitor** *and the* **Merrimack**? They were ironclad warships which fought one of the most important battles of the American Civil War – the first duel between armoured warships.

The *Merrimack* was a Union (Northern) ship, which was scuttled when Union forces abandoned a naval yard at Portsmouth, Virginia, in 1861, soon after the start of the Civil War. Confederate (Southern) sailors raised her, and partly rebuilt her. They covered her with thick iron plates. They renamed her *Virginia*, but she is always remembered as the *Merrimack*.

Impregnable This powerful and apparently impregnable ship began destroying the Union's wooden ships, whose guns were powerless to affect her. She was steam powered, so she needed no sails or wind to drive her along.

In the face of such a weapon the Union called for an armoured ship to fight *Merrimack*. The Swedish-born engineer, John Ericsson, obliged with a design that traditional naval engineers scoffed at initially. However, the ship was duly built and named *Monitor*. She was little more than an armoured floating gun-turret.

Encounter On March 9, 1862 the *Merrimack*, returning from a raid against the 'wooden walls' of the Union fleet, found the *Monitor* waiting for her. For hours the two ships pounded each other, their shells doing little or no damage.

Two months later the *Merrimack* was scuttled again, this time permanently, to keep her from falling into Union hands as Confederate forces withdrew.

The *Monitor* survived a few months longer, but as she was being towed towards Beaufort, North Carolina, she sank in a storm, with the loss of 16 lives. Her sunken wreck was found in 55 m (180 ft) of water in 1973, and underwater television cameras photographed her the following year.

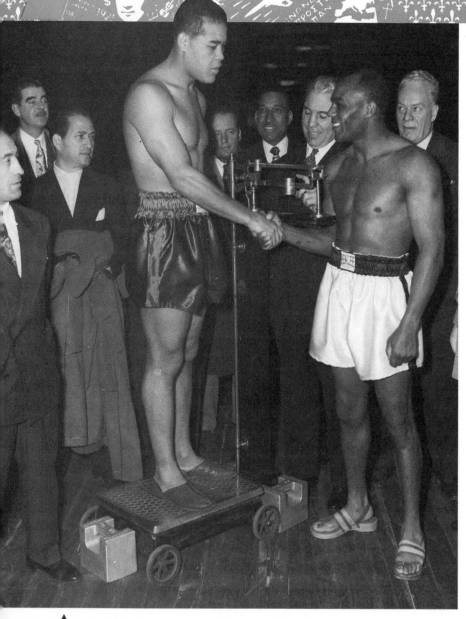

▲
Joe Louis, on the scales, and Jersey Joe Walcott in December 1947.

MAN WITH CLOUT

Who was the 'Brown Bomber'?
That was the nickname given to
American Joe Louis, who held
the world's heavyweight boxing
championship longer than
anyone else. His title lasted for
11 years and eight months. Louis
was born in Lexington,
Alabama, in 1914, and his full
name was Joseph Louis Barrow.
He had his first professional fight
in 1934, earning just $52 for it.

Louis won the heavyweight
title in 1937, and defended it
successfully 25 times. He retired
in 1949, still undefeated, and is
reputed to have earned over
$4,600,000 in the ring, much of
which he gave away. He died in
1981.

Louis' courage, skill and
dignity were an inspiration to
thousands of other Black
Americans. He was their hero,
and he ended among other
heroes, in Arlington National
Cemetery, along with John F.
Kennedy and the Unknown
Warriors of two world wars and
the Korean War.

NAME OF THE STATE

***Why is the Empire State
Building so called?*** It goes back
to a chance remark by George
Washington, the first president of
the United States. Visiting New
York, he commented that it might
become the seat of a new
empire. Ever since, New York
State has been known as the
'Empire State'.

So when the Empire State
Building was completed in New
York City in 1931, the State's
nickname seemed appropriate
for what was then the world's
tallest building. (This record was
retained by the 381-m (1750-ft)
tall building for over 40 years,
until 1972.)

PERSISTENT SPIDER

Was Robert Bruce really inspired by a spider? According to an old
legend, the Scottish leader, Robert Bruce, who was fighting to free
Scotland from English rule, suffered a disastrous defeat in 1306 and had
to flee to one of the western isles for safety. There he sought shelter in a
cave and despaired of ever succeeding in his struggle. But his hopes
were revived by seeing a spider try six times to climb up its web and fail,
only to try once more and succeed. Bruce resolved to carry on, and
within seven years he was master of Scotland.

This may be just a legend. But a zoologist, Dr W. S. Bristowe, was
visiting one of the caves which tradition says was used by Bruce, and
there he saw the webs of a spider known to scientists as *Zygiella
x-notata*. This spider is the only British species which regularly has
trouble climbing its own thread – so it could have been a descendant of
the spider that inspired Bruce.

FIERY CURTAIN

What was the Globe Theatre? It was the playhouse that stood on Bankside, Southwark, London just beside the River Thames. It was owned by William Shakespeare and a company of actors.

Originally the company to which Shakespeare belonged played at The Theatre, which stood in Shoreditch, north of the Thames. When their lease expired in 1598, the actors had the timber framework of the building pulled down and floated across the Thames, where it was rebuilt in a larger form as The Globe in 1599. The playhouse was a six-sided building, with three tiers of galleries. They and the stage were covered with thatch, but the pit (the main audience area) had no roof and was open to the sky.

Exit the globe The Globe came to a fiery end. In 1613 a new play called *All is True* was performed there – probably the play we now know as Shakespeare's *Henry VIII*. During the performance, cannon were shot off to mark the entrance of the king upon the stage. A piece of wadding from one of the guns settled on the thatch and set it alight. Within an hour the whole structure had gone up in flames.

▲
The original Globe Theatre.

ONE GIANT LEAP

Who was the first man on the Moon? 'That's one small step for a man, one giant leap for mankind'. With these words Neil Alden Armstrong placed his left foot on the fine, powdery surface of the Moon on July 20, 1969. It was the culmination of years of striving for the US space programme.

The astronauts Armstrong was then a few weeks short of his 39th birthday. He was a US Navy pilot from 1949 to 1952, and saw active service during the Korean War. He then became a civilian test pilot, before joining the small, select band of astronauts in 1962.

His companion on the Moon was Edwin Eugene Aldrin, who was a colonel in the US Air Force, also with experience of the Korean War. Aldrin was the scientist of the team, holding a doctorate in astronautics.

The third man in *Apollo 11* was Colonel Michael Collins, who did not have the privilege of setting foot on the Moon. He had the vital task of keeping the command module of the spacecraft in orbit round the Moon, ready to pick up the two Moon walkers at the end of their mission.

Near miss Altogether six American missions were sent to land on the Moon, the last – *Apollo 17* – in December 1972. There should have been seven, but *Apollo 13* had a near escape from disaster. An explosion damaged the spacecraft on takeoff, and it was only skill and daring that enabled the crew to take their craft round the Moon, rather than landing on it, and safely back to Earth.

The future Will there be any more Moon landings? None is planned at present, and the astronomical cost of such voyages has probably ruled them out for many years to come. The Apollo Space Programme cost about $22,000 million dollars up to the first Moon landing, and costs have escalated sharply ever since.

Neil Armstrong walks on the Moon in July 1969. ▶

▲
Martin Luther King addresses the Washington crowd in March, 1963.

MAN OF PEACE

Who was Martin Luther King? He was a Black American civil rights leader, who won the Nobel prize for peace and was assassinated for his beliefs.

Born in 1929, Martin Luther King Jr became a Baptist minister, settling in Montgomery, Alabama. In 1955 he began a civil rights campaign to try to end discrimination against Blacks on buses in Southern States. Like Mahatma Gandhi in India, King believed in non-violent campaigning; but violence was used against him.

Several times he was arrested and jailed for acts of civil disobedience. His enemies threw stones at him, on one occasion stabbed him, and tried to blow up his house. But King carried on with his crusade. He said: 'Every man should have something he'd be willing to die for'.

A dream In 1963 he told a crowd of 200,000 in Washington, DC: 'I have a dream that one day this nation will rise up and live out the true meaning of its creed, "We hold truths to be self-evident, that all men are created equal"' – a quotation from the American Declaration of Independence of 1776.

King's campaigns resulted in two important pieces of legislation: the Civil Rights Act of 1964, which outlawed discrimination, and the Voting Rights Acts of 1965, which gave increased protection to Blacks to vote in elections.

In 1968 Martin Luther King was about to mount a new campaign, to draw attention to the plight of poor Americans of all races, when a white escaped convict, James Earl Ray, gunned him down.

TWINKLE, TWINKLE

What was the star system? It was a phenomenon of Hollywood at the height of the film industry's success. Studios built up the public image of some of their leading actors and actresses by clever and sometimes ruthless publicity, with stunts and stories about their personal lives.

Publicity men even invented fictional life stories for some of their 'victims'. The studios, having placed their players under contract, then proceeded to supervise every aspect of their lives – clothes, make-up, diet and friends. The stars often had no say in the kinds of roles they were expected to play.

Some stars found this treatment intolerable. Judy Garland and Marilyn Monroe were two actresses who found their star status, as defined by their studios, hard to adapt to; both died from an overdose of sleeping pills.

▲
Betty Grable, a Hollywood star.

▲ The Grand Entrance to the Great Exhibition in the Crystal Palace.

GLASSHOUSE EXTRAORDINARY

What was the Crystal Palace?

This was the nickname given by the people of London to the huge pavilion that was erected in Hyde Park for the Great Exhibition of 1851. It was designed by Joseph Paxton, who was a gardener and architect employed at Chatsworth in Derbyshire.

Paxton, having built a large conservatory at Chatsworth, produced a similar design for his exhibition building. It was constructed of cast-iron girders and arches, filled in with glass. The building was so popular that, instead of demolishing it at the end of the exhibition, as intended, it was moved to a permanent site at Sydenham, in south-east London. It was reopened there in 1854 and known officially as the Crystal Palace. In 1936 the building and its contents were destroyed by fire, the cause of which remains a mystery.

QUIZ: TRANSPORT

1. Which important part of a vehicle was invented in 1845, and reinvented in 1888?
2. What was the *Graf Zeppelin*?
3. What was the name of the submarine that made the first under-the-ice crossing of the North Pole?
4. Who were the brothers who made the first balloon to carry a man aloft?
5. What is the name of the rail link between Moscow and Vladivostok, on the Pacific coast?
6. What did Gottlieb Daimler and Karl Benz do in 1885?
7. Which canal was begun by the Emperor Nero in AD 67 and finished in 1893?
8. What was a tea clipper?

ANSWERS
1 The pneumatic tyre (invented by Robert William Thomson in 1845, forgotten, and reinvented by John Boyd Dunlop in 1888). 2 A German airship, in service from 1928 to 1937. 3 USS *Nautilus*. 4 Jacques and Joseph Montgolfier. 5 The Trans-Siberian Railway. 6 They built the first petrol-driven motor-cars. 7 The Corinth Canal in Greece. 8 A fast sailing ship, used to carry tea from the East to Europe.

Acknowledgements
The publishers thank the following for providing the photographs in this book:

Ace Photo Library 167 right, 170, 172 centre, 215 above; Aldus Archive 140 below; Aquarius Picture Library 259 below, 312 below; Ardea London Ltd 88, 93, 97 above, 98 left, 100 above, 119, 144 below, 145 left, 146 above, 152 centre; Associated Sports Photography 225 above, 235 above; Barnabys Picture Library 17 above; Biofotos 212; The Bridgeman Art Library 242 right, 249, 259 above, 262, 264 below, 267 above, 275, 292, 297; Paul Brierley Science Photography 182, 222 above; British Antarctic Survey 72; British Waterways Board 187; Camera Press Ltd 59 above, 253 below; J. Allan Cash Photolibrary 180; Celtic Picture Library 270 below; Bruce Coleman Ltd 89-91, 95 below, 98 right, 101, 103 right, 104 left, 106 right below, 109-110, 111 below, 112 below right, 115 above right, 118, 122 left, 123 below, 124, 125 above right, 127, 128 above, 129, 133 below, 137, 138, 141, 142, 145 right, 146 below, 147-151, 155 above, 156 left, 159 above & centre, 308 below; Colorsport 4/5, 186, 191 below, 233 below, 302; Daily Telegraph Colour Library 134 above, 164 above, 166 below, 188, 197 below, 199 below, 206, 219, 222 below, 223 below, 226, 230; The Design Council Picture Library 172 above; ET Archive 283; Greg Evans Photo Library 68; Mary Evans Picture Library 12 below, 29 above, 45 above, 80, 242 left, 244 below, 246, 251, 254 above, 256 below, 260 below, 264 above, 269, 273, 277, 278 left, 278 right, 288, 289 above, 291, 294 below, 300 above, 309, 311 above, 313; John Frost Historical Newspaper Service 244 above; Robert Harding Picture Library 6/7, 8-9, 11, 13 above, 15, 16 above, 19, 22, 24 below, 25 below, 26, 28, 31, 35, 37, 38 below, 40 above, 44, 52 below, 53, 55 centre, 57 above, 61, 62, 64, 73-7, 79 inset; 255 above, 263, 266, 284, 286 right, 287, 289 below, 290, 298 right, 303 left; Michael Holford Photographs 247, 256 above, 260 above, 261, 279, 281, 293, 294, 295-6; Eric & David Hosking 130 below; The Hutchison Library 17 below, 18 centre, 21 left, 25 above, 29 below, 32, 35 inset, 39, 40 below, 46, 47 above, 48 above, 52 above, 59 left, 67 below, 70, 81, 162/3, 218, 240/1; Illustrated London News 268 below; Impact Photos 282 below; Independent Television News Ltd 183; Institute of Optometry 220 above; Keystone Press Agency 164 below; The Kobal Collection 253 above, 257-8, 265, 272 below, 308 above; Roger Kohn 82, 105, 225 below; The Frank Lane Agency 13 below, 22 above, 63, 83, 94, 112 left & above right, 139, 160 above; L.F.I. Ltd 305 below; M.A.R.S. 203; Neill Meneer 84/5; N.H.P.A. 92, 100 below, 104 right, 111 above left, 113, 114, 115 above left & below, 128, 130, 132, 134 below, 135, 140 above, 143, 152 above & below, 155 below, 158; The National Trust Photo Library 270 above; Nature Photography 95 above, 103 left, 131, 144 above, 154, 159 below, 160 below; Octopus Prop. (Ian O'Leary) 166 centre, (Paul Williams) 169 below, (George Wright) 47 below; The Photo Source 168 above, 174, 178 above, 193, 196 above, 208 above, 209 above, 211 below, 223 above, 229, 236, 246 right, 248 below, 267 below, 274, 276, 280 left, 282 above, 300 below, 303 right, 304 above, 305 above, 306, 310, 312 above; Photographers Library 2/3; Planet Earth Pictures 86, 106, 108, 111 above right, 120, 122 right, 125 below left, 126, 156-7, 175, 198 below; Public Records Office 184; Retna Ltd 307; Ann Ronan Picture Library 177, 271, 272 above, 304 below; Royal Geographical Soc. 133 above; Science Photo Library 16 below, 20, 24 above, 30 above, 33, 38 above, 43 above, 45 below, 48 below, 54, 55 right, 58, 66, 74, 165 above, 166 above, 168 below, 169 above, 179, 189, 191 above, 192, 194-5, 196 below, 197 above, 198 above, 199 above, 200-2, 205, 207 below, 209 below, 210, 211 above, 213-4, 216, 220 below, 221, 224, 228, 232, 233 above, 234, 235 below, 239; Ronald Sheridan's Photo Library 252, 256 below, 286 left; Spacecharts 217, 311 below; Spectrum Colour Library 165 centre, 173, 231; Tony Stone Associates 33 above, 82; Survival Anglia Ltd 137 above; Telefocus 227; Topham Picture Library 167 left, 207 above, 245, 254 below, 298 left; Woburn Abbey 285; Zefa Picture Library 10, 12 above, 18 above, 21 right, 27, 30, 36, 42, 43 below, 49-50, 53 left, 57 below, 59 right, 60 above, 65, 66, 67 above, 71, 72, 78, 79 below, 178 below, 208 below, 238, 248 above, 250, 268 above, 229.

The publishers thank the following for permission to reproduce works of art in this book:

© ADAGP/1987 242; © DACS/1987 264, 279, 303; Bridget Riley 259; The Tate Gallery 242.